A Nation of Nations

edited by THEODORE L. GROSS

A Nation Of Nations

Ethnic Literature in America

F P | THE FREE PRESS · New York
Collier-Macmillan Limited · London

THE FREE PRESS
A DIVISION OF THE MACMILLAN COMPANY
866 Third Avenue, New York, New York 10022

Collier-Macmillan Canada Ltd., Toronto, Ontario

Library of Congress Catalog Card Number: 79–142365

printing number
1 2 3 4 5 6 7 8 9 10

To Mrs. IDA BELL

CONTENTS

RELIGION

IDENTITY

PREJUDICE

THE COMMUNITY
FACES IN THE CROWD   427

INTO THE MAINSTREAM
AND OBLIVION   499

PREFACE

America is a nation of immigrants. No other land has been so informed with the myth of men creating their own futures from their individual attributes. The American dream is a collective dream, and it has haunted the sleep of every child in this country. This book is an expression of that dream and the ways in which it has possessed, liberated, and often frustrated the minorities of America.

In the history of nations, America speaks for the common man. Spaniards, Italians, Swedes, Irish, Norwegians, Jews, Armenians—these and other ethnic groups have traveled to this country "to put up something proud to look at," in Carl Sandburg's words, "a tower from the flat land of earth." For some that tower has indeed reached "up through the ceiling into the top of the sky"; for others—Blacks, Puerto Ricans, and immigrants just entering American society—their tower has often seemed a "Tower of Babel." Ethnic authors have measured America against their private ideals, and the record of their encounters with this "promised land" is a remarkable revelation of what it means to become an American.

I have arranged the literature of minorities thematically so that the reader may experience the diverse reactions of these writers toward their families, childhoods, education, religion, and communities, as well as toward themselves as "hypenated Americans," the prejudices against them, and their relationship to the American "mainstream." By juxtaposing authors of various backgrounds in terms of the major aspects of American life, I have sought to reflect the rich human complexity of our society.

"Here is not merely a nation," wrote Whitman a century ago, "but a teeming nation of nations." Whitman celebrated the cultural pluralism of America, the opportunity for a man to claim his individuality through his ethnic heritage even as he became that new man in the New World—an American. At no other time in history has the threat been so great as now to man's sense of human worth. One way to remind the American of his humanity is to insist upon the ethnic diversity that has always characterized his country. The melting pot has not quite forced everyone to be alike; in the differences of Americans lie their strength and, as the following pages testify, some of their most meaningful literature.

I would like to thank my friends and colleagues Leo Hamalian and Arthur Zeiger for various suggestions in the preparation of this manuscript. My son Jonathan was of great assistance, and I am grateful for his enthusiasm and co-operation.

New York City   T.L.G.

CREDITS AND ACKNOWLEDGMENTS

"Angel Levine" from *The Magic Barrel* by Bernard Malamud.
Copyright © 1955, 1958 by Bernard Malamud.
Reprinted with the permission of Farrar, Straus & Giroux, Inc.

"How Much Are We American"? (pp. 32–33) from *Selected Poems* by
Muriel Rukeyser.
Copyright © 1951 by Muriel Rukeyser.
Reprinted by permission of International Famous Agency, Inc.

"To Be a Jew in the Twentieth Century" (pp. 49–50) from *Letter to the
Front* by Muriel Rukeyser.
Copyright © 1951 by Muriel Rukeyser.
Reprinted by permission of International Famous Agency, Inc.

"The Refugees" (pp. 80–82) from *Fourth Elegy* by Muriel Rukeyser.
Copyright © 1951 by Muriel Rukeyser.
Reprinted by permission of International Famous Agency, Inc.

"A Turning Wind" (pp. 82–85) from *Fifth Elegy* by Muriel Rukeyser.
Copyright © 1951 by Muriel Rukeyser.
Reprinted by permission of International Famous Agency, Inc.

"22 Miles . . ." from *El Grito* by Josue A. Gonzalez.
Copyright and reprinted by permission of Quinto Sol Publications, Inc.

"Now That the Buffalo's Gone" Words and Music by Buffy Sainte-Marie.
Copyright © 1965 by Gypsy Boy Music, Inc.
Used by permission of the author and publisher.

"The Return to the Source" by Jo Pagano.
Copyright and reprinted by permission of the author.

"The American Irish" (pp. 24–26) by William Shannon.
Reprinted by permission of The Macmillan Company.

"Well, My Father Was an Armenian, Yes" by John Hagopian.
Copyright and reprinted by permission of the author.

"Incident" from *On These I Stand* by Countee Cullen.
Copyright © 1925 by Harper & Brothers; renewed, 1953 by Ida M.
Cullen.
Reprinted by permission of Harper & Row, Publishers.

"Battle Royal" from *Invisible Man* by Ralph Ellison.
Copyright © 1952 by Ralph Ellison.
Reprinted by permission of Random House, Inc.

"The Alarm Clock" by Mari Evans.
Copyright and reprinted by permission of Negro Digest and author.

"Negro and Jew: Encounter in America" from *No! In Thunder* by Leslie
Fiedler.
Copyright © 1960 by Leslie A. Fiedler.
From the book *No! In Thunder*.
Reprinted with permission of Stein and Day Publishers.

"Slant-Eyed Americans" (pp. 127–135) from *Yokohama California* by Toshio Mori.
From Toshio Mori's *Yokohama*, California. 1949. Caldwell, Idaho, The Caxton Printers, Ltd.

"The Country That Is My Country" by Jose Garcia Villa.
Copyright and reprinted by permission of the author.

"A Brief History of Any Country" by Jose Garcia Villa.
Copyright and reprinted by permission of the author.

"A Brief History of the Philippines" by Jose Garcia Villa.
Copyright and reprinted by permission of the author.

"Lines Against a Loved American Poet After Hearing an Irish One's Nickname" from *Ghosts of the Heart* by John Logan.
Copyright © 1960 by John Logan.
Reprinted by permission of the author.

"Things in Common" is reprinted with the permission of Charles Scribner's Sons from *Half Sun, Half Sleep* by May Swenson.
Copyright © 1967 May Swenson.

From *America Is in the Heart* by Carlos Bulosan, copyright © 1943, 1946 by Harcourt, Brace Jovanovich, Inc. and reprinted with their permission.

"The Well" by Scott Momaday.
Copyright Ramparts Magazine, Inc., © 1963. By permission of the Editors.

From *Beyond the Melting Pot* by Nathan Glazer and Daniel P. Moynihan.
Copyright © 1963 by permission of The M.I.T. Press, Cambridge, Massachusetts.

Keep on Pushing (Harlem Riots/Summer/1964)
"From the book *De Mayor Harlem* by David Henderson.
Copyright © 1970 by David Henderson. Published by E. P. Dutton & Co., Inc. and reprinted with their permission.

"City of Harlem" from *Home:* Social Essays by LeRoi Jones.
Reprinted by permission of William Morrow and Company, Inc.
Copyright © 1962, 1966 by LeRoi Jones.

"Cruz Moves to a Housing Project" from *La Vida,* by Oscar Lewis.
Copyright © 1965 by Oscar Lewis.
Reprinted by permission of Random House, Inc.

"Beyond Delinquency" from *Long Live Man* by Gregory Corso.
Copyright © 1959, 1962 by New Directions Publishing Corporation.
Related by permission of New Directions Publishing Corporation.

"Writ on the Steps of Puerto Rican Harlem" from *Long Live Man* by Gregory Corso.

ORIGINS

THE OLD MASTER EUROPE,
THE MASTERLESS AMERICA

*That's why most people have come to
America, and still do come. To get away
from everything they are and have been.
"Henceforth be masterless."*

D. H. Lawrence

The history of America is a history of immigrants: explorers, missionaries, colonizers, victims of religious and
economic oppression, dreamers of a new Jerusalem and
a New World. Diverse as the many countries they represent, immigrants manifest distinctive origins which shape
the varied pattern of America. What are their roots? Why
have they come to this country? Where have they settled?
What has America meant to them?

The Indians were the first people to migrate to America. Traveling from Asia, Mexico, and Peru, they had established fairly complex cultures by the time Columbus arrived in the new world. But the Indians were overridden in
turn by Spanish, English, and French explorers who coveted
America's vast resources. In their desire to appropriate the
wealth of this land, the European colonizers turned to
Africa for slaves to work the numerous plantations created
in the South and in the Carribean. By the late eighteenth
century, after struggles with the Spanish and French, the
British dominated America. As the chief bearers of western
European thought, they gave this nation its language, law,

and political institutions; and they exerted the deepest influence on its literary artists. Indeed, when we think of the "mainstream" in American life, we usually refer to the British heritage that had so strong an impact on New England and the South and created many customs in American life.

New ethnic groups began to arrive in the early nineteenth century, producing a succession of "minorities" in addition to the Indians and the Negroes. Germans came during the revolutions of 1848; Irish Catholics fled famine and economic deprivation at the same time; Jews sought to escape the Russian pogroms of the 1880s; Norwegians and Spaniards, Italians and Greeks, Armenians and Poles, Chinese, Japanese, and Filipinos migrated to America in the twentieth century. The distinctive languages, customs, and folkways they brought transformed Americian into the most heterogeneous and culturally diverse nation in modern history. The Germans and Norwegians went to the Midwest; the Irish settled in Boston; the Jews formed a large community in New York; the Orientals lived in San Francisco.

What origins did American minorities have in common? Why did they leave their native land? What promises did this country offer, and what sort of Americans did these immigrants finally become? Answers to these questions can never be absolute; but certain conclusions may be drawn. In the essays of John F. Kennedy, Oscar Handlin, James Baldwin, and Max Lerner, we begin to sense the origins and promises of America, the roots from which the immigrants were torn, and the nation of nations which they welcomed as a new world of infinite possibilities.

A NATION OF NATIONS

John F. Kennedy

On May 11, 1831, Alexis de Tocqueville, a young French aristocrat, disembarked in the bustling harbor of New York City. He had crossed the ocean to try to understand the implications for European civilization of the new experiment in democracy on the far side of the Atlantic. In the next nine months, Tocqueville and his friend Gustave de Beaumont traveled the length and breadth of the eastern half of the continent—from Boston to Green Bay and from New Orleans to Quebec—in search of the essence of American life.

Tocqueville was fascinated by what he saw. He marveled at the energy of the people who were building the new nation. He admired many of the new political institutions and ideals. And he was impressed most of all by the spirit of equality that pervaded the life and customs of the people. Though he had reservations about some of the expressions of this spirit, he could discern its workings in every aspect of American society —in politics, business, personal relations, culture, thought. This commitment to equality was in striking contrast to the class-ridden society of Europe. Yet Tocqueville believed "the democratic revolution" to be irresistible.

"Balanced between the past and the future," as he wrote of himself, "with no natural instinctive attraction toward either, I could without effort quietly contemplate each side of the question." On his return to France, Tocqueville delivered his dispassionate and penetrating judgment of the American experiment in his great work *Democracy in America*. No one, before or since, has written about the United States with such insight. And, in discussing the successive waves of immigration from England, France, Spain and other European countries,

Tocqueville identified a central factor in the American democratic faith:

All these European colonies contained the elements, if not the development, of a complete democracy. Two causes led to this result. It may be said that on leaving the mother country the emigrants had, in general, no notion of superiority one over another. The happy and powerful do not go into exile, and there are no surer guarantees of equality among men than poverty and misfortune.

To show the power of the equalitarian spirit in America, Tocqueville added: "It happened, however, on several occasions, that persons of rank were driven to America by political and religious quarrels. Laws were made to establish a gradation of ranks; but it was soon found that the soil of America was opposed to a territorial aristocracy."

What Alexis de Tocqueville saw in America was a society of immigrants, each of whom had begun life anew, on an equal footing. This was the secret of America: a nation of people with the fresh memory of old traditions who dared to explore new frontiers, people eager to build lives for themselves in a spacious society that did not restrict their freedom of choice and action.

Since 1607, when the first English settlers reached the New World, over 42 million people have migrated to the United States. This represents the largest migration of people in all recorded history. It is two and a half times the total number of people now living in Arizona, Arkansas, Colorado, Delaware, Idaho, Kansas, Maine, Montana, Nevada, New Hampshire, New Mexico, North Dakota, Oregon, Rhode Island, South Dakota, Utah, Vermont and Wyoming.

Another way of indicating the importance of immigration to America is to point out that every American who ever lived, with the exception of one group, was either an immigrant himself or a descendant of immigrants.

The exception? Will Rogers, part Cherokee Indian, said that his ancestors were at the dock to meet the *Mayflower*. And some anthropologists believe that the Indians themselves were immigrants from another continent who displaced the original Americans—the aborigines.

In just over 350 years, a nation of nearly 200 million people has grown up, populated almost entirely by persons who either came from other lands or whose forefathers came from other lands. As President Franklin D. Roosevelt reminded a convention of the Daughters of the American Revolution, "Remember, remember always, that all of us, and you and I especially, are descended from immigrants and revolutionists."

Any great social movement leaves its mark, and the massive migration of peoples to the New World was no exception to this rule. The interaction of disparate cultures, the vehemence of the ideals that led the immigrants here, the opportunity offered by a new life, all gave America a flavor and a character that make it as unmistakable and as remarkable to people today as it was to Alexis de Tocqueville in the early part of the nineteenth century. The contribution of immigrants can be seen in every aspect of our national life. We see it in religion, in politics, in business, in the arts, in education, even in athletics and in entertainment. There is no part of our nation that has not been touched by our immigrant background. Everywhere immigrants have enriched and strengthened the fabric of American life. As Walt Whitman said,

> These States are the amplest poem,
> Here is not merely a nation but
> a teeming Nation of nations.

To know America, then, it is necessary to understand this peculiarly American social revolution. It is necessary to know why over 42 million people gave up their settled lives to start anew in a strange land. We must know how they met the new land and how it met them, and, most important, we must know what these things mean for our present and for our future.

PEASANT ORIGINS

Oscar Handlin

The immigrant movement started in the peasant heart of
Europe. Ponderously balanced in a solid equilibrium for centuries, the old structure of an old society began to crumble at
the opening of the modern era. One by one, rude shocks weakened the aged foundations until some climactic blow suddenly
tumbled the whole into ruins. The mighty collapse left without homes millions of helpless, bewildered people. These were
the army of emigrants.

The impact was so much the greater because there had
earlier been an enormous stability in peasant society. A granite-
like quality in the ancient ways of life had yielded only slowly
to the forces of time. From the westernmost reaches of Europe,
in Ireland, to Russia in the east, the peasant masses had maintained an imperturbable sameness; for fifteen centuries they
were the backbone of a continent, unchanging while all about
them radical changes again and again recast the civilization
in which they lived.

Stability, the deep, cushiony ability to take blows, and yet
to keep things as they were, came from the special place of
these people on the land. The peasants were agriculturists; their
livelihood sprang from the earth. Americans they met later
would have called them "farmers," but that word had a different meaning in Europe. The bonds that held these men to
their acres were not simply the personal ones of the husband-
man who temporarily mixes his sweat with the soil. The ties
were deeper, more intimate. For the peasant was part of a community and the community was held to the land as a whole.

Always, the start was the village. "I was born in such a

village in such a parish"—so the peasant invariably began the account of himself. Thereby he indicated the importance of the village in his being; this was the fixed point by which he knew his position in the world and his relationship with all humanity.

The village was a place. It could be seen, it could be marked out in boundaries, pinned down on a map, described in all its physical attributes. Here was a road along which men and beasts would pass, reverence the saint's figure at the crossing. There was a church, larger or smaller, but larger than the other structures about it. The burial ground was not far away, and the smithy, the mill, perhaps an inn. There were so many houses of wood or thatch, and so built, scattered among the fields as in Ireland and Norway, or, as almost everywhere else, huddled together with their backs to the road. The fields were round about, located in terms of river, brook, rocks, or trees. All these could be perceived; the eye could grasp, the senses apprehend the feel, the sound, the smell, of them. These objects, real, authentic, true, could come back in memories, be summoned up to rouse the curiosity and stir the wonder of children born in distant lands.

Yet the village was still more. The aggregate of huts housed a community. Later, much later, and very far away, the Old Countrymen also had this in mind when they thought of the village. They spoke of relationships, of ties, of family, of kinship, of many rights and obligations. And these duties, privileges, connections, links, had each their special flavor, somehow a unique value, a meaning in terms of the life of the whole.

They would say then, if they considered it in looking backward, that the village was so much of their lives because the village *was* a whole. There were no loose, disorderly ends; everything was knotted into a firm relationship with every other thing. And all things had meaning in terms of their relatedness to the whole community.

In their daily affairs, these people took account of the relationships among themselves through a reckoning of degrees of kinship. The villagers regarded themselves as a clan connected within itself by ties of blood, more or less remote. That they did so may have been in recollection of the fact that the village was anciently the form the nomadic tribe took when it settled down to a stable agricultural existence. Or it may have been a reflection of the extent of intermarriage in a place where contact with outsiders was rare. In any case, considerations of kinship had heavy weight in the village, were among the most important determinants of men's actions.

But the ties of blood that were knotted into all the relationships of communal life were not merely sentimental. They were also functional; they determined or reflected the role of individuals in the society.

No man, for instance, could live alone in the village. Marriage was the normal expected state of all but the physically deformed. If death deprived a person of his marriage partner, all the forces of community pressure came into play to supply a new helpmate. For it was right and proper that each should have his household, his place in a family.

The family, being functional, varied somewhat to suit the order of local conditions. But always the unit revolved about the husband and wife. The man was head of the household and of its enterprises. He controlled all its goods, made the vital decisions that determined its well-being, had charge of the work in the fields, and was the source of authority and discipline within the home. His wife was mother, her domain the house and all that went on in and about it. She was concerned with the garden and the livestock, with domestic economy in its widest sense—the provision of food, shelter, and clothing for all. The children had each their task, as befitted their age and condition. Now they herded the cattle or assisted in the chores of cleaning and cookery; later they would labor by the side of mother and father, and prepare to set up families of their own. Other members too had their allotted and recognized roles. Grandparents, aunts and uncles, sometimes cousins up to the fourth degree with no establishments of their own, found a place and a job. The family felt the obligation of caring for all, but also knew that no one could expect food and a corner in which to sleep while doing nothing to earn it. In this respect such collateral relatives did not differ in condition from the hired servants, where they existed, who were also counted members of the family.

The family was then the operating economic unit. In a sense that was always recognized and respected, the land on which it worked was its own. The head of the household, it was true, held and controlled it; legally, no doubt, he had certain powers to waste or dispose of it. But he was subject to an overwhelming moral compulsion to keep it intact, in trust for those who lived from it and for their descendants who would take a place upon it.

The family's land was rarely marked out in a well-defined plot. The house, the garden, and the barnyard with its buildings were its own, but the bulk of agricultural lands were enmeshed in a wide net of relationships that comprehended the whole community.

Once, it seems, the village had held and used all the land communally; until very recent times recognizable vestiges of that condition persisted. The pastures and meadows, the waste, the bogs and woodlands, existed for the use of all. It hardly mattered at first that the nobility or other interlopers asserted a claim to ownership. The peasants' rights to graze their cattle, to gather wood for building and peat for fire, in practice remained undisturbed. In some parts of Europe, even the arable lands rested in the hands of the whole village, redivided on occasions among its families according to their rights and condition.

Even where particular pieces of land were permanently held, it was rarely in such consolidated plots as the peasants might later see on American farms. A holding consisted rather of numerous tiny strips that patched the slopes of the countryside in a bewildering, variegated design. A Polish peasant, rich in land, could work his nine acres in forty different places.

Agriculture conformed to the pattern of landholding. By long usage, the fields almost everywhere were divided into thirds, a part for winter crops—wheat, rye; another for summer crops—barley, oats, and potatoes; and another to lie fallow. Since no man's lands were completely apart from his neighbor's, there was no room for individuality in working the soil. Every family labored on its own and kept the fruit of its own labors. Yet all labor had to be directed toward the same ends, in the same way, at the same time.

Many important aspects of agriculture, moreover, were altogether communal. The pastures were open to all villagers; in the common fields, the boys tended the cattle together or a hired herdsman had their oversight. Women, working in groups at the wearisome indoor tasks, spinning or plucking cabbage leaves, could turn chores into festive occasions, lighten their labors with sociable gossip. The men were accustomed to give aid to each other, to lend or exchange as an expression of solidarity. After all, folk must live with each other.

So the peasants held together, lived together, together drew the stuff of life from an unwilling earth. Simple neighborliness, mutual assistance, were obligations inherent in the conditions of things, obligations which none could shirk without fear of cutting himself off from the whole. And that was the community, that the village—the capacity to do these things together, the relationships that regulated all. . . .

The calls on the land for its produce grew more insistent as the eighteenth century drew to a close and continued as the nineteenth century advanced toward its middle. It was not only that the population as a whole grew, but particularly that the urban population grew. The peasants could not know it, but those who went to the cities, in effect, increased the pressures on those who stayed behind. Townsfolk could not raise their own food; more numerous at the market place, they multiplied the demands upon agriculture.

You cannot make the land to stretch, the peasants said; and that was true enough in their own experience. But others witnessed with impatience the multitude of buyers, calculated the advance in prices and the prospect of profit, and disagreed. What if the land could be made to stretch under a more efficient organization of production? In the more advanced, that is, the more densely settled, areas of the continent there were significant attempts to answer that question. In the Netherlands and in England experiments tested the utility of new crops. Perhaps there were ways of eliminating the fallow year that had kept one third of the land annually out of production. Perhaps it was possible to bring more meat to the butcher not only by increasing the number of beasts, but also by increasing the weight of each through scientific breeding.

Landlords everywhere were quick to sense the potentialities. In region after region, England, Ireland, France, the Rhineland, Italy, Prussia, Hungary, Poland, Russia, there were excited speculations, eager efforts to apply the new developments.

But everywhere the old wasteful peasant village stood in the way. In these minuscule plots too many men followed stubbornly their traditional communal ways. As long as they remained, there could be no innovations. Sometimes the landlords tried to introduce the changes on their own lands, using outsiders as intermediaries, English farmers in Ireland, for instance, or Germans in Poland. But such compromises left untouched the great common meadows and forests, to say nothing of the arable lands in the grip of the peasants themselves. The ultimate solution, from the viewpoint of efficient exploitation, was consolidation of all the tiny plots into unified holdings and the liquidation of the common fields.

Only the power of government could effect the transition, for the dissolution of vested rights, centuries old, called for the sanctions of law. From England to Russia, in the century or so after 1750, a series of enactments destroyed the old agricultural order. The forms were varied; there were statutes by parliament, decrees from the Crown. The terms varied—enclosure, reform, liberation. But the effect did not vary.

Men drove into the village. They had the appearance of officers and the support of law. They were heavy with documents and quick in reckoning. They asked questions, wished to see papers, tried to learn what had been in time beyond the memory of man. There came with them also surveyors to measure the land. Then the peasants were told: they were now to be landowners, each to have his own farm proportionate to his former share and in one piece. The communal holdings were to disappear; every plot would be individual property, could be fenced around and dealt with by each as he liked.

Whether or not strict justice was done the peasant depended upon local circumstances and the conscience of the executing officials; it was not always possible to supply precise legal proof for property traditionally held. But in every case, the change undermined the whole peasant position. They were indeed now owners of their own farms; but they were less able than ever to maintain their self-sufficiency. The cost of the proceedings, in some places the requirement of fencing, left them in debt; they would have to find cash to pay. When the wastes disappeared there disappeared also the free wood for fire or building; there would have to be cash now to buy. If there were no longer common meadows, where would the cows graze?

All now found themselves compelled to raise crops that could be offered for sale. Confined to their own few acres and burdened with obligations, the peasants had no other recourse. The necessity was cruel for these were in no position to compete on the traders' market with the old landlords whose great holdings operated with the efficiency of the new methods and ultimately of the new machinery. Steadily the chill of mounting debt blanketed the village. Like the chill of winter, it extinguished growth and hope, only worse, for there seemed no prospect of a spring ahead.

The change, which weakened all, desolated those whose situation was already marginal. The cottiers, the crop-sharers, the tenants on short-term leases of any kind could be edged out at any time. They had left only the slimmest hopes of remaining where they were.

Some early gave up and joined the drift to the towns, where, as in England, they supplied the proletariat that manned the factories of the Industrial Revolution. Others swelled the ranks of the agricultural labor force that wandered seasonally to the great estates in search of hire. Still others remained, working the land on less and less favorable terms, slaving to hold on.

A few emigrated. Those who still had some resources but feared a loss of status learned with hope of the New World where land, so scarce in the Old, was abundantly available. Younger sons learned with hope that the portions which at home would not buy them the space for a garden, in America would make them owners of hundreds of acres. Tempted by the prospect of princely rewards for their efforts, they ventured to tear themselves away from the ancestral village, to undertake the unknown risks of transplantation. The movement of such men was the first phase of what would be a cataclysmic transfer of population.

But this phase was limited, involved few peasants. A far greater number were still determined to hold on; mounting adversities only deepened that determination. In addition, the costs of emigration were high, the difficulties ominous; few had the energy and power of will to surmount such obstacles. And though the landlords were anxious to evict as many as possible, there was no point in doing so without the assurance that the evicted would depart. Otherwise the destitute would simply remain, supported by parish charity, in one way or another continue to be a drain upon the landlords' incomes.

Soon enough disaster resolved the dilemma. There was no slack to the peasant situation. Without reserves of any kind these people were helpless in the face of the first crisis. The year the crops failed there was famine. Then the alternative to flight was death by starvation. In awe the peasant saw his fields barren, yielding nothing to sell, nothing to eat. He looked up and saw the emptiness of his neighbors' lands, of the whole village. In all the country round his startled eyes fell upon the same desolation. Who would now help? The empty weeks went by, marked by the burial of the first victims; at the workhouse door the gentry began to ladle out the thin soup of charity; and a heartsick weariness settled down over the stricken cottages. So much striving had come to no end.

Now the count was mounting. The endless tolling of the sexton's bell, the narrowing family circle, were shaping an edge of resolution. The tumbled huts, no longer home to anyone, were urging it. The empty road was pointing out its form. It was time.

He would leave now, escape; give up this abusive land his fathers had never really mastered. He would take up what remained and never see the sight of home again. He would become a stranger on the way, pack on back, lead wife and children toward some other destiny. For all about was evidence of the consequences of staying. Any alternative was better.

What sum the sale of goods and land would bring would pay the cost. And if nothing remained, then aid would come from the gentry or the parish, now compassionate in the eagerness to rid the place of extra hands, now generous in the desire to ease the burden on local charity. So, in the hundreds of thousands, peasants came to migrate. This was the second phase in the transfer of a continent's population.

It was not the end. Years of discontent followed. The burdens of those who stayed grew no lighter with the going of those who went. Grievances fed on the letters from America of the departed. From outposts in the New World came advice and assistance. Across the Atlantic the accumulation of immigrants created a magnetic pole that would for decades continue to draw relatives and friends in a mighty procession. This was the third phase.

With the peasants went a host of other people who found their own lives disrupted by the dislocation of the village. The empty inn now rarely heard the joy of wedding celebrations. The lonely church ministered to a handful of communicants. The tavernkeeper and priest, and with them smith and miller, followed in the train of those they once had served. There was less need now for the petty trade of Jews, for the labor of wandering artisans, for the tinkering of gypsies. These too joined the migration.

And toward the end, the flow of peoples received additions

as well from the factories and mines. Often these were peasants or the sons of peasants whose first remove had been to the nearby city, men who had not yet found security or stability and who, at last, thought it better to go the way their cousins had earlier gone.

So Europe watched them go—in less than a century and a half, well over thirty-five million of them from every part of the continent. In this common flow were gathered up people of the most diverse qualities, people whose rulers had for centuries been enemies, people who had not even known of each other's existence. Now they would share each other's future.

Westward from Ireland went four and a half million. On that crowded island a remorselessly rising population, avaricious absentee landlords, and English policy that discouraged the growth of industry early stimulated emigration. Until 1846 this had been largely a movement of younger sons, of ambitious farmers and artisans. In that year rot destroyed the potato crop and left the cottiers without the means of subsistence. Half a million died and three million more lived on only with the aid of charity. No thought then of paying rent, of holding on to the land; the evicted saw their huts pulled down and with bitter gratitude accepted from calculating poor-law officials the price of passage away from home. For decades after, till the end of the nineteenth century and beyond, these peasants continued to leave, some victims of later agricultural disasters, some sent for by relatives already across, some simply unable to continue a way of life already thoroughly disrupted.

Westward from Great Britain went well over four million. There enclosure and displacement had begun back in the eighteenth century, although the first to move generally drifted to the factories of the expanding cities. By 1815, however, farmers and artisans in substantial numbers had emigration in mind; and after midcentury they were joined by a great mass of landless peasants, by operatives from the textile mills, by laborers from the potteries, and by miners from the coal fields. In this number were Scots, Welsh, and Englishmen, and also the sons of some Irishmen, sons whose parents had earlier moved across the Irish Sea.

From the heart of the continent, from the lands that in 1870 became the German Empire, went fully six million. First to leave were the free husbandmen of the southwest, then the emancipated peasants of the north and east. With them moved, in the earlier years, artisans dislocated by the rise of industry, and later some industrial workers.

From the north went two million Scandinavians. Crop failures, as in 1847 in Norway, impelled some to leave. Others found their lots made harsher by the decline in the fisheries and by the loss of the maritime market for timber. And for many more, the growth of commercial agriculture, as in Sweden, was the indication no room would remain for free peasants.

From the south went almost five million Italians. A terrible cholera epidemic in 1887 set them moving. But here, as elsewhere, the stream was fed by the deeper displacement of the peasantry.

From the east went some eight million others—Poles and Jews, Hungarians, Bohemians, Slovaks, Ukrainians, Ruthenians —as agriculture took new forms in the Austrian and Russian Empires after 1880.

And before the century was out perhaps three million more were on the way from the Balkans and Asia Minor: Greeks and Macedonians, Croatians and Albanians, Syrians and Armenians.

In all, thirty-five million for whom home had no place fled to Europe's shores and looked across the Atlantic.

What manner of refuge lay there?

IS THERE AN AMERICAN STOCK?

Max Lerner

Every traveler in the tropics comes away with an unforgettable sense of the pervasive jungle enclosing him. America's jungle is its ethnic environment of a myriad of peoples. In such a tropical luxuriance every ethnic type is present, everything grows fast and intertwines with everything else, anything is ethnically possible.

The best vantage points for observing the variety of American ethnic strains are on a subway in New York or a San Francisco street or at an Army induction center. Each is a broad channel through which the human material of America streams. Every people in Europe, most of the varied stocks of European and Asian Russia; peoples from Israel and the Arabs of the Middle East; peoples from China and Southeast Asia, from the Philippines, Hawaii, Australia, from the farthest reaches of India, from Liberia and Nigeria, from the Gold Coast and the Ivory Coast, from Kaffirland and the Witwatersrand, from every country in South and Central America, from every Caribbean island, from British and French Canada, from Greenland and Iceland—there is scarcely a stock on the ethnic map of the world that is not represented in America.

Let me make my use of terms clear. I use "stock" rather than "race," and "ethnic" rather than "racial," because in both cases I mean something in which race is only one ingredient. I have in mind a compound of influences from race, nationality, language, religion, region or sub-region—any recognizable strain which not only by its common descent but by its length of living on the same soil, under the same sky, and in the same community has formed a relatively stable biopsychological and cultural type.

In any one of these ethnic stocks more "American" than

the others? To say of someone that "he is of American stock" has come to mean that he is white, probably Protestant and of Anglo-Saxon descent, and that his forebears emigrated to America some generations back. But there is little of solace here for the distinction-hunters. In most civilizations the conquering stock has tried to set itself off on the one hand from the conquered natives, on the other from the newcomers who may want to get in on the power and the glory. In America this has been difficult on several scores: the natives were too few and were so ruthlessly stripped of land, home, and livelihood that the deed trailed little glory behind it. If "American stock" is to mean descent from those who were most immediately in on the kill, the leaders of the Great Predation, it would carry a guilt of which many would be gladly rid. The real conquest of America was not a military conquest, to deck out a boast that the strength of killers flows in one's blood: it was a conquest of forest and plain, of mountain and valley and river, of new technologies and new social forms; and in it every wave of immigrants took part. Although the largest single group came from the British Isles, there was no one stock that pre-empted the glory of settling America: even in the early decades of the Republic, there was a variety of stocks shaping the amalgam of "this new man, the American." Finally, the leveling force of the democratic idea has resulted in a crossbreeding and mingling of stocks which have made the task of the racial purist a hopeless one.

This effort to pre-empt the term "American" for a single strain out of many, and exclude from it all the others, is a familiar device in the technique of prescriptive prestige. Whatever meaning it may have in the case of a more inbred and homogeneous people, in America it is meaningless. Yet there are some who recoil from racism but regard the length of settlement as a crucial distinguishing mark. "Wouldn't European stocks which have been here longer," a friend writes me, "be more 'American' than the recent ones? Isn't a Lowell or a Roosevelt, for example, likely to be more 'American' than my Chinese laundryman's son?" By the test of time the most "American" stocks would be the American Indians, the descendants of the Pilgrims, and the descendants of the early Negro slaves—which is not exactly what was meant. The idea that European stocks are more "American" not by the fact of long settlement but by the fact of being European (West European, not Mediterranean or Slavic), is an idea easy to succumb to. Its strength derives from the fact that the English, Scottish, French Huguenot, and Dutch influences are interwoven with early American history. It is easier and more natural to think of a Lowell or Roosevelt as American than of a recent Chinese immigrant or a descendant of an early Indian or Negro family, but this is because the West Europeans have run the show in America since early times and have therefore made the rules and set the admission price. They feel more at home and have made others feel less at home.

Our thinking will be clearer if we say that there are three levels of meaning attached to "American": the links of family and stock with American history over time; the equal or unequal claims to rights and privileges under the law; the sense of commitment to American life. Only on the first level does the question of stock enter, however irrationally. On the second level there can be no discrimination between a Lowell or Roosevelt and the Chinese laundryman's son. On the third level the problem is one of individuals, not of stock: Americans belonging to the newer stocks may be as committed to the obligations and meanings of the American experience as the older ones, and many have enriched it greatly.

Yet in the world's most notable ethnic democracy there remains a hierarchy of prestige depending partly on stock—black, yellow, brown, and red at the bottom, white Protestant, West European on top, with the lines between the rest drawn partly in terms of closeness to Colonial descent, partly of geographic closeness to the British center of origin of the early settlements. A roughly chronological chart of the sequence of waves of immigration—English, Dutch, German, Scotch-Irish, French, Scandinavian, Irish, Mediterranean, Jewish, Balkan, Slavic, Mexican and Latin American, Filipino, Middle Eastern, Oriental—would correspond roughly to the descending scale of prestige in the ethnic hierarchy. The big divergences are that the Indians, who came first, are not at the top but toward the bottom of the pyramid; and the Negroes who were brought over early, are not near the top but at the very bottom. On the prestige chart of the ethnic hierarchy, one could superimpose a residence map showing which stocks are distributed in slum areas, in tolerable living quarters, in middle-class districts, in residential areas. Over that one could draw an occupational chart of the functions to which the ethnic groups have been more or less specialized.

This is fluid, but the correspondences are roughly there. Making allowance for the constant breaking of the mold and the emergence of many Negroes as doctors, lawyers, teachers, ministers, businessmen, it remains true that in the South the Negroes have done and still do the heavy labor in the fields, and everywhere the dirty jobs in the factories and on the roads and wharves, in digging ditches and laying tracks and building tunnels, while their women are domestics. The Chinese, Filipinos, and Puerto Ricans are also still specialized to do domestic and routine jobs. The Mexicans (or "Spanish-speaking Americans") work at sweated labor in the factories of the Southwest and as migratory workers on the farms of the Southwest and California. The Poles, Czechs, Magyars, and Slovaks are in the coal mines of Pennsylvania, West Virginia, and Illinois, in the steel mills and at the open-hearth furnaces of Gary and Pittsburgh and Buffalo. The Scandinavians are farmers in the Midwest and loggers in the lumber camps. The Irish of the later immigration are policemen, saloonkeepers, and bartenders in New York and Boston, but also day laborers and building-trades workers, transport workers, longshoremen. The Italians and the Jews work in the garment trades of New York and the other Eastern centers; the Italians are also barbers and shoeshine boys and musicians, and they work the truck gardens in New Jersey and the vineyards of California, as do the Japanese; while the Jews move from the sweatshops into the small trades and the middlemen functions, and into medicine, law, dentistry, teaching, and the entertainment world.

But in the fluid life of America, the specialization does not stick. Cutting across the ethnic occupation map is the fact that it is the new arrivals of most stocks who do the menial and dirty work and drift to the peripheral occupations, while the earlier and resourceful ones break out of their cultural molds, buy farms and houses, get university training, attain skills, and move up to become members of the middle class. The epithets do often stick—"Wop," "Dago," "Sheeny," "Kike," "Nigger," "Norske," "Mick," "Spick," "Polack," "Hunkie," "Bohunk," "Chink," "Jap," "wetback," "greaser"—betraying a class and xenophobe animus as well as a racist one.

Sometimes, in overcompensation for this prevalent animus, one is tempted to ask whether we can in fact distinguish stock from stock, or whether there are not simply *individuals* in a rich and bewildering variety?

It is true that the differences between the stocks are not

clear-cut, that one could find within one of them—say the
Jews—wider differences of physiognomy, height, bone structure, skull structure, temperament, than between particular
Jews on the one hand and particular Italians or Irish or Portuguese or Syrians on the other. It is also true that ethnic differences do not carry with them the differences of superiority
or inferiority that the racists ascribe to them. Although there
are no supermen in America, there are Americans who hunger
for a cult of the blond Anglo-Saxon gods; although there are
no sub-men in America, there are whites who cling to their
color out of a panic sense of emptiness and who pant to assign
Negroes or Puerto Ricans or Mexicans or Chinese to the category of inferior men. There are no Americans who belong to
radically different branches of the human family, in the sense
that their blood is of a different genus, or that some are closer
to apes and others closer to gods, some born to work and others
to lord it over them. There is not even an ethnically pure group
in America (unless we speak of ethnic sub-pockets like the Hut-
terites from Russia who settled in South Dakota and have been
almost completely endogamous) for at this point in history the
chromosomes of any group contain also some genes from most
of the others.

Yet it would be foolish to deny the reality of ethnic stocks
in America and the differences between them. Those who came
to America came from relatively stable ethnic groups. They
brought with them obvious physical hereditary differences and
habits of life that set them off from the others, and the social
hostility they encountered often made them huddle together in
more or less isolated ethnic communities. Many of them thus
retained and even froze their sense of separateness, while
others kept themselves open to every influence from other
groups, including interbreeding. If we recognize that there is no
stigma to membership in any one of the ethnic stocks of America the whole question of stock can be taken with realism and
without passion.

The fact is that America is more than an agglomerate of
individuals jumbled in hopeless confusion. America is a myriad
of stocks, each with some identity maintained from the earliest
to the latest migration. What gives America its biological rich-
ness is that it is a mingling of traditions and temperaments.
Unless the stocks had brought an identity of their own, it
would be meaningless to talk of their mingling. Unless those

identities were changed and dissolved in the process, shaped and reshaped, caught up in the ever-flowing stream of the life of all of them together, it would be meaningless to talk of America.

Does the unlimited crossbreeding of ethnic stocks hurt or help the quality of American life? True, there are some valid objections to be raised against unlimited crossbreeding. In the process of mixture, the groups with the higher birth rate will predominate, biologically and culturally, and while a high birth rate may be one of the indices of vitality, the crucial question is that of the quality of the individuals and cultures which are crossed. There is, however, a double and contradictory line of reasoning in the "pure America" argument. One is that the more recent immigrants are clannish, refuse to intermarry, and should therefore be kept out. The other is that they will flood into the country and overwhelm and corrupt the "native" stock by the weight of numbers and birth rate and by interbreeding. One argument rests on the theory that they do not mix, the other on the theory that they mix all too much. I suspect that logic is less important here than emotion—the emotions of invidiousness, guilt, pride, and fear that dominate the thinking of the "pure America" group.

On biological grounds alone, if these emotions can be ruled out, the central argument for an exclusive concept of American stock is the argument that unlimited crossbreeding will mean the mongrelization of America. Even reputable writers seem to have been made panicky by the possible biological and cultural corruption of pure Anglo-Saxonism by the Negroes, Asians, Slavs, Jews, and Mediterranean peoples. If mongrelization has any meaning, it assumes a "pure" (but non-existent) stock thinned out and corrupted by unlimited crossbreeding. The fear of mongrelization is the fear of strange blood and ways on the part of groups that believe their economic and social supremacy threatened by outsiders, and fix upon the racial invaders as the enemy.

This fear reaches nightmare proportions in the Southern states, where the governing group has sought to protect its "white supremacy" by a set of state miscegenation laws. States like Mississippi and Georgia, in a triumph of paranoia, enacted laws making any marriage felonious and void if it involves a white person and one with an "ascertainable trace" of African, West Indian, Asian Indian, or Mongolian blood. One of the wider aspects of the miscegenation laws, if they are regarded in terms of any rational threat of mongrelization, is that they are found in the North as well as the South, and that in eight of the states covered by them the Negroes against whom they are directed form less than 1 per cent of the population.

This is not to deny the reality of crossbreeding in America. But there can be no question of mongrelization because there is no norm of purity. Each ethnic strain, in the process of crossbreeding, "corrupts" the other; each dilutes and enriches the other. The fact is that crossbreeding is in itself neither good nor bad. Its chief effect is to increase variations at both ends of the curve of inherited traits: in other words, we may dilute the quality of what is transmitted as a result of the vast interchange of genes, but we may also get more geniuses on the top level. The range of potentials is widened in both directions. Everything depends, as I have said, on the individuals and cultures entering into the mixture. The characteristic ethnic quality of America is the outcome of the mingling of stocks and traditions on a scale unparalleled in history. Although some cultural historians maintain that the dilution of native stock is followed by cultural decadence, the example of the Italian city-states, Spain, Holland, Britain, and now Russia and India as well as America indicates that the most vigorous phase may come at the height of the mingling of many stocks. The greater danger lies in closing the gates.

No stock, once it has come to America, remains what it was. Each breeds away from type, both by the influence of the new physical environment and by the fact of intermingling. Every stock, by its migration, breaks with its past environment and enters a new one. Continued migration from one American region to another and mobility from one class and therefore one set of living standards to another continue the process of environmental reconditioning. How substantial the changes may be was shown in 1912 in the classic study by Franz Boas, *Changes in Bodily Form of Descendants of Immigrants*. Despite the prevailing view that skull measurements are an unchanging racial characteristic, Boas showed that the skull indices of the children of Jewish and Italian immigrants differed appreciably from those of the parents. This is environmental change away from ethnic type, whether due to diet, living standards, climate, or other factors in the natural and cultural environment. Boas was dealing with the physical factor that one would expect to be most resistant to change. What applied to skull changes would apply more easily to psychic and cultural changes; and what applied under the influence of environmental and standard-of-living change would apply more easily as the result of biological mixture.

I find a surprising misreading of Boas's meaning in Arnold Toynbee's *Study of History* (Vol. I, 220–1), which argues that Boas is, like his opponents, an adherent of race thinking. Boas writes that his study is suggestive "because it shows that not even those characteristics of a race which have proved to be most permanent in their old home remain the same under the new surroundings; and we are compelled to conclude that when these features of the body change, the whole bodily and mental make-up of the immigrants may change." Toynbee gathers from this "what is the fundamental postulate of all race theories: that is, the postulate that physical and psychical characteristics are correlated." But this is to miss the meaning of the phrase "*may* change," which carries with it an emphasis on the plasticity of *both* the cultural-psychic and the physical traits under environmental pressure. The whole point of racist thinking is that there is no such plasticity but that a given set of inherent physical traits of a superior or inferior caste carries with it a rigid set of psychic traits of a similarly superior or inferior caste. Boas proved the plasticity (although he felt it was a limited one) and rejected the moral hierarchy. The racists assert the moral hierarchy and reject the plasticity.

The process of plasticity has been described in Paul Engle's *America Remembers.*

> *The ancient features of the type were changed*
> *Under a different sun, in a clearer air*
> *That entered the lungs like wine, the swarthy face*
> *Paled, cheekbones lifted and narrowed, hair*
> *Straightened and faded, and the body moved*
> *With a lighter step, the toes springy, the eyes*
> *Eager as a bird's, and every man*
> *Had a coiled spring in his nerves that drove him*
> *In a restless fury of life.*
> >>>>>>>>>>>>>> *The bloods mingled*
> Madly . . . . (Who knows
> What strange multi-fathered child will come
> Out of the nervous travail of these bloods
> To fashion in a new world continent
> A newer breed of men?)

Given conditions making for rapid change, the question thus put is the question of how far the plasticity of the American stock is likely to lead. Clearly, every ethnic stock in America, unless it is caught and isolated in some eddy of the American stream, is breeding toward a new form of its own type, where it will be more or less stabilized? Or is the process of change a continuing and cumulative one resulting in the emergence of an inclusive new ethnic type, like a loose sort of tent to cover the existing types which will survive yet be transformed?

The probabilities point to something less defined than either of these. We do not yet know what ethnic future lies ahead for America, since genetics is changing its insights and outlook so rapidly. Earnest Hooton, a physical anthropologist who liked to make bold forays into the future, predicted that "the stubby, bone-and-muscle Mr. Americas of today" are doomed to disappear or to be "reduced to the ranks of the institutionalized malefactors." They will be replaced (said Hooton) by a more "attentuated" body build, "taller and more gangling than ever, with big feet, horse faces, and deformed dental arches"; the women "less busty and buttocky than those of our generation." There are other guesses of the future stock, some of them less unattractive. But their common premise is that a new ethnic entity is forming which will carry with it the multiform freightage of all past generations, but in which there will also be some central cast of temperament, physique, and lineament that crops up more and more frequently.

This does not mean that the old stocks will disappear or that America will become ethnically uniform. The processes of heredity and their interplay with the physical and cultural environment are too complex to allow for uniformity. The gene variants of so heterogeneous a population as the American are fantastically large in number, and the potential directions of American stock are great. This is the first great instance in history where ethnic abundance has combined with so great a freedom in marriage, to produce an unimaginable ethnic future.

If then we ask again, "Is there an American stock?" the answer must be that there are many stocks in America—more than have ever been gathered together before within a national unit; that none of them, whatever its claims and arrogance, is more American than the others, and none, whatever its sense of inferiority, less American; that each is different from what it was in its area of ethnic origin—each touched and changed by the alchemy of the American environment, by the fact of living and mingling with all the others on the American continent. America has become a great biological and psychological laboratory, whose experiments may issue in undreamed-of results. In all the stocks there has been, whether obviously or subtly, a breeding away from type; there has also been, subtly rather than obviously, slowly, ever so slowly, and yet unmistakably, a breeding *toward* new types that have not yet emerged.

When they emerge they will be the creature of America, not America *their* creature. Yet as we watch the yeast working in the ever-re-created human material of America, can we doubt that the determiners of a not unimaginable American future are at work here? "There is but one victory that I know is sure," wrote Saint-Exupéry, "and that is the victory that is lodged in the energy of the seed." Given what we know about American stock, we must take this to mean the victory not of the seed's rigidity but of its plasticity.

IN SEARCH OF A MAJORITY:
AN ADDRESS

James Baldwin

I am supposed to speak this evening on the goals of American society as they involve minority rights, but what I am really going to do is to invite you to join me in a series of speculations. Some of them are dangerous, some of them painful, all of them are reckless. It seems to me that before we can begin to speak of minority rights in this country, we've got to make some attempt to isolate or to define the majority.

Presumably the society in which we live is an expression—in some way—of the majority will. But it is not so easy to locate this majority. The moment one attempts to define this majority one is faced with several conundrums. Majority is not an expression of numbers, of numerical strength, for example. You may far outnumber your opposition and not be able to impose your will on them or even to modify the rigor with which they impose their will on you, i.e., the Negroes in South Africa or in some counties, some sections, of the American South. You may have beneath your hand all the apparatus of power, political, military, state, and still be unable to use these things to achieve your ends, which is the problem faced by de Gaulle in Algeria and the problem which faced Eisenhower when, largely because of his own inaction, he was forced to send paratroopers into Little Rock. Again, the most trenchant observers of the scene in the South, those who are embattled there, feel that the Southern mobs are not an expression of the Southern majority will. Their impression is that these mobs fill, so to speak, a moral vacuum and that the people who form these mobs would be very happy to be released from their pain, and their ignorance, if someone arrived to show them the way. I would be inclined to agree with this, simply from what we know of human nature. It is not my impression that people wish to become worse; they really wish to become better but very often do not know how. Most people assume the position, in a way, of the Jews in Egypt, who really wished to get to the Promised Land but were afraid of the rigors of the journey; and, of course, before you embark on a journey the terrors of whatever may overtake you on that journey live in the imagination and paralyze you. It was through Moses, according to legend, that they discovered, by undertaking this journey, how much they could endure.

These speculations have led me a little bit ahead of myself. I suppose it can be said that there was a time in this country when an entity existed which could be called the majority, let's say a class, for the lack of a better word, which created the standards by which the country lived or which created the standards to which the country aspired. I am referring or have in mind, perhaps somewhat arbitrarily, the aristocracies of Virginia and New England. These were mainly of Anglo-Saxon stock and they created what Henry James was to refer to, not very much later, as our Anglo-American heritage, or Anglo-American connections. Now at no time did these men ever form anything resembling a popular majority. Their importance was that they kept alive and they bore witness to two elements of a man's life which are not greatly respected among us now: (1) the social forms, called manners, which prevent us from rubbing too abrasively against one another and (2) the interior life, or the life of the mind. These things were important; these things were realities for them and no matter how roughhewn or dark the country was then, it is important to remember that this was also the time when people sat up in log cabins studying very hard by lamplight or candlelight. That they were better educated than we are now can be proved by comparing the political speeches of that time with those of our own day.

Now, what I have been trying to suggest in all this is that the only useful definition of the word "majority" does not refer to numbers, and it does not refer to power. It refers to influence. Someone said, and said it very accurately, that what is honored in a country is cultivated there. If we apply this touchstone to American life we can scarcely fail to arrive at a very grim view of it. But I think we have to look grim facts in the face because if we don't, we can never hope to change them.

These vanished aristocracies, these vanished standard bearers, had several limitations, and not the least of these limitations was the fact that their standards were essentially nostalgic. They referred to a past condition; they referred to the achievements, the laborious achievements, of a stratified society; and what was evolving in America had nothing to do with the past. So inevitably what happened, putting it far too simply, was that the old forms gave way before the European tidal wave, gave way before the rush of Italians, Greeks, Spaniards, Irishmen, Poles, Persians, Norwegians, Swedes, Danes, wandering Jews from every nation under heaven, Turks, Armenians, Lithuanians, Japanese, Chinese, and Indians. Everybody was here suddenly in the melting pot, as we like to say, but without any intention of being melted. They were here because they had wanted to leave wherever they had been and they were here to establish a new identity. I doubt if history has ever seen such a spectacle, such a conglomeration of hopes, fears, and desires. I suggest, also, that they presented a problem for the Puritan God, who had never heard of them and of whom they had never heard. Almost always as they arrived, they took their places as a minority, a minority because their influence was so slight and because it was their necessity to make themselves over in the image of their new and unformed country. There were no longer any universally accepted forms or standards, and since all the roads to the achievement of an identity had vanished, the problem of status in American life became and it remains today acute. In a way, status became a kind of substitute for identity, and because money and the things money can buy is the universally accepted symbol here of status, we are often condemned as materialists. In fact, we are much closer to being metaphysical because nobody has ever expected from things the miracles that we expect.

Now I think it will be taken for granted that the Irish, the Swedes, the Danes, etc., who came here can no longer be considered in any serious way as minorities; and the question of anti-Semitism presents too many special features to be profitably discussed here tonight. The American minorities can be placed on a kind of color wheel. For example, when we think of the American boy, we don't usually think of a Spanish, Turkish, a Greek, or a Mexican type, still less of an Oriental type. We usually think of someone who is kind of a cross between the Teuton and the Celt, and I think it is interesting to consider what this image suggests. Outrageous as this image is, in most cases, it is the national self-image. It is an image which suggests hard work and good clean fun and chastity and piety and success. It leaves out of account, of course, most of the people in the country, and most of the facts of life, and there is not much point in discussing those virtues it suggests, which are mainly honored in the breach. The point is that it has almost nothing to do with what or who an American really is. It has nothing to do with what life is. Beneath this bland, this conqueror-image, a great many unadmitted despairs and confusions, and anguish and unadmitted crimes and failures hide. To speak in my own person, as a member of the nation's most oppressed minority, the oldest oppressed minority, I want to suggest most seriously that before we can do very much in the way of clear thinking or clear doing as relates to the minorities in this country, we must first crack the American image and find out and deal with what it hides. We cannot discuss the state of our minorities until we first have some sense of what we are, who we are, what our goals are, and what we take life to be. The question is not what we can do now for the hypothetical Mexican, the hypothetical Negro. The question is what we really want out of life, for ourselves, what we think is real.

Now I think there is a very good reason why the Negro in this country has been treated for such a long time in such a cruel way, and some of the reasons are economic and some of them are political. We have discussed these reasons without ever coming to any kind of resolution for a very long time. Some of them are social, and these reasons are somewhat more important because they have to do with our social panic, with our fear of losing status. This really amounts sometimes to a kind of social paranoia. One cannot afford to lose status on this peculiar ladder, for the prevailing notion of American life seems to involve a kind of rung-by-rung ascension to some hideously desirable state. If this is one's concept of life, obviously one cannot afford to slip back one rung. When one slips, one slips back not a rung but back into chaos and no longer knows who he is. And this reason, this fear, suggests to me one of the real reasons for the status of the Negro in this country. In a way, the Negro tells us where the bottom is: *because he is there*, and *where* he is, beneath us, we know where the limits are and how far we must not fall. We must not fall beneath him. We must never allow ourselves to fall that low, and I am not trying to be cynical or sardonic. I think if one examines the myths which have proliferated in this country concerning the Negro, one discovers beneath these myths a kind of sleeping terror of some condition which we refuse to imagine. In a way if the Negro were not here, we might be forced to deal within ourselves and our own personalities, with all those vices, all those conundrums, and all those mysteries with which we have invested the Negro race. Uncle Tom is, for example, if he is called uncle, a kind of saint. He is there, he endures, he will forgive us, and this is a key to that image. But if he is not uncle, if he is merely Tom he is a danger to everybody. He will wreak havoc on the countryside. When he is Uncle Tom he has no sex—when he is Tom, he does—and this obviously says much more about the people who invented this myth than it does about the people who are the object of it.

If you have been watching television lately, I think this is unendurably clear in the faces of those screaming people in the South, who are quite incapable of telling you what it is they are afraid of. They do not really know what it is they are afraid of, but they know they are afraid of something, and they are so frightened that they are nearly out of their minds. And this same fear obtains on one level or another, to varying degrees, throughout the entire country. We would never, never allow Negroes to starve, to grow bitter, and to die in ghettos all over the country if we were not driven by some nameless fear that has nothing to do with Negroes. We would never victimize, as we do, children whose only crime is color and keep them, as we put it, in their place. We wouldn't drive Negroes mad as we do by accepting them in ball parks, and on concert stages, but not in our homes and not in our neighborhoods, and not in our churches. It is only too clear that even with the most malevolent will in the world Negroes can never manage to achieve one-tenth of the harm which we fear. No, it has every-thing to do with ourselves and this is one of the reasons that for all these generations we have disguised this problem in the most incredible jargon. One of the reasons we are so fond of sociological reports and research and investigational committees is because they hide something. As long as we can deal with the Negro as a kind of statistic, as something to be manipulated, something to be fled from, or something to be given something to, there is something we can avoid, and what we can avoid is what he really, really means to us. The question that still ends these discussions in an extraordinary question: Would you let your sister marry one? The question, by the way, depends on several extraordinary assumptions. First of all it assumes, if I may say so, that I *want* to marry your sister and it also assumes that if I asked your sister to marry me, she would immediately say yes. There is no reason to make either of these assumptions, which are clearly irrational, and the key to why these assumptions are held is not to be found by asking Negroes. The key to why these assumptions are held has something to do with some insecurity in the people who hold them. It is only, after all, too clear that everyone born is going to have a rather difficult time getting through his life. It is only too clear that people fall in love according to some principle that we have not as yet been able to define, to discover or to isolate, and that marriage depends entirely on the two people involved; so that this objection does not hold water. It certainly is not justification for segregated schools or for ghettos or for mobs. I suggest that the role of the Negro in American life has something to do with our concept of what God is, and from my point of view, this concept is not big enough. It has got to be made much bigger than it is because God is, after all, not anybody's toy. To be with God is really to be involved with some enormous, overwhelming desire, and joy, and power which you cannot control, which controls you. I conceive of my own life as a journey toward something I do not understand, which in the going toward, makes me better. I conceive of God, in fact, as a means to control others. Love does not begin and end the way we seem to think it does. Love is a battle, love is a war; love is a growing up. No one in the world—in the entire world —knows more—knows Americans better or, odd as this may sound, loves them more than the American Negro. This is because he has had to watch you, outwit you, deal with you, and bear you, and sometimes even bleed and die with you, ever since we got here, that is, since both of us, black and white, got here—and this is a wedding. Whether I like it or not, or whether you like it or not, we are bound together forever. We are part of each other. What is happening to every Negro in the country at any time is also happening to you. There is no way around this. I am suggesting that these walls—these artificial walls—which have been up so long to protect us from something we fear, must come down. I think that what we really have to do is to create a country in which there are no minorities—for the first time in the history of the world. The one thing that all Americans have in common is that they have no other identity apart from the identity which is being achieved on this continent. This is not the English necessity, or the Chinese necessity, or the French necessity, but they are born into a framework which allows them their identity. The necessity of Americans to achieve an identity is a historical and a present personal fact and this is the connection between you and me.

This brings me back, in a way, to where I started. I said that we couldn't talk about minorities until we had talked about majorities, and I also said that majorities had nothing to do with numbers or with power, but with influence, with moral influence,· and I want to suggest this: that the majority for which everyone is seeking which must reassess and release us from our past and deal with the present and create standards worthy of what a man may be—this majority is you. No one else can do it. The world is before you and you need not take it or leave it as it was when you came in.

THE PROMISED LAND

STRANGERS IN A NEW WORLD

I pray thee ask no questions
This is that Golden Land.
Henry Roth

The promise of America has always been an important theme in our literature; for ethnic authors it has been a dominant, compelling subject. The meeting of the American dream and the American reality—the promise and, for some, the failure of that promise—is a central conflict in the work of our greatest writers. For ethnic artists the conflict arises naturally from immigration to the New World —it is their first subject, their most personal subject.

In the nineteenth and early twentieth centuries, ethnic writers informed their work with an idealism that transcended the harsh conditions of migration to America or, in the case of the Negro, the difficult adjustment from slave to free man; later authors were less tolerant of prejudice and injustice. Emma Lazarus and Mary Antin celebrated "the new colossus" and "the promised land"; but Henry Roth viewed this "vast incredible land" with less than sympathetic eyes, and Michael Gold wrote bluntly of Jews without money. Booker T. Washington anticipated a better life for black people if only they adopted the puritanic values of hard work, cleanliness, earnestness, and thrift; but sixty years later Claude Brown depicted what it meant to be a "manchild in the promised land," and Langston Hughes suggested the anxieties that attend migration from the South to the North in his "Evenin' Air Blues."

The conflicts that arise from the promise of America and the inevitable frustrations of living here are reflected in the following works by strangers in a new world. For these immigrants America was "that Golden Land," the last place in the world that could be asked to speak for the family of man.

THE NEW COLOSSUS*

Emma Lazarus

Not like the brazen giant of Greek fame,
With conquering limbs astride from land to land;
Here at our sea-washed, sunset gates shall stand
A mighty woman with a torch, whose flame
Is the imprisoned lightning, and her name
Mother of Exiles. From her beacon-hand
Glows world-wide welcome; her mild eyes command
The air-bridged harbor that twin cities frame.
"Keep, ancient lands, your storied pomp!" cries she
With silent lips. "Give me your tired, your poor,
Your huddled masses yearning to breathe free,
The wretched refuse of your teeming shore.
Send these, the homeless, tempest-tost to me,
I lift my lamp beside the golden door!"

---

* Written in aid of Bartholdi Pedestal Fund, November 1883 [now inscribed on a plaque on the Statue of Liberty.-M.U.S.]

THE PROMISED LAND

Mary Antin

Having made such good time across the ocean, I ought to be able to proceed no less rapidly on *terra firma,* where, after all, I am more at home. And yet here is where I falter. Not that I hesitated, even for the space of a breath, in my first steps in America. There was no time to hesitate. The most ignorant immigrant, on landing, proceeds to give and receive greetings, to eat, sleep, and rise, after the manner of his own country; wherein he is corrected, admonished, and laughed at, whether by interested friends or the most indifferent strangers; and his American experience is thus begun. The process is spontaneous on all sides, like the education of the child by the family circle. But while the most stupid nursery maid is able to contribute her part toward the result, we do not expect an analysis of the process to be furnished by any member of the family, least of all by the engaging infant. The philosophical maiden aunt alone, or some other witness equally psychological and aloof, is able to trace the myriad efforts by which the little Johnnie or Nellie acquires a secure hold on the disjointed parts of the huge plaything, life.

Now I was not exactly an infant when I was set down, on a May day some fifteen years ago, in this pleasant nursery of America. I had long since acquired the use of my faculties, and had collected some bits of experience, practical and emotional and had even learned to give an account of them. Still, I had very little perspective, and my observations and comparisons were superficial. I was too much carried away to analyze the forces that were moving me. My Polotzk I knew well before I began to judge it and experiment with it. America was bewilderingly strange, unimaginable complex, delightfully unexplored. I rushed impetuously out of the cage of my provincialism and looked eagerly about the brilliant universe. My question was, What have we here?—not, What does this mean? That query came much later. When I now become retrospectively introspective, I fall into the predicament of the centipede in the rhyme, who got along very smoothly until he was asked which leg came after which, whereupon he became so rattled that he couldn't take a step. I know I have come on a thousand feet, on wings, winds, and American machines,—I have leaped and run and climbed and crawled,—but to tell which step came after which I find a puzzling matter. Plenty of maiden aunts were present during my second infancy, in the guise of immigrant officials, school-teachers, settlement workers, and sundry other unprejudiced and critical observers. Their statistics I might properly borrow to fill the gaps in my recollections, but I am prevented by my sense of harmony. The individual, we know, is a creature unknown to the statistician, whereas I undertook to give the personal view of everything. So I am bound to unravel, as well as I can, the tangle of events, outer and inner, which made up the first breathless years of my American life.

During his three years of probation, my father had made a number of false starts in business. His history for that period is the history of thousands who come to America, like him, with pockets empty, hands untrained to the use of tools, minds cramped by centuries of repression in their native land. Dozens of these men pass under your eyes every day, my American friend, too absorbed in their honest affairs to notice the looks of suspicion which you cast at them, the repugnance with which you shrink from their touch. You see them shuffle from door to door with a basket of spools and buttons, or bending over the sizzling irons in a basement tailor shop, or rummaging in your ash can, or moving a pushcart from curb to curb, at the command of burly policeman. "The Jew peddler!" you say, and dismiss him from your premises and from your thoughts, never dreaming that the sordid drama of his days may have a moral that concerns you. What if the creature with the untidy beard carries in his bosom his citizenship papers? What if the cross-legged tailor is supporting a boy in college who is one day going to mend your state constitution for you? What if the ragpicker's daughters are hastening over the ocean to teach your children in the public schools? Think, every time you pass the greasy alien on the street, that he was born thousands of

years before the oldest native American; and he may have
something to communicate to you, when you two shall have
learned a common language. Remember that his very physiognomy is a cipher the key to which it behooves you to search
for most diligently.

By the time we joined my father, he had surveyed many
avenues of approach toward the coveted citadel of fortune. One
of these, heretofore untried, he now proposed to essay, armed
with new courage, and cheered on by the presence of his family. In partnership with an energetic little man who had an
English chapter in his history, he prepared to set up a refreshment booth on Crescent Beach. But while he was completing
arrangements at the beach we remained in town, where we
enjoyed the educational advantages of a thickly populated
neighborhood; namely, Wall Street, in the West End of Boston.

Anybody who knows Boston knows that the West and
North Ends are the wrong ends of that city. They form the
tenement district, or, in the newer phrase, the slums of Boston.
Anybody who is acquainted with the slums of any American
metropolis knows that that is the quarter where poor immigrants foregather, to live, for the most part, as unkempt, half-
washed, toiling, unaspiring foreigners; pitiful in the eyes of
social missionaries, the despair of boards of health, the hope of
ward politicians, the touchstone of American democracy. The
well-versed metropolitan knows the slums as a sort of house of
detention for poor aliens, where they live on probation till they
can show a certificate of good citizenship.

He may know all this and yet not guess how Wall Street,
in the West End, appears in the eyes of a little immigrant from
Polotzk. What would the sophisticated sight-seer say about
Union Place, off Wall Street, where my new home waited for
me? He would say that it is no place at all, but a short box of
an alley. Two rows of three-story tenements are its sides, a
stingy strip of sky is its lid, a littered pavement is the floor, and
a narrow mouth its exit.

But I saw a very different picture on my introduction to
Union Place. I saw two imposing rows of brick buildings, loftier
than any dwelling I had ever lived in. Brick was even on the
ground for me to tread on, instead of common earth or boards.
Many friendly windows stood open, filled with uncovered heads
of women and children. I thought the people were interested in
us, which was very neighborly. I looked up to the topmost row

of windows, and my eyes were filled with the May blue of an American sky!

In our days of affluence in Russia we had been accustomed to upholstered parlors, embroidered linen, silver spoons and candlesticks, goblets of gold, kitchen shelves shining with copper and brass. We had featherbeds heaped halfway to the ceiling; we had clothes presses dusky with velvet and silk and fine woollen. The three small rooms into which my father now ushered us, up one flight of stairs, contained only the necessary beds, with lean mattresses; a few wooden chairs; a table or two; a mysterious iron structure, which later turned out to be a stove; a couple of unornamental kerosene lamps; and a scanty array of cooking utensils and crockery. And yet we were all impressed with our new home and its furniture. It was not only because we had just passed through our seven lean years, cooking in earthern vessels, eating black bread on holidays and wearing cotton; it was chiefly because these wooden chairs and tin pans were American chairs and pans that they shone glorious in our eyes. And if there was anything lacking for comfort or decoration we expected it to be presently supplied—at least, we children did. Perhaps my mother alone, of us newcomers, appreciated the shabbiness of the little apartment, and realized that for her there was as yet no laying down of the burden of poverty.

Our initiation into American ways began with the first step on the new soil. My father found occasion to instruct or correct us even on the way from the pier to Wall Street, which journey we made crowded together in a rickety cab. He told us not to lean out of the windows, not to point, and explained the word "greenhorn." We did not want to be "greenhorns," and gave the strictest attention to my father's instructions. I do not know when my parents found opportunity to review together the history of Polotzk in the three years past, for we children had no patience with the subject; my mother's narrative was constantly interrupted by irrelevant questions, interjections, and explanations.

EVENIN' AIR BLUES

Langston Hughes

Folks, I come up North
Cause they told me de North was fine.
I come up North.
Cause they told me da North was fine.
Been up here six months—
I'm about to lose my mind.

This mornin' for breakfast
I chawed de mornin' air.
This mornin' for breakfast
Chawed de mornin' air.
But this evenin' for supper,
I got evenin' air to spare.

Believe I'll do a little dancin'
Just to drive my blues away—
A little dancin'
To drive my blues away,
Cause when I'm dancin'
De blues forgets to stay.

But if you was to ask me
How de blues they come to be,
Says if you was to ask me
How de blues they come to be—
You wouldn't need to ask me:
Just look at me and see!

MANCHILD IN THE PROMISED LAND

Claude Brown

Foreword

I want to talk about the first Northern urban generation of Negroes. I want to talk about the experiences of a misplaced generation, of a misplaced people in an extremely complex, confused society. This is a story of their searching, their dreams, their sorrows, their small and futile rebellions, and their endless battle to establish their own place in America's greatest metropolis—and in America itself.

The characters are sons and daughters of former Southern sharecroppers. These were the poorest people of the South, who poured into New York City during the decade following the Great Depression. These migrants were told that unlimited opportunities for prosperity existed in New York and that there was no "color problem" there. They were told that Negroes lived in houses with bathrooms, electricity, running water, and indoor toilets. To them, this was the "promised land" that Mammy had been singing about in the cotton fields for many years.

Going to New York was good-bye to the cotton fields, good-bye to "Massa Charlie," good-bye to the chain gang, and, most of all, good-bye to those sunup-to-sundown working hours. One no longer had to wait to get to heaven to lay his burden down; burdens could be laid down in New York.

So, they came, from all parts of the South, like all the black chillun o' God following the sound of Gabriel's horn on that long-overdue Judgment Day. The Georgians came as soon as they were able to pick train fare off the peach trees. They came from South Carolina where the cotton stalks were bare.

The North Carolinians came with tobacco tar beneath their finger-nails.

They felt as the Pilgrims must have felt when they were coming to America. But these descendants of Ham must have been twice as happy as the Pilgrims, because they had been catching twice the hell. Even while planning the trip, they sang spirituals as "Jesus Take My Hand" and "I'm On My Way" and chanted, "Hallelujah, I'm on my way to the promised land!"

It seems that Cousin Willie, in his lying haste, had neglected to tell the folks down home about one of the most important aspects of the promised land: it was a slum ghetto. There was a tremendous difference in the way life was lived up North. There were too many people full of hate and bitterness crowded into a dirty, stinky, uncared-for closet-size section of a great city.

Before the soreness of the cotton fields had left Mama's back, her knees were getting sore from scrubbing "Goldberg's" floor. Nevertheless, she was better off; she had gone from the fire into the frying pan.

The children of these disillusioned colored pioneers inherited the total lot of their parents—the disappointments, the anger. To add to their misery, they had little hope of deliverance. For where does one run to when he's already in the promised land?

As a child, I remember being morbidly afraid. It was a fear that was like a fever that never let up. Sometimes it became so intense that it would just swallow you. At other times, it just kept you shaking. But it was always there. I suppose, in Harlem, even now, the fear is still there.

When I first moved away from the folks, it seemed as though I was moving deeper into the Harlem life that I had wanted to become a part of and farther away from what Mama and Dad wanted me to become a part of. I think, as time went on, they both became aware that the down-home life had kind of had its day. But they didn't know just what was to follow, so how could they tell me?

I didn't realize it until after I had gotten out, but there were other cats in Harlem who were afraid too. They were afraid of getting out of Harlem; they were afraid to go away from their parents. There were some cats who would stay at home; they wouldn't work; they wouldn't do anything. I didn't see how they could do it, but they seemed to manage. They just didn't feel anything about it, but it was pretty evident that they were afraid of not being able to turn to their parents when things got rough. And they were afraid of getting out there and not being able to make it.

When I moved up on Hamilton Terrace, I suppose I still had my fears, but it was something. I was a move away from fear, toward challenges, toward the positive anger that I think every young man should have. All the time before, I thought I was angry. I guess I was, but the anger was stifled. It was an impotent anger because it was stifled by fear. I was more afraid than I was angry. There were many times when I wondered if Rock would have hurt anybody if he hadn't been in Harlem . . . or if Johnny Wilkes would have been so mean if he hadn't been in Harlem. I was afraid of what Harlem could bring out in a person. When I decided to move, I was trying to get away from the fear.

Everybody I knew in Harlem seemed to have some kind of dream. I didn't have any dreams, not really. I didn't have any dreams for hitting the number. I didn't have any dreams for getting a big car or a fine wardrobe. I bought expensive clothes because it was a fad. It was the thing to do, just to show that you had money. I wanted to be a part of what was going on, and this was what was going on.

I didn't have any dreams of becoming anything. All I knew for certain was that I had my fears. I suppose just about everybody else knew the same thing. They had their dreams, though, and I guess that's what they had over me. As time went by, I was sorry for the people whose dreams were never realized.

When Butch was alive, sometimes I would go uptown to see him. He'd be sick. He'd be really messed up. I'd give him some drugs, and then he'd be more messed up than before. He wouldn't be sick, but I couldn't talk to him, I couldn't reach him. He'd be just sitting on a stoop nodding. Sometimes he'd be slobbering over himself.

I used to remember Butch's dream. Around 1950, he used to dream of becoming the best thief in Harlem. It wasn't a big dream. To him, it was a big dream, but I don't suppose too many people would have seen it as that. Still, I felt sorry for him because it was his dream. I suppose the first time he put the spike in his arm every dream he'd ever had was thrown out the window. Sometimes I wanted to shout at him or snatch him by the throat and say, "Butch, what about your dream?" But there were so many dreams that were lost for a little bit of duji.

I remember Reno used to say that all he wanted was two bars in Harlem and two Cadilllacs. It sounded like something that was all right to me. I used to envy Reno for his dream.

When he first told me, I thought to myself, Wow, if I could just want two bars and two Cadillacs. I was hoping all the time that he'd make it. Once I asked him, "Reno, what's the two Cadillacs for, man? You can only drive one at a time."

He said, "One I'm gon get for my woman."

I said, "Oh, then the other one'll be hers."

"No, man, you can't expect but so much out of a bitch, not any bitch, I don't care how good she is."

"Uh-huh. So what?"

Reno said, "Every time a bitch fucks up, I'm gonna just cut her loose and get another one. Every time I get a new bitch, the other Cadillac's gon be hers. You dig it?"

"Yeah, I dig it. It sounds like a pretty hip life."

"I don't know, man, but that's what I want to do, Sonny."

"Yeah, Reno, I guess that's all that matters, that a cat does what he wants to do."

I used to feel that I belonged on the Harlem streets and that, regardless of what I did, nobody had any business to take me off the streets.

I remember when I ran away from shelters, places that they sent me to, here in the city. I never ran away with the thought in mind of coming home. I always ran away to get back to the streets. I always thought of Harlem as home, but I never thought of Harlem as being in the house. To me, home was the streets. I suppose there were many people who felt that. If home was so miserable, the street was the place to be. I wonder if mine was really so miserable, or if it was that there was so much happening out in the street that it made home seem such a dull and dismal place.

When I was very young—about five years old, maybe younger—I would always be sitting out on the stoop. I remember Mamma telling me and Carole to sit on the stoop and not to move away from in front of the door. Even when it was time to go up and Carole would be pulling on me to come upstairs and eat, I never wanted to go, because there was so much out there in that street.

You might see somebody get cut or killed. I could go out in the street for an afternoon, and I would see so much that, when I came in the house, I'd be talking and talking for what seemed like hours. Dad would say, "Boy, why don't you stop that lyin'? You know you didn't see all that. You know you didn't see nobody do that." But I knew I had.

UP FROM PUERTO RICO

Elena Padilla

Many Hispanos see their lives and those of their children as unfolding in this country. To them, Puerto Rico is something of the past, and for many of the children who are growing up or have grown up in the United States, Puerto Rico is less than an echo; it is a land they have never visited, a "foreign country." Some migrants consciously decide at some point or other to make their homes here, to stay in this country permanently, never again turning back to look at Puerto Rico. These are to be found even among recent migrants. They are the people who view their future as being tied up with whatever life in New York may offer. We can call these Hispanos settlers, and can distinguish them from transients or those who regard their future life as gravitating toward Puerto Rico and who hope to return to live there later on, after their children have grown up or when they have enough savings to buy a house or start a business.

Settlers who have migrated to New York as adults are those who have lost or who give little importance to their relationships with their home towns, their friends and relatives who are still in Puerto Rico or are recent migrants to New York. They have cut off their emotional ties with the homeland, but they may still have significant interpersonal relationships with their kin and within cliques that may consist largely of persons from their own home town who are residents of New York. The settler fulfills or expects to fulfill his social needs in relation to living in New York.

One sort of settler has in his formative years moved away from his home town, rural or urban, in Puerto Rico to another town or city in the island itself. He started to break away from the primary relations and bonds of his home town then. By the time he comes to New York, he has already experienced life situations in which primary groups derived from his home town contexts have no longer operated for him, in which he has developed new social bonds, wherever he may have been. The primary group relationships of this kind of settler lack the continuity and history of those of the settler who, throughout his life, whether in Puerto Rico or New York, has been able to continue depending and relying on persons known to him for many years.

The consequent social adjustments that the settlers here have made are the outcome of a gradual process of adaptation to living in New York, and of recognizing that home, friends, and other interests are here and not in Puerto Rico. The settler may be oriented within the ethnic group of Puerto Ricans in New York, partially by his participation in the cliques and other small groups of people from his home town and in those of his New York neighbors. But the one who has lost his primary ties with a home town and has been exposed to a greater variety of group experiences in Puerto Rico through moving about there is likely to become involved in New York in groups and cliques that are not derived from any particular home town context. The kinds of adjustments he can make to these changing group situations is related to his own background experiences as a migrant in Puerto Rico itself. There he may have reacted to and resolved the social stresses of the uprooting he underwent as a migrant, acquiring as a result the social techniques for making it easier to establish satisfactory social relationships outside of home town and family settings.

The migrant who is essentially a transient, on the other hand, still maintains ties with the homeland: he has a strong feeling of having a country in Puerto Rico, a national identity there, and there he has friends and relatives whom he writes, visits, and can rely upon. "If things get bad" (*si las cosas se ponen malas*), he can go back to Puerto Rico and get sympathy and help from those he grew up with. The transient migrants can be expected to feel obligated to their Puerto Rican friends and relatives, should these come to New York. The settler, on the other hand, is likely to say that he will "not return to Puerto Rico even if I have to eat stones in New York," and he will feel less bound to friends and relatives left in the island.

But becoming a settler does not necessarily involve a conscious decision. Transients may change into settlers as life orientations and social relations that are satisfactory and meaningful to them become part of their life in New York. The fundamental difference between settlers and transients is that the settler's life is organized in New York, while that of the transient is both in New York and in Puerto Rico.

In New York the lives of Puerto Ricans must, obviously, undergo profound changes. For those who learn American life in a slum like Eastville, the experience is one thing. For Puerto Ricans who were in better circumstances and had better life-chances in the island, it is another: they can begin life in New York as members as the middle class and avoid the particular cultural and social difficulties that beset the residents of Eastville. Yet all have their difficulties. Many overcome them. Many Eastvillers have made their way out of the slum into satisfactory fulfillment of their aspirations for themselves and their children. Others have returned to Puerto Rico.

One of the matters that concern Eastville Puerto Ricans is what has happened and is happening to Puerto Ricans in New York. Among migrants, social and cultural changes among Hispanos are a conscious preoccupation. They see the results of change in their own lives and in those of their friends. It is on this basis that they evaluate social behavior. Their awareness also reflects the conflicting values, orientations, and ambivalence of New York Hispanos.

True, old migrants and Hispanos who have grown up in New York regard recent migrants as representing a departure from their culture and as being socially inferior; on the other hand, recent migrants, in turn, express discontent with the ways Hispanos "are"—behave—in this country. George Espino, a New York-born man of Puerto Rican parents voiced a sentiment frequently heard from others who like himself have grown up in New York: "The Puerto Ricans that are coming over today, well, they're the most hated people . . . the most hated people." Migrants, particularly those who have come as adults, contrast and evaluate the changes they experienced in their lives in Puerto Rico with those they are experiencing in New York. To them, changes here in family life, in the expectancies of what family members can demand of each other, in the ways children are brought up, in marital behavior, and in the behavior of men, women, and children—all these factors that govern daily life—are of concern. Migrants are conscious of these changes and speak of how they have something to do both with modern life and with living in New York. Some of these changes are acceptable and "good," while others are disapproved of and considered "bad."

Migrants write of their experiences in New York, tell of them on visits to Puerto Rico, or show in their behavior the new ways they have adopted. In Puerto Rico some of these types of behavior are considered to be for the best, others for the worst. Potential migrants in the island know their future life in New York is going to be different from their life in Puerto Rico. How, and to what extent, however, is part of the adventure and "changing environment" they will find in New York.

The impact of New York life on Puerto Rican migrants is described in fact and popular fancy, but whether it is described glowingly, soberly, or depressingly, depends on the aspirations, frustrations, hopes, and anxieties of the one who is speaking. Men, women, and children change in New York, it is said. How?

Clara Fredes, now a mother of three, who migrated after the Second World War when she was a teen-ager, replied to a member of the field team when asked if there were any differences between "the way people act here and in Puerto Rico," that "when women get here they act too free. They go out and stand in the street and don't cook dinner or anything. Puerto Rican women in New York City are bad. They talk to other men beside their husband, and just aren't nice. They boss the men. In Puerto Rico a wife obeys her husband, and keeps house, and takes care of her children. But here they run wild. [They are] all day long in the candy store talking and forgetting about their houses. Men here don't always support their wives and children. They are too free too. They think they can get away with everything, but I think it's the woman's fault. They are so bad. They don't take care of the children right. The children [are] out on the streets at all hours of the night."

Another informant, Gina Ortiz, said that Puerto Rican women in New York like to go dancing the mambo and drinking and that "they don't do it in Puerto Rico. In Puerto Rico the woman who smokes and drinks is a bad woman."

Rosa Burgos also explained changes in the behavior of women migrants. "[It is] because they work and they have too much freedom. In Puerto Rico the wife is always in the house.

Here they go out, they go to work, get together with another girl, drink beer, and so on. In Puerto Rico they don't do that."

Women who want to be rated as "good" do not admit to having changed in these directions. They would claim that they do not drink, smoke, or work outside the home, though they may acknowledge having changed in such areas as child-rearing, including giving greater freedom to their children.

Among changes that men undergo in New York, Dolores Miro mentioned that "some of them take friends. The friends like to drink and has women in the street. They change. They like to do same thing the friends do. . . . In Puerto Rico they have the same friends always, but here they have friends from other places, other towns. Some of them are good friends, some bad."

Good men are expected not to change in New York, but to continue recognizing their obligations to their wives and children. They may say they do not have friends in New York because friends get a man in trouble.

A couple that consider themselves good and as having a satisfactory relationship with each other and their children may deny changes in their lives in New York. Manuel and Sophia Tres, in telling a fieldworker about themselves, said, "We don't have any change. We still the same." Manuel continued, "Some of them [Hispanos] when they come here they want to go to the bar and drink, are drunk people and have plenty girl friends," to which Sophia added, "because they make more money to spend. We are not changed, we have the same customs."

In New York children also change, in a variety of ways. It is more difficult to make them respect their parents and elders, and one must keep them upstairs in order to prevent their becoming too uncontrollable and bad. For Juana Roman: "In Puerto Rico the fathers don't want the children to do what they want. They are strict; is better there. In Puerto Rico if your kids do anything wrong, the father punishes. Here you can't punish a big boy. . . . One day my boy went with another boy and they took a train and got lost, and when I got to the Children's Shelter, the lady said, 'Don't punish the boy' and I said, 'Oh yes [I will punish him], I don't want him to do it again.' I see many kids that they do what they want."

Antonio Velez, now in her mid-thirties, finds that in this country people are nice to old people, but says that in Puerto

Rico old people are more respected. Her children do not respect in the same way she respected her father and mother in Puerto Rico when she was a child. Yet she is acceptant to some of the changes in patterns of respect she finds among her children. Says she, "Everybody is nice with the old people here in this country. They take care better of the old people and the children. I didn't pay too much attention to it in Puerto Rico. They are nice too. Everybody respects old people. The children are more respectful to old people in Puerto Rico than here . . . I know. I never used to argue with my mother in Puerto Rico. If she had a reason or no, I keep quiet. And with my father too. The word that he said was the only word to me. If he said not to go to a movie, I didn't discute [argue] that with him. I didn't go. No here. The children are more free here. Tommy, when I say, do that, and he don't want to and he explains me why, I don't mind that. I think it is better for him. You know, we didn't do that but it was not good inside. I think so, because they are human beings too. I love my father and mother because they are so good to me. If I didn't go to movies they may have the reason to say no, but I don't know it. Maybe that way, if I know it, I would have been better."

Children who have migrated recently at ages when they had friends and were allowed to play in the yards and streets in their home towns and now are being reared "upstairs in the home" speak of their past life in Puerto Rico with nostalgia. Lydia Rios, age twelve, says that "here one cannot do anything," referring to having to remain at home, sitting and watching from a window the play of other children, except when she goes to church or school.

Advantages listed of living in New York are the higher wages and income, better opportunities to educate the children, better medical care, more and better food, more and better clothes, furniture, and material things here than in Puerto Rico. In New York one can even save money to go back to Puerto Rico and purchase a house. Which place is better to live in is contingent on whether the migrant has realized or is on his way to realizing the aspirations and hopes connected with his coming to New York.

For Emilio Cruz it is better to live in New York than in Puerto Rico. "I think life in New York is better. We have better living in New York and can give the children the food they want and need. When we work we have more money. We spend more here but we earn more so we can live better. In Puerto Rico we rent a house [for] $10.00 or $12.00 a month, and here we [pay] so much [more] money and [must have] a lease too, [of] two or three years in New York."

Migrants speak of the future with reference to a good life, and a good life can be realized either in New York or in Puerto Rico, though one must search for it. As Rafael Dorcas put it, "A good life is when we work and we has the things we need for all the family. I think that's a good life."

THE FORTUNATE PILGRIM

Mario Puzo

While the war raged over the world, the Italians living along the western wall of the city finally grasped the American dream in their callused hands. Money rolled over the tenements like a flood. Men worked overtime and doubletime in the railroad, and those whose sons had died or been wounded worked harder than all the rest, knowing grief would not endure as long as poverty.

For the clan of Angeluzzi-Corbo the magic time had come. The house on Long Island was bought, for cold cash, from people mysteriously ruined by the war. A two-family house, so that Larry and Louisa and their children could live in one apartment under the watchful eye of Lucia Santa. There would be separate, doored bedrooms for everyone, even Gino when he came home from the war.

On the last day Lucia Santa could not bear to help her children strip the apartment, fill the huge barrels and wooden boxes. That night, lying all alone in her bed, she could not sleep. The wind whistled softly through the window cracks that had always been shielded by drapes. Lighter patches of wall that had held pictures gleamed in the darkness. There were strange sounds in the apartment, in the empty cupboards and closets, as if all the ghosts of forty years had been set free.

Staring up at the ceiling Lucia Santa finally became drowsy. She put out her arm to trap a child against the wall. Falling into dreams she listened for Gino and Vincenzo to go to bed and for Frank Corbo to come through the hallway door. And where had Lorenzo gone again? Never fear, she told little Octavia, no harm can come to my children while I live, and then, trembling, she stood before her own father and begged

53

linen for her bridal bed. And then she was weeping and her father would not comfort her and she was alone forever.

She had never meant to be a pilgrim. To sail a fearful ocean.

The apartment turned cold and Lucia Santa awoke. She got up and dressed in the dark, then put a pillow on the window sill. Leaning out over Tenth Avenue she waited for light and for the first time in years really heard the railroad engines and freight cars grinding against each other in the yards across the street. Sparks flew through the darkness and there was the clear ringing of steel clashing on steel. Far away on the Jersey shore there were no lights because of war, only stars caught on the shade of night.

In the morning there was a long wait for the moving vans. Lucia Santa greeted neighbors who came to wish the family good luck. But none of the old friends came, none were left on Tenth Avenue. The *Panetierre* had sold his bakery when his son, Guido, came home wounded too badly for work. He had moved far out on Long Island, as far out as Babylon or West Islip. The mad barber with his houseful of daughters had retired; with so few male heads to cut because of the war, he too had moved out to Long Island to a town called Massapequa, near enough the *Panetierre* for a game of cards on Sundays. And others too had left for all those strange towns dreamed of for so many years.

Dr. Barbato, to everyone's surprise, had volunteered for the Army and in Africa had become a hero of some sort, with his pictures in the magazines and a story of his exploits so terrifying that his father suffered a stroke from sheer exasperation at his son's foolishness. Poor Teresina Coccalitti never moved out of her apartment, fiercely guarding the countless tins of olive oil and fat that would some day ransom her sons from death. Gino's childhood friend, Joey Bianco, had in some clever fashion escaped the Army, no one knew how, had become rich, and bought a palace for his mother and father in New Jersey. So now it was really time for the Angeluzzi-Corbo family to leave.

Finally Piero Santini came with his trucks from Tuckahoe. The war made such services dear to arrange, but Santini came as a favor to a native of his very own village in Italy. And because, mellowed now, it gladdened his heart to help the happy end to this story.

Lucia Santa had shrewdly left out a pot and some scarred cups. She gave Santini coffee and they drank it while looking down on Tenth Avenue, balancing their drinks on the window sill. Octavia and Sal and Lena carried light packages down to the waiting vans while two old muscular Italians, grunting like donkeys, let their backs be saddled with enormous bureaus and beds.

After a time the only thing left in the apartment was the backless kitchen chair deemed too worthless for the fine house on Long Island. Louisa and her three little children came up the stairs then to wait with them, the little villains wading through a sea of discarded clothing and the litter of stripped cupboards and left-over newspaper.

And then the final moment had come. Mr. di Lucca's limousine, now Larry's, was waiting in front of the tenement. Octavia and Louisa swept the little children down the row of dirty, deserted bedrooms and out the door. Then Octavia said to Lucia Santa, "Come on, Ma, let's get out of this dump."

To everyone's surprise a dazed look came over Lucia Santa's face, as if she had never really believed she must leave this house forever. Then instead of going toward the door, she sat on the backless kitchen chair and began to weep.

Octavia shooed Louisa and her children down the stairs before turning on her mother. Her voice was shrill, exasperated. "Ma, what the hell's the matter now? Come on, you can cry in the car. Everybody's waiting." But Lucia Santa bowed her head into her hands. She could not stop her tears.

Then the mother heard Lena's angry voice say, "Leave her alone"; and Sal, who never spoke, said, "We'll bring her down, you go ahead."

Octavia went down the stairs and the mother raised her head. Her two youngest children guarded her on each side. She had not realized they were so grown. Lena was very pretty, very dark, with her father's blue eyes, but her face was like Gino's. Then she felt Salvatore's hand on her shoulder. He had the eyes of a man who could never get angry. In that moment the mother remembered how Sal and Lena, silent in their corner, had watched and surely judged them all. She could not know that to them their mother had been a heroine in some frightening play. They had watched her suffer the blows of fate, their father's fury, her hopeless struggles with Larry and Gino and the terrible grief of Vinnie's death. But as she reached out to touch their bodies she knew that they had judged her and found her innocent.

Then why does Lucia Santa weep in these empty rooms? Who is better than her?

She goes to live in the house on Long Island, her grandchildren beneath her feet. Salvatore and Lena will become doctors or schoolteachers. Her daughter Octavia is a forelady in the dress shops, and her son Lorenzo is the president of a union, giving out jobs as grandly as a duke in Italy. Her son Gino is still alive while millions die. There will always be enough food and money for an old age surrounded by respectful and loving children. Who is better than her?

In Italy forty years ago her wildest dream had not gone so far. And now a million secret voices called out, "Lucia Santa, Lucia Santa, you found your fortune in America," and Lucia Santa weeping on her backless kitchen chair raised her head to cry out against them, "I wanted all this without suffering. I wanted all this without weeping for two lost husbands and a beloved child. I wanted all this without the hatred of that son conceived in true love. I wanted all this without guilt, without sorrow, without fear of death and the terror of a judgment day. In innocence."

America, America, blasphemous dream. Giving so much, why could it not give everything? Lucia Santa wept for the inevitable crimes she had committed against those she loved. In her world, as a child, the wildest dream had been to escape the fear of hunger, sickness and the force of nature. The dream was to stay alive. No one dreamed further. But in America wilder dreams were possible, and she had never known of their existence. Bread and shelter were not enough.

Octavia had wanted to be a teacher. What had Vinnie wanted? Something she would never know. And Gino—what dreams he must have had, surely the wildest of them all. But even now through the tears, through the anguish, a terrible hatred rose, and she thought, most of all he wanted his own pleasure. He had wanted to live like a rich man's son. Then she remembered how she had broken her own father's heart to win linen for her marriage bed.

With terrible clarity she knew Gino would never come home after the war. That he hated her as she had hated her father. That he would become a pilgrim and search for strange Americas in his dreams. And now for the first time Lucia Santa begged for mercy. *Let me hear his footsteps at the door and I will live those forty years again. I will make my father weep and become a pilgrim to sail the fearful ocean. I will let my husband die and stand outside that house in Jersey to scream curses at Filomena with Vincenzo in my arms and then I will weep beside his coffin. And then I will do it once again.*

But having said this, it was all too much. Lucia Santa raised her head and saw that Salvatore and Lena were watching her anxiously. Their grave faces made her smile. Strength surged back into her body, and she thought how handsome her last two children were. They looked so American, too, and this amused her for some reason, as if they had escaped her and the rest of the family.

Salvatore held her coat open so that she could rise easily into it. Lena murmured, "I'll write Gino the new address as soon as we get there." Lucia Santa glanced at her sharply, sure she herself had said nothing aloud. But the young girl's face, so like Gino's, made her want to weep again. She took one last look at the naked walls and then left her home of forty years forever.

Out on Tenth Avenue three women clad in black waited for her with folded arms. She knew them well. One raised her withered hand to salute her, called out, "Lucia Santa, *buona fortuna.*" Truly meant, without malice, yet on a warning note, as if to say, "Beware, there are years to come, life is not over." Lucia Santa bowed her head in thanks.

Larry tapped the steering wheel with impatience as they all scrambled into the limousine. Then he moved it forward slowly so that the two moving vans could follow, moving east toward the Queensborough Bridge. At first, because of the mother's tears, there was a heavy silence, then the three little children squirmed and began fighting. Louisa shouted and slapped them quiet. The tension relaxed and they all talked about the house. Larry said it would take an hour to get there. Every two minutes the children asked, "Are we in Long Island yet?" and Sal or Lena would say, "No, not yet."

Lucia Santa rolled down the window to enjoy the fresh air. She took one of the little boys on her lap and Larry smiled at her and said, "It'll be great living together, huh, Ma?" Lucia Santa caught Lena's eye, but that innocent was like Gino, too simple to understand her mother's grin. Octavia smiled. They had always seen through Larry. They both understood. Larry

was delighted that Louisa and the children would have company, while, he, animal that he was, chased young girls starved
by the war.

Then they were ascending the slope of Queensborough
Bridge, running through the slanted, flashing shadows of
suspended cables. The children stood up to see the slate-gray
water below, but in just a few moments they were off the
bridge and rolling down a wide, tree-lined boulevard. The
children began to shriek, and Lucia Santa told them, yes, now
they were on Long Island.

WHAT THE INDIAN MEANS TO AMERICA

Chief Standing Bear

The feathered and blanketed figure of the American Indian has come to symbolize the American continent. He is the man who through centuries has been moulded and sculped by the same hand that shaped its mountains, forests, and plains, and marked the course of its rivers.

The American Indian is of the soil, whether it be the region of forests, plains, pueblos, or mesas. He fits into the landscape, for the hand that fashioned the continent also fashioned the man for his surroundings. He once grew as naturally as the wild sunflowers; he belongs just as the buffalo belonged.

With a physique that fitted, the man developed fitting skills—crafts which today are called American. And the body had a soul, also formed and moulded by the same master hand of harmony. Out of the Indian approach to existence there came a great freedom—an intense and absorbing love for nature; a respect for life; enriching faith in a Supreme Power; and principles of truth, honesty, generosity, equity, and brotherhood as a guide to mundane relations.

Becoming possessed of a fitting philosophy and art, it was by them that native man perpetuated his identity; stamped it into the history and soul of this country—made land and man one.

By living—struggling, losing, meditating, imbibing, aspiring, achieving—he wrote himself into ineraceable evidence—an evidence that can be and often has been ignored, but never totally destroyed. Living—and all the intangible forces that constitute that phenomenon—are brought into being by Spirit, that which no man can alter. Only the hand of the Supreme Power can transform man; only Wakan Tanka can transform the Indian. But of such deep and infinite graces finite man has little comprehension. He has, therefore, no weapons with which to slay the unassailable. He can only foolishly trample.

The white man does not understand the Indian for the reason that he does not understand America. He is too far removed from its formative processes. The roots of the tree of his life have not yet grasped the rock and soil. The white man is still troubled with primitive fears; he still has in his consciousness the perils of this frontier continent, some of its fastnesses not yet having yielded to his questing footsteps and inquiring eyes. He shudders still with the memory of the loss of his forefathers upon its scorching deserts and forbidding mountain-tops. The man from Europe is still a foreigner and an alien. And he still hates the man who questioned his path across the continent.

But in the Indian the spirit of the land is still vested; it will be until other men are able to divine and meet its rhythm. Men must be born and reborn to belong. Their bodies must be formed of the dust of their forefathers' bones.

The attempted transformation of the Indian by the white man and the chaos that has resulted are but the fruits of the white man's disobedience of a fundamental and spiritual law. The pressure that has been brought to bear upon the native people, since the cessation of armed conflict, in the attempt to force conformity of custom and habit has caused a reaction more destructive than war, and the injury has not only affected the Indian, but has extended to the white population as well. Tyranny, stupidity, and lack of vision have brought about the situation now alluded to as the "Indian Problem."

There is, I insist, no Indian problem as created by the Indian himself. Every problem that exists today in regard to the native population is due to the white man's cast of mind, which is unable, at least reluctant, to seek understanding and achieve adjustment in a new and a significant environment into which it has so recently come.

The white man excused his presence here by saying that he had been guided by the will of his God; and in so saying absolved himself of all responsibility for his appearance in a land occupied by other men.

Then, too, his law was a written law; his divine decalogue reposed in a book. And what better proof that his advent into this country and his subsequent acts were the result of divine will! He brought the Word! There ensued a blind worship of written history, of books, of the written word, that has denuded the spoken word of its power and sacredness. The written word became established as a criterion of the superior man— a symbol of emotional fineness. The man who could write his name on a piece of paper, whether or not he possessed the spiritual fineness to honor those words in speech, was by some miraculous formula a more highly developed and sensitized person than the one who had never had a pen in hand, but whose spoken word was inviolable and whose sense of honor and truth was paramount. With false reasoning was the quality of human character measured by man's ability to make with an implement a mark upon paper. But granting this mode of reasoning be correct and just, then where are to be placed the thousands of illiterate whites who are unable to read and write? Are they, too, 'savages'? Is not humanness a matter of heart and mind, and is it not evident in the form of relationship with men? Is not kindness more powerful than arrogance; and truth more powerful than the sword?

True, the white man brought great change. But the varied fruits of his civilization, though highly colored and inviting, are sickening and deadening. And if it be the part of civilization to maim, rob, and thwart, then what is progress?

I am going to venture that the man who sat on the ground in his tipi meditating on life and its meaning, accepting the kinship of all creatures, and acknowledging unity with the universe of things was infusing into his being the true essence of civilization. And when native man left off this form of development, his humanization was retarded in growth.

Another most powerful agent that gave native man promise of developing into a true human was the responsibility accepted by parenthood. Mating among Lakotas was motivated, of course, by the same laws of attraction that motivate all beings; however, considerable thought was given by parents of both boy and girl to the choosing of mates. And a still greater advantage accrued to the race by the law of self-mastery which the young couple voluntarily placed upon themselves as soon as they discovered they were to become parents. Immediately, and for some time after, the sole thought of the parents was in preparing the child for life. And true civilization lies in the dominance of self and not in the dominance of other men.

How far this idea would have gone in carrying my people upward and toward a better plane of existence, or how much of an influence it was in the development of their spiritual being, it is not possible to say. But it had its promises. And it cannot be gainsaid that the man who is rising to a higher estate is the man who is putting into his being the essence of humanism. It is self-effort that develops, and by this token the greatest factor today in dehumanizing races is the manner in which the machine is used—the product of one man's brain doing the work for another. The hand is the tool that has built man's mind; it, too, can refine it.

The Savage

After subjugation, after dispossession, there was cast the last abuse upon the people who so entirely resented their wrongs and punishments, and that was the stamping and the labeling of them as savages. To make this label stick has been the task of the white race and the greatest salve that it has been able to apply to its sore and troubled conscience now hardened through the habitual practice of injustice.

But all the years of calling the Indian a savage has never made him one; all the denial of his virtues has never taken them from him; and the very resistance he has made to save the things inalienably his has been his saving strength—that which will stand him in need when justice does make its belated appearance and he undertakes rehabilitation.

All sorts of feeble excuses are heard for the continued subjection of the Indian. One of the most common is that he is not yet ready to accept the society of the white man—that he is not yet ready to mingle as a social entity.

This, I maintain, is beside the question. The matter is not one of making-over the external Indian into the likeness of the white race—a process detrimental to both races. Who can say that the white man's way is better for the Indian? Where resides the human judgment with the competence to weigh and value Indian ideals and spiritual concepts; or substitute for them other values?

Then, has the white man's social order been so harmonious and ideal as to merit the respect of the Indian, and for that matter the thinking class of the white race? Is it wise to urge upon the Indian a foreign social form? Let none but the Indian answer!

Rather, let the white brother face about and cast his mental eye upon a new angle of vision. Let him look upon the Indian world as a human world; then let him see to it that human rights be accorded to the Indians. And this for the purpose of retaining for his own order of society a measure of humanity.

The Indian School of Thought

I say again that Indians should teach Indians; that Indians should serve Indians, especially on reservations where the older people remain. There is a definite need of the old for the care and sympathy of the young and they are today perishing for the joys that naturally belong to old Indian people. Old Indians are very close to their progeny. It was their delightful duty to care for and instruct the very young, while in turn they looked forward to being cared for by sons and daughters. These were the privileges and blessings of old age.

Many of the grievances of the old Indian, and his disagreements with the young, find root in the far-removed boarding-school which sometimes takes the little ones at a very tender age. More than one tragedy has resulted when a young boy or girl has returned home again almost an utter stranger. I have seen these happenings with my own eyes and I know they can cause naught but suffering. The old Indian cannot, even if he wished, reconcile himself to an institution that alienates his young. And there is something evil in a system that brings about an unnatural reaction to life; when it makes young hearts callous and unheedful of the needs and joys of the old.

The old people do not speak English and they never will be English-speaking. To place upon such people the burden of understanding and functioning through an office bound up with the routine and red tape of the usual Government office is silly and futile, and every week or so I receive letters from the reservation evidencing this fact. The Indian's natural method of settling questions is by council and conference. From time immemorial, for every project affecting their material, social, and spiritual lives, the people have met together to "talk things over."

To the end that young Indians will be able to appreciate

both their traditional life and modern life they should be doubly educated. Without forsaking reverence for their ancestral teachings, they can be trained to take up modern duties that relate to tribal and reservation life. And there is no problem of reservation importance but can be solved by the joint efforts of the old and the young Indians.

There certainly can be no doubt in the public mind today as to the capacity of the younger Indians in taking on white modes and manners. For many years, and particularly since the days of General Pratt, the young Indian has been proving his efficiency when entering the fields of white man's endeavor and has done well in copying and acquiring the ways of the white man.

The Indian liked the white man's horse and straightway became an expert horseman; he threw away his age-old weapons, the bow and arrow, and matched the white man's skill with gun and pistol; in the field of sports—games of strength and skill—the Indian enters with no shame in comparison; the white man's beads the Indian woman took, developed a technique and an art distinctly her own with no competitor in design; and in the white man's technique of song and dance the Indian has made himself a creditable exponent.

However, despite the fact that Indian schools have been established over several generations, there is a dearth of Indians in the professions. It is most noticeable on the reservations where the numerous positions of consequence are held by white employees instead of trained Indians. For instance, why are not the stores, post-offices, and Government office jobs on the Sioux Reservation held by trained Indians? Why cannot Sioux be reservation nurses and doctors; and road-builders too? Much road work goes on every summer, but the complaint is constant that it is always done by white workmen, and in such a manner as to necessitate its being done again in a short time. Were these numerous positions turned over to trained Indians, the white population would soon find reservation life less attractive and less lucrative.

With school facilities already fairly well established and the capability of the Indian unquestioned, every reservation could well be supplied with Indian doctors, nurses, engineers, road- and bridge-builders, draughtsmen, architects, dentists, lawyers, teachers, and instructors in tribal lore, legends, orations, song, dance, and ceremonial ritual. The Indian, by the very sense of duty, should become his own historian, giving his account of the race—fairer and fewer accounts of the wars and more of statecraft, legends, languages, oratory, and philosophical conceptions. No longer should the Indian be dehumanized in order to make material for lurid and cheap fiction to embellish street-stands. Rather, a fair and correct history of the native American should be incorporated in the curriculum of the public school.

Caucasian youth is fed, and rightly so, on the feats and exploits of their old-world heroes, their revolutionary forefathers, their adventurous pioneer trail-blazers, and in our Southwest through pageants, fiestas, and holidays the days of the Spanish *conquistador* is kept alive.

But Indian youth! They, too, have fine pages in their past history; they, too, have patriots and heroes. And it is not fair to rob Indian youth of their history, the stories of their patriots, which, if impartially written, would fill them with pride and dignity. Therefore, give back to Indian youth all, everything in their heritage that belongs to them and augment it with the best in the modern schools. I repeat, doubly educate the Indian boy and girl.

What a contrast this would make in comparison with the present unhealthy, demoralized place the reservation is today, where the old are poorly fed, shabbily clothed, divested of pride and incentive; and where the young are unfitted for tribal life and untrained for the world of white man's affairs except to hold an occasional job!

Why not a school of Indian thought, built on the Indian pattern and conducted by Indian instructors? Why not a school of tribal art?

Why should not America be cognizant of itself; aware of its identity? In short, why should not America be preserved?

There were ideals and practices in the life of my ancestors that have not been improved upon by the present-day civilization; there were in our culture elements of benefit; and there were influences that would broaden any life. But that almost an entire public needs to be enlightened as to this fact need not be discouraging. For many centuries the human mind labored under the delusion that the world was flat; and thousands of men have believed that the heavens were supported by the strength of an Atlas. The human mind is not yet free from fallacious reasoning; it is not yet an open mind and its deepest recesses are not yet swept free of errors.

But it is now time for a destructive order to be reversed,

and it is well to inform other races that the aboriginal culture of America was not devoid of beauty. Furthermore, in denying the Indian his ancestral rights and heritages the white race is but robbing itself. But America can be revived, rejuvenated, by recognizing a native school of thought. The Indian can save America.

The Living Spirit of the Indian—His Art

The spiritual health and existence of the Indian was maintained by song, magic, ritual, dance, symbolism, oratory (or council), design, handicraft, and folk-story.

Manifestly, to check or thwart this expression is to bring about spiritual decline. And it is in this condition of decline that the Indian people are today. There is but a feeble effort among the Sioux to keep alive their traditional songs and dances, while among other tribes there is but a half-hearted attempt to offset the influence of the Government school and at the same time recover from the crushing and stifling régime of the Indian Bureau.

One has but to speak of Indian verse to receive uncomprehending and unbelieving glances. Yet the Indian loved verse and into this mode of expression went his deepest feelings. Only a few ardent and advanced students seem interested; nevertheless, they have given in book form enough Indian translations to set forth the character and quality of Indian verse.

Oratory receives a little better understanding on the part of the white public, owing to the fact that oratorical compilations include those of Indian orators.

Hard as it seemingly is for the white man's ear to sense the differences, Indian songs are as varied as the many emotions which inspire them, for no two of them are alike. For instance, the Song of Victory is spirited and the notes high and remindful of an unrestrained hunter or warrior riding exultantly over the prairies. On the other hand, the song of the *Cano unye* is solemn and full of urge, for it is meant to inspire the young men to deeds of valor. Then there are the songs of death and the spiritual songs which are connected with the ceremony of initiation. These are full of the spirit of praise and worship, and so strong are some of these invocations that the very air seems as if surcharged with the presence of the Big Holy.

The Indian loved to worship. From birth to death he revered his surroundings. He considered himself born in the luxurious lap of Mother Earth and no place was to him humble. There was nothing between him and the Big Holy. The contact was immediate and personal, and the blessings of Wakan Tanka flowed over the Indian like rain showered from the sky. Wakan Tanka was not aloof, apart, and ever seeking to quell evil forces. He did not punish the animals and the birds, and likewise He did not punish man. He was not a punishing God. For there was never a question as to the supremacy of an evil power over and above the power of Good. There was but one ruling power, and that was *Good.*

Of course, none but an adoring one could dance for days with his face to the sacred sun, and that time is all but done. We cannot have back the days of the buffalo and beaver; we cannot win back our clean blood-stream and superb health, and we can never again expect that beautiful *rapport* we once had with Nature. The springs and lakes have dried and the mountains are bare of forests. The plow has changed the face of the world. Wi-wila is dead! No more may we heal our sick and comfort our dying with a strength founded on faith, for even the animals now fear us, and fear supplants faith.

And the Indian wants to dance! It is his way of expressing devotion, of communing with unseen power, and in keeping his tribal identity. When the Lakota heart was filled with high emotion, he danced. When he felt the benediction of the warming rays of the sun, he danced. When his blood ran hot with success of the hunt or chase, he danced. When his heart was filled with pity for the orphan, the lonely father, or bereaved mother, he danced. All the joys and exaltations of life, all his gratefulness and thankfulness, all his acknowledgments of the mysterious power that guided life, and all his aspirations for a better life, culminated in one great dance—the Sun Dance.

Today we see our young people dancing together the silly jazz—dances that add nothing to the beauty and fineness of our lives and certainly nothing to our history, while the dances that record the life annals of a people die. It is the American Indian who contributes to this country its true folk-dancing, growing, as we did, out of the soil. The dance is far older than his legends, songs, or philosophy.

Did dancing mean much to the white people they would better understand ours. Yet at the same time there is no attraction that brings people from such distances as a certain tribal dance, for the reason that the white mind senses its mystery, for even the white man's inmost feelings are unconsciously stirred by the beat of the tomtom. They are heart-beats, and once all men danced to its rhythm.

When the Indian has forgotten the music of his fore-fathers, when the sound of the tomtom is no more, when noisy jazz has drowned the melody of the flute, he will be a dead Indian. When the memory of his heroes are no longer told in story, and he forsakes the beautiful white buckskin for factory shoddy, he will be dead. When from him has been taken all that is his, all that he has visioned in nature, all that has come to him from infinite sources, he then, truly, will be a dead Indian. His spirit will be gone, and though he walk crowded streets, he will, in truth, be—*dead!*

But all this must not perish; it must live, to the end that America shall be educated no longer to regard native produc-tion of whatever tribe—folk-story, basketry, pottery, dance, song, poetry—as curios, and native artists as curiosities. For who but the man indigenous to the soil could produce its song, story, and folk-tale; who but the man who loved the dust be-neath his feet could shape it and put it into undying, ceramic form; who but he who loved the reeds that grew beside still waters, and the damp roots of shrub and tree, could save it from seasonal death, and with almost superhuman patience weave it into enduring objects of beauty—into timeless art!

Regarding the 'civilization' that has been thrust upon me since the days of reservation, it has not added one whit to my sense of justice; to my reverence for the rights of life; to my love for truth, honesty, and generosity; nor to my faith in Wakan Tanka—God of the Lakotas. For after all the great religions have been preached and expounded, or have been revealed by brilliant scholars, or have been written in books and embellished in fine language with finer covers, man—all man—is still confronted with the Great Mystery.

So if today I had a young mind to direct, to start on the journey of life, and I was faced with the duty of choosing between the natural way of my forefathers and that of the white man's present way of civilization, I would, for its welfare, unhesitatingly set that child's feet in the path of my forefathers. I would raise him to be an Indian!

AMERIKANCI IN CARNIOLA

Louis Adamic

I

As a boy of nine, and even younger, in my native village of Blato, in Carniola—then a Slovenian duchy of Austria and later a part of Yugoslavia—I experienced a thrill every time one of the men of the little community returned from America.

Five or six years before, as I heard people tell, the man had quietly left the village for the United States, a poor peasant clad in homespun, with a mustache under his nose and a bundle on his back; now, a clean-shaven *Amerikanec*, he sported a blue-serge suit, buttoned shoes very large in the toes and with india-rubber heels, a black derby, a shiny celluloid collar, and a loud necktie made even louder by a dazzling horseshoe pin, which, rumor had it, was made of gold, while his two suitcases of imitation leather, tied with strips, bulged with gifts from America for his relatives and friends in the village. In nine cases out of ten, he had left in economic desperation, on money borrowed from some relative in the United States; now there was talk in the village that he was worth anywhere from one to three thousand American dollars. And to my eyes he truly bore all the earmarks of affluence. Indeed, to say that he thrilled my boyish fancy is putting it mildly. With other boys in the village, I followed him around as he went visiting his relatives and friends and distributing presents, and hung onto his every word and gesture.

Then, on the first Sunday after his homecoming, if at all possible, I got within earshot of the nabob as he sat in the winehouse or under the linden in front of the winehouse in Blato, surrounded by village folk, ordering wine and *klobase*— Carniolan sausages—for all comers, paying for accordion-players, indulging in tall talk about America, its wealth and vastness, and his own experiences as a worker in the West Virginia or Kansas coal-mines or Pennsylvania rolling-mills, and comparing notes upon conditions in the United States with other local *Amerikanci* who had returned before him.

Under the benign influence of *cvichek*—Lower Carniolan wine—and often even when sober, the men who had been in America spoke expansively, boastfully, romantically of their ability and accomplishments as workers and of the wages they had earned in Wilkes-Barre or Carbondale, Pennsylvania, or Wheeling, West Virginia, or Pueblo, Colorado, or Butte, Montana, and generally of places and people and things and affairs in the New World. The men who returned to the village, either to stay or for a visit, were, for the most part, natural men of labor—men with sinewy arms and powerful backs—"Bohunks," or "Hunkies," so called in the United States—who derived a certain brawny joy and pride from hard toil. Besides, now that they had come home, they were no longer mere articles upon the industrial labor market, "working stiffs" or "wage slaves," as radical agitators in America referred to them, but adventurers, distant kinsmen of Marco Polo safely returned from a far country, heroes in their own eyes and the eyes of the village; and it was natural for them to expand and to exaggerate their own exploits and enlarge upon the opportunities to be found in America. Their boasting, perhaps, was never wholly without basis in fact. . . .

I remember that, listening to them, I played with the idea of going to America when I was but eight or nine.

My notion of the United States then, and for a few years after, was that it was a grand, amazing, somewhat fantastic place—the Golden Country—a sort of Paradise—the Land of Promise in more ways than one—huge beyond conception, thousands of miles across the ocean, untellably exciting, explosive, quite incomparable to the tiny, quiet, lovely Carniola; a place full of movement and turmoil, wherein things that were unimaginable and impossible in Blato happened daily as a matter of course.

In America one could make pots of money in a short time, acquire immense holdings, wear a white collar, and have polish on one's boots like a *gospod*—one of the gentry—and eat white bread, soup, and meat on weekdays as well as on Sundays, even if one were but an ordinary workman to begin with.

In Blato no one ate white bread or soup and meat, except on Sundays and holidays, and very few then.

In America one did not have to remain an ordinary workman. There, it seemed, one man was as good as the next. There were dozens, perhaps scores, or even hundreds of immigrants in the United States, one-time peasants and workers from the Balkans—from Carniola, Styria, Carinthia, Croatia, Banat, Dalmatia, Bosnia, Montenegro, and Serbia—and from Poland, Slovakia, Bohemia, and elsewhere, who, in two or three years, had earned and saved enough money working in the Pennsylvania, Ohio, or Illinois coal-mines or steel-mills to go to regions called Minnesota, Wisconsin, and Nebraska, and there buy sections of land each of which was larger than the whole area owned by the peasants in Blato. . . . Oh, America was immense —*immense!*

I heard a returned *Amerikanec* tell of regions known as Texas and Oklahoma where single farms—*renche* (ranches), he called them—were larger than the entire province of Carniola! It took a man days to ride on horseback from one end of such a ranch to the other. There were people in Blato and in neighboring villages who, Thomas-like, did not believe this, but my boyish imagination was aflame with America, and I believed it. At that time I accepted as truth nearly everything I heard about America. I believed that a single cattleman in Texas owned more cattle than there were in the entire Balkans. And my credulity was not strained when I heard that there were gold-mines in California, and trees more than a thousand years old with trunks so enormous that it required a dozen men, clasping each other's hands, to encircle them wtih their arms.

In America everything was possible. There even the common people were "citizens," not "subjects," as they were in Austria and in most other European countries. A citizen, or even a non-citizen foreigner, could walk up to the President of the United States and pump his hand. Indeed, that seemed to be a custom in America. There was a man in Blato, a former steel-worker in Pittsburgh, who claimed that upon an occasion he had shaken hands and exchanged words with Theodore Roosevelt, to whom he familiarly referred as "Tedi" —which struck my mother very funny. To her it seemed as if some one had called the Pope of Rome or the Emperor of Austria by a nickname. But the man assured her, in my hear-

ing, that in America everybody called the President merely
"Tedi."

Mother laughed about this, off and on, for several days.
And I laughed with her. She and I often laughed together.

II

One day—I was then a little over ten—I said to Mother:
"Some day I am going to America."

Mother looked at me a long moment. . . . She was then a
healthy young peasant woman, not yet thirty, rather tall, with
a full bust and large hips; long arms and big, capable hands,
wide-spaced hazel eyes, mild and luminous with simple mirth;
and wavy auburn hair which stuck in little gold-bleached wisps
from under her colored kerchief, tied below her chin. She had
then four children, two boys and two girls; later she bore five
more, three boys and two girls. I was the oldest. Years after I
came to America my oldest sister wrote me that there was a
story in the village that Mother had laughed in her pains at my
birth—which probably is not true; mother herself, who is still
living, does not remember. But I know that when I was a boy
she had—and probably still has—the gift of laughter in a
greater measure than most people thereabouts; indeed, than
most people anywhere. Hers was the healthy, natural, visceral,
body-shaking laughter of Slovenian peasants in Carniola, especially of peasant women—variable laughter; usually mirthful
and humorous, clear and outright, but sometimes, too, mirthless
and unhumorous, pain-born, and pain-transcending. . . .

"I am going to America," I said again, as Mother continued
to look at me in silence.

I imagine she thought that I was a strange boy. Now and
then she had remarked in my hearing that I worried her. Often
she looked at me with silent concern. In some respects I was
a self-willed youngster. I usually had things my way, regardless of opposition.

Finally, Mother smiled at me, although I do not doubt
that what I said frightened her. She smiled with her whole
face—her mouth, her wrinkles, her eyes, especially her eyes.

I smiled, too. I was a healthy boy, tall and strong for my
age. Physically, as Mother often remarked, I resembled Father,
who was a peasant in body and soul; but evidently I was not
made to be a peasant. If necessary, I could work hard in the

fields, but I very much preferred not to. I liked to move about the village, roam in the woods, go to neighboring villages, stand by the side of the highway, and observe things.

With a little catch in her voice, Mother said: "To America? But when are you going?"

"I don't know," I said. "When I grow up, I guess. I am already ten." I had not thought of it in detail, but had merely decided to go some day.

Mother laughed. Her laughter was tremulous with apprehension. She could not make me out.

I realized then that she would not like me to go to America. A cousin of hers had gone there twenty-odd years before, when she was still a little girl. She scarcely remembered him, but had heard other relatives speak of him. The first year he had written a few times. Then Heaven only knew what became of him. And, as it occurred to me later, Mother knew of other men in Blato and the vicinity who had gone to America and had sunk, leaving no trace, in the vastness of America. She knew of men in villages not remote from our own who had returned from the United States without an arm or minus a leg, or in bad health. There was an *Amerikanec* in Gatina, the village nearest Blato, who had come home with a strange, sinful, and unmentionable disease, which he later communicated to his wife, who, in turn, gave birth to a blind child. There was a widow in Podgora, another village near by, whose husband had been killed in a mine accident in the United States. Mother had only a faint conception of what a mine was; there are no mines in Lower Carniola; but she dreaded the thought that some day one of her children might work underground.

III

All of us, parents and children, slept in the *izba*—the large room in a Slovenian peasant house—and that night, soon after we all went to bed, Mother called me by name in a low voice, adding, "Are you asleep?"

I was awake, and almost answered her, but then it occurred to me that she probably meant to discuss me with Father. I kept quiet. The bed which I shared with my brother was in the opposite corner from my parents'.

"He is asleep," mumbled Father. "Why do you call him?"

"I want to tell you what he said to me today," said Mother, in a half-whisper, which I heard clearly. "He said he would go to America when he grew up."

Father grunted vaguely. He was heavy with fatigue. He had worked hard all day. He was one of the better-to-do peasants in Blato, but, with Mother's aid, did nearly all the work on the farm, seldom hiring outside help. He was a large, hard man, in his late thirties; blue-eyed and light-haired; a simple, competent peasant.

He grunted again. "America? He is only a child. How old is he, anyhow?" he asked. He was too busy to keep up with the ages of his children.

"He is ten," said Mother. "But he is like no other boy in the village."

"Only a child," Father grunted again. "Childish talk."

"Sometimes I am afraid to talk with him," said Mother. "I don't know what is going on in his head. He asks me questions and tells me things. Nothing that occurs hereabouts escapes him. And he reads everything he finds in the village."

They were both silent a minute.

"I'll send him to city school, then," said Father, "even if he is our oldest." According to custom in Carniola, as the oldest son, I was supposed to stay home and work on the farm, and after my father's death become its master. "He isn't much good on the farm, anyhow," Father went on. "I'll send him to school in Lublyana"—the provincial capital. "Let him get educated if he has a head for learning."

"That's what Martin says we should do, too," said Mother. Martin was her brother, the priest in charge of the parish of Zhalna, which included the village of Blato.

"They say children are God's blessing," said Father, after a while, "but——"

"Oh, everything will be well in the end," Mother interrupted his misgiving. "There is little to worry about so long as God gives us health." She was a natural, earth-and-sky optimist; a smiling, laughing fatalist. Then, after a few moments, she added: "Maybe—maybe, if we send him to school in Lublyana, he will become a priest, like my brother Martin."

Father said nothing to this. Mother was silent, too. By and by I heard Father snore lightly, in the first stage of his slumber.

Mother, I believe, did not fall asleep till late that night.

She probably smiled to herself in the darkness, yielding her consciousness to delicious thoughts. It was absurd to think that I should go to America! I was only a child, and one should not take seriously a child's chatter. . . . They would send me to Lublyana; that was settled. Then, after years of schooling, I would become a priest and the bishop might send me to the parish church in Zhalna. "Oh, that would be beautiful!" she exclaimed to herself, half aloud. I heard her clearly, despite Father's snoring, and I imagine that this is what she was thinking to herself. She probably figured that by the time I would be ordained a priest, Uncle Martin would have been promoted to a bigger parish than Zhalna, making a vacancy for me.

In common with many peasant women in Carniola, Mother was not deeply religious in the ordinary sense. I believe that she scarcely concerned herself with the tenets of the Catholic faith. She was innately pagan. In her blood throbbed echoes of prayers that her ancestors—Old Slavs—had addressed a thousand years ago from their open-air sacrificial altars to the sun and to the wind- and thunder-gods. What largely appealed to her in Catholicism, although, of course, she was not conscious of the fact, were the ritual and the trappings. She loved the vestments that her brother and other priests wore at mass. She loved the solemn processions with bells tolling long and sonorously on big holidays or on hot, still days in midsummer when drought threatened to destroy or harm the crops. She loved the jubilant midnight mass at Christmas. She relished the incense, the smell of lighted candles, the pictures, the stations of the Way of the Cross, and the statues of saints at the main and side altars, and the organ music on Sundays. She sang in the choir with a strong and clear, although untrained, voice. Sometimes, when she sang solos, her fellow parishioners from Blato said they detected a ring of laughter in her singing. She did not care for sermons, not even her brother's; at least, so far as I know, she never praised a sermon; but I think it was deeply satisfying to her to see Uncle Martin stand in the pulpit and read the Gospel and preach. . . . And some day, perhaps—perhaps, I, her son, would stand in the pulpit at Zhalna and preach! She would be so proud of me. All the people of the parish would be proud of me, just as they were proud of Uncle Martin, who was also a native of the parish and a peasant's son.

In my father's life, too, religion was of no great moment.

He was essentially a practical man who had serious and constant business with the ancient earth. He went to church on Sundays and prayed to God every evening with his family, but I think he did so more because that was the conventional thing to do than because he felt it necessary. Basically, like most peasants in Carniola and elsewhere, he was a hard realist, a practical man, a fatalist, possessing a natural, almost biological good sense and a half-cynical earth knowledge older than any religion or system. . . . However, he probably figured, if a son of his was cut out to be a priest—why, well and good. Priests were an important part of the scheme of things. To have a priest in the family added to one's prestige. Father knew that. He felt that even now peasants in the parish showed him a special sort of deference because his wife's brother was a priest. To have his own son become one, he possibly said to himself, would be even better. At any rate, he decided to send me to city school which —for the time being—was agreeable to me.

IV

Late in the spring of 1909, four months before I was taken to school in Lublyana, and six or seven months after I had first announced my intention to go to America, there returned to Blato a man who had been in America for more than twenty years.

He was Peter Molek, brother of Francé Molek, a rather well-to-do peasant who was our nearest neighbor. Peter had no property in the village, and so he went to live in Francé's house. His brother had not heard from or of him for eight years. He had thought him dead. None of the returned *Amerikanci* had seen him in America. Then, of a sudden that spring, there came a letter from him that he was "coming home to die."

Peter Molek was an unusual *Amerikanec* to return to Blato.

At the supper table the day after his homecoming, I heard my parents discuss him. Father said that he remembered when Peter had gone to America. "He was one of the sturdiest and lustiest men in this parish, even stronger and taller than Francé," who, although in his fifty-seventh year, was still a big and powerful man. "Now look at him!"—and Father shook his head.

Although not yet fifty, Peter Molek was a gaunt, bent, and broken man, hollow-eyed, bald, mostly skin and bone, with a bitter expression on his face; suffering from rheumatism and asthma—two diseases till then all but unknown in Blato. He was eight or nine years younger than Francé, but only a shadow of his brother.

"America is an evil place," said Mother, glancing at me concernedly, although I had not spoken of going to America again. "They say Peter came home almost penniless. I guess Francé will have to keep him till he dies."

Which, to me, was the most extraordinary aspect of Peter Molek. With my ideas about America, I could not understand how anyone, after spending twenty years in that country—in the midst of abundance—could return home in such a state. And it doubtless was true what people said about Peter Molek having no money. He brought no presents even for his closest relatives. He did not go to the winehouse, nor talk about his adventures in America with anyone. He kept, for the most part, to himself. All day long he sat in the sun on the beach in front of his brother's house. He read books and papers which evidently were American publications. He took slow walks in the fields. Sometimes he coughed for ten or twenty minutes at a spell.

Peter Molek's cough was a great sensation among the children in Blato. When the asthmatic spasm seized him, his face turned purple, his deep-sunken eyes bulged and looked wide and terror-stricken; and bending over, he held his chest in desperation. The first two or three weeks after his return, as soon as one of the boys heard him cough, there was much yelling in the village and, with the heartless, unthinking curiosity of youth, ten or a dozen husky, barefooted urchins came dashing from all sides to Molek's house, to watch the strange *Amerikanec* choke, and listen to the wheezing sound that issued from his tortured chest. When he emitted an especially long wheeze, the boys looked at one another in wonder and smiled.

In this respect I was no better than the other boys, until Mother forbade me to go near Peter Molek when he coughed. Then I watched him from the distance. Our house was only a couple of hundred yards from Molek's.

But occasionally, when he was not coughing, I walked by him. I wanted to talk with him, but could not work up enough courage to address him first.

One day he smiled faintly and said to me, "You are the neighbor's boy, aren't you?"

"Yes," I said. "My father remembers you when you went to America."

Peter Molek nodded his head. "That was a long time ago," he said.

"Why do you cough like you do all the time?" I asked.

Peter Molek did not answer for a while. He stared at me in away that made me uneasy. Then he looked away and swung one of his large bony hands in a vague gesture. "America," he said. ". . . America."

I did not know what he meant.

"How old are you?" Peter Molek asked me.

"Ten," I said. "Soon I'll be eleven. I am going to city school in the fall."

Peter Molek smiled again and nodded his head. "You are *all right*." He said "all right" in English.

"I know what that means—'*all right*,'" I said, eagerly. "It means 'good' in the American language. I have often heard other men who came from America say '*all right*.' I also know other American words. '*Sure Mike!*' . . . '*Sonabitch.*' . . ." I was pleased with my knowledge.

Peter Molek peered at me from under his eyebrows. He seemed to want to touch me, but probably was afraid that I might draw away from him because he was a sick man. "You are *all right*," he said again.

I was delighted with his approval.

On the bench beside him I noticed some papers and books. I stepped close. "What are these?" I said.

"Books and papers from America," said Peter Molek. "I brought the books with me. The papers I get by mail once a week."

The newspapers were copies of the *Appeal to Reason,* a radical sheet then printed at Girard, Kansas. One of the books was *The Jungle,* by Upton Sinclair.

"Are there pictures in them?" I asked. "Pictures of America?"

"No," said Peter Molek. "But I have some pictures inside. Wait; I'll bring them out." He went into the house and presently returned with some photographs, postcards, and newspaper clippings.

I sat beside him.

"This," said Peter Molek, showing me the first picture, "is a coal town in Pennsylvania. Forest City. This, which looks like a mountain, is a pile of coal, dug out of the ground—thousands of feet below—mostly by our people from Carniola. Nearly all the miners in Forest City are Slovenians. I worked in one of the mines there for seven years."

He showed me the next picture. "A steel-mill in Pennsylvania. Once I worked here awhile, too. Most of the time I worked in the mines. I worked from one end of the country to the other—not only in Pennsylvania, but in Ohio, in West Virginia, in Illinois, in Montana, in Nevada—in places you have never heard of."

"I have heard of Pennsylvania"—pronouncing it *Panslovenia*—"and Ohio and—"

Peter Molek smiled wanly. He liked me, and I was happy that he did.

"This is New York," he said, showing me another picture. "You see these buildings? Some of them are many times higher than the highest church tower in Carniola."

"I know about the buildings of New York," I said.

"They are building them higher every year. *Skyscrapers,* they call them. You know what that means?"

"No," I said.

Peter Molek explained to me why the tall buildings in America were called skyscrapers. It was the most interesting talk I had ever heard.

Then I said, "Some day I am going to America."

Peter Molek looked at me, startled. He was about to say something, when another asthmatic spasm seized him. "This is what America did to me," said Peter Molek, after he had stopped coughing.

"What does this mean?" I said, pointing at the title of a book on the bench.

"*The Jungle,*" said Peter Molek. "That means *dzhungla* in Slovenian."

I did not even know what *dzhungla* meant. The forests around Blato were neat, thinned-out, idyllic groves where one went to pick berries or gather mushrooms.

"A jungle," Peter Molek explained, "is a wild place, a great forest, all tangled up with vegetation, everything growing crisscross, almost impenetrable, mysterious and terrible, infested with beasts and snakes, and spiders bigger than my fist. . . . This is a book about the United States, although there are no jungles in the United States, so far as I know. But the whole of America is a jungle. This is a story about people like me—foreigners—who go there and are swallowed by the jungle. Understand?"

I nodded in the affirmative, but I did not really understand.

"America swallowed me," continued Peter Molek, "but she did not digest me." He smiled, as if to himself, a peculiar, mirthless smile.

Peter Molek went on: "America the jungle swallows many people who go there to work. She squeezes the strength out of them, unless they are wise or lucky enough to escape before it is too late; unless they work in the mills or the mines only a few years and save every cent they can and return home, or buy themselves a piece of land where land is cheap."

My understanding of Peter Molek's words was scant, but I listened and remembered everything he said.

". . . I was there too long," he was saying. "I worked too hard. Here is New York," pointing at the picture he had shown me before. "I—we helped to build these buildings—we Slovenians and Croatians and Slovaks and other people who went to America to work. We helped to build many other cities there, cities of which you have never heard, and railroads, and bridges, all made of steel which our people make in the mills. Our men from the Balkans are the best steel-workers in America. The framework of America is made of steel. And this smoke that you see here—it comes from coal that we have dug up; we from the Balkans and from Galicia and Bohemia. We have also dug up much ore. I myself worked for a few years in the iron-mines of the West. I lost my health in the mines. Miners get asthma and rheumatism.

"Three times I was in accidents. Once, in Colorado, I was buried for four days three thousand feet underground. There were seven other men buried with me—three of them Slovenians like myself, two Poles, one Dalmatian, one American. When they dug us out, the Dalmatian and I were the only two still living. Once, in Pennsylvania, a rock fell on me in a mine and broke my right leg. The leg healed and I went back to work. I worked two months, and another rock fell on me. It almost broke my left leg.

"For many years I did not understand America. Then I began to read and understand. . . .

"The day before I sailed for home I walked in these streets"—he pointed at the picture—"where the buildings are tallest. Steel buildings—and I looked up, and I can hardly describe my feelings. I realized that there was much of our work and strength, my own work and strength, frozen in the greatness of America. I felt that, although I was going home to Blato, I was actually leaving myself in America."

V

That spring and summer I had more sessions with Peter Molek. Between asthmatic spasms he talked to me of the vast jungle that he conceived America to be. His view of the country, as I remember it now, was one-sided, bitter. He told me of accidents in the mines and iron-foundries which he had witnessed or of which he had merely read or heard; of labor upheavals; of powerful capitalists who owned immense industries and whom he sketched as "the beasts in the jungle"; of rich people's orgies in Chicago and New York at which, as reported in socialistic prints, men smoked cigarettes wrapped in hundred-dollar bills; of millionaires who wore diamonds in their teeth and had bands playing while they bathed in champagne; and of slums where people lived in rags and misery.

I listened open-mouthed.

"But for some people America is not a bad place," said Peter Molek one day. "Many foreigners have greatly bettered themselves there, but these fortunate ones are few when compared with the multitude of immigrants who, I believe, would be better off had they remained in the old country. American industries use them, then cast them off."

"More people go to America all the time," I said. Lately I had read in a newspaper to which my father subscribed that four thousand more persons had emigrated from Carniola to the United States in 1908 than in 1907.

"Yes," said Peter Molek. "They go because each thinks that he will get the better of America and not America the better of him. They listen to the few who return home from the United States with two or three thousand dollars. They hear that some one else who stayed there has succeeded on a big scale. And they think they will do the same. America is the Land of Promise to them. She lures them over by the thousands and hundreds of thousands—people from many countries, not only from Carniola. She needs their hands even more than they need her dollars, and makes use of them. Once upon a time immigrants were called 'dung' in America; that was a good name for them. They were the fertilizer feeding the roots of America's present and future greatness. They are still 'dung.' The roots of America's greatness still feed on them. . . . Life in America is a scramble. More people are swept under than rise to riches."

All of which, on top of what I had previously heard and thought of America, tended to bewilder me.

IMMIGRANTS

F. P. Dunne

"Well, I see Congress has got to wurruk again," said Mr. Dooley.

"The Lord save us fr'm harm," said Mr. Hennessy.

"Yes, sir," said Mr. Dooley, "Congress has got to wurruk again, an' manny things that seems important to a Congressman 'll be brought up befure thim. 'Tis sthrange that what's a big thing to a man in Wash'nton, Hinnissy, don't seem much account to me. Divvie a bit do I care whether they dig th' Nicaragoon Canal or cross th' Isthmus in a balloon; or whether th' Monroe docthrine is enfoorced or whether it ain't; or whether th' thrusts is abolished as Teddy Rosenfelt wud like to have thim or encouraged to go on with their neefaryous but magnificent entherprises as th' Prisidint wud like; or whether th' water is poured into th' ditches to reclaim th' arid lands iv th' West or th' money f'r thim to fertilize th' arid pocket-books iv th' conthractors; or whether th' Injun is threated like a depindant an' miserable thribesman or like a free an' indepindant dog; or whether we restore th' merchant marine to th' ocean or whether we lave it to restore itsilf. None iv these here questions inthrests me, an' be me I mane you an' be you I mane ivrybody. What we want to know is, ar-re we goin' to have coal enough in th' hod whin th' cold snap comes; will th' plumbin' hold out, an' will th' job last.

"But they'se wan question that Congress is goin' to take up that you an' me are intherested in. As a pilgrim father that missed th' first boats, I must raise me claryon voice again' th' invasion iv this fair land be th' paupers an' arnychists iv effete Europe. Ye bet I must—because I'm here first. 'Twas diff'-rent whin I was dashed high on th' stern an' rockbound coast.

In thim days America was th' refuge iv th' oppressed iv all th' wurruld. They cud come over here an' do a good job iv oppressin' thimsilves. As I told ye I come a little late. Th' Rosenfelts an' th' Lodges bate me be at laste a boat lenth, an' be th' time I got here they was stern an' rockbound thimsilves. So I got a gloryous rayciption as soon as I was towed off th' rocks. Th' stars an' sthripes whispered a welcome in th' breeze an' a shovel was thrust into me hand an' I was pushed into a sthreet excyvatin' as though I'd been born here. Th' pilgrim father who bossed th' job was a fine ol' puritan be th' name iv Doherty, who come over in th' Mayflower about th' time iv th' potato rot in Wexford, an' he made me think they was a hole in th' breakwather iv th' haven iv refuge an' some iv th' wash iv th' seas iv opprission had got through. He was a stern an' rockbound la-ad himsilf, but I was a good hand at loose stones an' wan day—but I'll tell ye about that another time.

"Annyhow, I was rayceived with open arms that sometimes ended in a clinch. I was afraid I wasn't goin' to assimilate with th' airlyer pilgrim fathers an' th' instichoochions iv th' counthry, but I soon found that a long swing iv th' pick made me as good an another man an' it didn't require a gr-reat intellect, or sometimes anny at all, to vote th' dimmycrat ticket, an' befure I was here a month, I felt enough like a native born American to burn a witch. Wanst in a while a mob iv intilligint collajeens, whose grandfathers had bate me to th' dock, wud take a shy at me Pathrick's Day procission or burn down wan iv me churches, but they got tired iv that befure long; 'twas too much like wurruk.

"But as I tell ye, Hinnissy, 'tis diff'rent now. I don't know why 'tis diff'rent but 'tis diff'rent. 'Tis time we put our back again' th' open dure an' keep out th' savage horde. If that cousin iv ye'ers expects to cross, he'd betther tear f'r th' ship. In a few minyits th' gates 'll be down an' whin th' oppressed wurruld comes hikin acrost to th' haven iv refuge, they'll do well to put a couplin' pin undher their hats, f'r th' Goddess iv Liberty 'll meet thim at th' dock with an axe in her hand. Congress is goin' to fix it. Me friend Shaughnessy says so. He was in yisterdah an says he: "Tis time we done something to make th' immigration laws sthronger,' says he. 'Thrue f'r ye, Miles Standish,' says I; 'but what wud ye do?' 'I'd keep out th' offscourin's iv Europe,' says he. 'Wud ye go back?" says I. 'Have ye'er joke,' says he. ' 'Tis not so seeryus as it was befure ye come,' says I. 'But what ar're th' immygrants doin' that's roonous to us?' I says. 'Well,' says he, 'they're arnychists,' he says; 'they don't assymilate with th' counthry,' he says. 'Maybe th' counthry's digestion has gone wrong fr'm too much rich food,' says I; 'perhaps now if we'd lave off thryin' to digest Rockyfellar an' thry a simple diet like Schwartzmeister, we wudden't feel th' effects iv our vittels,' I says. 'Maybe if we'd season th' immygrants a little or cook thim thurly, they'd go down betther,' I says.

" 'They're arnychists, like Parsons,' he says. 'He wud've been an immygrant if Texas hadn't been admitted to th' Union,' I says. 'Or Snolgosh, he says. 'Has Mitchigan seceded?' I says. 'Or Gittoo,' he says.* 'Who come fr'm th' effete monarchies iv Chicago, west iv Ashland Av'noo,' I says. 'Or what's-his-name, Wilkes Booth,' he says. 'I don't know what he was—maybe a Boolgharyen,' says I. 'Well, annyhow,' says he, 'they're th' scum iv th' earth.' 'They may be that,' says I; 'but we used to think they was th' cream iv civilization.' I says. 'They're off th' top annyhow. I wanst believed 'twas th' best man iv Europe come here, th' la-ads that was too sthrong and indepindant to be kicked around be a boorgmasther at home an' wanted to dig out f'r a place where they cud get a chanst to make their way to th' money. I see their sons fightin' into politics an' their daughters tachin' young American idee how to shoot too high in th' public school, an' I thought they was all right. But I see I was wrong. Thim boys out there towin' wan heavy foot afther th' other to th' rowlin mills is all arnychists. There's warrants out f'r all names endin' in 'inski, an I think I'll board up me windows, fr,' I says, "if immygrants is as dangerous to this counthry as ye an' I an' other pilgrim fathers believe they are, they'se enough iv thim sneaked in already to make us aborigines about as inflooential as the prohibition vote in th' Twenty-ninth Ward. They'll dash again' our stern an' rock-bound coast till they bust it,' says I.

" 'But I ain't so much afraid as ye ar-re. I'm not afraid iv me father an' I'm not afraid iv mesilf. An' I'm not afraid iv Schwartzmeister's father or Hinnery Cabin Lodge's grandfather.

---

* Albert Parsons, American-born defendant in the trial of anarchists for the historic Chicago bombing of 1886; he was executed in a miscarriage of justice. Leon Czolgosz assassinated President William McKinley in 1901. Charles J. Guiteau, a disappointed office-seeker, assassinated President James A. Garfield in 1881.

We all come over th' same way, an' if me ancestors were not what Hogan calls regicides, 'twas not because they were not ready an' willin', on'y a king niver come their way. I don't believe in killin' kings, mesilf. I niver wud've sawed th' block off that curly-headed potintate that I see in th' pitchers down town, but, be hivins, Presarved Codfish Shaughnessy, if we'd begun a few years ago shuttin' out folks that wudden't mind handin' a bomb to a king, they wudden't be enough people in Mattsachoosetts to make a quorum f'r th' Anti-Impeeryal S'ciety,' says I. 'But what wud ye do with th' offscourin' iv Europe?' says he. 'I'd scour thim some more,' says I.

"An' so th' meetin' iv th' Plymouth Rock Assocyation come to an end. But if ye wud like to get it together, Deacon Hinnissy, to discuss th' immygration question, I'll sind out a hurry call f'r Schwartzmeister an' Mulcahey an' Ignacio Sbarbaro an' Nels Larsen an' Petrus Gooldvink, an' we 'll gather tonight at Fanneilnoviski Hall at th' corner iv Sheridan an' Sigel sthreets. All th' pilgrim fathers is rayquested f'r to bring interpreters."

"Well," said Mr. Hennessy, "divvle th' bit I care, on'y I'm here first, an' I ought to have th' right to keep th' bus fr'm bein' overcrowded."

"Well," said Mr. Dooley, "as a pilgrim father on me gran' nephew's side. I don't know but ye're right. An' they'se wan sure way to keep thim out."

"What's that?" asked Mr. Hennessy.

"Teach thim all about our instichoochions befure they come," said Mr. Dooley.

THE PEOPLE, YES

Carl Sandburg

1

From the four corners of the earth
from corners lashed in wind
and bitten with rain and fire,
from places where the winds begin
and fogs are born with mist children,
tall men from tall rocky slopes came
and sleepy men from sleepy valleys,
their women tall, their women sleepy,
with bundles and belongings,
with little ones babbling, "Where to now?
     what next?"

The people of the earth, the family of man,
wanted to put up something proud to look at,
a tower from the flat land of earth
on up through the ceiling into the top of the sky.

    And the big job got going,
    the caissons and pilings sunk,
    floors, walls and winding staircases
    aimed at the stars high over,
    aimed to go beyond the ladders of the moon.

    And God Almighty could have struck them dead
    or smitten them deaf and dumb.

    And God was a whimsical fixer.
    God was an understanding Boss
    with another plan in mind,

And suddenly shuffled all the languages,
    changed the tongues of men
    so they all talked different
And the masons couldn't get what the hodcarriers
    said,
The helpers handed the carpenters the wrong tools,
Five hundred ways to say, ''W h o a r e y o u ?''
Changed ways of asking, "Where do we go from
    here?"
Or of saying, "Being born is only the beginning,"
Or, "Would you just as soon sing as make that noise?"
Or, "What you don't know won't hurt you."
And the material-and-supply men started disputes
With the hauling gangs and the building trades
And the architects tore their hair over the blueprints
And the brickmakers and the mule skinners talked
    back
To the straw bosses who talked back to the superin-
    tendents
And the signals got mixed; the men who shovelled
    the bucket
Hooted the hoisting men—and the job was wrecked.

Some called it the Tower of Babel job
And the people gave it many other names.
The wreck of it stood as a skull and a ghost,
a memorandum hardly begun,
swaying and sagging in tall hostile winds,
held up by slow friendly winds.

    2

From Illinois and Indiana came a later myth
Of all the people in the world at Howdeehow
For the first time standing together:
From six continents, seven seas, and several archipelagoes,
From points of land moved by wind and water
Out of where they used to be to where they are,
The people of the earth marched and travelled
To gather on a great plain.

At a given signal they would join in a shout,
    So it was planned,

One grand hosannah, something worth listening to.
    And they all listened.
    The signal was given.
    And they all listened.
    And the silence was beyond words.
They had come to listen, not to make a noise.
    They wanted to hear.
So they all stood still and listened,
Everybody except a little old woman from Kalamazoo
Who gave out a long slow wail over what she was missing
    because she was stone deaf.

This is the tale of the Howdeehow powpow,
One of a thousand drolls the people tell of themselves,
Of tall corn, of wide rivers, of big snakes,
Of giants and dwarfs, heroes and clowns,
Grown in the soil of the mass of the people.

14

The people is Everyman, everybody.
Everybody is you and me and all others.
What everybody says is what we all say.
    And what is it we all say?

Where did we get these languages?
Why is your baby-talk deep in your blood?
What is the cling of the tongue
To what it heard with its mother-milk?

They cross on the ether now.
They travel on high frequencies
Over the border-lines and barriers
Of mountain ranges and oceans.
When shall we all speak the same language?
And do we want to have all the same language?
Are we learning a few great signs and passwords?
Why should Everyman be lost for words?
The questions are put every day in every tongue:
        "Where you from, Stranger?
        Where were you born?
        Got any money?
        What do you work at?

Where's your passport?
Who are your people?"
Over the ether crash the languages.
And the people listen.
As on the plain of Howdeehow they listen.
They want to hear.
They will be told when the next war is ready.
The long wars and the short wars will come on the air,
How many got killed and how the war ended
And who got what and the price paid
And how there were tombs for the Unknown Soldier,
The boy nobody knows the name of,
The boy whose great fame is that of the masses,
The millions of names too many to write on a tomb,
The heroes, the cannonfodder, the living targets,
The mutilated and sacred dead,
The people, yes.

Two countries with two flags
are nevertheless one land, one blood, one people—
can this be so?
And the earth belongs to the family of man?
can this be so?

The first world war came and its cost was laid on the
people.
The second world war—the third—what will be the cost?
And will it repay the people for what they pay?

107

The people will live on.
The learning and blundering people will live on.
They will be tricked and sold and again sold
And go back to the nourishing earth for rootholds,
The people so peculiar in renewal and comeback,
You can't laugh off their capacity to take it.
The mammoth rests between his cyclonic dramas,

The people so often sleepy, weary, enigmatic,
is a vast huddle with many units saying:
"I earn my living.

I make enough to get by
and it takes all my time.
If I had more time
I could do more for myself
and maybe for others.
I could read and study
and talk things over
and find out about things.
It takes time.
I wish I had the time."

The people is a tragic and comic two-face:
hero and hoodlum: phantom and gorilla twisting to moan with a gargoyle mouth: "They
buy me and sell me . . . it's a game . . .
sometimes I'll break loose . . ."

Once having marched
Over the margins of animal necessity,
Over the grim line of sheer subsistence
Then man came
To the deeper rituals of his bones,
To the lights lighter than any bones,
To the time for thinking things over,
To the dance, the song, the story,
Or the hours given over to dreaming,
Once having so marched.

Between the finite limitations of the five senses
and the endless yearnings of man for the beyond
the people hold to the humdrum bidding of work and food
while reaching out when it comes their way
for lights beyond the prison of the five senses,
for keepsakes lasting beyond any hunger of death.
This reaching is alive.
The panderers and liars have violated and smutted it.
Yet this reaching is alive yet
for lights and keepsakes.

The people know the salt of the sea
and the strength of the winds
lashing the corners of the earth.

The people take the earth
as a tomb of rest and a cradle of hope.
Who else speaks for the Family of Man?
They are in tune and step
with constellations of universal law.

The people is a polychrome,
a spectrum and a prism
held in a moving monolith,
a console organ of changing themes,
a clavilux of color poems
wherein the sea offers fog
and the fog moves off in rain
and the labrador sunset shortens
to a nocturne of clear stars
serene over the shot spray
of northern lights.

The steel mill sky is alive.
The fire breaks white and zigzag
shot on a gun-metal gloaming.
Man is a long time coming.
Man will yet win.
Brother may yet line up with brother:

This old anvil laughs at many broken hammers.
There are men who can't be bought.
The fireborn are at home in fire.
The stars make no noise.
You can't hinder the wind from blowing.
Time is a great teacher.
Who can live without hope?

In the darkness with a great bundle of grief
    the people march.
In the night, and overhead a shovel of stars for
    keeps, the people march:
                    "Where to? what next?"

THE FAMILY

DESTINY IS IN THE HOME

The Child is Father of the Man.
Wordsworth

For the European of the nineteenth century, the family was clearly defined: The father dominated his household and gave economic security to his wife and children through his control of the farm or family business. For the American of the twentieth century, the family has lost its economic, social, and religious hold on children. Indeed, the institution of the family, as we have known it, is challenged by young people who often seek other forms of "tribal" identification. Fathers are no longer the exclusive wage-earners in a family; women are no longer willing to accept their traditionally passive role within the family unit; and children leave the home at increasingly earlier ages.

For minority groups in America, the family has had a special history. The children of immigrants have usually rebelled against their "foreign" heritage, seeking to Americanize themselves as quickly as possible; the grandchildren, however, have often regarded their ancestry with pride in their ethnic origins and the legacies of their Black and Jewish, Puerto Rican, Italian, Irish, Chinese, and Indian backgrounds.

The rejection of the family—and its minority way of life—has led to impressive works of ethnic literature. Richard Wright's first book, *Uncle Tom's Children,* stated quite emphatically that the children of Uncle Tom would not be servile and abject, self-denigrating and timid. Philip Roth's *Portnoy's Complaint* is a long diatribe against the Jewish family—particularly the Jewish mother—and its tendency to make the young Jew too self-conscious, guilty, and inhibited. Piri Thomas, Pietro diDonato, and Lin Yutang struggle with the special features of Spanish, Italian, and Chinese families in their attempt to establish a *modus vivendi* as second-generation Americans.

The American family has been confined, for the most part, to the married couple and their children. The Indian "joint family" in which older women are dominant; the Jewish patriarchy; the Negro matriarchy; the Chinese family, controlled by old men—these structures have yielded to the smaller and less cohesive American type of family in which the father is less authoritarian and the children more assertive than in its European counterpart. The transition from one type of family to the other forms one of the richest aspects of ethnic literature as well as a revealing commentary on contemporary American life.

THE NEGRO FAMILY
IN THE UNITED STATES

E. Franklin Frazier

Our account of the development of the Negro family in the United States traverses scarcely more than a century and a half of history. Yet, during that comparatively brief period, from the standpoint of human history, the Negro, stripped of the relatively simple preliterate culture in which he was nurtured, has created a folk culture and has gradually taken over the more sophisticated American culture. Although only three-quarters of a century has elapsed since the arrival of the last representative of preliterate African races, the type of culture from which he came was as unlike the culture of the civilized American Negro today as the culture of the Germans of Tacitus' day was unlike the culture of German-Americans.

Thus our first task has been to discover the process whereby his raw sexual impulses were brought under control not only through the discipline of the master race but also by association with his fellows. Next, we have undertaken to study the character of the restraints upon sex and family behavior which have evolved as a part of the Negro's folk culture. Our final task has been to analyze the process by which a favored few have escaped from the isolation of the black folk and gradually taken over the attitudes and sentiments as well as the external aspects of the culture of the dominant race.

When the Negro slave was introduced into American economic life, he was to all intents and purposes, to use the words of Aristotle, merely an "animate tool." But, as in all cases where slavery exists, the fact that the slave was not only animate but human affected his relations with his masters. To the slave-trader, who had only an economic interest in the slave, the

Negro was a mere utility. But, where master and slave had to live together and carry on some form of co-operation, the human nature of the slave had to be taken into account. Consequently, slavery developed into a social as well as an economic institution. The lives of the white master class became intertwined with the lives of the black slaves. Social control was not simply a matter of force and coercion but depended upon a system of etiquette based upon sentiments of superordination, on the one hand, and sentiments of submission and loyalty, on the other. Thus the humanization of the slave as well as his assimilation of the ideals, meanings, and social definitions of the master race depended upon the nature of his contacts with the master race. Where the slave was introduced into the household of the master, the process of assimilation was facilitated; but, where his contacts with whites were limited to the poor white overseer, his behavior was likely to remain impulsive and subject only to external control.

Yet, social interaction within the more or less isolated world of the slave did much to mold his personality. Although in some cases the slaves retained the conception of themselves which they had acquired in their own culture, their children were only slightly influenced by these fading memories. Consequently, their personalities reflected, on the whole, the role which they acquired in the plantation economy. Individual differences asserted themselves and influenced the responses of their fellow-slaves as well as their own behavior. The large and strong of body and those of nimble minds outstripped the weak and slow-witted. Some recognition was shown these varying talents and aptitudes by the slaves as well as by the masters. Within the world of the slave, social distinctions appeared and were appreciated.

When the sexual taboos and restraints imposed by their original culture were lost, the behavior of the slaves in this regard was subject at first only to the control of the masters and the wishes of those selected for mates. Hence, on the large plantations, where the slaves were treated almost entirely as instruments of production and brute force was relied upon as the chief means of control, sexual relations were likely to be dissociated on the whole from human sentiments and feelings. Then, too, the constant buying and selling of slaves prevented the development of strong emotional ties between the mates.

But, where slavery became a settled way of life, the slaves were likely to show preferences in sexual unions, and opportunity was afforded for the development of strong attachments. The permanence of these attachments was conditioned by the exigencies of the plantation system and the various types of social control within the world of the plantation.

Within this world the slave mother held a strategic position and played a dominant role in the family groupings. The tie between the mother and her younger children had to be respected not only because of the dependence of the child upon her for survival but often because of her fierce attachment to her brood. Some of the mothers undoubtedly were cold and indifferent to their offspring, but this appears to have been due to the attitude which the mother developed toward the unborn child during pregnancy as well as the burden of child care. On the whole, the slave family developed as a natural organization, based upon the spontaneous feelings of affection and natural sympathies which resulted from the association of the family members in the same household. Although the emotional interdependence between the mother and her children generally caused her to have a more permanent interest in the family than the father, there were fathers who developed an attachment for their wives and children.

But the Negro slave mother, as she is known through tradition at least, is represented as the protectress of the children of the master race. Thus tradition has symbolized in the relation of the black foster-parent and the white child the fundamental paradox in the slave system—maximum intimacy existing in conjunction with the most rigid caste system. Cohabitation of the men of the master race with women of the slave race occurred on every level and became so extensive that it nullified to some extent the monogamous mores. The class of mixed-bloods who were thus created formed the most important channel by which the ideals, customs, and mores of the whites were mediated to the servile race. Whether these mixed-bloods were taken into the master's house as servants, or given separate establishments, or educated by their white forebears, they were so situated as to assimilate the culture of the whites. Although a large number of this class were poor and degraded, fairly well-off communities of mixed-bloods who had assimilated the attitudes and culture of the whites to a high degree developed in various parts of the country. It was among this class that family traditions became firmly established before the Civil War.

Emancipation destroyed the *modus vivendi* which had become established between the two races during slavery. Although the freedmen were able to move about and thereby multiply the external contacts with the white man's world, many of the intimate and sympathetic ties between the two races were severed. As a result, Negroes began to build their own institutions and to acquire the civilization of the whites through the formal process of imitation and education. Then, too, despite their high hopes that their freedom would rest upon a secure foundation of landownership, the masses of illiterate and propertyless Negroes were forced to become croppers and tenants under a modified plantation system. In their relative isolation they developed a folk culture with its peculiar social organization and social evaluations. Within the world of the black folk, social relations have developed out of intimate and sympathetic contacts. Consequently, the maternal-family organization, a heritage from slavery, has continued on a fairly large scale. But the maternal-family organization has also been tied up with the widespread illegitimacy which one still finds in these rural communities. Illegitimacy among these folk is generally a harmless affair, since it does not disrupt the family organization and involves no violation of the mores. Although formal education has done something in the way of dispelling ignorance and superstition, it has effected little change in the mores and customs of these folk communities.

The stability and the character of the social organization of the rural communities has depended upon the fortunes of southern agriculture. Up until the opening of the present century, the more ambitious and energetic of the former slaves and their descendants have managed to get some education and buy homes. This has usually given the father or husband an interest in his family and has established his authority. Usually such families sprang from the more stable, intelligent, and reliable elements in the slave population. The emergence of this class of families from the mass of the Negro population has created small nuclei of stable families with conventional standards of sexual morality all over the South. Although culturally these families may be distinguished from those of free ancestry, they have intermarried from time to time with the latter families. These families represented the highest development of Negro family life up to the opening of the present century.

The urbanization of the Negro population since 1900 has brought the most momentous change in the family life of the Negro since emancipation. This movement, which has carried over a million Negroes to southern cities alone, has torn the Negro loose from his cultural moorings. Thousands of these migrants have been solitary men and women who have led a more or less lawless sex life during their wanderings. But many more illiterate or semi-illiterate and impoverished Negro families, broken or held together only by the fragile bonds of sympathy and habit, have sought a dwellingplace in the slums of southern cities. Because of the dissolution of the rural folkways and mores, the children in these families have helped to swell the ranks of juvenile delinquents. Likewise, the bonds of sympathy and community of interests that held their parents together in the rural environment have been unable to withstand the disintegrating forces in the city. Illegitimacy, which was a more or less harmless affair in the country, has become a serious economic and social problem. At times students of social problems have seen in these various aspects of family disorganization a portent of the Negro's destruction.

During and following the First World War, the urbanization of the Negro population was accelerated and acquired even greater significance than earlier migrations to cities. The Negro was carried beyond the small southern cities and plunged into the midst of the modern industrial centers in the North. Except for the war period, when there was a great demand for his labor, the migration of the Negro to northern cities has forced him into a much more rigorous type of competition with whites than he has ever faced. Because of his rural background and ignorance, he has entered modern industry as a part of the great army of unskilled workers. Like the immigrant groups that have preceded him, he has been forced to live in the slum areas of northern cities. In vain social workers and others have constantly held conferences on the housing conditions of Negroes, but they have been forced finally to face the fundamental fact of the Negro's poverty. Likewise, social and welfare agencies have been unable to stem the tide of family disorganization that has followed as a natural consequence of the impact of modern civilization upon the folkways and mores of a simple peasant folk. Even Negro families with traditions of stable family life have not been unaffected by the social and economic forces in urban communities. Family traditions and social distinctions that had meaning and significance in the relatively simple and stable southern communities have lost their meaning in the new world of the modern city.

By accelerating once again the cityward movement of Negroes, World War II brought within the orbit of urban civilization a larger sector of the Negro population. It is estimated that about a quarter of a million Negroes were attracted to the cities of the West where there had been relatively few Negroes. In the urban areas of the West as well as in the cities of the North, the Negro family faced the same economic and social problems. During the war period the Negro family enjoyed considerable economic security. But in its adjustment to an urban way of life, the Negro family revealed the same weakness in organization which was revealed during other periods of initial contacts with city life. There was considerable family desertion on the part of fathers and husbands; there was an increase in illegitimacy and juvenile delinquency. Consequently, World War II did not cause the Negro family to face new problems; it caused new strata of the Negro population to face the same problems of family adjustment which had been faced by former migrants to the city.

Although the problems facing the Negro family were the same as those it faced during and following the first World War, the impact of these problems on the Negro family were different. Because of the opportunities for employment, including the service of men in the armed forces, Negro men and women were more able to support their families. Ther was considerable upgrading of Negro workers partly because of the President's Committee on Fair Employment Practice and perhaps more especially because of the manpower shortage. The improved economic status of the Negro did not always bring greater stability to the family since children and even wives were often able to escape their dependence upon the father and husband in the family. However, the economic basis of family life was made more secure and the physical setting for normal family living was improved through the housing projects subsidized by the federal government. Before the outbreak of World War II, Negro families with low incomes had been the chief beneficiaries of the low-rent housing programs. Although

Negro families did not fare so well in regard to the war-housing projects, their share in these projects helped to make normal family living possible for Negroes drawn into defense areas.

One of the most important consequences of the urbanization of the Negro has been the rapid occupational differentiation of the population. A Negro middle class has come into existence as the result of new opportunities and greater freedom as well as the new demands of the awakened Negro communities for all kinds of services. This change in the structure of Negro life has been rapid and has not had time to solidify. The old established families, generally of mulatto origin, have looked with contempt upon the new middle class which has come into prominence as the result of successful competition in the new environment. With some truth on their side, they have complained that these newcomers lack the culture, stability in family life, and purity of morals which characterized their own class when it graced the social pyramid. In fact, there has not been sufficient time for these new strata to form definite patterns of family life. Consequently, there is much confusion and conflict in ideals and aims and patterns of behavior which have been taken over as the result of the various types of suggestion and imitation in the urban environment. This confusion has been increased by the fact that the middle class has been affected with an upper class outlook because of the segregation of the Negro. With incomes derived from occupations which would normally give them a middle class status, many families are influenced by extraneous values and attempt to maintain a style of life of a leisured upper class. But with the increase in the size of the middle class as the result of World War II, the upper class fringe is becoming more sharply differentiated from the middle class proper which is developing its own pattern of family life.

The most significant element in the new social structure of Negro life is the black industrial proletariat that has been emerging since the Negro was introduced into Western civilization. Its position in industry in the North was insecure and of small consequence until, with the cessation of foreign immigration during the first World War, it became a permanent part of the industrial proletariat. This development has affected tremendously the whole outlook on life and the values of the masses of Negroes. Heretofore, the Negro was chiefly a worker in domestic and personal services, and his ideals of family and other aspects of life were a crude imitation of the middle-class standards which he saw. Very often in the hotel or club he saw the white man during his leisure and recreation and therefore acquired leisure-class ideals which have probably been responsible for the "sporting complex" and the thriftlessness which are widespread among Negroes. But thousands of Negroes are becoming accustomed to the discipline of modern industry and are developing habits of consumption consonant with their new role. As the Negro has become an industrial worker and received adequate compensation, the father has become the chief breadwinner and assumed a responsible place in his family. Although World War II did not offer the same opportunities for large masses of unskilled Negro laborers as did the first World War, the black worker's position in industry was improved. Since the cessation of the War, the black worker has lost some of his gains but he has not lost his foothold in American industry.

As the result of the drafting of large numbers of Negro men into the armed forces, the lower strata of the Negro population developed a new attitude toward legal marriage. The legal and institutional meaning of marital relations became meaningful for thousands of Negro men for the first time when they were faced with the problem of making allowances for their wives and children. During the early years of the War there was among Negroes as among whites an increase in the birthrate. Following the War there was an increase in the illegitimacy rate at least in some cities. At the same time there has been a growing interest among Negroes in the program of planned parenthood. In various parts of the country Negro college and high school students are becoming interested in the question of planning for family life. Moreover, where clinics have been set up, working class Negro mothers are responding in ever increasing numbers to the advice provided concerning birth control.

When one views in retrospect the waste of human life, the immorality, delinquency, desertions, and broken homes which have been involved in the development of Negro family life in the United States, they appear to have been the inevitable consequences of the attempt of a preliterate people, stripped of their cultural heritage, to adjust themselves to civilization. The very fact that the Negro has succeeded in adopting habits of living that have enabled him to survive in a civilization based upon laissez faire and competition, itself bespeaks a degree of success in taking on the folkways and mores of the white race. That the Negro has found within the patterns of the white man's culture a purpose in life and a significance for his strivings which have involved sacrifices for his children and the curbing of individual desires and impulses indicates that he has become assimilated to a new mode of life.

However, when one undertakes to envisage the probable course of development of the Negro family in the future, it appears that the travail of civilization is not yet ended. First it appears that the family which evolved within the isolated world of the Negro folk will become increasingly disorganized. Modern means of communication will break down the isolation of the world of black folk, and, as long as the bankrupt system of southern agriculture exists, Negro families will continue to seek a living in the towns and cities of the country. They will crowd the slum areas of southern cities or make their way to northern cities where their family life will become disrupted and their poverty will force them to depend upon charity. Of course, the ordeal of civilization will be less severe if there is a general improvement in the standard of living and racial barriers to employment are broken down. Moreover, the chances for normal family life will be increased if large scale modern housing facilities are made available for the masses of the Negro population in cities. Nevertheless, those families which possess some heritage of family traditions and education will resist the destructive forces of urban life more successfully than the illiterate Negro folk and in either case their family life will adapt itself to the secular and rational organization of urban life. Undoubtedly, there will be a limitation of offspring; and men and women who associate in marriage will use it as a means for individual development.

The process of assimilation and acculturation in a highly mobile and urbanized society will proceed on a different basis from that in the past. There are evidences at present that in the urban environment, where caste prescriptions lose their force, Negroes and whites in the same occupational classes are being drawn into closer association than in the past. Such associations, to be sure, are facilitating the assimilation of only the more formal aspects of white civilization; but there are signs that intermarriage in the future will bring about a fundamental type of assimilation. Although there is no reliable measure of the extent of intermarriage at present, it appears that with the increasing mobility of the Negro intermarriage is slowly increasing. But, in the final analysis, the process of assimilation and acculturation will be limited by the extent to which the Negro becomes integrated into the economic organization and participates in the life of the community. The gains in civilization which result from participation in the white world will in the future as in the past be transmitted to future generations through the family.

PORTNOY'S COMPLAINT

Philip Roth

. . . I am so small I hardly know what sex I am, or so you would imagine. It is early in the afternoon, spring of the year Four. Flowers are standing up in purple stalks in the patch of dirt outside our building. With the windows flung open the air in the apartment is fragrant, soft with the season—and yet electric too with my mother's vitality: she has finished the week's wash and hung it on the line; she has baked a marble cake for our dessert tonight, beautifully bleeding—there's that blood again! there's that knife again!—anyway expertly bleeding the chocolate in and out of the vanilla, an accomplishment that seems to me as much of a miracle as getting those peaches to hang there suspended in the shimmering mold of jello. She has done the laundry and baked the cake; she has scrubbed the kitchen and bathroom floors and laid them with newspapers; she has of course dusted; needless to say, she has vacuumed; she has cleared and washed our luncheon dishes and (with my cute little assistance) returned them to their place in the *milchiks* cabinet in the pantry—and whistling like a canary all the morning through, a tuneless melody of health and joy, of heedlessness and self-sufficiency. While I crayon a picture for her, she showers—and now in the sunshine of her bedroom, she is dressing to take me downtown. She sits on the edge of the bed in her padded bra and her girdle, rolling on her stockings and chattering away. Who is Mommy's good little boy? Who is the best little boy a mommy ever had? Who does Mommy love more than anything in the whole wide world? I am absolutely punchy with delight, and meanwhile follow in their tight, slow, agonizingly delicious journey up her legs the transparent stockings that give her flesh a hue of stirring

dimensions. I sidle close enough to smell the bath powder on
her throat—also to appreciate better the elastic intricacies of
the dangling straps to which the stockings will presently be
hooked (undoubtedly with a flourish of trumpets). I smell the
oil with which she has polished the four gleaming posts of the
mahogany bedstead, where she sleeps with a man who lives
with us at night and on Sunday afternoons. My father they
say he is. On my fingertips, even though she has washed each
one of those little piggies with a warm wet cloth, I smell my
lunch, my tuna fish salad. Ah, it might be cunt I'm sniffing.
Maybe it is! Oh, I want to growl with pleasure. Four years
old, and yet I sense in my blood—uh-huh, again with the blood
—how rich with passion is the moment, how dense with possibility. This fat person with the long hair whom they call my
sister is away at school. This man, my father, is off somewhere making money, as best he is able. These two are gone,
and who knows, maybe I'll be lucky, maybe they'll never come
back . . . In the meantime, it is afternoon, it is spring, and
for me and me alone a woman is rolling on her stockings and
singing a song of love. Who is going to stay with Mommy forever and ever? *Me.* Who is it who goes with Mommy wherever
in the whole wide world Mommy goes? *Why me, of course.*
What a silly question—but don't get me wrong, I'll play the
game! Who had a nice lunch with Mommy, who goes downtown like a good boy on the bus with Mommy, who goes into
the big store with Mommy . . . and on and on and on . . . so
that only a week or so ago, upon my safe return from Europe,
Mommy had this to say—

"Feel."

"*What?*"—even as she takes my hand in hers and draws
it toward her body—"Mother—"

"I haven't gained five pounds," she says, "since you were
born. Feel," she says, and holds my stiff fingers against the
swell of her hips, which aren't bad . . .

And the stockings. More than twenty-five years have
passed (the game is supposed to be over!), but Mommy still
hitches up the stockings in front of her little boy. Now, however, he takes it upon himself to look the other way when
the flag goes fluttering up the pole—and out of concern not
just for his own mental health. That's the truth, I look away
not for me but for the sake of that poor man, my father! Yet

what preference does Father really have? If there in the living room their grown-up little boy were to tumble all at once onto the rug with his mommy, what would Daddy do? Pour a bucket of boiling water on the raging, maddened couple? Would he draw *his* knife—or would he go off to the other room and watch television until they were finished? "What are you looking away—?" asks my mother, amused in the midst of straightening her seams. "You'd think I was a twenty-one-year-old girl; you'd think I hadn't wiped your backside and kissed your little tushy for you all those years. Look at him"—this to my father, in case he hasn't been giving a hundred percent of his attention to the little floor show now being performed—"look, acting like his own mother is some sixty-year-old beauty queen."

But you *are* a Jew, my sister says. You are a Jewish boy, more than you know, and all you're doing is making yourself miserable, all you're doing is hollering into the wind . . . Through my tears I see her patiently explaining my predicament to me from the end of my bed. If I am fourteen, she is eighteen, and in her first year at Newark State Teacher's College, a big sallow-faced girl, oozing melancholy at every pore. Sometimes with another big, homely girl named Edna Tepper (who has, however, to recommend her, tits the size of my head), she goes to a folk dance at the Newark Y. This summer she is going to be crafts counselor in the Jewish Community Center day camp. I have seen her reading a paperback book with a greenish cover called *A Portrait of the Artist as a Young Man*. All I seem to know about her are these few facts, and of course the size and smell of her brassiere and panties. What years of confusion! And when will they be over? Can you give me a tentative date, please? When will I be cured of what I've got!

Do you know, she asks me, where you would be now if you had been born in Europe instead of America?

That isn't the issue, Hannah.

Dead, she says.

That isn't the issue!

Dead. Gassed, or shot, or incinerated, or butchered, or buried alive. Do you know that? And you could have screamed all you wanted that you were not a Jew, that you were a human being and had nothing whatever to do with their stupid suffering heritage, and still you would have been taken away to be disposed of. You would be dead, and I would be dead, and

But that isn't what I'm talking about!

And your mother and your father would be dead.

But why are you taking their side!

I'm not taking anybody's side, she says. I'm only telling you he's not such an ignorant person as you think.

And she isn't either, I suppose! I suppose the Nazis make everything she says and does smart and brilliant too! I suppose the Nazis are an excuse for everything that happens in this house!

Oh, I don't know, says my sister, maybe, maybe they are, and now she begins to cry too, and how monstrous I feel, for she sheds her tears for six million, or so I think, while I shed mine only for myself. Or so I think.

KADDISH FOR
NAOMI GINSBERG 1894–1956

Allen Ginsberg

Strange now to think of you, gone without corsets & eyes, while
I walk on the sunny pavement of Greenwich Village.
downtown Manhattan, clear winter noon, and I've been up all
night, talking, talking, reading the Kaddish aloud, listening to Ray Charles blues shout blind on the phonograph
the rhythm the rhythm—and your memory in my head three
years after—And read Adonais' last triumphant stanzas
aloud—wept, realizing how we suffer—
And how Death is that remedy all singers dream of, sing,
remember, prophesy as in the Hebrew Anthem, or the
Buddhist Book of Answers—and my own imagination of
a withered leaf—at dawn—
Dreaming back thru life, Your time—and mine accelerating
toward Apocalypse,
the final moment—the flower burning in the Day—and what
comes after,
looking back on the mind itself that saw an American city
a flash away, and the great dream of Me or China, or you and
a phantom Russia, or a crumpled bed that never existed—
like a poem in the dark—escaped back to Oblivion—
No more to say, and nothing to weep for but the Beings in the
Dream, trapped in its disappearance,
sighing, screaming with it, buying and selling pieces of
phantom, worshipping each other,
worshipping the God included in it all—longing or inevitability?—while it lasts, a Vision—anything more?
It leaps about me, as I go out and walk the street, look back
over my shoulder, Seventh Avenue, the battlements of

window office buildings shouldering each other high under
a cloud, tall as the sky an instant—and the sky above—
an old blue place.

or down the Avenue to the South, to—as I walk toward the
Lower East Side—where you walked 50 years ago, little
girl—from Russia, eating the first poisonous tomatoes of
America—frightened on the dock—

then struggling in the crowds of Orchard Street toward what?
—toward Newark—

toward candy store, first home-made sodas of the century,
hand-churned ice cream in backroom on musty brownfloor-
boards—

Toward education, marriage nervous breakdown, operation,
teaching school, and learning to be mad, in a dream—
what is this life?

Toward the Key in the window—and the great Key lays its
head of light on top of Manhattan, and over the floor,
and lays down on the sidewalk—in a single vast beam,
moving, as I walk down First toward the Yiddish Theater
—and the place of poverty

you knew, and I know, but without caring now—Strange to
have moved thru Paterson, and the West, and Europe and
here again,

with the cries of Spaniards now in the doorstoops doors and
dark boys on the street, fire escapes old as you

—Tho you're not old now, that's left here with me—

Myself, anyhow, maybe as old as the universe—and I guess
that dies with us—enough to cancel all that comes—
What came is gone forever every time—

That's good! That leaves it open for no regret—no fear radiators, lacklove, torture even toothache in the end—

Though while it comes it is a lion that eats the soul—and the
lamb, the soul, in us, alas, offering itself in sacrifice to
change's fierce hunger—hair and teeth—and the roar of
bonepain, skull bare, break rib, rot-skin, braintricked
Implacability.

Ai! ai! we do worse! We are in a fix! And you're out, Death
let you out, Death had the Mercy, you're done with your
century, done with God, done with the path thru it—
Done with yourself at last—Pure—Back to the Babe dark
before your Father, before us all—before the world—

There, rest. No more suffering for you. I know where you've
gone, it's good.

No more flowers in the summer fields of New York, no joy now,
no more fear of Louis,

and no more of his sweetness and glasses, his high school
decades, debts, love, frightened telephone calls, conception
beds, relatives, hands—

No more of sister Elanor,—she gone before you—we kept it
secret—you killed her—or she killed herself to bear with
you—an arthritic heart—But Death's killed you both—
No matter—

Nor your memory of your mother, 1915 tears in silent movies
weeks and weeks—forgetting, agrieve watching Marie
Dressler address humanity, Chaplin dance in youth,

or Boris Godinov, Chaliapin's at the Met, halling his voice of a
weeping Czar—by standing room with Elanor & Max—
watching also the Capitalists take seats in Orchestra,
white furs, diamonds,

with the YPSL's hitch-hiking thru Pennsylvania, in black baggy
gym skirts pants, photograph of 4 girls holding each other
round the waste, and laughing eye, too coy, virginal
solitude of 1920

all girls grown old, or dead, now, and that long hair in the
grave—lucky to have husbands later—

You made it—I came too—Eugene my brother before (still
grieving now and will gream on to his last stiff hand, as
he goes thru his cancer—or kill—later perhaps—soon
he will think—)

And it's the last moment I remember, which I see them all
thru myself, now—tho not you

I didn't foresee what you felt—what more hideous gape of
bad mouth came first—to you—and were you prepared?

To go where? In that Dark—that—in that God? a radiance?
A Lord in the Void? Like an eye in the black cloud in a
dream? Adonoi at last, with you?

Beyond my remembrance! Incapable to guess! Not merely the
yellow skull in the grave, or a box of worm dust, and
a stained ribbon—Deathshead with Halo? can you believe
it?

Is it only the sun that shines once for the mind, only the flash
of existence, than none ever was?

Nothing beyond what we have—what you had—that so pitiful
    —yet Triumph,
to have been here, and changed, like a tree, broken, or flower—
    fed to the ground—but mad, with its petals, colored,
    thinking Great Universe, shaken, cut in the head, leaf-
    stript, hid in an egg crate hospital, cloth wrapped, sore
    —freaked in the moon brain, Naughtless.
No flower like that flower, which knew itself in the garden, and
    fought the knife—lost
Cut down by an idiot Snowman's icy—even in the Spring—
    strange ghost thought—some Death—Sharp icicle in his
    hand—crowned with old roses—a dog for his eyes—cock
    of a sweatshop—heart of electric irons.
All the accumulations of life, that wear us out—clocks, bodies,
    consciousness, shoe, breasts—begotten sons—your Com-
    munism—'Paranoia' into hospitals.
You once kicked Elanor in the leg, she died of heart failure
    later. You of stroke. Asleep? within a year, the two of
    you, sisters in death. Is Elanor happy?
Max grieves alive in an office on Lower Broadway, lone large
    mustache over midnight Accountings, not sure. His life
    passes—as he sees—and what does he doubt now? Still
    dream of making money, or that might have made money,
    hired nurse, had children, found even your Immortality,
    Naomi?
I'll see him soon. Now I've got to cut through—to talk to you
    —as I didn't when you had a mouth.
Forever. And we're bound for that, Forever—like Emily Dickin-
    son's horses—headed to the End.
They know the way—These Steeds—run faster than we think
    —it's our own life they cross—and take with them.

    Magnificent, mourned no more, marred of heart, mind
behind, married dreamed, mortal changed—Ass and face done
with murder.
    In the world, given, flower maddened, made no Utopia,
shut under pine, almed in Earth, balmed in Lone, Jehovah,
accept.
    Nameless, One Faced, Forever beyond me, beginningless,
endless, Father in death. Tho I am not there for this Prophecy,
I am unmarried, I'm hymnless, I'm Heavenless, headless in
blisshood I would still adore

Thee, Heaven, after Death, only One blessed in Nothing-
ness, not light or darkness, Dayless Eternity—

Take this, this Psalm, from me, burst from my hand in
a day, some of my Time, now given to Nothing—to praise Thee
—But Death

This is the end, the redemption from Wilderness, way for
the Wonderer, House sought for All, black handkerchief washed
clean by weeping—page beyond Psalm—Last change of mine
and Naomi—to God's perfect Darkness—Death, stay thy
phantoms!

III

Only to have not forgotten the beginning in which she drank
    cheap sodas in the morgues of Newark,
only to have seen her weeping on grey tables in long wards of
    her universe
only to have known the weird ideas of Hitler at the door, the
    wires in her head, the three big sticks
rammed down her back, the voices in the ceiling shrieking out
    her ugly early lays for 30 years,
only to have seen the time-jumps, memory lapse, the crash of
    wars, the roar and silence of a vast electric shock,
only to have seen her painting crude pictures of Elevateds
    running over the rooftops of the Bronx
her brothers dead in Riverside or Russia, her lone in Long
    Island writing a last letter—and her image in the sun-
    light at the window
'The key is in the sunlight at the window in the bars the key
    is in the sunlight,'
only to have come to that dark night on iron bed by stroke when
    the sun gone down on Long Island
and the vast Atlantic roars outside the great call of Being to
    its own
to come back out of the Nightmare—divided creation—with
    her head lain on a pillow of the hospital to die
—in one last glimpse—all Earth one everlasting Light in the
    familiar blackout—no tears for this vision—
But that the key should be left behind—at the window—the
    key in the sunlight—to the living—that can take
that slice of light in hand—and turn the door—and look
    back see

Creation glistening backwards to the same grave, size of
    universe,
size of the tick of the hospital's clock on the archway over the
    white door—

IV

O mother
what have I left out
O mother
what have I forgotten
O mother
farewell
with a long black shoe
farewell
with Communist Party and a broken stocking
farewell
with six dark hairs on the wen of your breast
farewell
with your old dress and a long black beard around the vagina
farewell
with your sagging belly
with your fear of Hitler
with your mouth of bad short stories
with your fingers of rotten mandolines
with your arms of fat Paterson porches
with your belly of strikes and smokestacks
with your chin of Trotsky and the Spanish War
with your voice singing for the decaying overbroken workers
with your nose of bad lay with your nose of the smell of the
    pickles of Newark
with your eyes
with your eyes of Russia
with your eyes of no money
with your eyes of false China
with your eyes of Aunt Elanor
with your eyes of starving India
with your eyes pissing in the park
with your eyes of America taking a fall
with your eyes of your failure at the piano
with your eyes of your relatives in California
with your eyes of Ma Rainey dying in an ambulance
with your eyes of Czechoslovakia attacked by robots

with your eyes going to painting class at night in the Bronx
with your eyes of the killer Grandma you see on the horizon
    from the Fire-Escape
with your eyes running naked out of the apartment screaming
    into the hall
with your eyes being led away by policemen to an ambulance
with your eyes strapped down on the operating table
with your eyes with the pancreas removed
with your eyes of appendix operation
with your eyes of abortion
with your eyes of ovaries removed
with your eyes of shock
with your eyes of lobotomy
with your eyes of divorce
with your eyes of stroke
with your eyes alone
with your eyes
with your eyes
with your Death full of Flowers

V

Caw caw caw crows shriek in the white sun over grave stone
    in Long Island
Lord Lord Lord Naomi underneath this grass my halflife and
    my own as hers
caw caw my eye be buri'd in the same Ground where I stand
    in Angel
Lord Lord great Eye that stares on All and moves in a black
    cloud
caw caw strange cry of Beings flung up into sky over the waving
    trees
Lord Lord O Grinder of giant Beyonds my voice in a boundless
    field in Sheol
Caw caw the call of Time rent out of foot and wing an instant
    in the universe
Lord Lord an echo in the sky the wind through ragged leaves
    the roar of memory
caw caw all years my birth a dream caw caw New York the big
    the broken shoe the vast highschool caw caw all Visions
    of the Lord
Lord Lord Lord caw caw caw Lord Lord Lord caw caw caw
    Lord

PUERTO RICAN PARADISE

Piri Thomas

Poppa didn't talk to me the next day. Soon he didn't talk much to anyone. He lost his night job—I forget why, and probably it was worth forgetting—and went back on home relief. It was 1941, and the Great Hunger called Depression was still down on Harlem.

But there was still the good old WPA. If a man was poor enough, he could dig a ditch for the government. Now Poppa was poor enough again.

The weather turned cold one more time, and so did our apartment. In the summer the cooped-up apartments in Harlem seem to catch all the heat and improve on it. It's the same in the winter. The cold, plastered walls embrace that cold from outside and make it a part of the apartment, till you don't know whether it's better to freeze out in the snow or by the stove, where four jets, wide open, spout futile, blue-yellow flames. It's hard on the rats, too.

Snow was falling. "My *Cristo*," Momma said, "*qué frío.* Doesn't that landlord have any *corazón*? Why don't he give more heat?" I wondered how Pops was making out working a pick and shovel in that falling snow.

Momma picked up a hammer and began to beat the beat-up radiator that's copped a plea from so many beatings. Poor steam radiator, how could it give out heat when it was freezing itself? The hollow sounds Momma beat out of it brought echoes from other freezing people in the building. Everybody picked up the beat and it seemed a crazy, good idea. If everybody took turns beating on the radiators, everybody could keep warm from the exercise.

We drank hot cocoa and talked about summertime.

Momma talked about Puerto Rico and how great it was, and how she'd like to go back one day, and how it was warm all the time there and no matter how poor you were over there, you could always live on green bananas, *bacalao,* and rice and beans. *"Dios mío,"* she said, "I don't think I'll ever see my island again."

"Sure you will, Mommie," said Miriam, my kid sister. She was eleven. "Tell us, tell us all about Porto Rico."

"It's not Porto Rico, it's Puerto Rico," said Momma.

"Tell us, Moms," said nine-year-old James, "about Puerto Rico."

"Yeah, Mommie," said six-year-old José.

Even the baby, Paulie, smiled.

Moms copped that wet-eyed look and began to dream-talk about her *isla verde,* Moses' land of milk and honey.

"When I was a little girl," she said, "I remember the getting up in the morning and getting the water from the river and getting the wood for the fire and the quiet of the greenlands and the golden color of the morning sky, the grass wet from the *illuvia* . . . Ai, Dios, the *cuquís* and the *pajaritos* making all the *música* . . ."

"Mommie, were you poor?" asked Miriam.

"*Sí, muy pobre,* but very happy. I remember the hard work and the very little bit we had, but it was a good little bit. It counted very much. Sometimes when you have too much, the good gets lost within and you have to look very hard. But when you have a little, then the good does not have to be looked for so hard."

"Moms," I asked, "did everybody love each other—I mean, like if everybody was worth something, not like if some weren't important because they were poor—you know what I mean?"

"*Bueno hijo,* you have people everywhere who, because they have more, don't remember those who have very little. But in Puerto Rico those around you share la *pobreza* with you and they love you, because only poor people can understand poor people. I like *los Estados Unidos,* but it's sometimes a cold place to live—not because of the winter and the landlord not giving heat but because of the snow in the hearts of the people."

"Moms, didn't our people have any money or land?" I leaned forward, hoping to hear that my ancestors were noble princes born in Spain.

"Your grandmother and grandfather had a lot of land, but they lost that."

"How come, Moms?"

"Well, in those days there was nothing of what you call *contratos*, and when you bought or sold something, it was on your word and a handshake, and that's the way your *abuelos* bought their land and then lost it."

"Is that why we ain't got nuttin' now?" James asked pointedly.

"Oh, it—"

The door opened and put an end to the kitchen yak. It was Poppa coming home from work. He came into the kitchen and brought all the cold with him. Poor Poppa, he looked so lost in the clothes he had on. A jacket and coat, sweaters on top of sweaters, two pairs of long johns, two pairs of pants, two pairs of socks and a woolen cap. And under all that he was cold. His eyes were cold; his ears were red with pain. He took off his gloves and his fingers were stiff with cold.

"*Cómo está?*" said Momma. "I will make you coffee."

Poppa said nothing. His eyes were running hot frozen tears. He worked his fingers and rubbed his ears, and the pain made him make faces. "Get me some snow, Piri," he said finally.

I ran to the window, opened it, and scraped all the snow on the sill into one big snowball and brought it to him. We all watched in frozen wonder as Poppa took that snow and rubbed it on his ears and hands.

"Gee, Pops, don't it hurt?" I asked.

"*Sí*, but it's good for it. It hurts a little first, but it's good for the frozen parts."

I wondered why.

"How was it today?" Momma asked.

"Cold. My God, ice cold."

Gee, I thought, *I'm sorry for you, Pops. You gotta suffer like this.*

"It was not always like this," my father said to the cold walls. "It's all the fault of the damn depression."

"Don't say 'damn,'" Momma said.

"Lola, I say 'damn' because that's what it is—*damn*."

And Momma kept quiet. She knew it was "damn."

My father kept talking to the walls. Some of the words came out loud, others stayed inside. I caught the inside ones—

the damn WPA, the damn depression, the damn home relief, the damn poorness, the damn cold, the damn crummy apartments, the damn look on his damn kids, living so damn damned and his not being able to do a damn thing about it.

And Momma looked at Poppa and at us and thought about her Puerto Rico and maybe being there where you didn't have to wear a lot of extra clothes and feel so full of damns, and how when she was a little girl all the green was wet from the *lluvias*.

And Poppa looking at Momma and us, thinking how did he get trapped and why did he love us so much that he dug in damn snow to give us a piece of chance? And why couldn't he make it from home, maybe, and keep running?

And Miriam, James, José, Paulie, and me just looking and thinking about snowballs and Puerto Rico and summertime in the street and whether we were gonna live like this forever and not know enough to be sorry for ourselves.

The kitchen all of a sudden felt warmer to me, like being all together made it like we wanted it to be. Poppa made it into the toilet and we could hear everything he did, and when he finished, the horsey gurgling of the flushed toilet told us he'd soon be out. I looked at the clock and it was time for "Jack Armstrong, the All-American Boy."

José, James, and I got some blankets and, like Indians, huddled around the radio digging the all-American Jack and his adventures, while Poppa ate dinner quietly. Poppa was funny about eating—like when he ate, nobody better bother him. When Poppa finished, he came into the living room and stood there looking at us. We smiled at him, and he stood there looking at us.

All of a sudden he yelled, "How many wanna play 'Major Bowes' Amateur Hour'?"

"Hoo-ray Yeah, we wanna play," said José.

"Okay, first I'll make some taffy outta molasses, and the one who wins first prize gets first choice at the biggest piece, okay?"

"Yeah, hoo-ray, *chevere*."

Gee, Pops, you're great, I thought, *you're the swellest, the bestest Pops in the whole world, even though you don't understand us too good.*

When the candy was all ready, everybody went into the living room. Poppa came in with a broom and put an empty can over the stick. It became a microphone, just like on the radio.

"Pops, can I be Major Bowes?" I asked.

"Sure, Piri," and the floor was mine.

"Ladies and gentlemen," I announced, "tonight we present 'Major Bowes' Amateur Hour,' and for our first number—"

"Wait a minute, son, let me get my ukelele," said Poppa. "We need music."

Everybody clapped their hands and Pops came back with his ukelele.

"The first con-tes-t'nt we got is Miss Miriam Thomas."

"Oh no, not me first, somebody else goes first," said Miriam and she hid behind Momma.

"Let me! Let me!" said José.

Everybody clapped.

"What are you gonna sing, sir?" I asked.

"Tell the people his name," said Poppa.

"Oh yeah. Presenting Mr. José Thomas. And what are you gonna sing, sir?"

I handed José the broom with the can on top and sat back. He sang well and everybody clapped.

Everyone took a turn, and we all agreed that two-year-old Paulie's "gurgle, gurgle" was the best song, and Paulie got first choice at the candy. Everybody got candy and eats and thought how good it was to be together, and Moms thought that it was wonderful to have such a good time time even if she wasn't in Puerto Rico where the grass was wet with *lluvia*. Poppa thought about how cold it was gonna be tomorrow, but then he remembered tomorrow was Sunday and he wouldn't have to work, and he said so and Momma said "*Sí*," and the talk got around to Christmas and how maybe things would get better.

The next day the Japanese bombed Pearl Harbor.

"My God," said Poppa. "We're at war."

"*Dios mío*," said Momma.

I turned to James. "Can you beat that." I said.

"Yeah," he nodded. "What's it mean?"

"What's it mean?" I said said. "You gotta ask, dopey? It means a rumble is on, and a big one, too."

I wondered if the war was gonna make things worse than they were for us. But it didn't. A few weeks later Poppa got a job in an airplane factory. "How about that?" he said happily. "Things are looking up for us."

Things *were* looking up for us, but it had taken a damn

war to do it. A lousy rumble had to get called so we could start to live better. I thought, *How do you figure this crap out?*

I couldn't figure it out, and after a while I stopped thinking about it. Life in the streets didn't change much. The bitter cold was followed by the sticky heat; I played stickball, marbles, and Johnny-on-the-Pony, copped girls's drawers and blew pot. War or peace—what difference did it really make?

CHRIST IN CONCRETE

Pietro di Donato

March whistled stinging snow against the brick walls and up the gaunt girders. Geremio, the foreman, swung his arms about, and gaffed the men on.

Old Nick, the "Lean," stood up from over a dust-flying brick pile, and tapped the side of his nose.

"Master Geremio, the devil himself could not break his tail any harder than we here."

Burly Vincenzo of the walrus moustache, and known as the "Snoutnose," let fall the chute door of the concrete hopper and sang over the Lean's direction: "Mari-Annina's belly and the burning night will make of me once more a milk-mouthed stripling lad . . ."

The Lean loaded his wheelbarrow and spat furiously. "Sons of two-legged dogs . . . despised of even the devil himself! Work! Sure! For America beautiful will eat you and spit your bones into the earth's hole! Work!" And with that his wiry frame pitched the barrow violently over the rough floor.

Snoutnose waved his head to and fro and with mock pathos wailed, "Sing on, oh guitar of mine . . ."

Short, cherry-faced Joe Chiappa, the scaffoldman, paused with hatchet in hand and tenpenny spike sticking out from small dice-like teeth to tell the Lean as he went by, in a voice that all could hear, "Ah, father of countless chicks, the old age is a carrion!"

Geremio chuckled and called to him: "Hey, little Joe, who are you to talk? You and big-titted Cola can't even hatch an egg, whereas the Lean has just to turn the doorknob of his bedroom and old Philomena becomes a balloon!"

Coarse throats tickled and mouths opened wide in laughter.

Mike, the "Barrel-mouth," pretended he was talking to himself and yelled out in his best English . . . he was always speaking English while the rest carried on in their native Italian: "I don't know myself, but somebodys whose gotta bigga buncha keeds and he alla times talka from somebody's elsa!"

Geremio knew it was meant for him and he laughed. "On the tomb of Saint Pimplelegs, this little boy my wife is giving me next week shall be the last! Eight hungry Christians to feed is enough for any man."

Joe Chiappa nodded to the rest. "Sure, Master Geremio had a telephone call from the next bambino. Yes, it told him it had a little bell there instead of a rosebush . . . It even told him its name!"

"Laugh, laugh all of you," returned Geremio, "but I tell you that all my kids must be boys so that they some day will be big American builders. And then I'll help them to put the gold away in the basements for safe keeping!"

A great din of riveting shattered the talk among the fast-moving men. Geremio added a handful of "Honest" tobacco to his corncob, puffed strongly, and cupped his hands around the bowl for a bit of warmth. The chill day caused him to shiver, and he thought to himself, "Yes, the day is cold, cold . . . but who am I to complain when the good Christ himself was crucified?

"Pushing the job is all right (when has it been otherwise in my life?) but this job frightens me. I feel the building wants to tell me something; just as one Christian to another. I don't like this. Mr. Murdin tells me, 'Push it up!' That's all he knows. I keep telling him that the underpinnings should be doubled and the old material removed from the floors, but he keeps the inspector drunk and . . . 'Hey, Ashes-ass! Get away from under that pilaster! Don't pull the old work. Push it way from you or you'll have a nice present for Easter if the wall falls on you!' . . . Well, with the help of God I'll see this job through. It's not my first, nor the . . . 'Hey, Patsy number two! Put more cement in that concrete; we're putting up a building, not an Easter cake!' "

Patsy hurled his shovel to the floor and gesticulated madly. "The padrone Murdin-sa tells me, 'Too much! Lil' bit is plenty!' And you tell me I'm stingy! The rotten building can fall after I leave!"

Six floors below, the contractor called: "Hey Geremio! Is your gang of dagos dead?"

Geremio cautioned to the men: "On your toes, boys. If he writes out slips, someone won't have big eels on the Easter table."

The Lean cursed that "the padrone could take the job and shove it . . . !"

Curly-headed Sandino, the rougish, pigeon-toed scaffold-man, spat a clod of tobacco-juice and hummed to his own music.

"Yes, certainly yes to your face, master padrone . . . and behind, this to you and all your kind!"

The day, like all days, came to an end. Calloused and bruised bodies sighed, and numb legs shuffled towards shabby railroad flats. . . .

"Ah, *bella casa mio*. Where my little freshlets of blood, and my good woman await me. Home where my broken back will not ache so. Home where midst the monkey chatter of my piccolinos I will float off to blessed slumber with my feet on the chair and the head on the wife's soft full breast."

These great child-hearted ones leave each other without words or ceremony, and as they ride and walk home, a great pride swells the breast. . . .

"Blessings to Thee, oh Jesus. I have fought winds and cold. Hand to hand I have locked dumb stones in place and the great building rises. I have earned a bit of bread for me and mine."

The mad day's brutal conflict is forgiven, and strained limbs prostrate themselves so that swollen veins can send the yearning blood coursing and pulsating deliciously as though the body mountained leaping streams.

The job alone remained behind . . . and yet, they too, having left the bigger part of their lives with it. The cold ghastly beast, the Job, stood stark, the eerie March wind wrapping it in sharp shadows of falling dusk.

That night was a crowning point in the life of Geremio. He bought a house! Twenty years he had helped to mould the New World. And now he was to have a house of his own! What mattered that it was no more than a wooden shack? It was his own!

He had proudly signed his name and helped Annunziata to make her X on the wonderful contract that proved them owners. And she was happy to think that her next child, soon to come, would be born under their own rooftree. She heard the church chimes, and cried to the children: "Children, to bed! It

is near midnight. And remember, shut-mouth to the *paesanos!*
Or they will send the evil eye to our new home even before we
put foot."

The children scampered off to the icy yellow bedroom
where three slept in one bed and three in the other. Coltishly
and friskily they kicked about under the covers; their black
iron-cotton stockings not removed . . . what! and freeze the
peanut-little toes?

Said Annunziata, "The children are so happy, Geremio;
let them be, for even I would a Tarantella dance." And with
that she turned blushing. He wanted to take her on her word.
She patted his hands, kissed them, and whispered, "Our children will dance for us . . . in the American style some day."

Geremio cleared his throat and wanted to sing. "Yes, with
joy I could sing in a richer feeling than the great Caruso." He
babbled little old country couplets and circled the room until
the tenant below tapped the ceiling.

Annunziata whispered: "Geremio, to bed and rest. Tomorrow is a day for great things . . . and the day on which our
Lord died for us."

The children were now hard asleep. Heads under the
cover, over . . . moist noses whistling, and little damp legs
entwined.

In bed Geremio and Annunziata clung closely to each
other. They mumbled figures and dates until fatigue stilled
their thoughts. And with chubby Johnnie clutching fast his
bottle and warmed between them . . . life breathed heavily,
and dreams entertained in far, far worlds, the nation-builder's
brood.

But Geremio and Annunziata remained for a while staring
into darkness, silently.

"Geremio?"

"Yes?"

"This job you are now working. . . ."

"So?"

"You used always to tell about what happened on the
jobs . . . who was jealous, and who praised. . . ."

"You should know by now that all work is the same. . . ."

"Geremio The month you have been on this job, you have
not spoken a word about the work . . . And I have felt that I am
walking in a dream. Is the work dangerous? Why don't you
answer . . .?"

Job loomed up damp, shivery grey. Its giant members waiting.

Builders quietly donned their coarse robes, and waited.

Geremio's whistle rolled back into his pocket and the symphony of struggle began.

Trowel rang through brick and slashed mortar rivets were machine-gunned fast with angry grind Patsy number one check Patsy number two check the Lean three check Vincenzo four steel bellowed back at hammer donkey engines coughed purple Ashes-ass Pietro fifteen chisel point intoned stone thin steel whirred and wailed through wood liquid stone flowed with dull rasp through iron veins and hoist screamed through space Carmine the Fat twenty-four and Giacomo Sangini check . . . The multitudinous voices of a civilization rose from the surroundings and welded with the efforts of the Job.

To the intent ear, Nation was voicing her growing pains, but, hands that create are attached to warm hearts and not to calculating minds. The Lean as he fought his burden on looked forward to only one goal, the end. The barrow he pushed, he did not love. The stones that brutalized his palms, he did not love. The great God Job, he did not love. He felt a searing bitterness and a fathomless consternation at the queer consciousness that inflicted the ever mounting weight of structure that he HAD TO! HAD TO! raise above his shoulders! When, when and where would the last stone be? Never . . . did he bear his toil with the rhythm of song! Never . . . did his gasping heart knead the heavy mortar with lifting melody! A voice within him spoke a wordless language.

The language of worn oppression and the despair of realizing that his life had been left on brick piles. And always, there had been hunger and her bastard, the fear of hunger.

Murdin bore down upon Geremio from behind and shouted:

"Goddamnit, Geremio, if you're givin' the men two hours off today with pay, why the hell are they draggin' their tails? And why don't you turn that skinny old Nick loose, and put a young wop in his place?"

"Now, listen-a to me. Mister Murdin——"

"Don't give me that! And bear in mind that there are plenty of good barefoot men in the streets who'll jump for a day's pay!"

"Padrone—padrone, the underpinning gotta be make safe and——"

"Lissenyawopbastard! If you don't like it, you know what you can do!"

And with that he swung swaggering away.

The men had heard, and those who hadn't knew instinctively.

The new home, the coming baby, and his whole background, kept the fire from Geremio's mouth and bowed his head. "Annunziata speaks of scouring the ashcans for the children's bread in case I didn't want to work on a job where . . . But am I not a man, to feed my own with these hands? Ah, but day will end and no boss in the world can then rob me of the joy of my home!"

Murdin paused for a moment before descending the ladder.

Geremio caught his meaning and jumped to, nervously directing the rush of work . . . No longer Geremio, but a machine-like entity.

The men were transformed into single, silent beasts. Snoutnose steamed through ragged moustache whip-lashing sand into mixer. Ashes-ass dragged under four by twelve beam Lean clawed wall knots jumping in jaws masonry crumbled dust billowed thundered choked. . . .

At noon, Geremio drank his wine from an old-fashioned magnesia bottle and munched a great pepper sandwich . . . no meat on Good Friday. Said one, "Are some of us to be laid off? Easter is upon us and communion dresses are needed and . . ."

That, while Geremio was dreaming of the new house and joys he could almost taste. Said he: "Worry not. You should know Geremio." It then all came out. He regaled them with his wonderful joy of the new house. He praised his wife and children one by one. They listened respectfully and returned him well wishes and blessings. He went on and on. . . . "Paul made a radio—all by himself, mind you! One can hear Barney Google and many American songs! How proud he."

The ascent to labour was made, and as they trod the ladder, heads turned and eyes communed with the mute flames of the brazier whose warmth they were leaving, not with willing heart, and in that fleeting moment, the breast wanted so, so much to speak of hungers that never reached the tongue.

About an hour later, Geremio called over to Pietro: "Pietro see if Mister Murdin is in the shanty and tell him I must see him! I will convince him that the work must not go on like this . . . just for the sake of a little more profit!"

Pietro came up soon. "The padrone is not coming up. He was drinking from a large bottle of whiskey and cursed in American words that if you did not carry out his orders—"

Geremio turned away disconcerted, stared dumbly at the structure and mechanically listed in his mind's eye the various violations of construction safety. An uneasy sensation hollowed him. The Lean brought down an old piece of wall and the structure palsied. Geremio's heart broke loose and outthumped the floor's vibrations, a rapid wave of heat swept him and left a chill touch in its wake. He looked about to the men, a bit frightened. They seemed usual, life-size, and moved about with the methodical deftness that made the moment then appear no different than the task of toil had ever been.

Snoutnose's voice boomed into him. "Master Geremio, the concrete is rea—dy!"

"Oh, yes, yes, Vincenz." And he walked gingerly towards the chute, but, not without leaving behind some part of his strength, sending out his soul to wrestle with the limbs of Job, who threatened in stiff silence. He talked and joked with Snoutnose. Nothing said anything, nor seemed wrong. Yet a vague uneasiness was to him as certain as the foggy murk that floated about Job's stone and steel.

"Shall I let the concrete down now, Master Geremio?"

"Well, let me see—no, hold it a minute. Hey, Sandino! Tighten the chute cables!"

Snoutnose straightened, looked about, and instinctively rubbed the sore small of his spine. "Ah," sighed he, "all the men feel as I—yes, I can tell. They are tired but happy that today is Good Friday and we quit at three o'clock . . ." And he swelled in human ecstasy at the anticipation of food, drink, and the hairy flesh-tingling warmth of wife, and then, extravagant rest. In truth, they all felt as Snoutnose, although perhaps with variations on the theme.

It was the Lean only who had lived, and felt otherwise. His soul, accompanied with time, had shredded itself in the physical war to keep the physical alive. Perhaps he no longer had a soul, and the corpse continued from momentum. May he not be the Slave, working on from the birth of Man—He of whom it was said, "It was not for Him to reason?" And probably He who, never asking, taking, nor vaunting, created God and the creatable? Nevertheless, there existed in the Lean a sense of oppression suffered, so vast that the seas of time could never wash it away.

Geremio gazed about and was conscious of seeming to understand many things. He marvelled at the strange feeling which permitted him to sense the familiarity of life. And yet —all appeared unreal, a dream pungent and nostalgic. Life, dream, reality, unreality, spiralling ever about each other. "Ha," he chuckled, "how and from where do these thoughts come?"

Snoutnose had his hand on the hopper latch and was awaiting the word from Geremio. "Did you say something, Master Geremio?"

"Why, yes, Vincenz, I was thinking—funny! A—yes, what is the time—yes, that is what I was thinking."

"My American can of tomatoes says ten minutes from two o'clock. It won't be long now, Master Geremio."

Geremio smiled. "No, about an hour . . . and then, home."

"Oh, but first we stop at Mulberry Street, to buy their biggest eels, and the other finger-licking stuffs."

Geremio was looking far off, and for a moment happiness came to his heart without words, a warm hand stealing over. Snoutnose's words sang to him pleasantly, and he nodded.

"And Master Geremio, we ought really to buy the seafruits with the shells—you know, for the much needed steam they put into the——"

He flushed despite himself and continued. "It is true, I know it—especially the juicy clams . . . uhmm, my mouth waters like a pump."

Geremio drew on his unlit pipe and smiled acquiescence. The men around him were moving to their tasks silently, feeling of their fatigue, but absorbed in contemplations the very same as Snoutnose's. The noise of labour seemed not to be noise, and as Geremio looked about, life settled over him a grey concert—grey forms, atmosphere, and grey notes . . . Yet his off-tone world felt so near, and familiar.

"Five minutes from two," swished through Snoutnose's moustache.

Geremio automatically took out his watch, rewound, and set it. Sandino had done with the cables. The tone and movement of the scene seemed to Geremio strange, differently strange, and yet, a dream familiar from a timeless date. His hand went up in motion to Vincenzo. The molten stone gurgled low, and then with heightening rasp. His eyes followed the stone-cementy pudding, and to his ears there was no other sound than its flow. From over the roofs somewhere, the tinny voice of *Barney Google* whined its way, hooked into his consciousness and kept itself a revolving record beneath his skull-plate.

"Ah, yes, Barney Google, my son's wonderful radio machine . . . wonderful Paul." His train of thought quickly took in his family, home and hopes. And with hope came fear. Something within asked, "Is it not possible to breathe God's air without fear dominating with the pall of unemployment? And the terror of production for Boss, Boss and Job? To rebel is to lose all of the very little. To be obedient is to choke. Oh, dear Lord, guide my path."

Just then, the floor lurched and swayed under his feet. The slipping of the underpinning below rumbled up through the undetermined floors.

Was he faint or dizzy? Was it part of the dreamy afternoon? He put his hands in front of him and stepped back, and looked up wildly. "No! No!"

The men poised stricken. Their throats wanted to cry out and scream but didn't dare. For a moment they were a petrified and straining pageant. Then the bottom of their world gave way. The building shuddered violently, her supports burst with the crackling slap of wooden gunfire. The floor vomited upward. Geremio clutched at the air and shrieked agonizingly. "Brothers, what have we done? Ahhhh-h, children of ours!" With the speed of light, balance went sickeningly awry and frozen men went flying explosively. Job tore down upon them madly. Walls, floors, beams became whirling, solid, splintering waves crashing with detonations that ground man and material in bonds of death.

The strongly shaped body that slept with Annunziata nights and was perfect in all the limitless physical quantities, thudded as a worthless sack amongst the giant debris that crushed fragile flesh and bone with centrifugal intensity.

Darkness blotted out his terror and the resistless form twisted, catapulted insanely in its directionless flight, and shot down neatly and deliberately between the empty wooden forms of a foundation wall pilaster in upright position, his blue swollen face pressed against the form and his arms outstretched, caught securely through the meat by the thin round bars of reinforcing steel.

The huge concrete hopper that was sustained by an independent structure of thick timber, wavered a breath or so, its heavy concrete rolling uneasily until a great sixteen-inch wall caught it squarely with all the terrific verdict of its dead weight and impelled it downward through joists, beams and masonry, until it stopped short, arrested by two girders, an arm's length above Geremio's head: the grey concrete gushing from the hopper mouth, and sealing up the mute figure.

Giacomo had been thrown clear of the building and dropped six floors to the street gutter, where he lay writhing.

The Lean had evinced no emotion. When the walls descended, he did not move. He lowered his head. One minute later he was hanging in mid-air, his chin on his chest, his eyes tearing loose from their sockets, a green foam bubbling from his mouth and his body spasming, suspended by the shreds left of his mashed arms pinned between a wall and a girder.

A two-by-four hooked little Joe Chiappa up under the back of his jumper and swung him around in a circle to meet a careening I-beam. In the flash that he lifted his frozen cherubic face, its shearing edge sliced through the top of his skull.

When Snoutnose cried beseechingly, "Saint Michael!" blackness enveloped him. He came to in a world of horror. A steady stream, warm, thick, and sickening as hot wine bathed his face and clogged his nose, mouth, and eyes. The nauseous syrup that pumped over his face, clotted his moustache red and drained into his mouth. He gulped for air, and swallowed the rich liquid scarlet. As he breathed, the pain shocked him to oppressive semiconsciousness. The air was wormingly alive with cries, screams, moans and dust, and his crushed chest seared him with a thousand fires. He couldn't see, nor breathe enough to cry. His right hand moved to his face and wiped at the gelatinizing substance, but it kept coming on, and a heart-breaking moan wavered about him, not far. He wiped his eyes in subconscious despair. Where was he? What kind of dream was he having? Perhaps he wouldn't wake up in time for work, and then what? But how queer; his stomach beating him, his chest on fire, he sees nothing but dull red, only one hand moving about, and a moaning in his face!

The sound and clamour of the rescue squads called to him from far off.

Ah, yes, he's dreaming in bed, and far out in the streets,

engines are going to a fire. Oh poor devils! Suppose his house were on fire? With the children scattered about in the rooms he could not remember! He must do his utmost to break out of this dream! He's swimming under water, not able to raise his head and get to the air. He must get back to consciousness to save his children!

He swam frantically with his one right hand, and then felt a face beneath its touch. A face! It's Angelina alongside of him! Thank God, he's awake! He tapped her face. It moved. It felt cold, bristly, and wet. "It moves so. What is this?" His fingers slithered about grisly sharp bones and in a gluey, stringy, hollow mass, yielding as wet macaroni. Grey light brought sight, and hysteria punctured his heart. A girder lay across his chest, his right hand clutched a grotesque human mask, and suspended almost on top of him was the twitching, faceless body of Joe Chiappa. Vincenzo fainted with an inarticulate sigh. His fingers loosed and the bodyless-headless face dropped and fitted to the side of his face while the drippings above came slower and slower.

The rescue men cleaved grimly with pick and axe.

Geremio came to with a start . . . far from their efforts. His brain told him instantly what had happened and where he was. He shouted wildly. "Save me! Save me! I'm being buried alive!"

He paused exhausted. His genitals convulsed. The cold steel rod upon which they were impaled froze his spine. He shouted louder and louder. "Save me! I am hurt badly! I can be saved, I can—save me before it's too late!" But the cries went no farther than his own ears. The icy wet concrete reached his chin. His heart was appalled. "In a few seconds I shall be entombed. If I can only breathe, they will reach me. Surely they will!" His face was quickly covered, its flesh yielding to the solid, sharp-cut stones. "Air! Air!" screamed his lungs as he was completely sealed. Savagely, he bit into the wooden form pressing upon his mouth. An eighth of an inch of its surface splintered off. Oh, if he could only hold out long enough to bite even the smallest hole through to air! He must! There can be no other way! He is responsible for his family! He cannot leave them like this! He didn't want to die! This could not be the answer to life! He had bitten half way through when his teeth snapped off to the gums in the uneven conflict. The pressure of the concrete was such, and its effectiveness so thorough, that the wooden splinters, stumps of teeth, and blood never left his choking mouth.

Why couldn't he go any farther?

Air! Quick! He dug his lower jaw into the little hollowed space and gnashed in choking agonized fury. "Why doesn't it go through? Mother of Christ, why doesn't it give? Can there be a notch, or two-by-four stud behind it? Sweet Jesu! No! No! Make it give. . . . Air! Air!"

He pushed the bone-bare jaw maniacally; it splintered, cracked, and a jagged fleshless edge cut through the form opening a small hole to air. With a desperate burst the lung-prisoned air blew an opening through the shredded mouth and whistled back greedily a gasp of fresh air. He tried to breathe, but it was impossible. The heavy concrete was settling immutably, and its rich cement-laden grout ran into his pierced face. His lungs would not expand, and were crushing in tighter and tighter under the settling concrete.

"Mother mine—mother of Jesu-Annunziata—children of mine—dear, dear, for mercy, Jesu-Giuseppe e 'Maria," his blue-foamed tongue called. It then distorted in a shuddering coil and mad blood vomited forth. Chills and fire played through him and his tortured tongue stuttered, "Mercy, blessed Father—salvation, most kind Father—Saviour—Saviour of His children help me—adored Saviour—I kiss your feet eternally—you are my Lord—there is but one God—you are my God of infinite mercy—Hail Mary divine Virgin—our Father who art in heaven hallowed be thy—name—our Father—my Father," and the agony excruciated with never-ending amount, "our Father— Jesu, Jesu, soon Jesu, hurry dear Jesu Jesu Je-sssu . . . !" His mangled voice trebled hideously, and hung in jerky whimperings.

The unfeeling concrete was drying fast, and shrinking into monolithic density. The pressure temporarily de-sensitized sensation; leaving him petrified, numb, and substanceless. Only the brain remained miraculously alive.

"Can this be death? It is all too strangely clear. I see nothing nor feel nothing, my body and senses are no more, my mind speaks as it never did before. Am I or am I not Geremio? But I am Geremio! Can I be in the other world? I never was in any other world except the one I knew of; that of toil, hardship, prayer . . . of my wife who awaits with child for me, of my children and the first home I was to own. Where do I begin in this world? Where do I leave off? Why? I recall only a baffled life of cruelty from every direction. And hope was always as painful as fear, the fear of displeasing, displeasing the people and ideas whom I could never understand; laws, policemen, priests, bosses, and a rag with colours waving on a stick. I never did anything to these things. But what have I done with my life? Yes, my life! No one else's! Mine—mine—MINE— Geremio! It is clear. I was born hungry, and have always been hungry for freedom—life! I married and ran away to America so as not to kill and be killed in Tripoli for things they call 'God and Country.' I've never known the freedom I wanted in my heart. There was always an arm upraised to hit at me. What have I done to them? I did not want to make them toil for me. I did not raise my arm to them. In my life I could never breathe, and now without air, my mind breathes clearly for me. Wait! There has been a terrible mistake! A cruel crime! The world is not right! Murderers! Thieves! You have hurt me and my kind, and have taken my life from me! I have long felt it—yes, yes, yes, they have cheated me with flags, signs and fear . . . I say you can't take my life! I want to live! My life! To tell the cheated to rise and fight! Vincenz! Chiappa! Nick! Men! Do you hear me? We must follow the desires within us for the world has been taken from us; we, who made the world! Life!"

Feeling returned to the destroyed form.

"Ahhh-h, I am not dead yet. I knew it—you have not done with me. Torture away! I cannot believe you, God and Country, no longer!" His body was fast breaking under the concrete's closing wrack. Blood vessels burst like mashed flower stems. He screamed. "Show yourself now, Jesu! Now is the time! Save me! Why don't you come! Are you there! I cannot stand it—ohhh, why do you let it happen—it is bestial—where are you! Hurry, hurry, hurry! You do not come! You make me suffer, and what have I done! Come, come—come now—now save me, save me now! Now, now, now! If you are God, save me!"

The stricken blood surged through a weltering maze of useless pipes and exploded forth from his squelched eyes and formless nose, ears and mouth, seeking life in the indifferent stone.

"Aie—aie, aie—devils and Saints—beasts! Where are you —quick, quick, it is death and I am cheated—cheat—ed! Do you hear, you whoring bastards who own the world? Ohhh-

ohhhh aie-aie—hahahaha!" His bones cracked mutely and his sanity went sailing distorted in the limbo of the subconscious.

With the throbbing tones of an organ in the hollow background, the fighting brain disintegrated and the memories of a baffled lifetime sought outlet.

He moaned the simple songs of barefoot childhood, scenes flashed desperately on and off in disassociated reflex, and words and parts of words came pitifully high and low from his inaudible lips, the hysterical mind sang cringingly and breathlessly, "Jesu my Lord my God my all Jesu my Lord my God my all Jesu my Lord my God my all Jesu my Lord my God my all," and on as the whirling tempo screamed now far, now near, and came in soul sickening waves as the concrete slowly contracted and squeezed his skull out of shape.

PAPA, MAMA AND ECONOMICS

George Panetta

Papa couldn't read and write when he came off the boat, but in those days it was just as it is now in America, and the first thing Papa did was go in business. He opened a big dress factory on Lafayette Street and began making money like an Irishman. It even looked as if he was smarter than the Irishmen, because although they were making money, too, they were always breaking their heads or falling off scaffolds and forgetting to come out of a hole before the backfill. Besides, there was more dignity to what Papa was doing, and once in a while he wore a clean shirt.

But as Papa made the money, Mama spent it by having one of us every year, and by lending Clara to Uncle George in Italy so that after that Mamma could make three trips to Italy to see if she couldn't get Clara back. Papa couldn't get over all the money he was making, and for years he had Mama write letters to everybody in Italy, telling them to come quick because the gold was in the streets. And in 1926, when Papa was ruined, he was glad he had Mama write the letters, because from 1927 to 1931 he was able to live on what he borrowed from fifty or sixty of his friends that came over. After that they all came bothering Papa with sad stories; they didn't mind so much that he had brought them to this country in the first place, but please as a favor give them back some of the money they lent him so that they could go back to Italy.

That was in 1930, when everybody except Hoover wanted to go and die somewhere.

But up to 1926 Papa made money as if he were born here, and he could afford to have the seven of us—and almost anything else. In the summer we would go to the country, in South

Beach, Staten Island. All the years before 1926 we lived in that big apartment on Kenmare Street where we had four rooms and a toilet of our own. We had three beds and didn't have to sleep mixed. The boys slept in the bedroom which faced Mulberry Street, Aly near the wall because he was the youngest. The girls slept in the living-room, and when Grandpa took Clara on that loan to Uncle George, Grandma came over because there was plenty of room. There was even room on the kitchen floor for uncles that were always coming off the boat.

While Papa made the money he spent it, and if he had made it long enough all of us would be big people today. At supper every night Papa used to call on each of us to recite what we were going to be when we grew up; it was what Papa was giving us for the future and he liked to hear it over and over again. I was going to be a doctor. I had a big chest and could make a long noise with my mouth, so Papa thought I should be a doctor. Viola was going to be a great music teacher because one week Papa was making so much money that he happened to buy a piano. Nothing ever came out of it except La Donna Mobile one finger by Papa himself, and later, when Papa was ruined, Jenny began playing it by ear. Jenny had become a pianist, but when she was sitting at the supper table with us she was going to be a kindergarten teacher. Peter, PJ, was going to be a doctor too and, because he was older, it looked as if he would beat me to it, but I kept making those long noises and PJ would be a little afraid and wonder if it wasn't better to be a lawyer.

Only little Aly never wanted to be anything. He always had convulsions and Lando was always bopping him on the head and calling him half-cigar, and I suppose poor Aly thought it was better just to try and keep alive. Lando himself was Papa's pride, and when all the wine was drunk Papa would tell everybody to keep quiet and listen to what Lando was going to be. He was going to be an actor because he had blue eyes and nobody thought he was Italian. Mama used to take him to an actors' school on 44th Street every Tuesday and Thursday. Papa paid ten dollars a lesson, and Lando went to the school for nine weeks.

Nobody became anything, although Clara came back from Italy in 1925 with kidney trouble and a bald head.

Still, it wasn't Papa's fault. Up to 1926 he had no idea that the reason a man had children was to support him when he was old. He worked hard. He never saved any money, but look at all the money you could always make in America, and what were you going to do with it all? When he came home at night and had us talk about what we were going to be, it was what he was giving us, and it made him happy.

One day in 1926 the bank sent Papa's check back even though it had the cross on. He couldn't make the payroll to pay the people. It wasn't Papa's fault.

"What happen, Domenick?" Uncle Louie asked him.

"Who know?" said Papa. "Crazy man at bank."

"You sure you got money, Domenick?"

"Louie, shut up you too."

"Fix up with bookkeep, Domenick."

"Fix nothing. The bank send tomorrow."

"Fix up with bookkeep. Make sure."

"Louie, shut up. Go home."

Uncle Louie knew Papa was broke; he was a little smarter than Papa, had learned to shoot pool and had become a citizen when his wife explained the widow's pension they give you in this country. He was even smart enough to get in the Army in the first war, become a cook, and get shot in the behind when his company was retreating. He could figure it all out how Papa was broke, and as he was going home he kept saying it over. . . . The wife three times Italy . . . coupla thousan, another coupla just kids born, and twenn thousan just kids eat, sleep, dress him up like somebody. Summer comes—country—South Beach. Gotta go country? Jeesa, how can have money! And then the doctors, Jeesa! The small one get the convulsion, the fat one falls swamp, the big one puts bean in nose. Gotta call doctors. Say five thousan just call lousa doctor. And the girl gotta go college? That's coupla thousan more. And factory. Fifty dollar bookkeep, make check, telephone, hello, goodbye, fifty dollar. . . .

Uncle Louie kept talking to himself all the way home, and by the time he was home he figured that Papa had spent two hundred thousand dollars since he had come to America.

"Jeesa," Uncle Louie said, "how can have money my brother?"

The next day Papa went to the bank, first thing. "Whatsa matter no money?" he said.

"Your checking account is overdrawn," said the bank. "You

owe us a dollar and sixty-two cents. You haven't made a deposit in two months."

"I don't want know deposits," Papa said. "When I get money pay people?"

"You don't understand, Mr. Caparooti."

"I understand all about. I put in put in put in. Now I wants to take out."

The bank looked at Papa as if it were almost human, as if it were sorry for all these human beings who were mad.

"Isa right?" Papa asked, looking back.

"But, Mr. Caparooti, you must check your account."

"Damma who know this account? For twenn years I look book? I see whats all this? No. Whats got to do book? The people want money; they work, no? Can tell go home people, no money? For twenn years Mr. Caparooti no do this thing. Now you talk account account. What's got to do account?"

"I'm sorry, Mr. Caparooti, the check is no good with your account in this condition."

Papa looked at the bank right in the eye and in Italian he told the bank first of all to go to hell, then he said it was no wonder we had bank robbers and that he hoped they would come around that night with sacks and take everything, even the pennies.

Papa smoked out of the bank, back to the factory, and right into the bookkeeper's face.

"Why you no tell me?"

"I told you a dozen times, Mr. Caparooti."

"You tell me? What, you liar now too?"

"Even when I was writing out the check, I told you there was no money."

"You crazy, Antonette? You tell me?"

It wasn't Papa's fault. When he came off the boat, he couldn't read and write, but he opened this factory and got in the habit of making money. Every time he put his cross on the check, they sent the money. Now all of a sudden they didn't send it. And even if the bookkeeper did tell him, it wasn't his fault. Could you believe a thing like that after twenty years? How could it be?

It wasn't Papa's fault. And when Uncle Louie came over one night and talked about putting fire to the factory, that wasn't Papa's fault either.

"Domenick, that's we do," Uncle Louie said.

"But you sure money comes?"

"Sure, Domenick. Sure."

It wasn't Uncle Louie's fault either. How could he know the factory was not insured?

One night Uncle Louie forgot his cigar between forty yards of cloth. He came running home to Papa that the factory was on fire.

Together they stood on the corner of Broome and Lafayette looking at the fire.

After that Papa began sitting around the house waiting for Them to send the check. They didn't send the check right away so Mama started buying everything on credit. It was the beginning of our credit system and the way we got to know everybody. Mama started with the poor grocer on the corner of Mulberry. At first Mama used to go down herself, but after a week the grocer was looking at her as if he were wondering, and Mama decided she had too much cooking and cleaning to do and began sending Aly down. It had to be Aly. It couldn't be Viola because she was going to college and was getting intelligent enough to be ashamed. It couldn't be Clara because she had just come back from Italy with a bald head. And Jenny was twelve and just starting in with the piano and learning to faint any time anybody asked her to do anything. And none of the other boys could go because PJ could fight me and I could fight Lando and Lando could fight Aly. It had to be Aly.

He used to go down every day with four or five of Mama's lists, written on both sides of a paper bag, with a promise on the bottom of each—don't worry, as soon as the check comes Mama will be down. The grocer didn't mind at first, because now that Papa was out of work, we were spending five or six dollars more every day. But after a few weeks he began to shake his head, scratch out items like provolone and salami, and send notes back to Mama. Then Mama would ask Papa when the check was coming.

"Shut up, do you cook," Papa would say.

One day the grocer sent Aly back with nothing, and Mama sent Aly right back with a long letter written by Viola.

The grocer's name was Max, but he spoke Italian, all dialects, and he ate macaroni like the Italians, had as many children, and the only reason he wasn't a Christian was because nobody really wanted to know.

"Who understands this?" he said. "Here, take, take. I should worry."

After all, why should he worry? People owed him, he owed the people. If people bought more retail, he bought more wholesale. If the people had no money for him, he had no money for the other people.

He shrugged and filled the bags up for Aly. "Here, take the salami, too."

Aly came up with the stuff that day smiling for the first time since he had the convulsions. Mama smiled too, and I think if it wasn't for Max giving us all that food and showing Mama how easy it was to get everything for nothing, we would have starved many times all the while Papa was waiting for the check. It taught Mama the economics of small business. We kept eating just as if Papa still had the factory, but at the end of the month the landlord kept coming every day to the door. One day Papa got out of the chair in which he was waiting for the check and answered the door.

"The rent, Mr. Caparooti?"

Papa wanted to kill him. "How long I here?"

"Twenty years," the landlord said.

"How long I pay you?"

"You always pay before."

"Well, whatch you want?"

"This is a new month. I've got taxes to pay."

"Figure out whatch I pay you twenn years."

At thirty-five dollars a month it came to about eight or nine thousand dollars, and it was hard to understand you didn't own the rooms, even if you weren't Papa who had come off the boat without knowing how to read and write.

"Get out my house," Papa said. "Come back I throw you downstairs."

The landlord went down the stairs, walking, and stayed away for two months.

When Mama asked Papa about the check again, he just said "What the hell what's matter with you? Sure check come. Go cook and shut up." Papa was patient and waited another month for it. When it came he was going to Boston to see "what's going be" and Mama was going to get a new bed and

Viola was going to get money for college and we were going to find a doctor who could put the hair back on Clara's head. Meanwhile, Mama learned how to get more and more on credit.

A little old man named Blau was beginning to come around every Monday for six petticoats that Mama had bought for the girls. Mama started with Blau in 1926 with a bill of twelve dollars, and in 1936 poor Blau was still coming around and Mama owed him three hundred and sixty-two dollars. Blau disappeared in 1936, and after that Mama got Mr. Klide. The first two dollars Mama spent with Mr. Klide was cash, but now, in 1944, Mama owes him three hundred and forty-eight dollars and thirty-two cents, and she has forgotten all about Blau.

Still, when Papa got the check Mama was going to pay everybody, even Max the grocer, although when the check never came she realized she never had to. But Mama worried a little and one night she got after Papa about the check, and they had one of those fights Grandma used to tell us about. He grabbed Mama by the hair and pulled and if Mama hadn't screamed we would have had another bald head around the house.

The boys and girls all got up, and PJ, who was eighteen and five feet three, asked what was the matter. Papa banged him on the head with one of the pots on the stove. Viola was his favorite then and she pleaded with Papa to stop and he told us all to go to bed before he threw us all out the window. That night he went out to see Uncle Louie.

"When hell come this check?" Papa said.

"Check no come?" Uncle Louie said.

Aunt Angie, Uncle Louie's big wife, was in the kitchen moving around like a giant. They had a big house but if Aunt Angie fell over straight, she would fall on Uncle Louie talking with Papa in the living-room.

"Why no come?" said Uncle Louie. "You send policy, all right?"

"Powicy?" Papa said.

"The policy for fire," said Uncle Louie.

"What the hell this powicy?"

"Isa insurance, Domenick. You no get check without policy."

"Dope, lousa," Papa cried, putting out a hand to strangle Uncle Louie. "You say that when burn factory? I tell you burn?

I break you head."

Aunt Anglie called "What's this? You put fire to Domenick's shop?"

"Was cigar, Angie," Uncle Louie said. "Cigar in goods. Was accident."

"Was nothing accident," said Papa. "Lousa dope, no you say, Domenick, go head burn factory, no worry? No you say send check?"

"No policy," said Uncle Louie.

"Listen, Angie. This better no fooling. Louie burn factory. I want pay."

Aunt Angie put out her arm and caught Uncle Louie's right ear. She began twisting it and Uncle Louie hollered blue murder. "Was cigar, Angie. I swear Blessed Virgin."

"This true?" she asked, still twisting.

"I swear on God," Uncle Louie cried, kicking his legs from the pain in the ear. "I swear, swear, swear. . . ."

Aunt Angie let go the ear. "Go home, Domenick," she said. "I believe my husband."

Papa left, and Uncle Louie was happy that his wife was convinced he had told the truth about the cigar, but when he began to talk to her she didn't answer him and later, when he turned around, he got a boot in the behind he didn't know what for.

Papa waited for Uncle Louie to pay. He sat around talking to himself about breaking Uncle Louie's head if he didn't come with the money. But Uncle Louie had nothing, only nine children, and they ate like horses.

"He pay," Papa said to himself. "He get money from Angie's father."

Angie's father had worked steady as a pantsmaker, and Papa figured he had a lot of money. When the old man died in 1934, Uncle Louie had to pay for half the funeral.

Once while he was waiting, Papa got up to chase the landlord up the roof, and that scared him for four more months. Mama keeps saying Papa never wanted to work after the fire, but it wasn't Papa's fault. He waited for the fire check and then for Uncle Louie to pay up, and that kept him worried almost all of 1926. Then from 1927 to about 1931, when we began moving all over Brooklyn with the piano, Papa was borrowing from all the friends he had invited to America, and you couldn't expect him to look for work while he had that on his mind all the time. And after 1931, when nobody had money any more, Papa spent most of his time learning to sign his name because he didn't want to take chances with the relief checks the way he did with the factory; and while he was doing this, you couldn't expect him to look for work and make it seem he was putting something over on the Government. And in 1935, when Mama got a new refrigerator on her credit and the Government thought it was the same as money and stopped the relief checks, didn't Papa ask somebody if somebody was building a building somewhere because he was thinking of being a watchman? And wasn't he getting more active, leaving his chair every five or ten minutes, surprising everybody? It wasn't Papa's fault that it happened to be diabetes.

LETTER TO MOTHER

John Ciardi

It was good. You found your America. It was worth all
The coming: the fading figures in the never-again
      doorway,
The rankness of steerage, the landing in fog.
Yes, and the tenement, the reek and the shouting in the
      streets
All that night and the terror. It was good, it was all good.
It is important only that you came.

And it is good to remember that this blood, in another
      body, your body, arrived.
There is dynastic example in a single generation of this
      blood, and the example good,
But, Mother, I can promise you nothing.

This traveling is across the sprung longitudes of the mind
And the blood's latitudes. I have made a sextant of heart
And nailed my bearings to sun, but from the look-out
There is no hailing yet of the hoped-for land.
Only the enormous, wheeling, imperative sea,
And the high example of this earlier coming—

But there will be no Americas discovered by analogy.

ELEGY

My father was born with a spade in his hand and traded it
for a needle's eye to sit his days cross-legged on tables
till he could sit no more, then sold insurance, reading
the ten-cent-a-week lives like logarithms from
the Tables of Metropolitan to their prepaid tombstones.

Years of the little dimes twinkling on kitchen tables
at Mrs. Fauci's at Mrs. Locatelli's at Mrs. Cataldo's
(*Arrividerla, signora. A la settimana prossima. Mi saluta,
la prego, il marito. Ciao, Anna. Bye-bye.*)
—known as a Debit. And with his ten-year button

he opened a long dream like a piggy bank, spilling the
      dimes
like mountain water into the moss of himself, and bought
ten piney lots in Wilmington. Sunday by Sunday
he took the train to his woods and walked under the trees
to leave his print on his own land, a patron of seasons.

I have done nothing as perfect as my father's Sundays
on his useless lots. Gardens he dreamed from briar tangle
and the swampy back slope of his ridge rose over him
more flowering than Brazil. Maples transformed to figs,
and briar to blood-blue grapes in his look around

when he sat on a stone with his wine-jug and cheese beside
      him,
his collar and coat on a branch, his shirt open,
his derby back on his head like a standing turtle. A big
man he was. When he sang *Celeste Aida* the woods
filled as if a breeze were swelling through them.

When he stopped, I thought I could hear the sound still
    moving.
—Well, I have lied. Not so much lied as dreamed it.
I was three when he died. It was someone else—my
    sister—
went with him under the trees. But if it was her
memory then, it became mine so long since

I will owe nothing on it, having dreamed it from all
the nights I was growing, the wet-pants man of the family.
I have done nothing as perfect as I have dreamed him
from old-wives tales and the running of my blood.
God knows what queer long darks I had no eyes for

followed his stairwell weeks to his Sunday breezeways.
But I will swear the world is not well made that rips
such gardens from the week. Or I should have walked
a saint's way to the cross and nail by nail
hymned out my blood to glory, for one good reason.

MY FATHER DIED
IMPERFECT AS A MAN

My father died imperfect as a man.
My mother lied him to perfections. I
knew nothing, and had to guess we all mean
our lives in honor of the most possible lie.

She was no more herself than a gull is
its own idea to make on any air
precisions of itself. What instinct does
for the egg in nature, history did for her.

So Italy's dark duplicating spines
bred her precisely herself, instinctual as
peasantry breeds in any Apennines.
Those centuries repeat; they do not pass.

And everywhere at their end which is always again,
always present, and everywhere the same—
as alike as gulls, as grass, bred on the chain
that breeds its likeness back through any name,

the ritual women sweep their Italies,
move step by step from grave to birth to grave,
scrub clothes and speak to God on the same knees,
and take exactly the shape of how they live.

So history lied my father from his death,
she having no history that would let him be
imperfect and worth keeping vigils with.
She made a saint of him. And she made me

kneel to him every night. When I was bad,
he shadowed me. And always knew my lies.
I was too young to know him, but my bed
lay under him and God, and both their eyes

bored through the dark to damn me as I was,
imperfect as a boy and growing worse.
Somehow I loved her in that haunted house
she made of her own flesh. And so, in course,

forgave myself and learned how to forgive.
Love must intend realities. I can
be anything but saintly and still live
my father's love, imperfect as a man.

ON THE DEATH OF THE POET'S
MOTHER THIRTY-THREE YEARS LATER

John Logan

To Isabella Gardner

The tongue fits to the teeth and the palate by Number,
pouring forth letters and words.   ST. AUGUSTINE

Years ago I came to the conclusion that poetry too is
nothing but an oral outlet.   A. A. BRILL, M.D.

I

My mother died because
I lived or so
I always chose to believe.
At any rate I nursed
At a violent teat with the boys
Of the bronzed picture. In my
Memories of taste I find
Bits of the tart hairs
Of an Irish dog that hangs
Its red arch over me; I'm not
So sure of that beast
That it has stole as much from me
As I shall suck from it.

It had an eye of milky
Glass with a very
Reddened spot that sent
About the eye's globe
And this eye moved
Among the long red hairs
At the skull of the dog as it
Threads or streams of red

Leaped in the childhood grass,
As it springs in the childhood
Trace, as it arched and pulled
And arched and pulled the sheath of its livid
Tongue through the wisps of its breath.

July began with the Fourth
And the moon in a box
Like a flaming house in the grass
At the edge of the fair with the frames
Of the fireworks there, but next
It floats, like a carnival balloon
That drops out weights of men,
And turns the festival tips
Of the sparklers hot: fear
Shot up in a kite when it burned
My throat white—like an eye
My friend once cooked in his head, as he mixed
Carnivals of fluids in a shed.

Yet I was not so scared
Or scarred I could not
Scream and climb to find
My aunt to cry for help
High in the mounts of bleachers:
I saw a face and told it
All my needs, but my hot
Throat beat with fright
As a strange mother bent
From the stands—her flanks were blood
In the moon and festive light
As she heard my plea of hurt and
Saw my burnt neck twitch,

Arched over me a God-like Bitch.

CHINATOWN FAMILY

Lin Yutang

1

Tom lay in bed, his limbs tired and all the muscles of his body sweetly relaxed, ready to fall asleep on this memorable first night after his arrival in America. His mother had just clicked off the switch triumphantly, and the light of the globe hanging over the middle of the bed had gone out, leaving for a second a streak of liver red that danced across his eyes. His toes hurt slightly, pleasantly, a new sensation for Tom. He did not often have new shoes, whether leather or cloth, and his father had bought him that day a new pair that cost three dollars and twenty-five cents and had insisted on his putting them on. The nerves across his arches tingled, and his ankles felt stiff, but from the middle of his heel came a sensation that really hurt.

He was drowsy, as a boy of thirteen can be healthily drowsy after a day of excitement. He wanted to sleep. His sister Eva, one year younger, was lying beside him. As he turned on his mattress and let his fingers fall curled on the edge of the bed, he saw the moon above the jagged, square, unfamiliar roofs of the houses across the avenue. For a time, his bed seemed to rock as if he were still on the ship which had docked that morning. He had not been seasick, as Eva had been, but the swaying motion of his bed continued. The moon seemed to swing in the sky, but when he opened his eyes wide, it stood still over the rooftops. Then he knew he was on land in a strange city in a strange country.

He had eaten too much that day, a Chinese lunch followed by a Chinese dinner, after being starved on the freighter for forty-five days. His mind was dim and a little giddy, and only the recollection remained of the swallowing of mouthfuls of inexhaustible rice, oiled by rich gravy and voluptuous hunks of bean curd fried in fat. The sleepy feeling crept over him, dark, sweet, and tender.

But Eva was awake.

"Are you asleep?" she whispered.

"Yes, I am."

"No, you are not."

Eva moved to rise from the bed. The mattress rolled and rocked again.

"What are you doing?" Tom asked.

He saw Eva's shape tiptoe across the room.

Click, click! Click, click! The light over his head went on and off three times.

"Oh, Eva!"

Giggling and triumphant, Eva jumped into bed again and pulled the sheet over her.

From across the room came the old father's voice. "Children, stop playing with the light. It is electricity!" The Cantonese word, *tin*, had a heavy thumping tone—*"Hai tinnn!"*

It was electricity! Momentous word in Tom's mind, symbolic of all that was new and marvelous in this new world of miracles. The brother and sister had been playing with the switch in the afternoon. Tom had scrutinized the crisscross pattern of the filaments; he had known electric light in Canton and on the ship, but they had not had it at home and the wonder never ceased. He knew he was going to explore that incomprehensible marvel someday; just now he only wanted to understand that nice, neat infallible click. Tom was very impressionable; he liked to puzzle things out for himself, things that didn't puzzle Eva. His father had said, "It is electricity," pronouncing the word with great respect. Electricity was lightning, and he had lightning over his bed. The thought was tremendously exciting.

Out of the silence of the night there had come at regular intervals a mad rushing sound that boomed and rumbled past the bedroom window and rocketed into the dark distance. As the sound approached, the rails wailed like demons in the night, the windowpanes shook, and he saw a succession of bizarre lighted train windows rush by in orderly procession, and then he heard the wheels of the Third Avenue El train screech to a halt at the Eighty-fourth Street station.

A train flying in midair before his window! Tom was fully

awake now. The noise did not surprise him. He had had a few notions about America before he came to this country. America was a country made all of machines, and machines were of course noisy, and, Tom reasoned, America should be noisy and full of that rushing motion, speeding motion, going somwhere—click—stopping—click—progress—click, click! What puzzled him was something else, something that left him no rest. He got up and peered down from the window. It was unbelievable. How could a flying demon with carloads of people be supported on such thin steel pillars? That was the miracle for Tom. A flying train whizzing in mid-air supported on matchsticks. Tom scratched his head. He wanted so much to know.

As he looked up, he saw men and women in their nightclothes, men with bald heads and women with almost bare bosoms, leaning on cushions and pillows out of the windows across the street.

He went back to bed. It was hot, noisy, strange, and all tremendous and wonderful. Eva was asleep already. His head was heavy, and his stomach was full.

The next thing he knew it was already morning.

2

"What do you think of Father?" whispered Eva, at the first movement Tom made in his bed. Tom was still in slumber. She shook him. "What do you think of Father?"

"What?" Tom rubbed his eyes. Without thinking, he knew that something good, something wonderful and exciting had happened to him. Then the realization that he was in the United States of America, in famous, fabulous New York, darted into his consciousness. He jumped up. "I am in New York! I am in New York!" It was like saying he was in Wonderland.

"Do you like Father?" asked Eva again.

"I like him," said Tom. "Isn't it strange to have a father?"

"It is not strange. He is our father," protested Eva.

"But it is strange to have a father.'

"Don't you like the feeling of it?" Eva always greatly respected Tom's opinions.

"Yes, the feeling is nice. It's like having a double roof. You've got a roof already, and you get another roof. It's nice."

"He works so hard for us," said Eva. "We didn't know."

Of the two, Tom was a little whiter and more slender. Eva, though still a child, had a more prominent jaw and cheekbones and a rather flat bony forehead above her little shining eyes. Her simple, direct smile and her queue made her look like a doll.

Tom had not seen his father since infancy, and Eva had not seen him since she was born. The "father" in their minds was a dream, a legend, a reality so remote that it was unreal.

In good years and bad, the father had sent them money. Family legends told that he had come to the United States with the Alaska gold rush. San Francisco was known to all Cantonese back home as Old Gold Mountain, and to the overseas Chinese in America as the Great Port. Their father had sent home what were called "gold dollars." What Cantonese villager on the south coast—in Toishan, Sunwei, Fanyu—had not heard of the gold country? The plain fact was that villagers whose sons were in America received remittances, had savings and could buy farms, and those who did not could not. Some had built "foreign houses" in Canton.

Twice had Tom Fong, Sr., gone home to China, to stay for little more than a year, and then had returned to America to earn more foreign gold.

But ever since the children had known anything, their father had been in New York. The fact that New York was not Old Gold Mountain did not make any difference—across the fabled Pacific, the two points merged in the distance. There were village legends that the Chinese were mobbed, robbed, killed, and many were driven out of the West Coast, and it was a family legend that their father, Tom Fong, Sr., had escaped to the East Coast after some thrilling adventures. But that was long ago; these stories always sounded like pirate tales. The fact remained that Tom Fong, Sr., survived, and that, year after year, he and the other villagers' sons continued to send gold dollars home to support parents, brothers, and wives and to send their nephews to school. It was a story of survival; it was success; it was struggle triumphant.

On and on the villagers' sons came, and the immigration officials were merely obstacles Heaven placed in the path of men determined to achieve success with patience and persistence. The immigration difficulties were nothing to laugh at, but you laugh at them when you have nothing to lose.

Look at Tom's second elder brother, Yiko. He had come as a seaman at the age of sixteen and jumped ship, and now he was Frederick A. T. Fong, Insurance Agent, representative of Cornelius United States Underwriters! The Department of Justice didn't know. Why it should be the business of the Department of Justice, Washington, D.C., to know his whereabouts, Frederick A. T. Fong never quite figured out. Frederick A. T. Fong always added Washington, D.C., when he mentioned the Department of Justice. He was friendly to everybody, and when he met an American, he always said, "I am Frederick A. T. Fong," without waiting to be introduced.

So while Tom and Eva grew up in their village in Sunwei, their eldest brother Daiko and the second brother Yiko were living with their father in New York. The family was neatly divided into two halves, one earning and the other spending. The mother was one roof, a perfect roof, for Tom and his sister, and the father provided the other roof. Now the two halves were united, and the two roofs overlapped.

To the younger children, the father had been a mystical entity. From all the evdences—the family letters that arrived about once in six months, sometimes at longer intervals; the drafts that usually came with them, especially when the New Year was drawing near; and the trips Tom sometimes made to town with his mother when the letters arrived and the amazing fact that the bank gave them real money when presented with that not too elaborate piece of paper—from all these evidences Tom was willing to conclude that the mystical entity existed, as Christians conclude from the rain and snow and birds and flowers that God exists. His father's letters were always brief and not very communicative. It was either times were good or times were bad, and "enclosed you will find a draft for——."

There were other evidences of the existence of the father. In the first place, the mother believed in him. In the second place, her own brother, Tom's Uncle Chan, was in New York, too. Uncle Chan did not live on Olympian heights, hidden in the clouds; he made his presence felt in their home across the seas; his letters were more frequent and more chatty, even loquacious; real things were happening in New York. It was from one of Uncle Chan's letters that the people at home learned of the dramatic marriage of the eldest son Daiko to an Italian girl named Flora. Tom's father had not thought the fact even worth mentioning. In the third place, there was another old man, also by the name of Fong, now over sixty, who had comfortably settled down in their home village after a lifetime in America and who told Tom, the inquisitive child, about things and customs in the United States, on which the old man was the unquestioned authority.

One of the unforgettable stories old Fong told was that in America there are restaurants without waiters where you put a nickel in a slot and, click, a whole chicken, roasted and brown, sprang into view. Nobody of course questioned such an authority. He would be offended if anybody did. He made a tremendous impression on Tom.

"And turkey?"

"Yes, and turkey. A whole big turkey."

Tom's mouth watered.

"You see what you want through a glass and put in the nickel, and out it jumps. Yes, Amelicans are clever. You go to Amelica when you grow up."

Tom, of course, had wanted to come to "Amelica." He wanted very much to. All the ancient stories about the killings and muggings of the railroad men could not scare him. All the tales about the big bugaboo, the Yiminkeok (Immigration Bureau), and its quiet, absurd tactics stimulated the boy's imagination. What was this Yiminkeok but a lot of officials? By the universally accepted dictum in China officials were a pest to the people anyway. They were no different from the Chinese officials he knew. Why should they be? So long as you have a relative in America you don't have to worry. An official may be an official, but a relative is a relative.

Tom Fong, Sr., had wanted his family to come. For ten long years he had been wanting them. But it was not easy. If his family should come across the continent by railroad, the traveling expenses of three people would come close to a thousand dollars. When was he going to earn and save so much money from his laundry? Some years ago, when he thought he had saved enough to send for his family, his bank had failed. Business was bad; fewer people sent their laundry. Those who remained his customers no longer sent their underwear, those who sent shirts seemed to change their shirts once instead of twice a week, and there was much work and little money in sheets. He lowered his prices; he worked long hours (heaven be thanked that there was no law against that!); he stood on his legs and sweated until eleven in the night; and he put all his money in a little cloth parcel inside a steel cabinet locked and hidden in a lower drawer. He had lost faith in all banks. He once prayed for delivery to come from fan-tan and was rewarded with the vision of winning two hundred dollars and then, in the hope of achieving all of his ambition, lost it all again. Thereafter he played moderately, but as a relaxation, not as a means of bringing his family over. But he continued to spend ten dollars systematically every year to take chances on the Irish sweepstakes.

A stroke of good fortune came in the person of his second son, who was beginning to do well as an insurance agent. Generous soul that he was, he handed over one day a check for five hundred dollars, his first savings, and said to his father, "Here, take this and send for Mother and the young children. Tell them Yiko sent the money. I know you want Mother here. It is all in the family."

Something stirred very deep in Tom senior's heart when he heard his son's offer, so deep that it took a long time for his feeling to come to the surface. The armor of patience and strength that he had worn for years had been pierced, and all his muscles relaxed. Slowly a contracted smile found its way to his face, and beads of moisture formed in his eyes. He was so touched that he could not say a word. He merely wiped his eyes. They seemed to say, "I appreciate it, my son. I have wanted very much to have your mother come."

With the money kept severely untouched in the bank, Tom's mother planned to go. For herself, she would rather have remained in China. The arrangement of living as the head of the family back home had been perfect for Mother Fong, and going at her age to America, where the language and customs were so strange, was hardly a pleasant prospect. But she wanted it for Tom and Eva, and there was unanimity of opinion in the family and great excitement among the children. They were not able to go until after the grandmother died. How long this was going to be nobody could tell. Leaving her alone would of course be outrageous, and they were willing to wait. But it could not be very long; Grandmother was in her eighties. Tom secretly wished it would happen soon and then blushed at the thought. But when Tom was thirteen, his grandmother died and was properly buried, and so they came.

No, it was not easy. There were those immigration officials, and there were immigration laws, laws made, it seemed, especially to keep Chinese out of America, or to let in as few as possible. But Chinese are used to officials and know of old that there are ways to get around laws. Yiko's way had been to jump ship. But a mother and her children could not do that. Neither could they be floated ashore in barrels on the California coast or smuggled across the Mexican border. A laundryman certainly could not bring his family into the country legally. But a merchant could if the children were not yet twenty-one years old. And Uncle Chan was a merchant, with a fine busy grocery store in Chinatown. Uncle Chan was glad to help to bring his sister and her children over.

So the legal procedures were taken to make Tom Fong joint owner of the grocery store with Uncle Chan. Thus in the somewhat blinking eye of the law, Tom Fong became a merchant. Both he and Uncle Chan knew that this was a temporary expedient, to satisfy the law. It was irregular. But the thing was done.

IMPRESSIONS OF AN INDIAN CHILDHOOD

Gertrude Bonnin (zitkala-sa)

A wigwam of weather-stained canvas stood at the base of some irregularly ascending hills. A footpath wound its way gently down the sloping land till it reached the broad river bottom; creeping through the long swamp grasses that bent over it on either side, it came out on the edge of the Missouri.

Here, morning, noon, and evening, my mother came to draw water from the muddy stream for our household use. Always, when my mother started for the river, I stopped my play to run along with her. She was only of medium height. Often she was sad and silent, at which times her full arched lips were compressed into hard and bitter lines, and shadows fell under her black eyes. Then I clung to her hand and begged to know what made the tears fall.

"Hush; my little daughter must never talk about my tears"; and smiling through them, she patted my head and said, "Now let me see how fast you can run today." Whereupon I tore away at my highest possible speed, with my long black hair blowing in the breeze.

I was a wild little girl of seven. Loosely clad in a slip of brown buckskin, and lightfooted with a pair of soft moccasins on my feet, I was as free as the wind that blew my hair, and no less spirited than a bounding deer. These were my mother's pride,—my wild freedom and overflowing spirits. She taught me no fear save that of intruding myself upon others.

Having gone many paces ahead I stopped, panting for breath, and laughing with glee as my mother watched my every movement. I was not wholly conscious of myself, but was more keenly alive to the fire within. It was as if I were the activity, and my hands and feet were only experiments for my spirit to work upon.

Returning from the river, I tugged beside my mother, with my hand upon the bucket I believed I was carrying. One time, on such a return, I remember a bit of conversation we had. My grown-up cousin, Warca-Ziwin (Sunflower), who was then seventeen, always went to the river alone for water for her mother. Their wigwam was not far from ours; and I saw her daily going to and from the river. I admired my cousin greatly. So I said: "Mother, when I am tall as my cousin Warca-Ziwin, you shall not have to come for water. I will do it for you."

With a strange tremor in her voice which I could not understand, she answered, "If the paleface does not take away from us the river we drink."

"Mother, who is this bad paleface?" I asked.

"My little daughter, he is a sham,—a sickly sham! The bronzed Dakota is the only real man."

I looked up into my mother's face while she spoke; and seeing her bite her lips, I knew she was unhappy. This aroused revenge in my small soul. Stamping my foot on the earth, I cried aloud, "I hate the paleface that makes my mother cry!"

Setting the pail of water on the ground, my mother stooped, and stretching her left hand out on the level with my eyes, she placed her other arm about me; she pointed to the hill where my uncle and my only sister lay buried.

"There is what the paleface has done! Since then your father too has been buried in a hill nearer the rising sun. We were once very happy. But the paleface has stolen our lands and driven us hither. Having defrauded us of our land, the paleface forced us away.

"Well, it happened on the day we moved camp that your sister and uncle were both very sick. Many others were ailing, but there seemed to be no help. We traveled many days and nights; not in the grand, happy way that we moved camp when I was a little girl, but we were driven, my child, driven like a herd of buffalo. With every step, your sister, who was not as large as you are now, shrieked with the painful jar until she was hoarse with crying. She grew more and more feverish. Her little hands and cheeks were burning hot. Her little lips were parched and dry, but she would not drink the water I gave her. Then I discovered that her throat was swollen and red. My poor child, how I cried with her because the Great Spirit had forgotten us!

"At last, when we reached this western country, on the first weary night your sister died. And soon your uncle died also, leaving a widow and an orphan daughter, your cousin Warca-Ziwin. Both your sister and uncle might have been happy with us today, had it not been for the heartless paleface."

My mother was silent the rest of the way to our wigwam. Though I saw no tears in her eyes, I knew that was because I was with her. She seldom wept before me.

THE CHILDREN
OF IMMIGRANTS

GROWING UP IN AMERICA

*I have a dream that my four little children
will one day live in a nation where they
will not be judged by the color of their
skin but by the content of their character.*

Martin Luther King

Americans have steadily mainifested the belief that their children possess the possibility of illimitable success. American myths inextricably involve the future, and the future is the child: He can rise from "rags to riches," from a ghetto to the Senate, from a log cabin to the White House. Important to all Americans, these myths have had for the the children of immigrants a central meaning. In this new country a child does not bear the burden of the past: He resembles Adam, creating a new world for himself and for the children who will follow him.

Growing up in America may be an onerous task indeed, for it often means—particularly among minority groups—the struggle by children to surpass their parents in education, economic advantages, and social status. At times the parents implant this hunger for success in their children, as Alfred Kazin points out in *A Walker in the City,* and the youngsters become their representatives in

America, those who can speak the language without an accent.

But the children of minority groups meet conflicts far beyond the small circle of the family, particularly when the child encounters the mainstream of American life. One feels this primary problem in the work of black authors like Gwendolyn Brooks, Ernest Gaines, Ralph Ellison, and Richard Wright; it is also central to the writing of ethnic writers as diverse in origin as Orlando Ortiz, Kay Bennett, and William Saroyan. For the child of a minority group, growing up in America often means growing into America: learning how to acculturate oneself into the general pattern of American life—or perhaps how to resist acculturation.

THE CHILDREN OF THE POOR

Gwendolyn Brooks

I:1

People who have no children can be hard:
Attain a mail of ice and insolence:
Need not pause in the fire, and in no sense
Hesitate in the hurricane to guard.
And when wide world is bitten and bewarred
They perish purely, waving their spirits hence
Without a trace of grace or of offense
To laugh or fail, diffident, wonder-starred.
While through a throttling dark we others hear
The little lifting helplessness, the queer
Whimper-whine; whose unridiculous
Lost softness softly makes a trap for us.
And makes a curse. And makes a sugar of
The malocclusions, the inconditions of love.

I:4

First fight. Then fiddle. Ply the slipping string
With feathery sorcery; muzzle the note
With hurting love; the music that they wrote
Bewitch, bewilder. Qualify to sing
Threadwise. Devise no salt, no hempen thing
For the dear instrument to bear. Devote
The bow to silks and honey. Be remote
A while from malice and from murdering.
But first to arms, to armor. Carry hate
In front of you and harmony behind.

Be deaf to music and to beauty blind.
Win war. Rise bloody, maybe not too late
For having first to civilize a space
Wherein to play your violin with grace.

II : —

Life for my child is simple, and is good.
He knows his wish. Yes, but that is not all.
Because I know mine too.
And we both want joy of undeep and unabiding things,
Like kicking over a chair or throwing blocks out of a
    window
Or tipping over an icebox pan
Or snatching down curtains or fingering an electric outlet
Or a journey or a friend or an illegal kiss.
No. There is more to it than that.
It is that he has never been afraid.
Rather, he reaches out and lo the chair falls with a
    beautiful crash,
And the blocks fall, down on the people's heads,
And the water comes slooshing sloppily out across the floor.
And so forth.
Not that success, for him, is sure, infallible.
But never has he been afraid to reach.
His lesions are legion.
But reaching is his rule.

FROM THE SUBWAY
TO THE SYNAGOGUE

Alfred Kazin

Every time I go back to Brownsville it is as if I had never been away. From the moment I step off the train at Rockaway Avenue and smell the leak out of the men's room, then the pickles from the stand just below the subway steps, an instant rage comes over me, mixed with dread and some unexpected tenderness. It is over ten years since I left to live in "the city"— everything just out of Brownsville was always "the city." Actually I did not go very far; it was enough that I could leave Brownsville. Yet as I walk those familiarly choked streets at dusk and see the old women sitting in front of the tenements, past and present become each other's faces; I am back where I began.

It is always the old women in their shapeless flowered housedresses and ritual wigs I see first; they give Brownsville back to me. In their soft dumpy bodies and the unbudging way they occupy the tenement stoops, their hands blankly folded in each other as if they had been sitting on these stoops from the beginning of time, I sense again the old foreboding that all my life would be like this. *Urim Yidn. Alfred, what do you want of us poor Jews?*

The early hopelessness burns at my face like fog the minute I get off the subway. I can smell it in the air as soon as I walk down Rockaway Avenue. It hangs over the Negro tenements in the shadows of the El-darkened street, the torn and flapping canvas sign still listing the boys who went to war, the stagnant wells of candy stores and pool parlors, the torches flaring at dusk over the vegetable stands and pushcarts, the neon-blazing fronts of liquor stores, the piles of *Halvah* and

chocolate kisses in the windows of the candy store next to the
News and *Mirror,* the dusty old drugstores where urns of rose
and pink and blue colored water still swing from chains, and
where next door Mr. A.'s sign still tells anyone walking down
Rockaway Avenue that he has pants to fit any color suit. It is
in the faces of the kids, who before they are ten have learned
that Brownsville is a nursery of tough guys and walk with
a springy caution, like boxers approaching the center of the
ring. Even the Negroes who have moved into the earliest slums
deserted by the Jews along Rockaway Avenue have been infected with the damp sadness of the place, and slouch along
the railings of their wormy wooden houses like animals in a
cage. The Jewish district drains out here, but eddies back again
on the next street; *they* have no connection with it. A Gypsy
who lives in one of the empty stores is being reproached by a
tipsy Negro in a sweater and new pearl-gray fedora who has
paid her to tell his fortune. *You promis' me, didnja? Didnja
promis', you lousy f . . . ?* His voice fills the street with the
empty rattle of a wooden wheel turning over and over.

The smell of damp out of the rotten hallways accompanies me all the way to Blake Avenue. Everything seems so
small here now, old, mashed-in, more rundown even than I
remember it, but with a heartbreaking familiarity at each door
that makes me wonder if I can take in anything new, so
strongly do I feel in Brownsville that I am walking in my
sleep. I keep bumping awake at harsh intervals, then fall back
into my trance again. In the last crazy afternoon light the
neons over the delicatessens bathe all their wares in a cosmetic
smile, but strip the street of every personal shadow and con-
cealment. The torches over the pushcarts hold in a single breath
of yellow flame the acid smell of half-sour pickles and herrings
floating in their briny barrels. There is a dry rattle of loose
newspaper sheets around the cracked stretched skins of the
"chiney" oranges. Through the kitchen windows along every
ground floor I can already see the containers of milk, the fresh
round poppy-seed evening rolls. Time for supper, time to go
home. The sudden uprooting I always feel at dusk cries out
in a crash of heavy wooden boxes; a dozen crates of old seltzer
bottles come rattling up from the cellar on an iron roller. Seltzer
is still the poor Jew's dinner wine, a mild luxury infinitely
prized above the water out of the faucets; there can be few
families in Brownsville that still do not take a case of it every

week. It sparkles, it can be mixed with sweet jellies and syrups; besides, the water in Europe was often unclean.

In a laundry window off Dumont Avenue a printed poster with a Star of David at the head proclaims solidarity with *"our magnificent brothers in Palestine."* A fiery breath of victory has come to Brownsville at last! Another poster calls for a demonstration against evictions. It is signed by one of those many subsidiaries of the Communist Party that I could detect if it were wrapped in twenty layers of disguise. "WORKERS AND PEOPLE OF BROWNSVILLE . . . !" Looking at that long-endured word *Landlord,* I feel myself quickening to the old battle cries.

And now I go over the whole route. Brownsville is that road which every other road in my life has had to cross.

When I was a child I thought we lived at the end of the world. It was the eternity of the subway ride into the city that first gave me this idea. It took a long time getting to "New York"; it seemed longer getting back. Even the I.R.T. got tired by the time it came to us, and ran up into the open for a breath of air before it got locked into its terminus at New Lots. As the train left the tunnel to rattle along the elevated tracks, I felt I was being jostled on a camel past the last way stations in the desert. Oh that ride from New York! Light came only at Sutter Avenue. First across the many stations of the Gentiles to the East River. Then clear across Brooklyn, almost to the brink of the ocean all our fathers crossed. All those first stations in Brooklyn—Clark, Borough Hall, Hoyt, Nevins, the junction of the East and West Side express lines—told me only that I was on the last leg home, though there was always a stirring of my heart at Hoyt, where the grimy subway platform was suddenly enlivened by Abraham and Straus's windows of ladies' wear. Atlantic Avenue was vaguely exciting, a crossroads, the Long Island railroad; I never saw a soul get in or out at Bergen Street; the Grand Army Plaza, with its great empty caverns smoky with dust and chewing-gum wrappers, meant Prospect Park and that stone path beside a meadow where as a child I ran off from my father one summer twilight just in time to see the lamplighter go up the path lighting from the end of his pole each gas mantle suddenly flaring within its corolla of pleated paper—then, that summer I first strayed off the block for myself, the steps leading up from the boathouse, the long stalks of grass wound between the steps thick with the dust and smell of summer—then, that great summer at sixteen, my discovery in the Brooklyn Museum of Albert Pinkham Ryder's cracked oily fishing boats drifting under the moon. Franklin Avenue was where the Jews began—but all middle-class Jews, *alrightniks,* making out "all right" in the New World, they were still Gentiles to me as they went out into the wide and tree-lined Eastern Parkway. For us the journey went on and on—past Nostrand, past Kingston, past Utica, and only then out into the open at Sutter, overlooking Lincoln Terrace Park, "Tickle-Her" Park, the zoo of our adolescence, through which no girl could pass on a summer evening without its being understood forever after that she was "in"; past the rickety "two-family" private houses built in the fever of Brownsville's last real-estate boom; and then into Brownsville itself—Saratoga, Rockaway, and home. For those who lived still beyond, in East New York, there was Junius, there was Pennsylvania, there was Van Siclen, and so at last into New Lots, where the city goes back to the marsh, and even the subway ends.

Yet it was not just the long pent-up subway ride that led me to think of Brownsville as the margin of the city, the last place, the car barns where they locked up the subway and the trolley cars at night. There were always raw patches of unused city land all around us filled with "monument works" where they cut and stored tombstones, as there were still on our street farmhouses and the remains of old cobbled driveways down which chickens came squealing into our punchball games— but most of it dead land, neither country nor city, with that look of prairie waste I have so often seen on my walks along the fringes of American cities near the freight yards. We were nearer the ocean than the city, but our front on the ocean was Canarsie—in those days the great refuse dump through which I made my first and grimmest walks into the city—a place so celebrated in New York vaudeville houses for its squalor that the very sound of the word was always good for a laugh. CAN-NARR-SIE! They fell into the aisles. But that was the way to the ocean we always took summer evenings— through silent streets of old broken houses whose smoky red Victorian fronts looked as if the paint had clotted like blood and had then been mixed with soot—past infinite weedy lots, the smell of freshly cut boards in the lumber yards, the junk yards, the marshland eating the pavement, the truck farms, the bungalows that had lost a window or a door as they tottered on their poles against the damp and the ocean winds. The place as I have it in my mind still reeks of the fires burning in the refuse dumps. Farms that had once been the outposts of settlers in Revolutionary days had crumbled and sunk like wet sand. Canarsie was where they opened the sluice gates to let the city's muck out into the ocean. But at the end was the roar of the Atlantic and the summer house where we stood outside watching through lattices the sports being served with great pitchers of beer foaming onto the red-checked tablecloths. Summer, my summer! Summer!

We were of the city, but somehow not in it. Whenever I went off on my favorite walk to Highland Park in the "American" district to the north, on the border of Queens, and climbed the hill to the old reservoir from which I could look straight across to the skyscrapers of Manhattan, I saw New York as a foreign city. There, brilliant and unreal, the city had its life, as Brownsville was ours. That the two were joined in me I never knew then—not even on those glorious summer nights of my last weeks in high school when, with what an ache, I would come back into Brownsville along Liberty Avenue, and, as soon as I could see blocks ahead of me the Labor Lyceum, the malted milk and Fatima signs over the candy stores, the old women in their housedresses sitting in front of the tenements like priestesses of an ancient cult, knew I was home.

We were the end of the line. We were the children of the immigrants who had camped at the city's back door in New York's rawest, remotest, cheapest ghetto, enclosed on one side by the Carnasie flats and on the other by the hallowed middle-class districts that showed the way to New York. "New York" was what we put last on our address, but first in thinking of the others around us. *They* were New York, the Gentiles, America; we were Brownsville—*Brunzvil,* as the old folks said —the dust of the earth to all Jews with money, and notoriously a place that measured all success by our skill in getting away from it. So that when poor Jews left, *even* Negroes, as we said found it easy to settle on the margins of Brownsville, and with the coming of spring, bands of Gypsies, who would rent empty stores, hang their rugs around them like a desert tent, and bring a dusty and faintly sinister air of carnival into our neighborhood.

They have built a housing project deep down the center of Brownsville, from Rockaway to Stone, cutting clean diagonal forms within the onlooking streets, and leaving at one end only the public school I attended as a boy. As I walked past those indistinguishable red prisms of city houses, I kept remembering what they had pulled down to make this *project*—and despite my pleasure in all the space and light in Brownsville, despite even my envious wonder what our own life would have been if *we* had lived, as soon all of New York's masses will live, just like everybody else, still, I could not quite believe that what I saw before me was real. Brownsville in that model quarter looks like an old crone who has had a plastic operation, and to my amazement I miss her old, sly, and withered face. I miss all those ratty little wooden tenements, born with the smell of damp in them, in which there grew up how many schoolteachers, city accountants, rabbis, cancer specialists, functionaries of the revolution, and strongarm men for Murder, Inc.; I miss that affected squirt who always wore a paste diamond on his left pinky and one unforgotten day, taught me to say *children* for *kids;* I miss the sinister "Coney Island" dives where before, during, and after the school day we all anxiously gobbled down hot dogs soggy in sauerkraut and mustard, and I slid along the sawdust floor fighting to get back the violin the tough guys always stole from my locker for a joke; I miss the poisonous sweetness I used to breathe in from the caramels melting inside the paper cartons every time I passed the candy wholesaler's on my way back from school; I miss the liturgical refrain *Kosher-Bosher* lettered on the windows of the butcher shops; the ducks at Thanksgiving hanging down the doorways of the chicken store; the clouds of white dust that rose up behind the windows of the mattress factory. Above all I miss the fence to the junk yard where I would wait with my store of little red volumes, THE WORLD'S GREATEST SELECTED SHORT STORIES, given us gratis by the *Literary Digest,* hoping for a glimpse of a girl named Deborah. At eleven or twelve I was so agonizedly in love with her, not least because she had been named after a prophetess in Israel, that I would stand at the fence for hours, even creep through the junk yard to be near her windows, with those little red books always in my hand. At home I would recite to myself in triumph the great lines from Judges: *Desolate were the open towns in Israel, they were desolate, until that I arose, Deborah. . . .* But near her I was afraid, and always took along volumes of THE WORLD'S GREATEST SELECTED SHORT STORIES as a gift, to ease my way into her house. She had five sisters, and every one of them always seemed to be home whenever I called. They would look up at me standing in their kitchen with the books in my hand, and laugh. "Look, boychik," the eldest once said to me in a kindly way, "you don't have to *buy* your way in here every time with those damned books just to see Deborah! Come on your own!"

There is something uncanny now about seeing the old vistas rear up at each end of that housing project. Despite those fresh diagonal walks, with their trees and children's sandboxes and Negro faces calmly at home with the white, so many of the old tenements have been left undisturbed on every side of the project, the streets beyond are so obviously just as they were when I grew up in them, that it is as if they had been ripped out of their original pattern and then pasted back again behind the unbelievable miniatures of the future.

To make that housing project they have torn away the lumber yard; the wholesale drygoods store where my dressmaker mother bought the first shirts I ever wore that she did not make herself; how many poolrooms; and that to me sinister shed that was so long a garage, but before that, in the days of the silents, a movie house where every week, while peddlers went up and down the aisles hawking ice-cream bricks and orange squeeze, I feasted in my terror and joy on the "episodes." It was there one afternoon, between the damp coldness in the movie house and the covetous cries of the peddlers, that I was first seized by that bitter guilt I always felt in the movies whenever there was still daylight outside. As I saw Monte Blue being locked into an Iron Maiden, it suddenly came on me that the penalty for my delicious reveries might be just such a death —a death as lonely, as sickeningly remote from all human aid, as the one I saw my hero calmly prepare to face against the yellow shadows of deepest Asia. Though that long-forgotten movie house now comes back on me as a primitive, folksy place —every time the main door was opened to let in peddlers with fresh goods, a hostile mocking wave of daylight fell against the screen, and in the lip-reading silence of the movies I could hear the steady whir and clacking of the machine and the screech of the trolley cars on Rockaway Avenue—I instantly saw in that ominous patch of light the torture box of life-in-death, some reproach calling out the punishment for my sin.

A sin, perhaps, only of my own devising; the sin I recorded against all idle enjoyment, looking on for its own sake alone; but a sin. The daylight was for grimness and labor.

I see that they have also torn out that little clapboard Protestant church that stood so long near the corner of Blake Avenue. It was the only church I ever saw in our neighborhood —the others were the Russian Orthodox meeting-house in East New York, and the Catholic church on East New York Avenue that marked the boundary, as I used to think of it, between us and the Italians stretching down Rockaway and Saratoga to Fulton. That little clapboard church must have been the last of its kind surviving from the days when all that land was owned by Scottish farmers. I remember the hymns that rolled out of the church on Sunday mornings, and how we sniffed as we went by. All those earnest, faded-looking people in their carefully brushed and strangely old-fashioned clothes must have come down there from a long way off. I never saw any of them except on Sunday mornings—the women often surprisingly quite fat, if not so fat as ours, and looking rather timid in their severe dresses and great straw hats with clusters of artificial flowers and wax berries along the brim as they waited for each other on the steps after the service; the men very stiff in their long four-buttoned jackets. They did not belong with us at all; I could never entirely believe that they were really there. One afternoon on my way back from school my curiosity got the better of me despite all my fear of Gentiles, and I stealthily crept in, never having entered a church in my life before, to examine what I was sure would be an exotic and idolatrous horror. It was the plainest thing I had ever seen— not, of course, homey, lived-in, and smelling of sour wine, snuff and old prayer books, like our little wooden synagogue on Chester Street, but so varnished-clean and empty and austere, like our school auditorium, and so severely reserved above the altar and in the set rows of wooden pews to the service of an enigmatic cult, that the chief impression it made on me, who expected all Christians to be as fantastic as albinos, was that these people were not, apparently, so completely different from us as I had imagined. I was bewildered. What really held me there was the number of things written in English. I had associated God only with a foreign language. Suspended from the ceiling over the altar was a great gold-wood sign on which the black Gothic letters read: I AM THE

RESURRECTION AND THE LIFE. I remember standing in the doorway, longing to go all the way up the aisle, then suddenly running away. The distance from that doorway to the altar was the longest gap in space I had ever seen.

All my early life lies open to my eye within five city blocks. When I passed the school, I went sick with all my old fear of it. With its standard New York public-school brown brick courtyard shut in on three sides of the square and the pretentious battlements overlooking that cockpit in which I can still smell the fiery sheen of the rubber ball, it looks like a factory over which has been imposed the façade of a castle. It gave me the shivers to stand up in that courtyard again; I felt as if I had been mustered back into the service of those Friday morning "tests" that were the terror of my childhood.

It was never learning I associated with that school: only the necessity to succeed, to get ahead of the others in the daily struggle to "make a good impression" on our teachers, who grimly, wearily, and often with ill-concealed distaste watched against our relapsing into the natural savagery they expected of Brownsville boys. The white, cool, thinly ruled record book sat over us from their desks all day long, and had remorselessly entered into it each day—in blue ink if we had passed, in red ink if we had not—our attendance, our conduct, our "effort," our merits and demerits; and to the last possible decimal point in calculation, our standing in an unending series of "tests"—surprise tests, daily tests, weekly tests, formal mid-term tests, final tests. They never stopped trying to dig out of us whatever small morsel of fact we had managed to get down the night before. We had to prove that we were really alert, ready for anything, always in the race. That white thinly ruled record book figured in my mind as the judgment seat; the very thinness and remote blue lightness of its lines instantly showed its cold authority over me; so much space had been left on each page, columns and columns in which to note down everything about us, implacably and forever. As it lay there on a teacher's desk, I stared at it all day long with such fear and anxious propriety that I had no trouble believing that God, too, did nothing but keep such record books, and that on the final day He would face me with an account in Hebrew letters whose phonetic dots and dashes looked strangely like decimal points counting up my every sinful thought on earth.

All teachers were to be respected like gods, and God Himself was the greatest of all school superintendents. Long after I had ceased to believe that our teachers could see with the back of their heads, it was still understood, by me, that they knew everything. They were the delegates of all visible and invisible power on earth—of the mothers who waited on the stoops every day after three for us to bring home tales of our daily triumphs; of the glacially remote Anglo-Saxon principal, whose very name was King; of the incalculably important Superintendent of Schools who would someday rubberstamp his name to the bottom of our diplomas in grim acknowledgment that we had, at last, given satisfaction to him, to the Board of Superintendents, and to our benefactor the City of New York—and so up and up, to the government of the United States and to the great Lord Jehovah Himself. My belief in teachers' unlimited wisdom and power rested not so much on what I saw in them—how impatient most of them looked, how wary—but on our abysmal humility, at least in those of us who were "good" boys, who proved by our ready compliance and "manners" that we wanted to get on. The road to a professional future would be shown us only as we pleased *them. Make a good impression the first day of the term, and they'll help you out. Make a bad impression, and you might as well cut your throat.* This was the first article of school folklore, whispered around the classroom the opening day of each term. You made the "good impression" by sitting firmly at your wooden desk, hands clasped; by silence for the greatest part of the live-long day; by sitting down noiselessly when you had answered a question; by "speaking nicely," which meant reproducing their painfully exact enunciation; by "showing manners," or an ecstatic submissiveness in all things; by outrageous flattery; by bringing little gifts at Christmas, on their birthdays, and at the end of the term—the well-known significance of these gifts being that they came not from us, but from our parents, whose eagerness in this matter showed a high level of social consideration, and thus raised our standing in turn.

It was not just our quickness and memory that were always being tested. Above all, in that word I could never hear without automatically seeing it raised before me in gold-plated letters, it was our *character*. I always felt anxious when I heard the word pronounced. Satisfactory as my "character" was, on the whole, except when I stayed too long in the playground reading; outrageously satisfactory, as I can see now, the very sound of the word as our teachers coldly gave it out from the end of their teeth, with a solemn weight on each dark syllable, immediately struck my heart cold with fear—they could not believe I really had it. Character was never something you had; it had to be trained in you, like a technique. I was never very clear about it. On our side *character* meant demonstrative obedience; but teachers already had it—how else could they have become teachers? They had it; the aloof Anglo-Saxon principal whom we remotely saw only on ceremonial occasions in the assembly was positively encased in it; it glittered off his bald head in spokes of triumphant light; the President of the United States had the greatest conceivable amount of it. Character belonged to great adults. Yet we were constantly being driven onto it; it was the great threshold we had to cross. *Alfred Kazin, having shown proficiency in his course of studies and having displayed satisfactory marks of character* . . . Thus someday the hallowed diploma, passport to my further advancement in high school. But there—I could already feel it in my bones—they would put me through even more doubting tests of character; and after that, if I should be good enough and bright enough, there would be still more. *Character* was a bitter thing, racked with my endless striving to please. The school—from every last stone in the courtyard to the battlements frowning down at me from the walls—was only the stage for a trial. I felt that the very atmosphere of learning that surrounded us was fake—that every lesson, every book, every approving smile was only a pretext for the constant probing and watching of me, that there was not a secret in me that would not be decimally measured into that white record book. All week long I lived for the blessed sound of the dismissal gong at three o'clock on Friday afternoon.

I was awed by this system, I believed in it, I respected its force. The alternative was "going bad." The school was notoriously the toughest in our tough neighborhood, and the dangers of "going bad" were constantly impressed upon me at home and in school in dark whispers of the "reform school" and in examples of boys who had been picked up for petty thievery, rape, or flinging a heavy inkwell straight into a teacher's face. Behind any failure in school yawned the great abyss of a criminal career. Every refractory attitude doomed you with the sound "Sing Sing." Anything less than absolute perfection in school always suggested to my mind that I might fall out of the daily race, be kept back in the working class forever, or—dared I think of it?—fall into the criminal class itself.

I worked on a hairline between triumph and catastrophe. Why the odds should always have felt so narrow I understood only when I realized how little my parents thought of their own lives. It was not for myself alone that I was expected to shine, but for them—to redeem the constant anxiety of their existence. I was the first American child, their offering to the strange new God; I was to be the monument of their liberation from the shame of being—what they were. And that there was shame in this was a fact that everyone seemed to believe as a matter of course. It was in the gleeful discounting of themselves—what do we know?—with which our parents greeted every fresh victory in our savage competition for "high averages," for prizes, for a few condescending words of official praise from the principal at assembly. It was in the sickening invocation of "Americanism"—the word itself accusing us of everything we apparently were not. Our families and teachers seemed tacitly agreed that we were somehow to be a little ashamed of what we were. Yet it was always hard to say why this should be so. It was certainly not—in Brownsville!—because we were Jews, or simply because we spoke another language at home, or were absent on our holy days. It was rather that a "refined," "correct," "nice" English was required of us at school that we did not naturally speak, and that our teachers could never be quite sure we would keep. This English was peculiarly the ladder of advancement. Every future young lawyer was known by it. Even the Communists and Socialists on Pitkin Avenue spoke it. It was bright and clean and polished. We were expected to show it off like a new pair of shoes. When the teacher sharply called a question out, then your name, you were expected to leap up, face the class, and eject those new words fluently off the tongue.

There was my secret ordeal: I could never say anything except in the most roundabout way; I was a stammerer. Although I knew all those new words from my private reading —I read walking in the street, to and from the Children's Library on Stone Avenue; on the fire escape and the roof; at every meal when they would let me; read even when I dressed in the morning, propping my book up against the drawers of the bureau as I pulled on my long black stockings—I could never seem to get the easiest words out with the right dispatch, and would often miserably signal from my desk that I did not know the answer rather than get up to stumble and fall and crash on every word. If, angry at always being put down as lazy or stupid, I did get up to speak, the black wooden floor would roll away under my feet, the teacher would frown at me in amazement, and in unbearable loneliness I would hear behind me the groans and laughter: *tuh-tuh-tuh-tuh.*

The word was my agony. The word that for others was so effortless and so neutral, so unburdened, so simple, so exact, I had first to meditate in advance, to see if I could make it, like a plumber fitting together odd lengths and shapes of pipe. I was always preparing words I could speak, storing them away, choosing between them. And often, when the word did come from my mouth in its great and terrible birth, quailing and bleeding as if forced through a thornbush, I would not be able to look the others in the face, and would walk out in the silence, the infinitely echoing silence behind my back, to say it all cleanly back to myself as I walked in the streets. Only when I was alone in the open air, pacing the roof with pebbles in my mouth, as I had read Demosthenes had done to cure himself of stammering; or in the street, where all words seemed to flow from the length of my stride and the color of the houses as I remembered the perfect tranquillity of a phrase in Beethoven's *Romance in F* I could sing back to myself as I walked—only then was it possible for me to speak without the infinite premeditations and strangled silences. I toiled through whenever I got up at school to respond with the expected, the exact answer.

It troubled me that I could speak in the fullness of my own voice only when I was alone on the streets, walking about. There was something unnatural about it; unbearably isolated. I was not like the others! I was not like the others! At midday, every freshly shocking Monday noon, they sent me away to a speech clinic in a school in East New York, where I sat in a circle of lispers and cleft palates and foreign accents holding a mirror before my lips and rolling difficult sounds over and over. To be sent there in the full light of the opening week, when everyone else was at school or going about his business, made me feel as if I had been expelled from the great normal body of humanity. I would gobble down my lunch on my way to the speech clinic and rush back to the school in

time to make up for the classes I had lost. One day, one unforgettable dread day, I stopped to catch my breath on a corner
of Sutter Avenue, near the wholesale fruit markets, where an
old drugstore rose up over a great flight of steps. In the window
were dusty urns of colored water floating off iron chains; card-
board placards advertising hairnets, Ex-Lax; a great illustrated
medical chart headed THE HUMAN FACTORY, which showed
the exact course a mouthful of food follows as it falls from
chamber to chamber of the body. I hadn't meant to stop there
at all, only to catch my breath; but I so hated the speech clinic
that I thought I would delay my arrival for a few minutes by
eating my lunch on the steps. When I took the sandwich out
of my bag, two bitterly hard pieces of hard salami slipped out
of my hand and fell through a grate onto a hill of dust below
the steps. I remember how sickeningly vivid an odd thread of
hair looked on the salami, as if my lunch were turning stiff
with death. The factory whistles called their short, sharp blasts
stark through the middle of noon, beating at me where I sat
outside the city's magnetic circle. I had never known, I knew
instantly I would never in my heart again submit to, such wild
passive despair as I felt at that moment, sitting on the steps
before THE HUMAN FACTORY, where little robots gathered and
shoveled the food from chamber to chamber of the body. They
had put me out into the streets, I thought to myself; with
their mirrors and their everlasting pulling at me to imitate
their effortless bright speech and their stupefaction that a boy
could stammer and stumble on every other English word he
carried in his head, they had put me out into the streets, had
left me high and dry on the steps of that drugstore staring at
the remains of my lunch turning black and grimy in the dust.

THE FRACTIONAL MAN

Vance Bourjaily

Now I must invent a scene, and knowing that you already know quite a lot. You know that mine was not the kind of family which preserved as anecdote or legend such a matter as how it got named.

I must invent my grandmother, too—invent her as a young woman, that is, for as I knew her she was always old, big and square as a monument, with a strong, swarthy face and a brooding, noncommittal forehead; the pain she knew showed only in her eyes.

I will remove the pain, for the purpose of my scene, and make her pretty. There is evidence for the prettiness in a photograph I saw once, but do not have.

She is twenty, the year is 1901, and the child whose hand she holds is my father, at five, for she married at fourteen a man whom she has left behind in Lebanon. She walked barefoot across mountains holding this child by the hand, worked in Beirut to save passage money, and now she is on the famous island, almost in New York, so that what she knew of girl's pain, in the bad marriage arranged by her parents and in the hard work it took to get here, is canceled now in the near realization of the immigrant's dream . . . opportunity, plenty, gold, all those words.

And liberty, for the land she has left is a province of the Turks.

I think I will put a heavy suitcase in my grandmother's other hand, as she stands with her child by the desk of some official. The suitcase is foreshadowing. She will spend many years carrying just such a dull, heavy, flat-sided bag from door to door in these United States, selling in broken English to the housewives of Lawrence, Massachusetts, and Syracuse, New York, the linens and laces which Syrian and Lebanese merchants, relatives, have consigned to her; she will be putting her child through private school. But she doesn't know about that other suitcase now, of course; she wants to get by the official and on to the opportunity, the plenty, and the gold.

The official asks her name. She is pretty and he is roguish. I rather hate him because he takes advantage, in my scene, of the fact that her hands are so completely engaged, beckoning her around to the side of the desk where he can pat her hip as he talks to her. She knows no English at all yet, and of course he knows no Arabic, this immigration official; he knows that her eyes are brown and her cheeks red. He has a mustache and sideburns since the year is 1901.

"Name? Name? What is your name?" He shows her a place on the form, and she says a word which is not intelligible to him. It is barely intelligible even to me, though it is our name in Arabic.

The official does not understand; when she writes it for him, in Arabic characters, putting down the suitcase (the child's hand can never be released), it makes him laugh. He pats her hip again.

Now a comic character enters the scene. He steps up to the desk, a fellow immigrant who has learned some English; he is a small man, with a small, funny hat on, and he means to be helpful. He repeats the unintelligible name.

"What?" says the official.

"Means quince," says the comic character. "Like fruit. Quince."

"Quince? Quincy." The official guesses, and laughs again. He is not a bad fellow, in spite of my dislike for the liberties he has taken with my grandmother's hip, and it is his job, in this good-natured era to get immigrants in, not keep them out. "Quincy." He writes it down, smiling.

Twenty-one years later I was born, and named, and it is time to explain the initials now—U. S. D. The first two are *Ulysses Snow,* my mother's father, a farmer whose people arrived in Ohio from New England; then *Davids,* Welsh, her mother's maiden name and coming from a wave of immigration not so much earlier than that which brought my father and my grandmother.

Ulysses Snow Davids Quincy—the fractions of my heritage

are in it: a quarter of what is more or less colonial American, of which my mother tried to teach me to be proud. A quarter Welsh, of which no one ever said anything much. Half Lebanese, the largest fraction, pretty well concealed by my unintending godfather, the sideburned Ellis Island man.

I was brought up not so much to conceal as to ignore that fraction; it was not particularly a secret, rather something which my father dismissed. He was busy being an American, a successful one which I guess means a good one, or used to. He spoke Arabic with his mother only when they quarreled; for normal conversation he wanted her to speak English, and he sent her to night school in her late forties, where she was supposed to learn to read and write it.

I remember her bringing her reader to me, when I was ten or twelve, for help with the one-syllable words: *cat, can, John can see the cat. . . .*

It wasn't until eight years afterwards that I could imagine what it cost her in pride, coming to a child for help, what profundity of dislocation it indicated. When a limb is dislocated it is painful; when a life is dislocated it produces the look I have described in my grandmother's eyes.

I myself was twenty, just the age at which she'd left it, when I finally found myself in Lebanon, at my grandmother's starting point, and once, just before the Corps left Syria, I tried going home, if that word can be used, to the mountain town that she grew up in, my father's birthplace. But I did not make this visit during the first three months in Baalbek; by the time I made it, I had been to El Tahog, Egypt, taken the driver-mechanic's course in Palestine, and was back in Baalbek once again.

It did not occur to me until much later—just now, even, as I write of it—that in going to my father's birthplace, I solved the riddle of my grandmother's eyes; always self-concerned, youth asks the idiot question, "What about me? What about me?"

I deserved no particular answer to that and I got none, except perhaps the negative answer that the fractions of my heritage were merely that, fractions, adding up to no Englishman, Welshman or Arab, so that for me, as for many, there is no heritage. Each of us is a fresh, a slightly different combination, with only his shaving mirror to tell him with what face he looks back at the face of the earth.

As a child I didn't care much; my interest as I went through school was precisely academic. In Geography the Lebanese were grouped with Syrians. In History the modern Syrians were not to be confused with Assyrians, who were ancient. In Arithmetic the Phoenicians had had something to do with numbers. I noted with interest Solomon's preference for Lebanese cedars, Zenobia made a noble footnote, but we seemed to be on the wrong sides in the Crusades, if we were on any side at all—mostly we were a supine little prize on the invasion route. My identification with such bits was extremely remote.

REFLECTIONS OF AN INARTICULATE CHILDHOOD

Orlando Ortiz

I

the caves were lit
by faces drawn
in a hazy pose
of urined dreams,
through the summer air
my drumbeat rang
like carousels of sound,
i heard and danced
a savage dance
knife-gleams at my feet,
you saw me run
over naked glass
eyes biting in the sun
a wolf-child speed
of rocks and bricks
as windows shattered gleaming sticks
gaping mouths exploding water,
gushed my skin, aware almost
of what it felt.
i bathed the flesh
of my animal self
alive to the instinct
of closing death,
white in law
and in fact
the old woman who bore me
came to terms

and a kind of peace.
but i ran to touch and seek
what must be there

II

ebon skin woman
she rattled the eyes
on loose summer days
when children clank
with shoes of tin
and sweepers push
against the noonday tar.
whoring games of youthful play
were sweated august days,
the first surprising touch
and mystery thereof grew
moistened by her warmth
and swelling visions
on summer beds,
played flaming walls
of rounded flesh
across the bricklike
prison of your mind,
you felt the need
to taste her flesh
and swim your head afire
across her chest
and pause reflect
upon the rising bone
and curve of shoulder warmth,
to reach her nervous thighs
engulfed in vaginal smiles
knowing her blackness
and your fantasy,
bitch of sensua
mother of our passion
distant crystal memory

III

curious how skies
infect the mind,
a faulted pearl

dogs your footsteps
the mind's eye
perceiving the closeness
despairs of hearing a song,
fairy castles
in the soot
gingerbread baking
on the tar
curious how the
phantom child
weaves his tale
among the young,
curious too
the broken kite
ripped by the wind
useless on a rainswept roof

IV

snowflake afternoon,
crystal winds sharp
upon my face,
pastoral silence
of abandoned streets,
my boots intrude
I crush the virgin white
unconscious of an art.
lifeless cat upon a snowbank
stiffened fur soon to disappear,
wino huddled in a doorway
a feeble gesture,
impassively I stride
self importance
written on my tracks

OUT OF THE MOUTH OF BABES

Arturo Giovanitti

Milady was sitting at the table under the pink wax-light, alone
in the resplendent hall.

I looked in from the street and knew not what resplended the
most, whether the young, blue-clad sweetness of milady
or the chaste sheen of the tablecloth, or the luster of the
candelabra, the silver, the gold, the crystal, or, mayhap,
the lucid head of the severe and solemn waiter.

But I knew that the waiter was there because of milady and
not milady because of the waiter, as some may think.

Milady was there only because of the little, fragile, shivering
bitch she held in her arms, and the little bitch had her
little paws on the white tablecloth while milady fed to her,
delicately and amorously, the soul and the brain of the
waiter diluted with a little spoon of gold in a creamy fluid,
in a noble silver bowl.

Alone milady sat in the great hall under the pink wax-light
as I watched her through the frost-embroidered window,
and methought she was Hebe ministering the nectar to
the last god.

Outside, the great black carriage awaited under the nimble-
limbed portico of alabaster, and the little newsboy who
stood by me devoured with his eyes, perhaps the uncarnal
beauty of milady, perhaps the heavenly gruel of the
shivering bitch.

I looked at him and deeply I looked into his ravenous eyes, and
then I asked: "Of what are you thinking, my little friend?"

Said he: "I have sold six papers in four hours and the papers
are now wet and old, for they age and die in few hours,
the papers."

Said he: "My mother is dead, my father is in jail, my sister
is in the saloon and I have sold only six papers in four
hours."

Said he again: "I wish I was that dog."

Again I looked at him, and his eyes were full of tears, the
child tears that only the women understand, the young
tears that make men smile.

And I said: "Yea, boy, for if you were that dog you would
be sure to eat and to be petted to-night.

"And also, if you can kiss no more your mother, at least you
could lap the hand of your mistress, for she is very dear
and very sweet. Is it not so?"

He raised his eyes to me, his big blue eyes, his placid eyes full
of tears and he glared at me and answered through his
clenched teeth:

"No, damn you, no, I would tear her nose off."

And he darted away in the raging blizzard.

But I saw the sun, the sun, the great sun, the luminous warm
sun, right in the front of him.

DANNY O'NEILL WAS HERE

James T. Farrell

Standing at the parlor window, Danny looked out at Washington Park, bare under the heavy autumn sky. He had never imagined he would do this again. But here he was, and there was the park. Below him was South Parkway, and on the opposite side of the street the tennis courts, and the shrubbery without leaves, and the park, bleak and grassless, and in the distance the lagoon and a fragment of the boathouse.

The apartment was near Fifty-seventh Street. Years ago, they had lived a block away. At 5816½ he had so often stood by the parlor window; brooding and lacking in confidence, staring out at the park. He had seen it in all seasons, when it was green and when it was bare as it was now. There was the park now. It had become the source and stimulation for the brooding of others, of other boys, boys of another color.

He lit a cigarette. Bryan, a gentle colored lad in his twenties, stood silently behind Danny. Danny imagined that Bryan was trying to guess at what feelings and what thoughts he might be having now. Bryan couldn't guess that he was having almost no thoughts.

"I never thought I would stand by a window on South Park Avenue, and look out on Washington Park."

"Has it changed?" Bryan asked.

Danny shook his head and sat down on the sofa. The parlor was clean, the heavy furniture polished. There were framed pictures of flowers on the wall, and books in a bookcase at one side. There was work and pride in all this furniture, a will to dignity. It was the setting of the life of others, others whom he didn't know.

As he and Bryan talked, Danny thought of his trip out

here. He had got on the subway—there had been no subway in Chicago in the old days—and then had ridden out on the El, shooting along the express tracks, looking out at the same old, deteriorating buildings of the Black Belt, the yards full of junk and rubble, the back porches, the dirty-looking stone and wooden tenements, the junk yards, the narrow streets. There were so many of the nameless dead who had produced all this that was Chicago, and here, in this old neighborhood, he thought of the nameless dead who had built these streets and buildings. And those who were dead, but who had once lived and looked out at that park, and walked in it, and seen him and talked with him in it. He remembered a day when his eyes had ached, and he had lain in the grass of Washington Park, rejected and dispirited, thinking of the Middle Ages and of a Beatrice who had rejected him, and he had read Swinburne's "The Garden of Proserpine" aloud. That had been a summer day many years ago.

He sat back relaxed and comfortable, and said to Byran: "Just after we left this neighborhood, you moved into it. You went to the same grammar schools as I did, Crucifixion and St. Patrick's."

"Yes, I did."

"Do you like this neighborhood?"

"No, but it's home. It's always been home to me. I lived in New York, but I came back here. It's been my home. Has it changed since you were here, Danny?"

"Some of the streets are dirtier."

"I've seen that happen."

"It's overcrowded now, isn't it?"

Bryan told Danny of conditions of life in the neighborhood. The colored people were charged high rents, and most of the landlords had split up the apartments in order to get more rent.

"One of my brothers," Danny said, "was delivering a package out to the old building on Calumet Avenue where he used to live—it's the building where my father died. In the basement there was an old storeroom without any windows. They made an apartment out of it. That's where he delivered the parcel."

"I know. And the people are cynical and dissatisfied. They're cheated, and they don't care. Most of them know they'll never get anywhere. They don't care. They spend everything they get because they're cynical and don't care."

"The people who lived around here in my day," Danny said, "did care, and it didn't do them any good."

"The colored boys are as tough as the boys were in your days."

"They weren't such tough boys."

"These boys are afraid, so they have to be rough and tough," Bryan said. "If they aren't tough and cynical, where will they belong? That's the way they are. They gamble and play the numbers. My brother works in the post office, and he knows he can't ever do anything else. He's cynical too."

"Are you?"

"No."

"Why?"

"I'm not. I'm sorry my mother is working today. I wanted you to meet her. She's heard about you. I think she understands what I want to do. I think you'd like her."

"My mother died—not so far away from here either. It was last January. She didn't want to live anywhere else. She lived over past Wentworth Avenue near Garfield Boulevard. That's the boundary line now."

"I don't want to have to think I'm colored, Danny, a Negro. I want to think that I'm myself, another person, a poet, with my own feelings."

"Was growing up in this neighborhood too rough on you?" Danny asked Bryan.

"I don't know," Bryan answered.

Bryan was thoughtful.

"I don't know what to say," Bryan began. "I didn't like it. I don't know how I could like it, any more than you did. It all seems like your books. They were the same kind of boys that you knew. And I guess I just wasn't the same kind, that's all. You understand me, don't you?"

Danny nodded.

Bryan's aunt called them to lunch. They went through the hallway to the dining room in the rear of the apartment. The rather large, square dining room was very clean. There were many dishes in a cupboard on one side. The big round table was piled with dishes and food. Danny was touched at the display. He realized that here was a gesture of pride and friendliness. Bryan introduced Danny to his two aunts. They were both gray-haired, and wore clean, bright aprons. One was small and plump. The other was tall and fleshy but not fat. Like

Bryan, they had tannish brown skin. They looked maternal, and both glanced with tenderness at their nephew. Danny spoke with them about the neighborhood, mentioning that he had formerly lived here, and he told them a little about his grandmother and his mother.

He and Bryan sat down to eat, and the two women served them. The women were friendly but dignified, and with pride they accepted his thanks for the lunch they had prepared, and told him they were glad he liked it. Looking around the table with so much on it, the special dishes, the plate of rolls, the bowl of salad, the shining silver, the linen cloth, Danny was touched again and he thought of how all this also represented work, hours and hours of work. And this dignity of tablecloth and silver and dishes had been bought with the pride of these hours of work. This was obvious, and yet he remembered how there had been a time when he wouldn't have thought of this, and he wouldn't have been as touched as he was now.

Bryan was telling Danny how glad he was to have him out.

"I don't know whether or not I feel strange, being back here, Bryan. You know it's really the same neighborhood it always was, it's the same neighborhood in many ways."

"I know it is. The colored boys were no different than the white boys. I've seen them grow up, and they don't care. They don't care about much of anything, anything that you and I would care about."

"There's something more important than their not caring. They don't know. That's the point about the boys I grew up with—they didn't know. I ran into a fellow I knew around here when I was a boy. I met him on the I.C. the other day. Do you know what he does every night in bed before he falls asleep?"

"What?"

"He lies in bed and thinks of Fifty-eighth Street. He remembers every building on Fifty-eighth Street between South Park and Calumet Avenue. To him there never was a neighborhood like this one. It's his boyhood."

"You fought this neighborhood, Dan."

"That doesn't express it. I didn't know either and I wanted to know. The beginning of knowing, of finding out, was right here when I lived on South Park Avenue."

"I want to know, too, Danny."

There was something appealing but soft in Bryan. He was

sensitive and gifted, and something had been hurt in him. Danny wondered what had hurt Bryan most in life. Bryan kept mentioning his mother, how she worked so hard, and how she wanted him to become somebody. Nearly everyone else told Bryan he was wasting his time trying to get out of all this. It couldn't be done, they said. But his mother understood. Danny wished he had met her.

"Do you know what I mean, Danny?"

"About what?"

"Cynicism. How do you feel about cynicism and pessimism?"

"Pessimism signifies a lack of confidence in yourself and others. Cynicism is an extreme form of pessimism."

"I want to get out, I want to go back to New York, but I think of my mother. She doesn't have much in life. She never did have. She always worked hard, mostly for me. If it weren't for my mother I wouldn't go on. I was away in New York. I liked it. I came back here, because of my mother, and because I thought perhaps I could write better. I lost four years in the army."

"Did you like the army?"

"I don't know. Can any Negro like the army? Most of them don't. Danny, I think there are a lot of them around here who'll never go to bed thinking about Fifty-eighth Street the way your friend does. America is different to them, especially after they fought for it. That's why they're cynical. I don't like it all—I don't want to think I'm just a Negro. I don't want to have to think I'm just a Negro poet. I want to think—I guess it's just as well to say American as anything."

"Human being?" asked Danny.

"Yes—a human being. That's what my mother wants me to be, and that's what she wanted to be herself. She is that, and I know it, but hardly anyone cares if she's a human being or not. That's what they all want to be, and they're not, they're cynical."

"I don't think they want to be cynical."

"I don't know—maybe they don't. But you can't get them to read much or care much. If I tried to convince my brother, he'd only laugh. He was in the army. He laughs at me and says it was Jim Crow and it's a Jim Crow world, and what's the use. That's the way they are in this neighborhood now."

"I can well understand," Danny answered.

One of the gray-haired Negro women poured them second cups of coffee, and Danny thanked her.

"The problem of writing poetry is only the problem of feeling, of living," Danny said.

Bryan signaled agreement, but yet the expression on his face was such that Danny didn't think that Bryan really understood. Danny talked on, in a slow and quiet manner.

"How much feeling and hope they have to have to break out of this cynicism and despair! Because, Bryan, it's despair."

"My mother doesn't despair. I guess I don't, either. I just don't like to be the way many of the colored boys around here are, that's all. That's why I want to write," Bryan said.

Danny and Bryan left the apartment. There were some clumps of dirty snow along the dark patches of earth by the sidewalks, and scraps of paper were blowing on the sidewalk. A jitney taxicab passed, and some colored people walked by them on the street. Danny looked at the flat buildings between Fifty-seventh and Fifty-eighth Streets.

"I've walked this block, Bryan, perhaps as many times as you."

"I wouldn't doubt that."

"And yet, it's a different block we walked—this same block between Fifty-seventh and Fifty-eighth on South Park."

"It's South Parkway now."

"I've been around here often since I left Chicago. Every time I see those buildings and this neighborhood, it's different. These stones, the stones of all these buildings change for me. Sometimes they are like ghost houses and sometimes they are like mere dead and lifeless stones."

"What are they like now?"

"I'm merely trying to fix them in my memory. I knew a boy who lived in this place," Danny said, pointing to a red brick, three-story building. "His name was Lenny Bernstein. He was a rich boy, and had soft, flabby flesh. He used to try and lay every maid his mother hired. He always bragged about laying colored maids. He's a playboy now, and I see his name in gossip columns occasionally."

They were near Fifty-eighth Street now. More Negroes had passed them on the street. Danny had not seen another white person.

It was a warm muggy day with the threat of rain in the air.

"There are a lot of men on the streets. Is there much unemployment in this neighborhood?"

"Many of them work nights, and a lot of them have small rackets. Maybe I'll be able to point out some of the neighborhood pimps to you. One boy I went to St. Patrick's with, Doxey Dugan, has become a pimp. He dresses in loud, flashy clothes and hangs around Fifty-eighth Street and Prairie."

Danny glanced across the street at the park entrance. Slowly, he was beginning to invest everything he saw with something of his own emotions, and his own past. He thought of himself, lonely and brooding and, at times, filled with sorrow for himself, entering the park across the street. In those days these streets, the park, were a big world in which he had been lonely and out of place. They seemed bigger to him then than the entire world now seemed, and he had been more afraid in this smaller world than he could ever be in the bigger world. How big was this neighborhood world in Bryan's mind? He pondered the question as he and Bryan turned the corner at Fifty-eighth Street and South Parkway.

"This street has changed. It never used to be this dirty," Danny said.

He looked around him. He saw unswept sidewalks, and paper littering them and the street. There were eight or ten colored persons on the street. Under the dark sky, it looked like a dreary slum street.

"Bryan, I walked here so many times. All this is now dead. And yet, I momentarily catch the illusion that somewhere around here the past is lodged as though it possessed substance, as though it were a material thing."

"I sometimes think like that."

"That alley—the number of times I went down it," Danny said, pointing across the street at the alley entrance. "Let's go and look at the back yard of the building I used to live in."

They crossed the street and entered the alley. The alley, also, was littered. Papers, tin cans, rubbish everywhere. The alley had never been like this in the old days.

"God, it's dirty now," he said.

"Yes, it is."

"There's nothing to make them care, so they litter up the alley and the streets. That's what you mean by cynicism, isn't it, Bryan?"

"I guess it is."

They stopped at the back yard of the 5816½ building. The fence separating it from the alley was gone.

"There used to be a fence," Danny said. "And you can see that grass hasn't been grown here in a long time."

The yard was cluttered with more rubbish, tin cans, paper, rocks, junk. Danny thought of the back yards he had seen from the elevated train while riding out here to see Bryan. He looked up at the old back porch. He thought of his Airedale dog, Lib. She was dead so many years. Behind that porch, inside the door of that flat, so much of his life had been lived, and all that life with its agonies and fears and worries had gone into making him what he now was. He had used to think of the agonies of those days. Now, he thought that inside that flat up there on the second floor, he had dreamed and his ambition had flourished.

"Up there," Danny said, pointing, "in the rooms behind that back door on the second porch, I became a writer. That's where I was living. That's where I was living when I resolved to write."

"I admire you. I've often thought of you around here, as I would walk these streets."

"We're walking them together this afternoon," Danny said, thinking, however, that he was no longer involved here, but that Bryan was.

They turned to walk out of the alley, and they continued on over to Fifty-eighth Street.

"There's still a drugstore here, and there's still the same drugstore at Fifty-eighth and Prairie."

"Yes, and the young colored fellows hang out at the corner of Fifty-eighth Street."

"Across there, there used not to be stores in some of those basements," Danny said, pointing to the building on the south side of Fifty-eighth Street which ran between Calumet Avenue and the elevated station.

There were many colored people on Fifty-eighth Street. A number of the men were flashily dressed.

"Most of the stores have changed, of course," he told Bryan.

"I've seen changes in my time here. I was hoping I could see neighborhood characters to point out to you, Dan. I don't see any. It's too bad you haven't more time. We could go around and we could meet people. I could show you what the insides of some of these houses look like now. Most of the flats are overcrowded."

"Bryan, compare the clothes of the people with their surroundings. The clothes tell a story. The war of all vanities against all other vanities is to be seen in these zoot suits."

They walked all over the neighborhood. Danny's eyes darted one way and another, acquisitively taking in the streets, the people, the buildings. The fireplug stood at Fifty-eighth and Prairie Avenue. Once in his memory, it had seemed big, almost as though it were as high as his waist. It was a low plug, painted a brownish red, and it had once been painted black. A group of colored men stood in front of the Walgreen drugstore. Bryan commented on them. They hung around here a considerable part of their time, and some of them were tough characters.

"Are you afraid of them?" Danny asked.

Bryan was taken aback by the question, and he didn't answer immediately. They crossed Prairie Avenue and Danny knew that they were followed by the eyes of the group on the corner. In his day, it would have been white boys and men whose eyes would have followed a black and a white walking along here.

"I remember when that theater was being built. I used to play around the foundation of it in 1916," Danny said, pointing to the theater, down from the corner on Prairie Avenue. "It used to be called The Prairie."

They walked on along Fifty-eighth Street.

"That was before I was born," Bryan said.

Danny wondered about his sense of changes in this neighborhood. Was it that there were more changes in the neighborhood, or in him? The time between the present when he was walking along Fifty-eighth Street, and the past when he had walked along here, seemed dense and full and rich. It seemed to have been such a long time ago, and in such a different world. The realization that there was a connection between himself of then and himself of the present moment seemed to him utterly strange. His eyes kept darting about one way and another, and he took in store fronts and faces of colored people whom he passed. He didn't speak to Bryan for a while and they turned into Indiana Avenue, and stopped on the sidewalk before the vacant lot near Fifty-eighth Street. It seemed smaller and narrower than it had in his boyhood.

"You used to play here?" Bryan asked.

"Yes, I used to play indoor ball here, and touch football. Touch football wasn't as developed and as popular a game then as it is now."

"I want to write about this neighborhood, and describe the way life went on here after you left. It's the same in many ways as you described it. You licked this neighborhood. I want to."

They walked on along Indiana Avenue toward Fifty-seventh.

"It wasn't the neighborhood that I licked. It was some of the fears in myself. At least, as I look back on it now, that's the way it seems."

The old familiar houses, the old familiar homes, the building where Dan Donaghan had lived, the gray old stores where the Scanlans and Johnny O'Brien had lived, and the buildings on the corner where he had lived, and where Andy Le Gare had lived, Danny thought of these houses. He wondered what life was going on inside them now, and he briefly closed his eyes and visioned this street peopled with the kids of his boyhood. He told Bryan briefly of those kids, of himself dreaming in those days, and Bryan said: "I wanted something when I was a boy around here and I didn't know what I wanted."

"This neighborhood was a world to me, now it's only so many streets," Danny said.

"They're sad to me. The people underneath are sad."

"They look at it differently from us. I'm looking at it now from the outside. You're looking at it half from the inside and half from the outside. They're pretty much looking at it from the inside."

"I guess so. You escaped. I want to escape."

They walked around. The alley between Michigan and Indiana was as dirty as that between South Park and Calumet. The old play house in the Shires yard was gone. Michigan Avenue was cleaner and better kept up than most of the other streets. A wall of one of the red store buildings at Fifty-eighth and Michigan attracted Danny's attention. A boy had scribbled with chalk:

KILROY WAS HERE BUT LEFT
BECAUSE THE PLACE STANK.

They walked on and saw other streets, and Danny and Bryan stood before the building between Fifty-ninth and Six-tieth on Calumet Avenue in which has father had died. He was sad but in a restrained way. He was over forty now. They wandered on for almost a half hour.

Then they left the neighborhood to go over and around the University. In the past as in the present, he was going away from the old neighborhood in the same direction.

THE THREE SWIMMERS AND
THE EDUCATED GROCER

William Saroyan

The ditches were dry most of the year, but when they weren't dry, they were roaring. As the snows melted in the hills the ditches began to roar and from somewhere, God knows where, arrived frogs and turtles, water snakes and fish. In the spring of the year the water hurried, and with it the heart, but as the fields changed from green to brown, the blossoms to fruit, the shy warmth to arrogant heat, the ditches slowed down and the heart grew lazy. The first water from the hills was cold, swift, and frightening. It was too cold and busy to invite the naked body of a boy.

Alone, or in a group, a boy would stand on the bank of a ditch and watch the water for many minutes, and then, terribly challenged, fling off his clothes, make a running dive, come up gasping, and swim across to the other side. If the boy was the first of a group to dive, the others would soon follow, in order not to walk home in shame. It wasn't simply that the water was cold. It was more that it had no time for boys. The springtime water was as unfriendly as anything could be.

One day in April I set out for Thompson Ditch with my cousin Mourad and a pal of his named Joe Bettencourt, a Portuguese who loved nothing more than to be free and out-of-doors. A schoolroom made Joe stupid. It embarrassed him. But once out of school, once off the school-grounds, he was as intelligent, as good-natured, casual, sincere, and friendly as anyone could possibly be. As my cousin Mourad said, Joe ain't dumb—he just doesn't want an education.

It was a bright Saturday morning. We had two baloney sandwiches each, and ten cents between the three of us. We decided to walk to the ditch so that we would get there around noon, when the day would be warm. We walked along the railroad tracks to Calwa. Along the state highway to Malaga. And then east through the vineyard country to the ditch. When we said Thompson Ditch, we meant a specific place. It was an intersection of country roads, with a wooden bridge and a headgate. The swimming was south of the bridge. West of the ditch was a big fenced-in pasture, with cows and horses grazing in it. East of the ditch was the country road. The road and the ditch traveled together many miles. The flow was south, and the next bridge was two miles away. In the summertime a day of swimming was incomplete until a boy had gone downstream to the other bridge, rested a moment in the pasture land, and then came back up, against the stream, which was a good workout.

By the time we got out to Thompson Ditch the brightness of morning had changed to a gloom that was unmistakably wintry; in fact, the beginning of a storm. The water was roaring, the sky was gray, growing black, the air was cold and unfriendly, and the landscape seemed lonely and desolate.

Joe Bettencourt said, I came all this way to swim and rain or no rain I'm going to swim.

So am I, I said.

You wait, my cousin Mourad said. Me and Joe will see how it is. If it's all right, you can come in. Can you really swim?

Aw shut up, I said.

This is what I always said when it seemed to me that somebody had unwittingly insulted me.

Well, Joe said, *can* you?

Sure I can swim, I said.

If you ask *him,* my cousin Mourad said, he can do anything. Better than anybody in the world.

Neither of them knew how uncertain I was as to whether or not I could swim well enough to negotiate a dive and a swim across that body of cold roaring water. If the truth were known, when I saw the dark water roaring I was scared, challenged, and insulted.

I brought out my lunch and bit into one of the sandwiches. My cousin Mourad whacked my hand and almost knocked the sandwich into the water.

We eat after we swim, he said. Do you want to have cramps?

I had plumb forgotten. It was because I was so challenged and scared.

One sandwich won't give anybody cramps, I said.

It'll taste better after we swim, Joe said.

He was a very kind boy. He knew I was scared and he knew I was bluffing. I knew *he* was scared, but I knew he was figuring everything out a little more wisely than I was.

Let's see, he said. We'll swim across, rest, swim back, get dressed, eat, and unless the storm passes, start for home. Otherwise we'll swim some more.

This storm isn't going to pass, my cousin Mourad said. If we're going to swim, we're going to have to do it in a hurry and start for home.

By this time Joe was taking off his clothes. My cousin Mourad was taking off his, and I was taking off mine. We stood together naked on the bank of the ditch looking at the unfriendly water. It certainly didn't invite a dive, but there was no other honorable way to enter a body of water. If you tried to walk in, you were just naturally not a swimmer. If you jumped in feet first it wasn't exactly a disgrace, it was just bad style. On the other hand, the water was utterly without charm, altogether unfriendly, uninviting, and sinister. It was certainly challenging, though. The swiftness of the water made the distance to the opposite bank seem greater than it was.

Without a word Joe dived in. Without a word my cousin Mourad dived in. The second or two between splashes seemed like long days dreamed in a winter dream because I was not only scared but very cold. With a bookful of unspoken words on my troubled mind, I dived in.

The next thing I knew—and it wasn't more than three seconds later—I was listening to Joe yelling, my cousin Mourad yelling, and myself yelling. What had happened was that we had all dived into mud up to our elbows, had gotten free only with great effort, and had each come up worrying about what had happened to the other two. We were all standing in the cold roaring water, up to our knees in soft mud.

The dives had been standing dives. If they had been running dives we would have stuck in the mud up to our ankles, head first, and remained there until summer, or later.

This scared us a little on the one hand and on the other hand made us feel very lucky to be alive.

The storm broke while we stood in the mud of the ditch.

Well, Joe said, we're going to get caught in the rain any-how. We might as well stay in a little while anyway.

We were all shivering, but it seemed sensible that we should try our best to make a swim of it. The water wasn't three feet deep; nevertheless, Joe managed to leap out of the mud and swim across, and then back.

We swam for what seemed like a long time, but was prob-ably no more than ten minutes. Then we got out of the water and mud and dressed and, standing under a tree, ate our sand-wiches.

Instead of stopping, the rain increased, so we decided to set out for home right away.

We may get a ride, Joe said.

All the way to Malaga the country road was deserted. In Malaga we went into the general store and warmed ourselves at the stove and chipped in and bought a can of beans and a loaf of French bread. The proprietor of the store was a man named Darcous who wasn't a foreigner. He opened the can for us, divided the beans into three parts on three paper plates, gave us each a wooden fork, and sliced the bread for us. He was an old man who seemed funny and young.

Where you been, boys? he said.

Swimming, Joe said.

Swimming? he said.

Sure, Joe said. We showed that river.

Well, I'll be harrowed, the grocer said. How was it?

Not three feet deep, Joe said.

Cold?

Ice-cold.

Well, I'll be cultivated, the grocer said. Did you have fun?

Did we? Joe asked my cousin Mourad.

Joe didn't know whether it had been fun or something else.

I don't know, my cousin Mourad said. When we dived in we got stuck in the mud up to our elbows.

It wasn't easy to get loose from the mud, I said.

Well, I'll be pruned, the grocer said.

He opened a second can of beans, pitched an enormous forkful into his mouth, and then divided the rest onto the three paper plates.

We haven't got any more money, I said.

Now, tell me, boys, the grocer said, what made you do it?

Nothing, Joe said with the finality of a boy who has too

many reasons to enumerate at a moment's notice, and his mouth full of beans and French bread.

Well, I'll be gathered into a pile and burned, the grocer said. Now, boys, he said, tell me—of what race are you? Californians, or foreigners?

We're all Californians, Joe said. I was born on G street in Fresno. Mourad here was born on Walnut Avenue or someplace on the other side of the Southern Pacific tracks, I guess, and his cousin somewhere around in that neighborhood, too.

Well, I'll be irrigated, the grocer said. Now, tell me, boys, what sort of educations have you got?

We ain't educated, Joe said.

Well, I'll be picked off a tree and thrown into a box, the grocer said. Now, tell me, boys, what foreign languages do you speak?

I speak Portuguese, Joe said.

You ain't educated? the grocer said. I have a degree from Yale, my boy, and I can't speak Portuguese. And you, son, how about you?

I speak Armenian, my cousin Mourad said.

Well, I'll be cut off a vine and eaten grape by grape by a girl in her teens, the grocer said. I can't speak a word of Armenian and I'm a college graduate, class of 1892. Now, tell me, son, he said. What's *your* name?

Aram Garoghlanian, I said.

I think I can get it, he said. Gar-oghlan-ian. Is that it?

That's it, I said.

Aram, he said.

Yes, sir, I said.

And what strange foreign language do *you* speak? he said.

I speak Armenian, too, I said. That's my cousin. *Mourad Garoghlanian.*

Well, I'll be harrowed, he said, cultivated, pruned, gathered into a pile, burned, picked off a tree, and let me see what else? Thrown into a box, I think it was, cut off a vine and eaten grape by grape by a girl in her teens. Yes, sir. All of them things, if this doesn't beat everything. Did you encounter any reptiles?

What's reptiles? Joe said.

Snakes, the grocer said.

We didn't see any, Joe said. The water was black.

Black water, the grocer said. Any fish?

Didn't see any, Joe said.

A ford stopped in front of the store and an old man got out and came across the wood floor of the porch into the store.

Open me a bottle, Abbott, the man said.

Judge Harmon, the grocer said, I want you to meet three of the most heroic Californians of this great state.

The grocer pointed at Joe, and Joe said, Joseph Bettencourt—I speak Portuguese.

Stephen L. Harmon, the Judge said. I speak a little French.

The grocer pointed at my cousin Mourad and Mourad said, Mourad Garoghlanian.

What do you speak? the Judge said.

Armenian, my cousin Mourad said.

The grocer gave the Judge the opened bottle, the Judge lifted it to his lips, swallowed three swigs, beat his chest, and said, I'm mighty proud to meet a Californian who speaks Armenian.

The grocer pointed at me.

Aram Garoghlanian, I said.

Brothers? the Judge asked.

Cousins, I said.

Same thing, the Judge said. Now, Abbott, if you please, what's the occasion for this banquet and your poetic excitement, if not delirium?

The boys have just come from showing that old river, the grocer said.

The Judge took three more swigs, beat his chest three times slowly and said, Come from *what*?

They've just come from swimming, the grocer said.

Have any of you fevers? the Judge said.

Fever? Joe said. We ain't sick.

The grocer busted out with a roar of laughter.

Sick? he said. Sick? Judge, these boys dived naked into the black water of winter and came up glowing with the warmth of summer.

We finished the beans and the bread. We were thirsty but didn't know if we should intrude with a request for a drink of water. At least *I* didn't know, but Joe apparently didn't stop to consider.

Mr. Abbott, he said, could we have a drink of water?

Water? the grocer said. Water, my boy? Water's for swimming in, not for drinking.

He fetched three paper cups, went to a small barrel with a

tap, turned the tap, and filled each cup with a light golden fluid.

Here, boys, he said. Drink. Drink the lovely juice of the golden apple, unfermented.

The Judge poured the grocer a drink out of his bottle, lifted the bottle to his lips, and said, To your health, gentlemen.

Yes, sir, Joe said.

We all drank.

The Judge screwed the top onto the bottle, put the bottle into his back pocket, looked at each of us carefully, as if to remember us for the rest of his life, and said, Good-by, gentlemen. Court opens in a half hour. I must pass sentence on a man who says he *borrowed* the horse, *didn't* steal it. He speaks Mexican. The man who says he *stole* the horse speaks Italian. Good-by.

Good-by, we said.

By this time our clothes were almost dry, but the rain hadn't stopped.

Well, Joe said, thanks very much, Mr. Abbott. We've got to get home.

Not at all, the grocer said. *I* thank you.

The grocer seemed to be in a strange silence for a man who only a moment before had been so noisy with talk.

We left the store quietly and began to walk down the highway. The rain was now so light it didn't seem like rain at all. I didn't know what to make of it. Joe was the first to speak.

That Mr. Abbott, he said, he's some man.

The name on the sign is Darcous, I said. Abbott's his first name.

First or last, Joe said, he sure is some man.

That Judge was somebody too, my cousin Mourad said.

Educated, Joe said. I'd learn French myself, but who would I talk to?

We walked along the highway in silence. After a few minutes the black clouds parted, the sun came through, and away over in the east we saw the rainbow over the Sierra Nevadas.

We sure showed that old river, Joe said. Was he crazy?

I don't know, my cousin Mourad said.

It took us another hour to get home. We had all thoughts about the two men and whether or not the grocer was crazy. Myself, I believed he wasn't, but at the same time it seemed to me he had acted kind of crazy.

So long, Joe said.

So long, we said.

He went down the street. Fifty yards away he turned around and said something almost to himself.

What? my cousin Mourad shouted.

He was, Joe said.

Was what? I shouted.

Crazy, Joe shouted back.

Yeah? I shouted back. How do you know?

How can you be cut off a vine and eaten grape by grape by a girl in her teens? Joe shouted.

Suppose he was crazy? my cousin Mourad said. What of it?

Joe put his hand to his chin and began to consider. The sun was shining for all it was worth now and the world was full of light.

I don't think he was crazy, he shouted.

He went on down the street.

He was pretty crazy, my cousin Mourad said.

Well, I said, maybe he's not always.

We decided to let the matter rest at this point until we went swimming again, at which time we would visit the store again and see what happened.

A month later when, after swimming in the ditch, the three of us went into the store, the man who was in charge was a much younger man than Mr. Abbott Darcous. He wasn't a foreigner either.

What'll it be? he said.

A nickel's worth of baloney, Joe said, and a loaf of French bread.

Where's Mr. Darcous? my cousin Mourad said.

He's gone home, the young man said.

Where's that? I said.

Some place in Connecticut, I think, the young man said.

We made sandwiches of the baloney and French bread and began to eat.

At last Joe asked the question.

Was he crazy? Joe said.

Well, the young man said, that's hard to say. I thought he was crazy at first. Then I decided he wasn't. The way he ran this store made you think he was crazy. He gave away more than he sold. To hear him talk you'd think he was crazy. Otherwise he was all right.

Thanks, Joe said.

The store was all in order now, and a very dull place. We walked out, and began walking home.

He's crazy, Joe said.

Who? I said.

That guy in the store now, Joe said.

That young fellow? I said.

Yeah, Joe said. That new fellow in there that ain't got no education.

I think you're right, my cousin Mourad said.

All the way home we remembered the educated grocer.

Well, I'll be cultivated, Joe said when he left us and walked on down the street.

Well, I'll be picked off a tree and thrown in a box, my cousin Mourad said.

Well, I'll be cut off a vine and eaten grape by grape by a girl in her teens, I said.

He sure was some man. Twenty years later, I decided he had been a poet and had run that grocery store in that little run-down village just for the casual poetry in it instead of the paltry cash.

EDUCATION

LEARNING IN AMERICA

It was never learning I associated with that school: only the necessity to succeed, to get ahead of the others in the daily struggle to "make a good impression" on our teachers. . . .

Alfred Kazin

The immigrant father could not transform himself completely into an American; the language and customs he retained kept him a "hyphenated American." His child, he felt, could be converted into that new breed of man, the American. The element of the child's life which would provide him with new mores and folkways was public education.

The school defined America for the immigrant child. Far more than a place of academic training, it meant potential success, assimilation, and rejection of the father's way of life. The greater the father's desire to educate his children in the American schools, the more extreme the children's renunciation of the father as a guide and model. Indeed the division between the generations has seemed so deep that the change in the children's character has been called "the American mutation."

For many immigrant children, the school teacher personified what it meant to be an American. More modern and sophisticated than the parents, she seemed more aware of the specific social pressures the children would confront.

She represented the world the child wanted to enter, and her influence was consequently great in the development of the boy or girl who studied with her. One can feel this influence in Norman Podhoretz's *Making It* and James Baldwin's "Notes of a Native Son."

The transition from home to school was, of course, not simple. The emotional conflict that arises when one lives in an immigrant household during the night and in an American school during the day, when one speaks one language at home and learns another at school, when one shifts constantly from one set of values to another, can lead to bewilderment and frustration—and some of these reactions are expressed in the poetry of Langston Hughes and Gregory Corso, in the essays of Zitkala-Sa and Lin Yutang.

THEME FOR ENGLISH B

Langston Hughes

The instructor said,

> *Go home and write*
> *a page tonight.*
> *And let that page come out of you—*
> *Then, it will be true.*

I wonder if it's that simple?

I am twenty-two, colored, born in Winston-Salem.
I went to school there, then Durham, then here
to this college on the hill above Harlem.
I am the only colored student in my class.
The steps from the hill lead down into Harlem,
through a park, then I cross St. Nicholas,
Eighth Avenue, Seventh, and I come to the Y,
the Harlem Branch Y, where I take the elevator
up to my room, sit down, and write this page:

It's not easy to know what is true for you or me
at twenty-two, my age. But I guess I'm what
I feel and see and hear, Harlem, I hear you:
hear you, hear me—we two—you, me, talk on this page.
(I hear New York, too.) Me—who?
Well, I like to eat, sleep, drink, and be in love.
I like to work, read, learn, and understand life.
I like a pipe for a Christmas present,
or records—Bessie, bop, or Bach.
I guess being colored doesn't make me *not* like

the same things other folks like who are other races.
So will my page be colored that I write?
Being me, it will not be white.
But it will be
a part of you, instructor.
You are white—
yet a part of me, as I am a part of you.
That's American.
Sometimes perhaps you don't want to be a part of me.
Nor do I often want to be a part of you.
But we are, that's true!
As I learn from you,
I guess you learn from me—
although you're older—and white—
and somewhat more free.

This is my page for English B.

EDUCATION

Don L. Lee

I had a good teacher,
He taught me everything I know;
how to lie,
      cheat,
      and how to strike the softest blow.

My teacher thought himself to be wise and right
He taught me things most people consider nice;
      such as to pray,
            smile,
            and how not to fight.

My teacher taught me other things too.
Things that I will be forever looking at;
      how to berate,
            segregate,
            and how to be inferior without hate.

My teacher's wisdom forever grows,
He taught me things every child will know,
      how to steal,
            appeal,
            and accept most things against my will.

All these acts take as facts,
The mistake was made in teaching me
How not to be BLACK.

THE PROMISED LAND

Mary Antin

Father himself conducted us to school. He would not have delegated that mission to the President of the United States. He had awaited the day with impatience equal to mine, and the visions he saw as he hurried us over the sun-flecked pavements transcended all my dreams. Almost his first act on landing on American soil, three years before, had been his application for naturalization. He had taken the remaining steps in the process with eager promptness, and at the earliest moment allowed by the law, he became a citizen of the United States. It is true that he had left home in search of bread for his hungry family, but he went blessing the necessity that drove him to America. The boasted freedom of the New World meant to him far more than the right to reside, travel, and work wherever he pleased; it meant the freedom to speak his thoughts, to throw off the shackles of superstition, to test his own fate, unhindered by political or religious tyranny. He was only a young man when he landed—thirty-two; and most of his life he had been held in leading-strings. He was hungry for his untasted manhood.

Three years passed in sordid struggle and disappointment. He was not prepared to make a living even in America, where the day laborer eats wheat instead of rye. Apparently the American flag could not protect him against the pursuing Nemesis of his limitations; he must expiate the sins of his fathers who slept across the seas. He had been endowed at birth with a poor constitution, a nervous, restless temperament, and an abundance of hindering prejudices. In his boyhood his body was starved, that his mind might be stuffed with useless learning. In his youth this dearly gotten learning was sold, and the price was the bread and salt which he had not been trained to earn for himself. Under the wedding canopy he was bound for life to a girl whose features were still strange to him; and he was bidden to multiply himself, that sacred learning might be perpetuated in his sons, to the glory of the God of his fathers. All this while he had been led about as a creature without a will, a chattel, an instrument. In his maturity he awoke, and found himself poor in health, poor in purse, poor in useful knowledge, and hampered on all sides. At the first nod of opportunity he broke away from his prison, and strove to atone for his wasted youth by a life of useful labor; while at the same time he sought to lighten the gloom of his narrow scholarship by freely partaking of modern ideas. But his utmost endeavor still left him far from his goal. In business, nothing prospered with him. Some fault of hand or mind or temperament led him to failure where other men found success. Wherever the blame for his disabilities be placed, he reaped their bitter fruit. "Give me bread!" he cried to America. "What will you do to earn it?" the challenge came back. And he found that he was master of no art, of no trade; that even his precious learning was of no avail, because he had only the most antiquated methods of communicating it.

So in his primary quest he had failed. There was left him the compensation of intellectual freedom. That he sought to realize in every possible way. He had very little opportunity to prosecute his education, which, in truth, had never been begun. His struggle for a bare living left him no time to take advantage of the public evening school; but he lost nothing of what was to be learned through reading, through attendance at public meetings, through exercising the rights of citizenship. Even here he was hindered by a natural inability to acquire the English language. In time, indeed, he learned to read, to follow a conversation or lecture; but he never learned to write correctly, and his pronunciation remains extremely foreign to this day.

If education, culture, the higher life were shining things to be worshipped from afar, he had still a means left whereby he could draw one step nearer to them. He could send his children to school, to learn all those things that he knew by fame to be desirable. The common school, at least, perhaps high school; for one or two, perhaps even college! His children should be students, should fill his house with books and intellectual company; and thus he would walk by proxy in the Elysian Fields of liberal learning. As for the children them-

selves, he knew no surer way to their advancement and happiness.

So it was with a heart full of longing and hope that my
father led us to school on that first day. He took long strides
in his eagerness, the rest of us running and hopping to keep
up.

At last the four of us stood around the teacher's desk; and
my father, in his impossible English, gave us over in her
charge, with some broken word of his hopes for us that his
swelling heart could no longer contain. I venture to say that
Miss Nixon was struck by something uncommon in the group
we made, something outside of Semitic features and the
abashed manner of the alien. My little sister was as pretty as a
doll, with her clear pink-and-white face, short golden curls,
and eyes like blue violets when you caught them looking up.
My brother might have been a girl, too, with his cherubic con-
tours of face, rich red color, glossy black hair, and fine eyebrows. Whatever secret fears were in his heart, remembering
his former teachers, who had taught with the rod, he stood
up straight and uncringing before the American teacher, his
cap respectfully doffed. Next to him stood a starved-looking
girl with eyes ready to pop out, and short dark curls that
would not have made much of a wig for a Jewish bride.

All three children carried themselves rather better than
the common run of "green" pupils that were brought to Miss
Nixon. But the figure that challenged attention to the group
was the tall, straight father, with his earnest face and fine
forehead, nervous hands eloquent in gesture, and a voice full
of feeling. This foreigner, who brought his children to school
as if it were an act of consecration, who regarded the teacher
of the primer class with reverence, who spoke of visions, like
a man inspired, in a common schoolroom, was not like other
aliens, who brought their children in dull obedience to the law;
was not like the native fathers, who brought their unmanage-
able boys, glad to be relieved of their care. I think Miss Nixon
guessed what my father's best English could not convey. I think
she divined that by the simple act of delivering our school
certificates to her he took possession of America.

MR. K★A★P★L★A★N AND SHAKESPEARE

Leonard Q. Ross (Leo Rosten)

It was Miss Higby's idea in the first place, she had suggested to Mr. Parkhill that the students came to her grade unaware of the *finer* side of English, of its beauty and, as she put it, "the glorious heritage of our literature." She suggested that perhaps poetry might be worked into the exercises of Mr. Parkhill's class. The beginners' grade had, after all, been subjected to almost a year of English and might be presumed to have achieved some linguistic sophistication. Poetry would make the students conscious of precise enunciation; it would make them read with greater care and an ear for sounds. Miss Higby, who had once begun a master's thesis on Coventry Patmore, *loved* poetry. And, it should be said in all justice, she argued her cause with considerable force. Poetry *would* be excellent for the enunciation of the students, thought Mr. Parkhill.

So it was that when he faced the class the following Tuesday night, Mr. Parkhill had a volume of Shakespeare on his desk and an eager, almost an expectant, look in his eye. The love that Miss Higby bore for poetry in general was as nothing compared to the love that Mr. Parkhill bore for Shakespeare in particular. To Mr. Parkhill, poetry meant Shakespeare. Many years ago he had played Polonius in his senior-class play.

"Tonight, class," said Mr. Parkhill, "I am going to try an experiment."

The class looked up dutifully. They had come to regard Mr. Parkhill's pedagogical innovations as part of the natural order.

"I am going to introduce you to poetry—great poetry. You see—" Mr. Parkhill delivered a modest lecture on the beauty of poetry, its expression of the loftier thoughts of men, its economy of statement. He hoped it would be a relief from spelling and composition exercises to use poetry as the subject matter of the regular Recitation and Speech period. "I shall write a passage on the board and read it for you. Then, for Recitation and Speech, you will give short addresses, using the passage as the general topic, telling us what it has brought to your minds, what—er—thoughts and ideas."

The class seemed quite pleased by the announcement. Miss Mitnick blushed happily. (This blush was different from most of Miss Mitnick's blushes; there was aspiration and idealism in it.) Mr. Norman Bloom sighed with a businesslike air: you could tell that for him poetry was merely another assignment, like a speech on "What I Like to Eat Best" or a composition on "A Day at a Picnic." Mrs. Moskowitz, to whom any public performance was unpleasant, tried to look enthusiastic, without much success. And Mr. Hyman Kaplan, the heroic smile on his face as indelibly as ever, looked at Mr. Parkhill with admiration and whispered to himself: "Poyetry! Now is poyetry! My! Mus' be progriss ve makink awreddy!"

"The passage will be from Shakespeare," Mr. Parkhill announced, opening the volume.

An excited buzz ran through the class as the magic of that name fell upon them.

"Imachine!" murmured Mr. Kaplan. "Jakesbeer!"

"*Shake*speare, Mr. Kaplan!"

Mr. Parkhill took a piece of chalk and, with care and evident love, wrote the following passage on the board in large, clear letters:

> Tomorrow, and tomorrow, and tomorrow
> Creeps in this petty pace from day to day,
> To the last syllable of recorded time;
> And all our yesterdays have lighted fools
> The way to dusty death. Out, out, brief candle!
> Life's but a walking shadow, a poor player
> That struts and frets his hour upon the stage,
> And then is heard no more; it is a tale
> Told by an idiot, full of sound and fury,
> Signifying nothing.

A reverent hush filled the classroom, as eyes gazed with wonder on this passage from the Bard. Mr. Parkhill was pleased.

"I shall read the passage first," he said. "Listen carefully to my enunciation and—er—let Shakespeare's thoughts sink into your minds."

Mr. Parkhill read: "Tomorrow, and tomorrow, and tomorrow . . ." Mr. Parkhill read very well, and this night, as if some special fire burned in him, he read with rare eloquence. "Out, out, brief candle!" In Miss Mitnick's eyes there was inspiration and wonder. "Life's but a walking shadow . . ." Mrs. Moskowitz sat with a heavy frown, indicating cerebration. "It is a tale told by an idiot . . ." Mr. Kaplan's smile had taken on something luminous, but his eyes were closed: it was not clear whether Mr. Kaplan had surrendered to the spell of Shakespeare or to that of Morpheus.

"I shall—er—read the passage again," said Mr. Parkhill, clearing his throat vociferously until he saw Mr. Kaplan's eyes open. "Tomorrow, and tomorrow, and tomorrow. . . ."

When Mr. Parkhill had read the passage for the second time, he said: "That should be quite clear now. Are there any questions?"

There were a few questions. Mr. Scymzak wanted to know whether "frets" was "a little kind excitement." Miss Schneiderman asked about "struts." Mr. Kaplan wasn't sure about "cripps." Mr. Parkhill explained the words carefully, with several illustrative uses of each word. "No more questions? Well, I shall allow a few minutes for you all to—er—think over the meaning of the passage. Then we shall begin Recitation and Speech."

Mr. Kaplan promptly closed his eyes again, his smile beatific. The students sank into that reverie miscalled thought, searching their souls for the symbols evoked by Shakespeare's immortal words. Olga Tarnova was uttering those husky, throaty moans that, in her case, signified either speechlessness or rapture.

"Miss Caravello, will you begin?" asked Mr. Parkhill.

Miss Caravello went to the front of the room. "Da poem isa gooda," she said slowly. "Itsa have—"

"It *has*."

"It has a beautiful wordsa. Itsa lak Dante, Italian poet—"

"Ha!" cried Mr. Kaplan scornfully. "Shaksbeer you metchink mit Tante? *Shaksbeer? Mein Gott!*"

It was obvious that Mr. Kaplan had identified himself with Shakespeare and would tolerate no disparagement of his *alter ego*.

"Miss Caravello is merely expressing her own ideas," said

Mr. Parkhill pacifically. (Actually, he felt completely sympathetic to Mr. Kaplan's point of view.)

"Hau Kay," agreed Mr. Kaplan, with a generous wave of the hand. "But to me is no comparink a high-cless man like Shaksbeer mit a Tante, dat's all."

Miss Caravello, her poise shattered, said a few more words and returned to her seat.

Mrs. Yampolsky's contribution was brief. "This is full deep meanings," she said, her eyes on the floor. "Is hard for a person not so good in English to unnistand. But I like."

"*Like!*" cried Mr. Kaplan. "*Like?* Batter *love*, Yampolsky. Mit Shaksbeer mus' be *love!*"

Mr. Parkhill had to suggest that Mr. Kaplan control his aesthetic passions. He did understand how Mr. Kaplan felt, however, and sensed a new bond between them. Mrs. Yampolsky staggered through several more nervous ambiguities and retired.

Mr. Bloom was next. He gave a long declamation, ending: "So is passimistic ideas in the poem, and I am optimist. Life should be happy—so we should remember this is only a poem. Maybe is Shakespeare too passimistic."

"You wronk, Bloom!" cried Mr. Kaplan with prompt indignation. "Shaksbeer is passimist because is de *life* passimist also!"

Mr. Parkhill, impressed by this philosophical stroke, realized that Mr. Kaplan, afire with the glory of the Swan of Avon, could not be suppressed. Mr. Kaplan was the kind of man who brooked no criticism of his gods. The only solution was to call on Mr. Kaplan for his recitation at once. Mr. Parkhill was, indeed, curious about what fresh thoughts Mr. Kaplan would utter after his passionate defenses of the Bard. When Mr. Parkhill had corrected certain parts of Mr. Bloom's speech, emphasizing Mr. Bloom's failure to use the indefinite article, he said: "Mr. Kaplan, will *you* speak next?"

Mr. Kaplan's face broke into a glow; his smile was like a rainbow. "Soitinly," he said, walking to the front of the room. Never had he seemed so dignified, so eager, so conscious of a great destiny.

"Er—Mr. Kaplan," added Mr. Parkhill, suddenly aware of the possibilities which the situation (Kaplan on Shakespeare) involved: "Speak *carefully*."

"*Spacially* careful vill I be," Mr. Kaplan reassured him. He cleared his throat, adjusted his tie, and began: "Ladies an' gantleman, you hoid all kinds minninks abot dis piece poyetry, an'—"

"Poetry."

"—abot dis piece *poetry*. But to me is a difference minnink altogadder. Ve mus' tink abot Julius Scissor an' how *he* falt!"

Mr. Parkhill moved nervously, puzzled.

"In dese exact voids is Julius Scissor sayink—"

"Er—Mr. Kaplan," said Mr. Parkhill once he grasped the full import of Mr. Kaplan's error. "The passage is from *Macbeth*."

Mr. Kaplan looked at Mr. Parkhill with injured surprise. "*Not* fromm *Julius Scissor?*"

"No. And it's—er—'Julius C*ae*sar.' "

Mr. Kaplan waited until the last echo of the name had permeated his soul. "Podden me, Mr. Pockheel. Isn't '*see*zor' vat you cottink somting op mit?"

"That," said Mr. Parkhill quickly, "is 'scissor.' You have used 'Caesar' for 'scissor' and 'scissor' for 'Caesar.' "

"My!" Mr. Kaplan exclaimed, marvelling at his own virtuosity.

"But go on with your speech, please." Mr. Parkhill, to tell the truth, felt a little guilty that he had not announced at the very beginning that the passage was from *Macbeth*. "Tell us *why* you thought the lines were from *Julius Caesar*."

"Vell," said Mr. Kaplan to the class, his smile assuming its normal serenity, "I vas positif, becawss I can *see* the whole ting." He paused, debating how to explain this cryptic remark. Then his eyes filled with a certain enchantment. "I see de whole scinn. It's in a tant, on de night bafore dey makink Julius de Kink fromm Rome. So he is axcited an' ken't slip. He is layink in bad, tinking: 'Tomorrow an' tomorrow an' tomorrow. How slow dey movink! Almost cripps! Soch a pity de pace!' "

Before Mr. Parkhill could explain that "petty pace" did not mean "Soch a pity de pacee" Mr. Kaplan had soared on.

"De days go slow, fromm day to day, like leetle tsyllables on phonograph racords fromm time."

"Mr. Kap—"

" 'An' vat abot yestidday?' tinks Julius Scissor. Ha! 'All our yestiddays are only makink a good light for fools to die in de dost!' "

" 'Dusty death' doesn't mean—"

"An' Julius Scissor is so tired, an he vants to fallink aslip. So he hollers, mit fillink, 'Go ot! Go ot! Short candle!' So it goes ot."

Mr. Kaplan's voice dropped to a whisper. "But he ken't slip. Now is bodderink him de idea fromm life. 'Vat is de life altogadder?' tinks Julius Scissor. An' he gives enswer, de pot I like de bast. 'Life is like a bum actor, strottink an' hollerink around de stage for only vun hour bafore he's kicked ot. Life is a tale told by idjots, dat's all, full of fonny sonds an' phooey!"

" 'Full of sound and fury!' " Mr. Parkhill cried desperately. But inspiration, like an irresistible force, swept Mr. Kaplan on.

" 'Life is monkey business! It don' minn a ting. It signifies nottink!' An' den Julius Scissor closes his ice fest"—Mr. Kaplan demonstrated the Consul's exact ocular process in closing his "ice"—"an' falls don dad!"

The class was hushed as Mr. Kaplan stopped. In the silence, a tribute to the fertility of Mr. Kaplan's imagination and the power of his oratory, Mr. Kaplan went to his seat. But just before he sat down, as if adding a postscript, he sighed: "Dat was mine idea. But ufcawss is all wronk, becawss Mr. Pockheel said de voids ain't abot Julius Scissor altogadder. It's all abot an Irishman by de name Macbat."

It was some time before Mr. Parkhill could bring himself to criticize Mr. Kaplan's pronunciation, enunciation, diction, grammar, idiom, and sentence structure. For Mr. Parkhill discovered that he could not easily return to the world of reality. He was still trying to tear himself away from that tent outside Rome, where "Julius Scissor," cursed with insomnia, had thought of time and life—and philosophized himself to a strange and sudden death.

Mr. Parkhill was distinctly annoyed with Miss Higby.

MAKING IT

Norman Podhoretz

In his book about Columbia, *The Reforming of General Education*, Daniel Bell speaks of the "conversion experience" which the college seems to induce in many of its students. They are shocked, he says, into "a new appreciation of the dimensions of thought and feeling," and they are thereby converted, "so to speak, to culture." Certainly something of this kind happened to me at Columbia; I discovered, and really for the first time, that there were more things in heaven and earth than were dreamt of in the philosophy of Brownsville, that the world offered a greater range of possibilities than I or the people among whom I had been raised had ever imagined it to contain. And in time I came to see that some of these were possibilities for *me*.

Bell is also right in saying that the conversion was to "culture"—the more so in that he attaches no qualifying adjectives to the term. To be sure, Columbia itself did attach a qualifying adjective, no bones ever having been made there about the fact that it was the heritage of *Western* Civilization to which we were being introduced. And yet the idea of Western Civilization seemed so broad and generous, so all-embracing of whatever might be important or good or great or noble in the world, that most of us thought of the adjective as merely a polite tautology, a kind of elegantly liberal nod at the poor old Orient. To our minds, this culture we were studying at Columbia was not the creation or the possession of a particular group of people; it was a repository of the universal, existing not in space or time but rather in some transcendental realm of the spirit—that very realm I had dreamed of in the days of Mrs. K.

But if for me Columbia represented universality, the Seminary stood just as sharply for parochialism—and not only because of its continuity with the life I had always known. Unlike the Rabbinical School and the Teachers Institute, its sister divisions within the Jewish Theological Seminary, the Seminary College was theoretically committed to what Jewish tradition calls *Torah lishma*, learning for its own sake, but in actual fact its purposes were very far from being disinterestedly academic. The literal meaning of *Torah lishma* may be "learning for its own sake," but the true, the theological, meaning of the idea is "studying the revealed word of God for the sake of heaven." The Seminary College did not, I think, consider that it was teaching the revealed word of God for the sake of heaven; it did, however, consider that it was teaching the heritage of the Jewish people as a way of ensuring the survival of that people (my father knew what he was doing when he sent me there). This is not to imply that there was anything covert or devious going on; on the contrary, most professors at the Seminary simply and frankly took it for granted that their business was to deepen the Jewish commitment of their students by making them more fully aware of the glories of the Jewish heritage. They were not training minds or sensibilities; they were training Jews.

To my adolescent eyes, guided by several extraordinary teachers at Columbia (the greatest of whom, the late Moses Hadas, was a lapsed rabbi: the ironies here are manifold), Western Culture made what the Seminary had to offer look narrow, constricted, provincial, and finally less relevant to me personally than the heritage of what was, after all, a Christian civilization, and one which had up until—how long? a minute before?—been at literally murderous odds with the heritage, not to mention the bodies, of my own people. And in this sense, too, I suppose one might speak of a conversion in describing what happened to me at Columbia.

But whether or not the word is appropriate (and probably it is several shades too harsh), it was not long before I grew restless and resentful at having to attend the Seminary. I was determined, because of my father, to stay on to the end, but it all seemed utterly pointless. A few of the courses were easily equal to any at Columbia—Bible with H. L. Ginsberg, Jewish history with Abraham S. Halkin—and could even be thought of as fitting in with my beloved Western Civilization

(which—further proof of its universality—took even the best
of the Jewish tradition into its generous and transcendent
embrace). But the strident note of apologetics and defensive-
ness which entered into the least detail of almost every other
aspect of the Seminary curriculum, the endless pep talks disguised as scholarship, the endless harping on the sufferings of
the Jews: all this made my Columbia-trained sensibilities raw.
And the students: the bright ones who were going cynically
into the rabbinate because it offered an easy, protected way of
life; the dull ones who were going solemnly into the rabbinate
because they were afraid to dare the outside world; the fa-
natical Hebraists who would admonish one to "Speak Hebrew!"
as they marched by in the halls (one of these, it was rumored,
would announce to his wife, "*Hineh zeh bah*"—"Behold, it
cometh"—as he reached a climax in the act of love)—what
had I to do with such people or they with me?

And there is yet a third sense, deeper in the long run
than the other two, in which the word conversion might be
applied in describing what happened to me in the course of
those four years at Columbia. But here I must tread warily. I
have already said that the Seminary was frank in its parochialism, that it made no pretense either to itself or to its students as to the purposes it was pursuing. I knew perfectly well
that the Seminary was in the business of making Jews, and I
understood perfectly well what that meant. But the suggestion
that Columbia, High Temple of Culture and Civilization, might
be pursuing certain restricted social purposes of its own would
have struck me as an absurdity, a contradiction in terms. And
yet it was. "One of the commonest references that one hears
with regard to Columbia," wrote the Dean of the College,
Frederick P. Keppel, in 1914,

is that its position at the gateway of European immigration
makes it socially uninviting to students who come from homes
of refinement. The form which the inquiry takes in these days
of slowly dying race prejudice is, "Isn't Columbia overrun with
European Jews who are most unpleasant persons socially?" . . .
[But] what most people regard as a racial problem is really a
social problem. The Jews who have had the advantages of
decent social surroundings for a generation or two are entirely
satisfactory companions. . . . There are, indeed, Jewish students
of another type who have not had the social advantages of their
more fortunate fellows. Often they come from an environment

which in any stock less fired with ambition would have put the idea of higher education entirely out of the question. Some of these are not particularly pleasant companions, but the total number is not large, and every reputable institution aspiring to public service must stand ready to give to those of probity and good moral character the benefits which they are making great sacrifices to obtain.*

Of course, Keppel was writing at a time when Columbia was the college of Old New York society—a kind of finishing school for young gentlemen who would soon enter the governing elite of the nation. By the end of the Second World War, when I arrived, the composition of its student body had become more diverse, both geographically and ethnically, and the G.I. Bill had brought in many veterans who would otherwise have been unable to afford the tuition. To be sure, the number of Jews admitted to the college was still limited by an unacknowledged quota (about 17 percent), but the only anti-Semitism I personally ever encountered there was among some of the Jewish students themselves.

If, however, anti-Semitism as such was dead at Columbia, at least one of the major assumptions contained in Keppel's remarks of 1914 was still very much alive in 1946, and this was that the adoption of a liberalized admissions policy by Columbia, as a "reputable institution aspiring to public service," carried with it the responsibility to make "satisfactory companions" out of such of their students who had not "come from homes of refinement" and had not enjoyed "the social advantages of their more fortunate fellows." It was, then, the business of Columbia College to make a gentleman out of any young man of "foreign stock" on whom it chose to confer the benefits of a higher education. In other words, me.

Maurice Samuel once wrote a whole book, *The Gentleman and the Jew*, to show that the idea of the gentleman, however variously it might have been defined at different times and in different places, was always consistent in one detail: that it stood in opposition to the idea of the Jew. Keppel's remarks are a good example of how this opposition worked, but in subsequent Columbia usage of the term, the element of class disappears and the gentleman Columbia now wishes to produce

---

* Frederick P. Keppel, *Columbia*, New York, Oxford University Press, 1914.

is described as "the honorable and responsible citizen of enlightened and gracious mind."* These are fine and resounding abstractions, but if one wishes to determine whether they are quite so free of any class bias as they appear to be, one has only to ask what the type they envisage would in all probability look like. He would not, I imagine, be a person who ate with his fingers, or whose accent bore the traces of an immigrant slum, or whose manners clashed significantly with the oppressively genteel atmosphere of the Columbia Faculty Club. He might once have been such a person, and as such a person he would once have been barred altogether from the possibility of ever being considered a "gentleman." Now, however, in a more liberal and tolerant age, his origins would no longer be held against him—so long, that is, as he could learn to comport himself like a reasonable facsimile of an upper-class WASP.

When I was in college, the term WASP had not yet come into currency—which is to say that the realization had not yet become widespread that white Americans of Anglo-Saxon Protestant background are an ethnic group like any other, that their characteristic qualities are by no means self-evidently superior to those of the other groups, and that neither their earlier arrival nor their majority status entitles them to exclusive possession of the national identity. In the absence of this realization, Columbia had no need to be as fully conscious of the social implications of the purposes it was pursuing as, on its side, the Seminary necessarily was. The demand being made on me as a student of Jewish culture was concrete, explicit, and unambiguous: "Become a good Jew!" The demand being made on me as a student of Western Culture, by contrast, was seductively abstract and idealized: "Become a gentleman, a man of enlightened and gracious mind!" It is not that Columbia was being dishonest in failing to mention that this also meant "Become a facsimile WASP!" In taking that corollary for granted, the college was simply being true to its

---

* This is Lionel Trilling's paraphrase of Columbia thinking on the matter. It is perhaps worth noting that Trilling was the first Jew ever to be given a permanent appointment in the Columbia English department, which was among the last holdouts against Jews of all the departments in the university. As late as 1937, it was thought that a Jew could teach philosophy or even Greek, but that no one with such shallow roots in Anglo-Saxon culture could be entrusted with the job of introducing the young to its literary heritage.

own ethnic and class origins; and in nothing did this fidelity show itself more clearly than in the bland unconsciousness that accompanied it.

As for me, I was even less conscious of the social meaning of Columbia's intentions toward me than Columbia itself was—which, of course, only made those intentions easier to realize. My personal deportment did not change. Far from coming to look or act like a facsimile WASP, I continued to dress in the Brownsville manner, resisting my Columbia friends now, as I had resisted Mrs. K. before, when they tried to prod me into adopting the "proper" style. Similarly with the dietary laws, which I insisted on observing in spite of much ridicule and long after I had ceased to believe in them. So too with the obscenities I constantly used, after the Brownsville fashion, in casual conversation. And so especially with my ambitiousness, which only grew more ostentatious with every kindly counsel that I try to conceal it. Back home, on weekend nights and any others I could spare, I continued to bum around with the gang—most of them now working at menial jobs and some of them attending night-school classes in accountancy or engineering at one of the City Colleges—living the old life of street corners, pool rooms, crap games, poker games, sports talk, sex talk. I was, to all appearances, the same kid I had been before entering Columbia, only a little older, a little more sure of myself, a little less anxious over my status as one of "the boys." With my parents, also, relations were as good on the surface as ever. We still talked a great deal, I still went on dutiful visits to relatives with them, and I still did not complain about having to live at home without a room of my own to work in.

And yet and yet: we all knew that things were not the same. They knew—it was in their eyes—that I was already halfway out of their world and that it was only a matter of time before I would be out of it altogether. And I? What did I know? I knew that the neighborhood voices were beginning to sound coarse and raucous; I knew that our apartment was beginning to look tasteless and tawdry; I knew that the girls in quest of whom my friends and I hornily roamed the streets were beginning to strike me as too elaborately made up, too shrill in their laughter, too crude in their dress.

Notice: it was my *sensibilities* which were being offended, and by things which had been familiar to me my whole life long; it was the lower-classness of Brownsville to which I was responding with irritation. To wean me away from Brownsville, all Columbia had had to do was give me the superior liberal education it did: in giving me such an education it was working a radical change in my tastes, and in changing my tastes it was ensuring that I would no longer be comfortable in the world from which I had come. For taste is an overwhelmingly important sociological force, capable by itself of turning strangers into brothers and brothers into strangers. What did it matter that I genuinely loved my family and my friends, when not even love had the power to protect them from the ruthless judgments of my newly delicate, oh-so-delicate, sensibilities? What did it matter that I was still naïve enough and cowardly enough and even decent enough to pretend that my conversion to "culture" had nothing to do with class when I had already traveled so far along the road Mrs. K. had predicted I would—when I had to all intents and purposes already become a snob?

And finally there was a fourth conversion—this one to the Columbia code. Though largely social in its origins, the Columbia code was much reinforced among the literati in the college by the contemptuous attitude toward success which inevitably seems to develop out of the study of literature. There are several reasons for this, but the widely entertained idea that the Western literary heritage itself inculcates such an attitude is most assuredly not one of them. For the truth is that if Western literature teaches any consistent lesson on this score—which of course it does not—it would be that wealth, power, and especially fame are immensely desirable things to have. Certainly the Greeks thought so; certainly the Elizabethans thought so; and certainly the great nineteenth-century novelists thought so too. Contemporary literature is admittedly another matter, but even there the case is rather more ambiguous than many people appear to think.

What then are the reasons for the connection between the study of literature and the contempt for success? The noblest of them is undoubtedly that the study of literature encourages a great respect for activity which is its own reward (whereas the ethos of success encourages activity for the sake of extrinsic reward), and a great respect for the thing-in-itself (as opposed to the ethos of success which encourages a nihilistically reductive preoccupation with the "cash value" of all things). To acquire even a small measure of independent critical judgment is to understand that "successful" does not necessarily mean "good" and that "good" does not necessarily mean "successful." From there it is but a short step, the shortest step in the world, to the ardent conclusion that the two can *never* go together, particularly in America and particularly in the arts.

But there are other, more strictly sociological, reasons for the connection. In the first place, a young man who studies literature is in effect electing to join a kind of political party within the American cultural order: the party of opposition to the presumed values of the business world. A negative attitude toward success is a requirement of membership in this party, and it will be strengthened by much of the new recruit's reading in the social and literary criticism of the past hundred years which, unlike the literary tradition itself, definitely does inculcate such an attitude.

A second reason, flowing from the first, is that a young man who studies literature is doing something which has at best a modest market value. He may—he almost invariably will —have fantasies of becoming a great writer himself, thereby at least achieving fame (the ambition for which has always enjoyed a better reputation among moralists than the ambition for wealth or power). But he is also sensible enough to know that in electing to pursue a literary career, which for all practical purposes means teaching in a college, he can probably look forward only to a life of relatively modest means on the periphery of American society. Most young men who make this choice make it with the greatest enthusiasm, imagining that they are entering an existence rich in spiritual satisfaction and turning their backs on one that has nothing to offer but empty material comforts. Naturally high-minded anyway, the young find it difficult to appreciate the value of these "empty" comforts; being human, they are quick to denigrate what they have not learned to appreciate; and being inexperienced, they are slow to understand that making a living in the academic world has more in common with making a living in the business world than a superficial glance at either would reveal.

All this clashed sharply with the direct and simple belief in the desirability of success I had absorbed at home, and especially from my mother. But that did not prevent the new attitude from taking a powerful hold over me. It did not, to be specific, prevent it from leading me (with a prodding assist from my Columbia friends) to the miserable speculation that my success at Columbia, far from being a confirmation of my worth and a certification of my promise as a future critic of literature, might in reality be a sign that, like a best-selling author, I was corrupt, opportunistic, and ultimately incapable of serious work.

It was at Columbia, then, that I was introduced to the ethos—destined to grow more and more powerful in the ensuing years—in which success was replacing sex as the major "dirty little secret" of the age. By the values of this ethos, the hunger for sex was a natural and indeed an admirable passion, whereas the hunger for worldly success was regarded as low, ignoble, ugly: something to be concealed from others and preferably even from oneself, something to be ashamed of and guilty about. My own conversion to such values was yet another sign that the first lap in the long, blind journey I was making from Brooklyn to Manhattan had at last been completed.

P.S. 42

Gregory Corso

When I think back to grammar school
I am overcome with breathlessness and sweet feeling—
Freighted to that glorious mahogany time
when bluecoats cheered each other with pewter mugs
and snow-hunched sentries eyed young Washington
    dismount
and Indians covered their horses with Algonquin rugs
Where perhaps a goodly witch buying sassafras
rubbed shoulders with Ben Franklin picking
    half-pennies from a tiny purse—

I played Christopher Columbus aged ten
in the great assembly hall before all
and I clearly remember as I sat
dreamily on the docks of Genoa
the beautiful picture of Washington at Valley Forge
Quite disastrous that
because when Queen Isabella asked my name
I said George
I learned in grammar school
that Lincoln walked many miles for a book
which he read lying on his stomach
    before a bubbling-kettle fireplace
That's how I wanted to read a book!
So as soon as the class was over
I hurried a mile from my neighborhood library
    to another library
Of course they wouldn't issue me a card
"Use the library in your own neighborhood"

So I stole my book
and late that night
under my blanket with a little flashlight
I read
And I do not exaggerate when I say
I fully felt the joy that was Lincoln's

It was the fourth grade when the teacher
took us to Trinity Church to see
Alexander Hamilton's grave—
Carmine wanted to laugh
The way he laughed made me laugh
And the way we laughed made the whole class laugh
He did that at the Planetarium
and because of it the teacher denied us the stars
When I was young I was able to be serious if I wanted
I did not laugh
He made funny faces
        scratched himself in dirty places
He did his utmost to deny me Hamilton
With all my might I listened to what the teacher
had to say about a man whose life I hold in high esteem
I never cared much about Patrick Henry
and Paul Revere too
Nor was there anything about the redcoats I liked
They were the enemy
no different from the Germans and the Japs
        I was a year later taught to hate
Yet one redcoat there was
        made me see the majesty of the English
It was the death of General Wolfe
the biggest picture in the school
The battle was in full force
war at its loveliest
and he lay there
        dying in the arms of soldiers

I'd a D conduct in that school
Never the tack on the teacher's chair
but oh, I was bad when I was bad

THREE AMERICAN VICES

Lin Yutang

To the Chinese, therefore, with the fine philosophy that "Nothing matters to a man who says nothing matters," Americans offer a strange contrast. Is life really worth all the bother, to the extent of making our soul a slave to the body? The high spirituality of the philosophy of loafing forbids it. The most characteristic advertisement I ever saw was one by an engineering firm with the big words: "Nearly Right Is Not Enough." The desire for one hundred per cent efficiency seems almost obscene. The trouble with Americans is that when a thing is nearly right, they want to make it still better, while for a Chinese, nearly right is good enough.

The three great American vices seem to be efficiency, punctuality and the desire for achievement and success. They are the things that make the Americans so unhappy and so nervous. They steal from them their inalienable right of loafing and cheat them of many a good, idle and beautiful afternoon. One must start out with a belief that there are no catastrophes in this world, and that besides the noble art of getting things done, there is a nobler art of leaving things undone. On the whole, if one answers letters promptly, the result is about as good or as bad as if he had never answered them at all. After all, nothing happens, and while one may have missed a few good appointments, one may have also avoided a few unpleasant ones. Most of the letters are not worth answering, if you keep them in your drawer for three months; reading them three months afterwards, one might realize how utterly futile and what a waste of time it would have been to answer them all. Writing letters really can become a vice. It turns our writers into fine promotion salesmen and our college professors into good efficient business executives. In this sense, I can under-stand Thoreau's contempt for the American who always goes to the post office.

Our quarrel is not that efficiency gets things done and very well done, too. I always rely on American water-taps, rather than on those made in China, because American water-taps do not leak. That is a consolation. Against the old conten-tion, however, that we must all be useful, be efficient, become officials and have power, the old reply is that there are always enough fools left in the world who are willing to be useful, be busy and enjoy power, and so somehow the business of life can and will be carried on. The only point is who are the wise, the loafers or the hustlers? Our quarrel with efficiency is not that it gets things done, but that it is a thief of time when it leaves us no leisure to enjoy ourselves and that it frays our nerves in trying to get things done perfectly. An American editor worries his hair gray to see that no typographical mistakes appear on the pages of his magazine. The Chinese editor is wiser than that. He wants to leave his readers the supreme satisfaction of discovering a few typographical mistakes for themselves. More than that, a Chinese magazine can begin printing serial fiction and forget about it halfway. In America it might bring the roof down on the editors, but in China *it doesn't matter, simply because it doesn't matter*. American engineers in building bridges calculate so finely and exactly as to make the two ends come together within one-tenth of an inch. But when two Chinese begin to dig a tunnel from both sides of a mountain, both come out on the other side. The Chinese's firm conviction is that it doesn't matter so long as a tunnel is dug through, and if we have two instead of one, why, we have a double track to boot. Provided you are not in a hurry, two tunnels are as good as one, dug somehow, finished somehow and if the train can get through somehow. And the Chinese are extremely punctual, provided you give them plenty of time to do a thing. They always finish a thing on schedule, provided the schedule is long enough.

The tempo of modern industrial life forbids this kind of glorious and magnificent idling. But worse than that, it im-poses upon us a different conception of time as measured by the clock, and eventually turns the human being into a clock himself. This sort of thing is bound to come to China, as is evi-dent, for instance in a factory of twenty thousand workers.

The luxurious prospect of twenty thousand workers coming in at their own sweet pleasure at all hours is, of course, somewhat terrifying. Nevertheless, this is what makes life so hard and hectic. A man who has to be punctually at a certain place at five o'clock has the whole afternoon from one to five ruined for him already. Every American adult is arranging his time on the pattern of the schoolboy—three o'clock for this, five o'clock for that, six-thirty for change of dress; six-fifty for entering the taxi and seven o'clock for emerging into a hotel room. It just makes life not worth living.

And Americans have now come to such a sad state that they are booked up not only for the following day, or the following week, but even for the following month. An appointment three weeks ahead of time is a thing unknown in China. And when a Chinese receives an invitation card, happily he never has to say whether he is going to be present or not. He can put down on the invitation list "coming" if he accepts, or "thanks" if he declines, but in the majority of cases the invited party merely writes the word "know," which is a statement of fact that he knows of the invitation and not a statement of intention. An American or a European leaving Shanghai can tell me that he is going to attend a committee meeting in Paris on April 19, 1938, at three o'clock and that he will be arriving in Vienna on May 21st by the seven o'clock train. If an afternoon is to be condemned and executed, must we announce its execution so early? Cannot a fellow travel and be lord of himself, arriving when he likes and taking departure when he likes?

But above all, the American's inability to loaf comes directly from his desire for doing things and in his placing action above being. We should demand that there be character in our lives as we demand there be character in all great art worthy of the name. Unfortunately, character is not a thing which can be manufactured overnight. Like the quality of mellowness in wine, it is acquired by standing still and by the passage of time. The desire of American old men and women for action, trying in this way to gain their self-respect and the respect of the younger generation, is what makes them look so ridiculous to an Oriental. Too much action in an old man is like a broadcast of jazz music from a megaphone on top of an old cathedral. Is it not sufficient that the old people *are* something? Is it necessary that they must be forever *doing* something? The loss of the capacity for loafing is bad enough in men of middle age, but the same loss in old age is a crime committed against human nature.

Character is always associated with something old and takes time to grow, like the beautiful facial lines of a man in middle age, lines that are the steady imprint of the man's evolving character. It is somewhat difficult to see character in a type of life where every man is throwing away his last year's car and trading it in for the new model. As are the things we make, so are we ourselves. In 1937 every man and woman look 1937, and in 1938 every man and woman will look 1938. We love old cathedrals, old furniture, old silver, old dictionaries and old prints, but we have entirely forgotten about the beauty of old men. I think an appreciation of that kind of beauty is essential to our life, for beauty, it seems to me, is what is old and mellow and well-smoked.

Sometimes a prophetic vision comes to me, a beautiful vision of a millennium when Manhattan will go slow, and when the American "go-getter" will become an Oriental loafer. American gentlemen will float in skirts and slippers and amble on the sidewalks of Broadway with their hands in their pockets, if not with both hands stuck in their sleeves in the Chinese fashion. Policemen will exchange a word of greeting with the slow-devil at the crossings, and the drivers themselves will stop and accost each other and inquire after their grandmothers' health in the midst of traffic. Some one will be brushing his teeth outside his shopfront, talking the while placidly with his neighbors, and once in a while, an absent-minded scholar will sail by with a limp volume rolled up and tucked away in his sleeve. Lunch counters will be abolished, and people will be lolling and lounging in soft, low armchairs in an Automat, while others will have learned the art of killing a whole afternoon in some cafe. A glass of orange juice will last half an hour, and people will learn to sip wine by slow mouthfuls, punctuated by delightful, chatty remarks, instead of swallowing it at a gulp. Registration in a hospital will be abolished, "emergency wards" will be unknown, and patients will exchange their philosophy with their doctors. Fire engines will proceed at a snail's pace, their staff stopping on the way to gaze at and dispute over the number of passing wild geese in the sky. It is too bad that there is no hope of this kind of a millennium on Manhattan ever being realized. There might be so many more perfect idle afternoons.

RELIGION

BELIEF AND DISBELIEF

*Religions are obsolete when reforms do
not proceed from them.*

Emerson

In coming to America, immigrants sacrificed many of the
folkways and customs that had given them emotional security. The one aspect of their former lives which they
carried with them and which provided a basis for self-identity in the New World was their religious belief.

The church which represented the largest number of
immigrants was the Roman Catholic. In the nineteenth century, Catholics emigrated from Ireland, Germany, and
Italy, and from smaller nations like Poland, Lithuania,
Hungary, and Syria. By the 1890s, the Irish tended to dominate American Catholicism as the largest group of Catholics; their control of the faith continued for most of the
twentieth century. Catholics could not continue their religious life precisely as in the old countries, and differences
between minority groups led to many arguments within the
Church. However, for the average disoriented Catholic immigrant, the discipline and order of the Church provided
a source of strength.

Among Jews, two waves of immigrants, the Germans
in the mid-nineteenth century and the East-Europeans in
the 1890s and subsequent decades, were significant. These
two groups inevitably clashed, for the Germans were gen-

erally less religious than the East-Europeans and felt threatened by the large numbers of poverty-stricken people who came to these shores at the turn of the twentieth century. Most of the Jewish writers represented in this book— Alfred Kazin, Karl Shapiro, Bernard Malamud, and others —are either the children or the grandchildren of East-Europeans. Religion was often of great significance to their families, but they found themselves struggling with the relevance of Judaism in their lives, an attitude suggested by Arthur Cohen's "Why I Choose to be a Jew" and Howard Nemerov's "Debate With the Rabbi."

Writers of other ethnic groups also questioned the religious assumptions of their ancestors. The families of Richard Wright and James Baldwin, for example, were deeply religious, and in this sense they were representative of many Blacks for whom religion was a solace and an escape from the burdens of prejudice. However, both Wright and Baldwin rejected the Church, even though religion clearly influenced their work from an aesthetic point of view.

The stories of John Fante and Hisaye Yamamoto further suggest the conflicts that arise when young people seek to make their inherited religious attitudes pertinent to a new world. In this sense the authors' attitudes towards religion gives us still another perspective on their relationship to America itself.

BLACK BOY

Richard Wright

Granny was an ardent member of the Seventh-Day Adventist Church and I was compelled to make a pretense of worshiping her God, which was her exaction for my keep. The elders of her church expounded a gospel clogged with images of vast lakes of eternal fire, of seas vanishing, of valleys of dry bones, of the sun burning to ashes, of the moon turning to blood, of stars falling to the earth, of a wooden staff being transformed into a serpent, of voices speaking out of clouds, of men walking upon water, of God riding whirlwinds, of water changing into wine, of the dead rising and living, of the blind seeing, of the lame walking; a salvation that teemed with fantastic beasts having multiple heads and horns and eyes and feet; sermons of statues possessing heads of gold, shoulders of silver, legs of brass, and feet of clay; a cosmic tale that began before time and ended with the clouds of the sky rolling away at the Second Coming of Christ; chronicles that concluded with the Armageddon; dramas thronged with all the billions of human beings who had ever lived or died as God judged the quick and the dead . . .

While listening to the vivid language of the sermons I was pulled toward emotional belief, but as soon as I went out of the church and saw the bright sunshine and felt the throbbing life of the people in the streets I knew that none of it was true and that nothing would happen.

Once again I knew hunger, biting hunger, hunger that made my body aimlessly restless, hunger that kept me on edge, that made my temper flare, hunger that made hate leap out of my heart like the dart of a serpent's tongue, hunger that created in me odd cravings. No food that I could dream of seemed half so utterly delicious as vanilla wafers. Every time I had a nickel I would run to the corner grocery store and buy a box of vanilla wafers and walk back home slowly, so that I could eat them all up without having to share them with anyone. Then I would sit on the front steps and dream of eating another box; the craving would finally become so acute that I would force myself to be active in order to forget. I learned a method of drinking water that made me feel full temporarily whether I had a desire for water or not; I would put my mouth under a faucet and turn the water on full force and let the stream cascade into my stomach until it was tight. Sometimes my stomach ached, but I felt full for a moment.

No pork or veal was ever eaten at Granny's, and rarely was there meat of any kind. We seldom ate fish and then only those that had scales and spines. Baking powder was never used; it was alleged to contain a chemical harmful to the body. For breakfast I ate mush and gravy made from flour and lard and for hours afterwards I would belch it up into my mouth. We were constantly taking bicarbonate of soda for indigestion. At four o'clock in the afternoon I ate a plate of greens cooked with lard. Sometimes on Sundays we bought a dime's worth of beef which usually turned out to be uneatable. Granny's favorite dish was a peanut roast which she made to resemble meat, but which tasted like something else.

My position in the household was a delicate one; I was a minor, an uninvited dependent, a blood relative who professed no salvation and whose soul stood in mortal peril. Granny intimated boldly, basing her logic on God's justice, that one sinful person in a household could bring down the wrath of God upon the entire establishment, damning both the innocent and the guilty, and on more than one occasion she interpreted my mother's long illness as the result of my faithlessness. I became skilled in ignoring these cosmic threats and developed a callousness toward all metaphysical preachments.

But Granny won an ally in her efforts to persuade me to confess her God; Aunt Addie, her youngest child, had just finished the Seventh-Day Adventist religious school in Huntsville, Alabama, and came home to argue that if the family was compassionate enough to feed me, then the least I could do in return was to follow its guidance. She proposed that, when the fall school term started, I should be enrolled in the religious school rather than a secular one. If I refused, I was placing myself not only in the position of a horrible infidel but of a hardhearted ingrate. I raised arguments and objections, but my mother sided with Granny and Aunt Addie and I had to accept.

The religious school opened and I put in a sullen attendance. Twenty pupils, ranging in age from five to nineteen and in grades from primary to high school, were crowded into one room. Aunt Addie was the only teacher and from the first day an acute, bitter antagonism sprang up between us. This was the first time she had ever taught school and she was nervous, self-conscious because a blood relative of hers—a relative who would not confess her faith and who was not a member of her church—was in her classroom. She was determined that every student should know that I was a sinner of whom she did not approve, and that I was not to be granted consideration of any kind.

The pupils were a docile lot, lacking in that keen sense of rivalry which made the boys and girls who went to public school a crowd in which a boy was tested and weighed, in which he caught a glimpse of what the world was. These boys and girls were will-less, their speech flat, their gestures vague, their personalities devoid of anger, hope, laughter, enthusiasm, passion, or despair. I was able to see them with an objectivity that was inconceivable to them. They were claimed wholly by their environment and could imagine no other, whereas I had come from another plane of living, from the swinging doors of saloons, the railroad yard, the round-houses, the street gangs, the river levees, an orphan home; had shifted from town to town and home to home; had mingled with grownups more than perhaps was good for me. I had to curb my habit of cursing, but not before I had shocked more than half of them and had embarrassed Aunt Addie to helplessness.

As the first week of school drew to a close, the conflict that smoldered between Aunt Addie and me flared openly. One afternoon she rose from her desk and walked down the aisle and stopped beside me.

"You know better than that," she said, tapping a ruler across my knuckles.

"Better than what?" I asked, amazed, nursing my hand.

"Just look at that floor," she said.

I looked and saw that there were many tiny bits of walnut meat scattered about; some of them had been smeared into grease spots on the clean, white pine boards. At once I knew that the boy in front of me had been eating them; my walnuts were in my pocket, uncracked.

"I don't know anything about that," I said.

"You know better than to eat in the classroom," she said.

"I haven't been eating," I said.

"Don't lie! This is not only a school, but God's holy ground," she said with angry indignation.

"Aunt Addie, my walnuts are here in my pocket . . ."

"I'm Miss Wilson!" she shouted.

I stared at her, speechless, at last comprehending what was really bothering her. She had warned me to call her Miss Wilson in the classroom, and for the most part I had done so. She was afraid that if I called her Aunt Addie I would undermine the morale of the students. Each pupil knew that she was my aunt and many of them had known her longer than I had.

"I'm sorry," I said, and turned from her and opened a book.

"Richard, get up!"

I did not move. The room was tense. My fingers gripped the book and I knew that every pupil in the room was watching. I had not eaten the nuts; I was sorry that I had called her Aunt Addie; but I did not want to be singled out for gratuitous punishment. And, too, I was expecting the boy who sat in front of me to devise some lie to save me, since it was really he who was guilty.

"I asked you to get up!" she shouted.

I still sat, not taking my eyes off my book. Suddenly she caught me by the back of my collar and yanked me from the seat. I stumbled across the room.

"I spoke to you!" she shouted hysterically.

I straightened and looked at her; there was hate in my eyes.

"Don't you look at me that way, boy!"

"I didn't put those walnuts on the floor!"

"Then who did?"

My street gang code was making it hard for me. I had never informed upon a boy in the public school, and I was waiting for the boy in front of me to come to my aid, lying, making up excuses, anything. In the past I had taken punishment that was not mine to protect the solidarity of the gang, and I had seen other boys do the same. But the religious boy, God helping him, did not speak.

"I don't know who did it," I said finally.

"Go to the front of the room," Aunt Addie said.

I walked slowly to her desk, expecting to be lectured; but my heart quickened when I saw her go to the corner and select a long, green, limber switch and come toward me. I lost control of my temper.

"I haven't done anything!" I yelled.

She struck me and I dodged.

"Stand still, boy!" she blazed, her face livid with fury, her body trembling.

I stood still, feeling more defeated by the righteous boy behind me than by Aunt Addie.

"Hold out your hand!"

I held out my hand, vowing that never again would this happen to me, no matter what the price. She stung my palm until it was red, then lashed me across my bare legs until welts rose. I clamped my teeth to keep from uttering a single whimper. When she finished I continued to hold out my hand, indicating to her that her blows could never really reach me, my eyes fixed and unblinking upon her face.

"Put down your hand and go to your seat," she said.

I dropped my hand and turned on my heels, my palm and legs on fire, my body taut. I walked in a fog of anger toward my desk.

"And I'm not through with you!" she called after me.

She had said one word too much; before I knew it, I had whirled and was staring at her with an open mouth and blazing eyes.

"Through with me?" I repeated. "But what have I done to you?"

"Sit down and shut up!" Aunt Addie bellowed.

I sat. I was sure of one thing: I would not be beaten by her again. I had often been painfully beaten, but almost always I had felt that the beatings were somehow right and sensible, that I was in the wrong. Now, for the first time, I felt the equal of an adult; I knew that I had been beaten for a reason that was not right. I sensed some emotional problem in Aunt Addie other than her concern about my eating in school. Did my presence make her feel so insecure that she felt she had to punish me in front of the pupils to impress them? All afternoon I brooded, wondering how I could quit the school.

The moment Aunt Addie came into the house—I reached home before she did—she called me into the kitchen. When

I entered, I saw that she was holding another switch. My muscles tightened.

"You're not going to beat me again!" I told her.

"I'm going to teach you some manners!" she said.

I stood fighting, fighting as I had never fought in my life, fighting with myself. Perhaps my uneasy childhood, perhaps my shifting from town to town, perhaps the violence I had already seen and felt took hold of me, and I was trying to stifle the impulse to go to the drawer of the kitchen table and get a knife and defend myself. But this woman who stood before me was my aunt, my mother's sister, Granny's daughter; in her veins my own blood flowed; in many of her actions I could see some elusive part of my own self, and in her speech I could catch echoes of my own speech. I did not want to be violent with her, and yet I did not want to be beaten for a wrong I had not committed.

"You're just mad at me for something!" I said.

"Don't tell me I'm mad!"

"You're too mad to believe anything I say."

"Don't speak to me like that!"

"Then how can I talk to you? You beat me for throwing walnuts on the floor! But I didn't do it!"

"Then who did?"

Since I was alone now with her, and desperate, I cast my loyalties aside and told her the name of the guilty boy, feeling that he merited no consideration.

"Why didn't you tell me before?" she asked.

"I don't want to tell tales on other people."

"So you lied, hunh?"

I could not talk; I could not explain how much I valued my code of solidarity.

"Hold out your hand!"

"You're not going to beat me! I didn't do it!"

"I'm going to beat you for lying!"

"Don't, don't hit me! If you hit me I'll fight you!"

For a moment she hesitated, then she struck at me with the switch and I dodged and stumbled into a corner. She was upon me, lashing me across the face. I leaped, screaming, and ran past her and jerked open the kitchen drawer; it spilled to the floor with a thunderous sound. I grabbed up a knife and held it ready for her.

"Now, I told you to stop!" I screamed.

"You put down that knife!"

"Leave me alone or I'll cut you!"

She stood debating. Then she made up her mind and came at me. I lunged at her with the knife and she grasped my hand and tried to twist the knife loose. I threw my right leg about her legs and gave her a shove, tripping her; we crashed to the floor. She was stronger than I and I felt my strength ebbing; she was still fighting for my knife and I saw a look on her face that made me feel she was going to use it on me if she got possession of it. I bit her hand and we rolled, kicking, scratching, hitting, fighting as though we were strangers, deadly enemies, fighting for our lives.

"Leave me alone!" I screamed at the top of my voice.

"Give me that knife, you boy!"

"I'll kill you! I'll kill you if you don't leave me alone!"

Granny came running; she stood thunderstruck.

"Addie, what are you doing?"

"He's got a knife!" she gasped. "Make 'im put it down!"

"Richard, put down that knife!" Granny shouted.

My mother came limping to the door.

"Richard, stop it!" she shouted.

"I won't! I'm not going to let her beat me!"

"Addie, leave the boy alone," my mother said.

Aunt Addie rose slowly, her eyes on the knife, then she turned and walked out of the kitchen, kicking the door wide open before her as she went.

"Richard, give me that knife," my mother said.

"But, mamma, she'll beat me, beat me for nothing," I said. "I'm not going to let her beat me; I don't care what happens!"

"Richard, you are bad, bad," Granny said, weeping.

I tried to explain what had happened, but neither of them would listen. Granny came toward me to take the knife, but I dodged her and ran into the back yard. I sat alone on the back steps, trembling, emotionally spent, crying to myself. Grandpa came down; Aunt Addie had told him what had happened.

"Gimme that knife, mister," he said.

"I've already put it back," I lied, hugging my arm to my side to conceal the knife.

"What's come over you?" he asked.

"I don't want her to beat me," I said.

"You're a child, a boy!" he thundered.

"But I don't want to be beaten!"

"What did you do?"

"Nothing."

"You can lie as fast as a dog can trot," Grandpa said. "And if it wasn't for my rheumatism, I'd take down your pants and tan your backside good and proper. The very idea of a little snot like you threatening somebody with a knife!"

"I'm not going to let her beat me," I said again.

"You're bad," he said. "You better watch your step, young man, or you'll end up on the gallows."

I had long ceased to fear Grandpa; he was a sick old man and he knew nothing of what was happening in the house. Now and then the womenfolk called on him to throw fear into someone, but I knew that he was feeble and was not frightened of him. Wrapped in the misty memories of his young manhood, he sat his days out in his room where his Civil War rifle stood loaded in a corner where his blue uniform of the Union Army lay neatly folded.

Aunt Addie took her defeat hard, holding me in a cold and silent disdain. I was conscious that she had descended to my own emotional level in her effort to rule me, and my respect for her sank. Until she married, years later, we rarely spoke to each other, though we ate at the same table and slept under the same roof, though I was but a skinny, half-frightened boy and she was the secretary of the church and the church's day-school teacher. God blessed our home with the love that binds . . .

I continued at the church school, despite Aunt Addie's never calling upon me to recite or go to the blackboard. Consequently I stopped studying. I spent my time playing with the boys and found that the only games they knew were brutal ones. Baseball, marbles, boxing, running were tabooed recreations, the Devil's work; instead they played a wildcat game called popping-the-whip, a seemingly innocent diversion whose excitement came only in spurts, but spurts that could hurl one to the edge of death itself. Whenever we were discovered standing idle on the school grounds, Aunt Addie would suggest that we pop-the-whip. It would have been safer for our bodies and saner for our souls had she urged us to shoot craps.

One day at noon Aunt Addie ordered us to pop-the-whip. I had never played the game before and I fell in with good faith. We formed a long line, each boy taking hold of another boy's hand until we were stretched out like a long string of human beads. Although I did not know it, I was on the tip end of the human whip. The leading boy, the handle of the whip, started off at a trot, weaving to the left and to the right, increasing speed until the whip of flesh was curving at breakneck gallop. I clutched the hand of the boy next to me with all the strength I had, sensing that if I did not hold on I would be tossed off. The whip grew taut as human flesh and bone could bear and I felt that my arm was being torn from its socket. Suddenly my breath left me. I was swung in a small, sharp arc. The whip was now being popped and I could hold on no more; the momentum of the whip flung me off my feet into the air, like a bit of leather being flicked off a horsewhip, and I hurtled head-long through space and landed in a ditch. I rolled over, stunned, head bruised and bleeding. Aunt Addie was laughing, the first and only time I ever saw her laugh on God's holy ground.

In the home Granny maintained a hard religious regime. There were prayers at sunup and sundown, at the breakfast table and dinner table, followed by a Bible verse from each member of the family. And it was presumed that I prayed before I got into bed at night. I shirked as many of the weekday church services as possible, giving as my excuse that I had to study; of course, nobody believed me, but my lies were accepted because nobody wanted to risk a row. The daily prayers were a torment and my knees became sore from kneeling so long and often. Finally I devised a method of kneeling that was not really kneeling; I learned, through arduous repetition, how to balance myself on the toes of my shoes and rest my head against a wall in some convenient corner. Nobody, except God, was any the wiser, and I did not think that He cared.

Granny made it imperative, however, that I attend certain all-night ritualistic prayer meetings. She was the oldest member of her church and it would have been unseemly if the only grandchild in her home could not be brought to these important services; she felt that if I were completely remiss in religious conformity it would cast doubt upon the staunchness of her faith, her capacity to convince and persuade, or merely upon her abiilty to apply the rod to my backside.

Granny would prepare a lunch for the all-night praying session, and the three of us—Granny, Aunt Addie, and I—would be off, leaving my mother and Grandpa at home. During the passionate prayers and the chanted hyms I would sit squirming on a bench, longing to grow up so I could run away, listening indifferently to the theme of cosmic annihilation, loving the hymns for their sensual caress, but at last casting furtive glances at Granny and wondering when it would be safe for me to stretch out on the bench and go to sleep. At ten or eleven I would munch a sandwich and Granny would nod her permission for me to take a nap. I would awaken at intervals to hear snatches of hymns or prayers that would lull me to sleep again. Finally Granny would shake me and I would open my eyes and I see the sun streaming through stained-glass windows.

Many of the religious symbols appealed to my sensibilities and I responded to the dramatic vision of life held by the church, feeling that to live day by day with death as one's sole thought was to be so compassionately sensitive toward all life as to view all men as slowly dying, and the trembling sense of fate that welled up sweet and melancholy, from the hymns blended with the sense of fate that I had already caught from life. But full emotional and intellectual belief never came. Perhaps if I had caught my first sense of life from the church I would have been moved to complete acceptance, but the hymns and sermons of God came into my heart only long after my personality had been shaped and formed by uncharted conditions of life. I felt that I had in me a sense of living as deep as that which the church was trying to give me, and in the end I remained basically unaffected.

My body grew, even on mush and lard gravy, a miracle which the church certainly should have claimed credit for. I survived my twelfth year on a diet that would have stunted an average sized dog, and my glands began to diffuse through my blood, like sap rising upward in trees in spring, those strange chemicals that made me look curiously at girls and women. The elder's wife sang in the choir and I fell in love with her as only a twelve-year-old can worship a distant and unattainable woman. During the services I would stare at her, wondering what it was like to be married to her, pondering over how passionate she was. I felt no qualms about my first lust for the flesh being born on holy ground; the contrast between budding carnal desires and the aching loneliness of the hymns never evoked any sense of guilt in me.

It was possible that the sweetly sonorous hymns stimulated me sexually, and it might have been that my fleshy fantasies, in turn, having as their foundation my already inflated sensibility, made me love the masochistic prayers. It was highly likely that the serpent of sin that nosed about the chambers of my heart was lashed to hunger by hymns as well as dreams, each reciprocally feeding the other. The church's spiritual life must have been polluted by my base yearnings, by the leaping hunger of my blood for the flesh, because I would gaze at the elder's wife for hours, attempting to draw here eyes to mine, trying to hypnotize her, seeking to communicate with her with my thoughts. If my desires had been converted into a concrete religious symbol, the symbol would have looked something like this: a black imp with two horns; a long, curving, forked tail; cloven hoofs, a scaly, naked body; wet, sticky fingers; moist, sensual lips; and lascivious eyes feasting upon the face of the elder's wife . . .

A religious revival was announced and Granny felt that it was her last chance to bring me to God before I entered the precincts of sin at the public school, for I had already given loud and final notice that I would no longer attend the church school. There was a discernible lessening in Aunt Addie's hostility; perhaps she had come to the conclusion that my lost soul was more valuable than petty pride. Even my mother's attitude was: "Richard, you ought to know God through *some* church."

The entire family became kind and forgiving, but I knew the motives that prompted their change and it drove me an even greater emotional distance from them. Some of my classmates—who had, on the advice of their parents, avoided me— now came to visit and I could tell in a split second that they had been instructed in what to say. One boy, who lived across the street, called on me one afternoon and his self-consciousness betrayed him; he spoke so naïvely and clumsily that I could see the bare bones of his holy plot and hear the creaking of the machinery of Granny's maneuvering.

"Richard, do you know we are all worried about you?" he asked. "Worried about me? Who's worried about me?" I asked in feigned surprise.

"All of us," he said, his eyes avoiding mine.

"Why?" I asked.

"You're not saved," he said sadly.

"I'm all right," I said, laughing.

"Don't laugh, Richard. It's serious," he said.

"But I tell you that I'm all right."

"Say, Richard, I'd like to be a good friend of yours."

"I thought we were friends already," I said.

"I mean true brothers in Christ," he said.

"We know each other," I said in a soft voice tinged with irony.

"But not in Christ," he said.

"But don't you want to save your soul?"

"I simply can't feel religion," I told him in lieu of telling him that I did not think I had the kind of soul he thought I had.

"Have you really tried to feel God?" he asked.

"No. But I know I can't feel anything like that."

"You simply can't let the question rest there, Richard."

"Why should I let it rest?"

"Don't mock God," he said.

"I'll never feel God, I tell you. It's no use."

"Would you let the fate of your soul hang upon pride and vanity?"

"I don't think I have any pride in matters like this."

"Richard, think of Christ's dying for you, shedding His blood, His precious blood on the cross."

"Other people have shed blood," I ventured.

"But it's not the same. You don't understand."

"I don't think I ever will."

"Oh, Richard, brother, you are lost in the darkness of the world. You must let the church help you."

"I tell you, I'm all right."

"Come into the house and let me pray for you."

"I don't want to hurt your feelings . . ."

"You can't. I'm talking for God."

"I don't want to hurt God's feelings either," I said, the words slipping irreverently from my lips before I was aware of their meaning.

He was shocked. He wiped tears from his eyes. I was sorry.

"Don't say that. God may never forgive you," he whispered.

It would have been impossible for me to have told him how I felt about religion. I had not settled in my mind whether I believed in God or not; His existence or nonexistence never worried me. I reasoned that if there did exist an all-wise, all-powerful God who knew the beginning and the end, who meted out justice to all, who controlled the destiny of man, this God would surely know that I doubted His existence and He would laugh at my foolish denial of Him. And if there was no God at all, then why all the commotion? I could not imagine God pausing in His guidance of unimaginably vast worlds to bother with me.

Embedded in me was a notion of the suffering in life, but none of it seemed like the consequences of original sin to me; I simply could not feel weak and lost in a cosmic manner. Before I had been made to go to church, I had given God's existence a sort of tacit assent, but after having seen His creatures serve Him at first hand, I had had my doubts. My faith, such as it was, was welded to the common realities of life, anchored in the sensations of my body and in what my mind could grasp, and nothing could ever shake this faith, and surely not my fear of an invisible power.

"I'm not afraid of things like that," I told the boy.

"Aren't you afraid of God?" he asked.

"No. Why should I be? I've done nothing to Him."

"He's a jealous God," he warned me.

"I hope that He's a kind God," I told him.

"If you are kind to Him, He is a kind God," the boy said. "But God will not look at you if you don't look at Him."

During our talk I made a hypothetical statement that summed up my attitude toward God and the suffering in the world, a statement that stemmed from my knowledge of life as I had lived, seen, felt, and suffered it in terms of dread, fear, hunger, terror, and loneliness.

"If laying down my life could stop the suffering in the world, I'd do it. But I don't believe anything can stop it," I told him.

He heard me but he did not speak. I wanted to say more to him, but I knew that it would have been useless. Though older than I, he had neither known nor felt anything of life for himself; he had been carefully reared by his mother and father and he had always been told what to feel.

"Don't be angry," I told him.

Frightened and baffled, he left me. I felt sorry for him.

Immediately following the boy's visit, Granny began her phase of the campaign. The boy had no doubt conveyed to her my words of blasphemy, for she talked with me for hours, warning me that I would burn forever in the lake of fire. As the day of the revival grew near, the pressure upon me intensified. I would go into the dining room upon some petty errand and find Granny kneeling, her head resting on a chair, uttering my name in a tensely whispered prayer. God was suddenly everywhere in the home, even in Aunt Addie's scowling and brooding face. It began to weigh upon me. I longed for the time when I could leave. They begged me so continuously to come to God that it was impossible for me to ignore them without wounding them. Desperately I tried to think of some way to say no without making them hate me. I was determined to leave home before I would surrender.

Then I blundered and wounded Granny's soul. It was not my intention to hurt or humiliate her; the irony of it was that the plan I conceived had as its purpose the salving of Granny's frustrated feelings toward me. Instead, it brought her the greatest shame and humiliation of her entire religious life.

One evening during a sermon I heard the elder—I took my eyes off his wife long enough to listen, even though she slumbered in my senses all the while—describe how Jacob had seen an angel. Immediately I felt that I had found a way to tell Granny that I needed proof before I could believe, that I could not commit myself to something I could not feel or see. I would tell her that if I were to see an angel I would accept that as infallible evidence that there was a God and would serve Him unhesitatingly; she would surely understand an attitude of that sort. What gave me courage to voice this argument was the conviction that I would never see an angel; if I had ever seen one, I had enough common sense to have gone to a doctor at once. With my bright idea bubbling in my mind, wishing to allay Granny's fears for my soul, wanting to make her know that my heart was not all black and wrong, that I was actually giving serious thought to her passionate pleadings, I leaned to her and whispered:

"You see, granny, if I ever saw an angel like Jacob did, then I'd believe."

Granny stiffened and stared at me in amazement; then a glad smile lit up her old wrinkled white face and she nodded and gently patted my hand. That ought to hold her for a while, I thought. During the sermon Granny looked at me several times and smiled. Yes, she knows now that I'm not dismissing her pleas from my mind . . . Feeling that my plan was working, I resumed my worship of the elder's wife with a cleansed conscience, wondering what it would be like to kiss her, longing to feel some of the sensuous emotions of which my reading had made me conscious. The service ended and Granny rushed to the front of the church and began talking excitedly to the elder;

I saw the elder looking at me in surprise. *Oh, goddamn, she's telling him!* I thought with anger. But I had not guessed one-thousandth of it.

The elder hurried toward me. Automatically I rose. He extended his hand and I shook it.

"Your grandmother told me," he said in awed tones.

I was speechless with anger.

"I didn't want her to tell you that," I said.

"She says that you have seen an angel." The words literally poured out of his mouth.

I was so overwhelmed that I gritted my teeth. Finally I could speak and I grabbed his arm.

"No . . . N-nooo, sir! No, sir!" I stammered. "I didn't say that. She misunderstood me."

The last thing on earth I wanted was a mess like this. The elder blinked his eyes in bewilderment.

"What did you tell her?" he asked.

"I told her that if I ever saw an angel, then I would believe," I said, feeling foolish, ashamed, hating and pitying my believing granny. The elder's face became bleak and stricken. He was stunned with disappointment.

"You . . . you didn't see an angel?" he asked.

"No, sir!" I said emphatically, shaking my head vigorously so that there could be no possible further misunderstanding.

"I see," he breathed in a sigh.

His eyes looked longingly into a corner of the church.

"With God, you know, anything is possible," he hinted hopefully.

"But I didn't see *anything*," I said. "I'm sorry about this."

"If you pray, then God will come to you," he said.

The church grew suddenly hot. I wanted to bolt out of it and never see it again. But the elder took hold of my arm and would not let me move.

"Elder, this is all a mistake. I didn't want anything like this to happen," I said.

"Listen, I'm older than you are, Richard," he said. "I think that you have in your heart the gift of God." I must have looked dubious, for he said: "Really, I do."

"Elder, please don't say anything to anybody about this," I begged.

Again, his face lit with vague hope.

"Perhaps you don't want to tell because you are bashful?"

he suggested. "Look, this is serious. If you saw an angel, then tell me." I could not deny it verbally any more; I could only shake my head at him. In the face of his hope, words seemed useless.

"Promise me you'll pray. If you pray, then God will answer," he said.

I turned my head away, ashamed for him, feeling that I had unwittingly committed an obscene act in rousing his hopes so wildly high, feeling sorry for his having such hopes. I wanted to get out of his presence. He finally let me go, whispering:

"I want to talk to you sometime."

The church members were staring at me. My fists doubled. Granny's wide and innocent smile was shining on me and I was filled with dismay. That she could make such a mistake meant that she lived in a daily atmosphere that urged her to expect something like this to happen. She had told the other members and everybody knew it, including the elder's wife! There they stood, the church members, with joyous astonishment written on their faces, whispering among themselves. Perhaps at that moment I could have mounted the pulpit and led them all; perhaps that was to be my greatest moment of triumph!

Granny rushed to me and hugged me violently, weeping tears of joy. Then I babbled, speaking with emotional reproof, censuring here for having misunderstood me; I must have spoken more loudly and harshly than was called for—the others had now gathered about me and Granny—for Granny drew away from me abruptly and went to a far corner of the church and stared at me with a cold, set face. I was crushed. I went to her and tried to tell her how it had happened.

"You shouldn't've spoken to me," she said in a breaking voice that revealed the depths of her disillusionment.

On our way home she would not utter a single word. I walked anxiously beside her, looking at her tired old white face, the wrinkles that lined her neck, the deep, waiting black eyes, and the frail body, and I knew more than she thought I knew about the meaning of religion, the hunger of the human heart for that which is not and can never be, the thirst of the human spirit to conquer and transcend the implacable limitations of human life.

Later, I convinced her that I had not wanted to hurt her and she immediately seized upon my concern for her feelings

as an opportunity to have one more try at bringing me to
God. She wept and pleaded with me to pray, really to pray, to
pray hard, to pray until tears came . . .

"Granny, don't make me promise," I begged.

"But you must, for the sake of your soul," she said.

I promised; after all, I felt that I owed her something for
inadvertently making her ridiculous before the members of her
church.

Daily I went into my room upstairs, locked the door, knelt,
and tried to pray, but everything I could think of saying seemed
silly. Once it all seemed so absurd that I laughed out loud while
on my knees. It was no use. I could not pray. I could never
pray. But I kept my failure a secret. I was convinced that if I
ever succeeded in praying, my words would bound noiselessly
against the ceiling and rain back down upon me like feathers.

My attempts at praying became a nuisance, spoiling my
days, and I regretted the promise I had given Granny. But I
stumbled on a way to pass the time in my room, a way that
made the hours fly with the speed of the wind. I took the
Bible, pencil, paper, and a rhyming dictionary and tried to
write verses for hymns. I justified this by telling myself that,
if I wrote a really good hymn, Granny might forgive me. But I
failed even in that; the Holy Ghost was simply nowhere near
me . . .

One day while killing my hour of prayer, I remembered a
series of volumes of Indian history I had read the year before.
Yes, I knew what I would do; I would write a story about the
Indians . . . But what about them? Well, an Indian girl . . . I
wrote of an Indian maiden, beautiful and reserved, who sat
alone upon the bank of a still stream, surrounded by eternal
twilight and ancient trees waiting . . . The girl was keeping
some vow which I could not describe and, not knowing how to
develop the story, I resolved that the girl had to die. She rose
slowly and walked toward the dark stream, her face stately and
cold; she entered the water and walked on until the water
reached her shoulders, her chin; then it covered her. Not a murmur or a gasp came from her, even in dying.

"And at last the darkness of the night descended and softly
kissed the surface of the watery grave and the only sound was
the lonely rustle of the ancient trees," I wrote as I penned the
final line. I was excited; I read it over and saw that there was a
yawning void in it. There was no plot, no action, nothing save

atmosphere and longing and death. But I had never in my life done anything like it; I had made something, no matter how bad it was; and it was mine . . . Now, to whom could I show it? Not my relatives; they would think I had gone crazy. I decided to read it to a young woman who lived next door. I interrupted her as she was washing dishes and, swearing her to secrecy, I read the composition aloud. When I finished she smiled at me oddly, her eyes baffled and astonished.

"What's that for?" she asked.

"Nothing," I said.

"But why did you write it?"

"I just wanted to."

"Where did you get the idea?"

I wagged my head, pulled down the corners of my mouth, stuffed my manuscript into my pocket and looked at her in a cocky manner that said: Oh, it's nothing at all. I write stuff like this all the time. It's easy, if you know how. But I merely said in an humble, quiet voice:

"Oh, I don't know. I just thought it up."

"What're you going to do with it?"

"Nothing."

God only knows what she thought. My environment contained nothing more alien than writing or the desire to express one's self in writing. But I never forgot the look of astonishment and bewilderment on the young woman's face when I had finished reading and glanced at her. Her inability to grasp what I had done or was trying to do somehow gratified me. Afterwards whenever I thought of her reaction I smiled happily for some unaccountable reason.

A RELIGIOUS CONVERSION, MORE OR LESS

Eldridge Cleaver

Folsom Prison,
September 10, 1965

Once I was a Catholic. I was baptized, made my first Communion, my Confirmation, and I wore a Cross with Jesus on it around my neck. I prayed at night, said my Rosary, went to Confession, and said all the Hail Marys and Our Fathers to which I was sentenced by the priest. Hopelessly enamored of sin myself, yet appalled by the sins of others, I longed for Judgment Day and a trial before a jury of my peers—this was my only chance to escape the flames which I could feel already licking at my feet. I was in a California Youth Authority institution at the time, having transgressed the laws of man—God did not indict me that time; if He did, it was a secret indictment, for I was never informed of any charges brought against me. The reason I became a Catholic was that the rule of the institution held that every Sunday each inmate had to attend the church of his choice. I chose the Catholic Church because all the Negroes and Mexicans went there. The whites went to the Protestant chapel. Had I been a fool enough to go to the Protestant chapel, one black face in a sea of white, and with guerrilla warfare going on between us, I might have ended up a Christian martyr—St. Eldridge the Stupe.

It all ended one day when, at a catechism class, the priest asked if anyone present understood the mystery of the Holy Trinity. I had been studying my lessons diligently and knew by heart what I'd been taught. Up shot my hand, my heart throbbing with piety (pride) for this chance to demonstrate my knowledge of the Word. To my great shock and embarrassment, the Father announced, and it sounded like a thunderclap, that I was lying, that no one, not even the Pope, understood the Godhead, and why else did I think they called it the *mystery* of the Holy Trinity? I saw in a flash, stung to the quick by the jeers of my fellow catechumens, that I had been used, that the Father had been lying in wait for the chance to drop that thunderbolt, in order to drive home the point that the Holy Trinity was not to be taken lightly.

I had intended to explain the Trinity with an analogy to 3-in1 oil, so it was probably just as well.

WHY I CHOOSE TO BE A JEW

Arthur A. Cohen

Until the present day, the Jew could not *choose* to be a Jew—history forced him to accept what his birth had already defined.

During the Middle Ages he was expected to live as a Jew. He could escape by surrendering to Islam or Christianity, but he could *not* choose to remain anonymous. In the nineteenth century, with the growth of nationalism, Christianity became the ally of patriotism. The Jews of Europe were compelled to prove that their religion did not compromise their loyalty to King, Emperor, Kaiser, or Tsar. But no matter how desperately they tried to allay suspicion by assimilation or conversion, the fact of their birth returned to plague them. Finally, in the Europe of Nazism and Communism, the Jew could not choose —on any terms—to exist at all.

In the United States today, it is at last possible to choose *not* to remain a Jew. The mass migrations of Jews from Europe have ended and the immigrant generation which was tied to the European pattern of poverty and voluntary segregation is dying off. Their children, the second generation, were as suspicious of the gentile American society in which they grew up as they were condescending toward the ghetto world of their parents. The second generation, however, made the Jewish community economically secure and fought anti-Semitism so effectively that, though still present, it is no longer severe. *Their* children —the third generation of Jews now in its twenties and thirties —are able to choose.

For this generation the old arguments no longer hold. It was once possible to appeal to history to prove that Jewish birth was inescapable, but history is no proof to those who are—as many Jews are—indifferent to its evidence. Loyalty to the Jewish people and pride in the State of Israel are no longer enough to justify the choice to be a Jew. The post-war American Jew no longer needs the securities which European Jewry found in Jewish Socialism, Jewish Nationalism, the revival of Hebrew, and the Zionist Movement. *Fear*—the fear of anti-Semitism—and *hope*—the hope for the restoration of Israel—are no longer effective reasons for holding onto Jewish identity. The fear has waned and the hope has been fulfilled.

The irresistible forces of history no longer *compel* the Jew to choose Judaism. In many cases, moreover, he is choosing to repudiate Judaism or to embrace Christianity. I do not say the numbers are alarming. That they exist at all is, however, symptomatic. It is only the exceptional—those who are searching deeply or are moved profoundly, who ever reject or embrace. The majority tend more often to undramatic indifference—to slide into the routine of maturity without asking questions for which no meaningful answers have been offered.

Given the freedom to choose I have decided to embrace Judaism. I have not done so out of loyalty to the Jewish people or the Jewish state. My choice was religious. I chose to believe in the God of Abraham, Isaac, and Jacob; to acknowledge the law of Moses as the Word of God; to accept the people of Israel as the holy instrument of divine fulfillment; to await the coming of the Messiah and the redemption of history.

Many Jews will find my beliefs unfamiliar or unacceptable—perhaps outrageous. The manner in which I arrived at them is not very interesting in itself, but I think two aspects of my experience are worth noting because they are fairly common: I come from a fundamentally unobservant Jewish home and my first religious inclination was to become a Christian.

My parents are both second-generation American Jews whose own parents were moderately religious, but, newly come to America, lacked either the education or the opportunity, patience, and time to transmit to their children their own undering of Judaism. My parents went to synagogue to observe the great Jewish holidays—Passover, the New Year, and the Day of Atonement—but worship at home, knowledge of the liturgy, familiarity with Hebrew, concern with religious thought and problems, did not occupy them. Their real concern—and they were not unique—was adjusting to American life, achieving security, and passing to their children and those less fortunate the rewards of their struggle.

It would be ungrateful to deny the accomplishments of my

parents' generation. They managed to provide their children with secular education and security. But although the flesh was nourished, the spirit was left unattended. When I had finished high school and was ready to leave for college I took with me little sense of what my religion, or any religion, involved. I knew only that in these matters I would have to fend for myself.

When an American Jew studies at an American university it is difficult for him not to be overwhelmed—as I was at the University of Chicago—by the recognition that Western culture is a Christian culture, that Western values are rooted in the Greek and Christian tradition. He may hear such phrases as "Judaeo-Christian tradition" or "the Hebraic element in Western culture," but he cannot be deluded into thinking that this is more than a casual compliment. The University of Chicago, moreover, insisted that its students study seriously the philosophic sources of Western culture, which, if not outspokenly Christian, were surely non-Jewish. I soon found myself reading the classics of Christian theology and devotion—from St. Augustine and St. Anselm through the sermons of Meister Eckhart.

It was not long before my unreligious background, a growing and intense concern with religious problems, and the ready access to compelling Christian literature all combined to produce a crisis—or at least my parents and I flattered ourselves that this normal intellectual experience was a religious crisis. The possibility of being a Christian was, however, altogether real. I was rushed, not to a psychoanalyst, but to a Rabbi—the late Milton Steinberg, one of the most gifted and profound Jewish thinkers of recent years. Leading me gently, he retracted the path backwards through Christianity to Judaism, revealing the groundwork of Jewish thought and experience which supported what I have come to regard as the scaffolding of Christian "unreason."

It was extremely important to me to return to Judaism through the medium of Christianity—to choose after having first received the impress of Western education and Christian thought. Since it would have been possible to become a Christian—to accept Christian history as my history, to accept the Christian version of Judaism as the grounds of my own repudiation of Judaism, to believe that a Messiah had redeemed *me*—I could only conclude that Judaism was not an unavoidable fate, but a destiny to be chosen freely.

My own conversion and, I suspect, the conversion of many

other Jews to Judaism, was effected, therefore, through study, reflection, and thought. What first seized my attention was not the day-to-day religious life of the Jewish community around me, but rather principles, concepts, and values. I had first to examine the pressing theological claims of a seemingly triumphant Christianity, before I could accept the ancient claims of a dispersed, tormented, and suffering Jewry.

This may sound reasonable enough to a gentile, but I must point out that it is an extremely unconventional attitude for a Jew. Historically, Judaism has often looked with disfavor upon theology. And today, despite the fact that traditional emotional ties can no longer be relied upon to bind the third generation to Jewish life, American Jewish leadership has not seen fit to encourage the examination of the theological bases of Jewish faith. In fact, the leading rabbinical seminaries teach little Jewish theology as such, give scant attention to Jewish philosophic literature, and have allowed the apologetic comparison of religious beliefs to become a moribund discipline. Even practical problems involving some theological insight— the nature of marriage, the Jewish attitude toward converts, the life of prayer—are dispatched with stratospheric platitudes, or not discussed at all.

Why this distrust of theology? I suspect that some Jewish leaders fear—perhaps not unjustifiably—that theological scrutiny of what they mean by God, Israel, and Law might reveal that they have no theology at all. Others no doubt fear—again not unjustifiably—that their unbending interpretations of Jewish Law and life might have to be revised and re-thought. Theology often produces a recognition of insufficiency, an awareness that valid doctrine is being held for the wrong reasons and that erroneous doctrine is being used to rationalize right action. But the major Jewish argument against Jewish theology is that it is a Christian pastime—that it may, by insinuation and subtle influence, Christianize Judaism. In this view, Christianity is a religion of faith, dogma, and theology and Judaism is a religion which emphasizes *observance* of God's Law, not speculation about it.

For me this argument is a vast oversimplification. Christianity is not without its own structure of discipline, requirements, and laws—the Roman sacraments and the Lutheran and Anglican liturgy, for example—and this structure does not move with the Holy Spirit as easily as St. Paul might have wished. Judaism, on the other hand, is not tied to the pure act.

It has matured through the centuries a massive speculation and mystic tradition which attempts to explain the principles upon which right action are founded. Judaism need not, therefore, regret the renewal of theology. It already has one. It is merely a question of making what is now a minor chord in Jewish tradition sound a more commanding note.

As a "convert" who thinks that theology must come first, what do I believe?

The convert, I must point out, is unavoidably both a thinker and a believer—he thinks patiently and believes suddenly. Yet belief, by itself, cannot evict the demons of doubt and despair. As a believer I can communicate my beliefs, but as a thinker I cannot guarantee that they are certain or will never change. As all things that record the encounter of God and man, beliefs are subject to the conditions of time and history, and the pitiable limitation of our capacity to understand such enormous mysteries. As I shall try to show, however, the four beliefs which I have already set down lie at the center of my faith as a Jew. They depend upon one another; they form a whole; they differ profoundly from the substance of Christian belief.

First, I chose to believe in the God of Abraham, Isaac, and Jacob. This is to affirm the reality of a God who acts in history and addresses man. Although this God may well be the same as the abstract gods formulated by philosophers, he is still more than these—he is the God who commanded Abraham to quit the land of the Chaldeans and who wrestled with Jacob throughout the night.

The philosopher and the believer must differ in their method. The philosopher begins by examining that portion of reality to which reason allows him access. The believer, however, must at some point move beyond the limits which reason has defined. He may rightly contend that much in human life—evil, suffering, guilt, and love—is terrifyingly real without ever being rationally comprehensible.

Reason may thus push a man to belief, and it is inaccurate to speak of the believer as though he had deserted or betrayed reason. Informed belief demands philosophic criticism and refinement. The believer is bound to uphold his faith in things he cannot see or verify; but he is foolish if he does not try to define what that belief is and clarify the unique ways in which it makes reality meaningful for him.

For me then to believe in the Biblical God, the God of

the Patriarchs, the smoking mountain, the burning bush, was not to surrender reason, but to go beyond it. More than accepting the literal words of the Bible, it meant believing in the Lord of History—the God who creates and unfolds history, and observes its tragic rifts and displacements—from the Tower of Babel to the Cold War; who, in his disgust, once destroyed the world with flood and later repented his anger; who, forgoing anger, gave the world counsels of revelation, commencing with the gift of Torah to Moses and continuing through the inspired writings of the ancient rabbis; and who finally—through his involvement with the work of creation—prepares it for redemption.

It may seem difficult—indeed for many years it was—to consider the Bible, which is the source of this belief, as more than the unreliable account of an obscure Semitic tribe. But gradually I came to discover in it an authentic statement of the grandeur and misery of man's daily existence—a statement which I could accept only if I believed in a God who could be addressed as "Lord, Lord."

My second belief is an acknowledgment that *the Law of Moses is the Word of God.* The Bible tells us that the Word of God broke out over the six hundred thousand Hebrews who assembled at the foot of Sinai. That Word was heard by Moses —he who had been appointed to approach and receive. The Word became human—in its humanity, it undoubtedly suffers from the limitation of our understanding—but it lost none of its divinity.

The Law is always a paradox: it is both the free Word of God and the frozen formality of human laws. But the Law of Moses was vastly different from what we usually understand law to be. It is true that in the days before the Temple was destroyed by Titus in 70 A.D. divine law was the enforceable law of the judge and the court; but later the great rabbis who interpreted it conceived of the revelation of God to Israel, not as law in its common usage, but as *Torah*—teaching.

Torah is a fundamental concept for the Jew. Narrowly conceived, it refers to the Pentateuch—the first five books of the Bible which are the pristine source of all Jewish tradition. In them are the laws of the Sabbath and the festivals; the foundations of family and communal morality; and the essentials of Jewish faith—the unity of God, the election of Israel, and the definition of its special mission. But, broadly conceived, Torah refers to *any* teaching which brings man closer to the true God, who is the God of Israel and the Lord of History.

Torah has two aspects—the actual way of law and observance (the *halachah* as it is called in Hebrew) and the theology of the rabbis which interprets that way (called the *aggadah*). By means of both, according to Jewish tradition, God proposes to lead *all* of his creation to fulfillment, to perfect its imperfections, to mend the brokenness of his creatures. The Jewish people—the guardian of the *halachah* and the *aggadah*—has been elected to be pedagogue to all the nations of the world, to become on its behalf "a kingdom of priests and a holy people."

Jews can achieve holiness—the primary objective, I believe, of their religion—neither by prayer nor meditation alone. Judaism values prayer only in conjunction with the act; it praises study only in relation to life.

God does not propose or suggest ways to achieve holiness; he commands them. According to Torah, he lays upon each Jew "the yoke of the commandments." To observe the Sabbath is as much a commandment as is the obligation to daily prayer; the grace which accompanies eating as essential as the study of sacred literature. Although tradition distinguishes between practical and intellectual commandments, it considers both to be equally the expressed will of God. The arbitrary and the reasonable—the dietary laws and the prohibition of homosexuality for example—both proceed from God.

Judaism begins with an explicit fact: the revelation of Torah. Many of its commandments may seem trivial. But it should not be expected that God will leave the trivial to man and concern himself only with the broad, general, and universal. The corruption of man takes place not only in the province of principle, but in the small and petty routine of life. The Torah is therefore exalted and picayune, universal and particular, occupied equally with principle and the details of practice. It tolerates no separation between the holy and the profane— all that is secular must become sacred, all that is profane must be kept open to the transforming power of God.

The exact degree to which Jews should fulfill all the commandments of the Law is one of the most difficult and perplexing dilemmas for modern Jews. Orthodox Jews are in principle obligated to observe all of Jewish Law, Reform Jews

have cut observance to a minimum (though there is a movement to increase it), Conservative Jews stand somewhere in
between. I will not attempt it in this space, but I believe it is
possible to show that the fundamental question is not whether
the Jew performs the required acts of observance, but whether
he is truly aware of the sacred intention of these acts. One
can, for example, recite the blessings over the food one eats
and feel nothing of the sanctity of food; on the other hand one
can silently acknowledge the holiness of eating, and fulfill
the command of God. Both are needed—the blessing and the
inner acknowledgment, but the former is surely incomplete
without the latter.

The third of my beliefs is, as I have indicated, simply an
element of God's revelation in Torah—that *the Jewish people
have been chosen as a special instrument of God.*

The Jews did not request the attentions of God. There is
significant truth—truth moreover which the rabbis of the Tal-
mud endorse—in the popular couplet: "How odd of God, to
choose the Jews." Odd, and unsolicited. The ancient rabbis disclaim particular merit. If anyone possessed merit, they repeat,
it was not the generation that fled Egypt and braved the wilderness for forty years, but the generations of the Biblical patriarchs—Abraham, Isaac, and Jacob. They had no organizer
such as Moses, nor strength of numbers, nor the miracles of
the well, manna, and quail. They made a covenant with God
on sheer trust. The generation of Sinai was *compelled* to become the people of God or perish. A God of History grows impatient with delay. The God of Israel was profoundly impatient
on Sinai.

This tradition of election should not be confused with
racial pride or an attitude of arrogant exclusion toward others.
The Jew believes neither that the truth flows in his blood nor
that the gentile cannot come to possess it. Judaism is exclusive
only in the sense that we affirm we possess important truth
which is available to all—everyone can join but only on our
terms.

The election of Israel is not a conclusion drawn from history—the survival and endurance of the Jews through twenty
centuries of destructive persecution could be no more than
blind accident. At best it could be construed as a compliment
to the resiliency and stubbornness of the Jewish people. Judaism
has insisted, however—not as a declaration after the fact, but

as a principle of its very existence—that it is both a holy nation chosen by God to be his own and a suffering nation destined to endure martyrdom for his sake. God announces not only that "Ye shall be holy unto me; for I the Lord am Holy, and have separated you from the people, that ye should be mine" (Leviticus 20:26) but that "You only have I known of all the families of the earth: therefore I will visit upon you all your iniquities" (Amos 3:2).

Israel is thus called not only to be the example to the nations, but, being the example, is tried all the more sorely for its transgressions. To be sure, this is not a doctrine for the uncourageous. No one even slightly familiar with the agonies of Jewish history could claim that the election of Israel has brought with it particular reward and security. It is, however, precisely the fact of Jewish suffering which makes its election and mission all the more pertinent to the modern world. To have believed and survived in spite of history is perhaps the only evidence which Judaism can offer to the accuracy of its conviction that it is called to be a holy community.

In the face of Christendom and the obvious success which its claims have enjoyed, it may seem foolish or presumptuous for Judaism—a small and insignificant community of believers —to assert my fourth belief: that *Jesus is not the Messiah of which the Bible speaks*, that Christianity has conceived but one more imperfect image of the end, and that *a Messiah is yet to come who will redeem history.*

But there are enduring reasons why Jews cannot accept Jesus as the Messiah. Both Christian and Jew begin with the conviction of the imperfection of man. The Christian argues, however, that creation has been so corrupted by man as to be saved only through the mediation of Jesus. The Jew considers creation imperfect but, rather than corrupt, he finds it rich with unfulfilled possibility. The role of man is to bring creation to that point at which the Messiah can come to glorify man by bringing him the praise of God—not to save him from self-destruction, as Christianity would have it. According to Jewish tradition, Moses died from the kiss of God. It would be fitting to conceive the advent of the Messiah and the Kingdom of God as the bestowal of a kiss.

This does not mean that God congratulates man for his good works but rather that he shares both in the agony of history and in its sanctification. Judaism does not imagine that every day we are getting better and better, and that finally we will reach a point where the Messiah will come. As likely as not, it seems to me, history is coming closer each day to suicide. The mission of Judaism is not to stave off disaster but to enlarge man's awareness of the Divine Presence.

Jews believe, if they are to remain Jews, that the Messiah has not come. They can accept Jesus of Nazareth as little more than a courageous witness to truths to which his own contemporaries in Pharisaic Judaism by and large subscribed. Jesus was, as Martin Buber has suggested, one in the line of "suffering servants" whom God sends forth to instruct the nations. It is to the dogmatizing work of St. Paul that one must ascribe the transformation of "prophet" into "Christ"—and it is therefore St. Paul who severs Jesus from the life of Israel. The rejection of Jesus must now stand to the end of time.

The role of Israel and Judaism, until the advent of the true Messiah, is to outlast the world and its solutions—to examine its complacencies, to deflate its securities, to put its principles to the test of prophetic judgment. This is an aristocratic and painful mission, for though Judaism may address the world and lay claim to it, it does not seek to convert it.

Judaism does not say "The world is not changed—therefore we do not believe in the Messiah." This is only partially true, for the coming of the Messiah will mean more than a reformed world in which the wolf and lamb shall share bread together and war shall cease. This social image of salvation is true as far as it goes, but it does not go far enough. The Messiah is not a handyman or a plumber—his task does not consist in "mending" a world that is temporarily faulty but is essentially perfect. The world is to be transformed—not reformed—by the Messiah.

This transformation will come to pass, Judaism believes, only when the world wishes it so deeply that it cannot abide itself more a single moment. At that moment the Messiah may come. This moment of expectancy has not yet arrived. The rabbis have taught us that I, and all of the House of Israel, prevent him from coming. Of this there is no question, but we cannot avoid concluding that he has not come.

For the Jew who comfortably repeats the rituals of his religion without confronting the principles of faith which they express, and for the Jew who was not aware that Judaism had any principles of faith at all, this personal statement may seem shocking. But I do not think my position or my background are by any means unique. If, as I have argued, the present generation of American Jews is indeed the first generation of Jews in centuries who are free to choose to believe as Jews, then, in my terms at least, my argument is important. Now as never before it will be possible for the Jewish people and the State of Israel to survive, but for Jewish *religion* to perish. For me, and for other believing Jews, it is crucial for mankind that Judaism survive. The mission of Judaism is not completed nor the task of the Jewish people fulfilled. If the Jewish people is an instrument sharpened by God for his own purposes, it must go on serving that purpose, sustaining its burden, and keeping that trust which alone can bring all men to redemption.

THE SYNAGOGUE

Karl Shapiro

The synagogue dispirits the deep street,
Shadows the face of the pedestrian,
It is the adumbration of the Wall,
The stone survival that laments itself,
Our old entelechy of stubborn God,
Our calendar that marks a separate race.

The swift cathedral palpitates the blood,
The soul moves upward like a wing to meet
The pinnacles of saints. There flocks of thanks
In nooks of holy tracery arrive
And rested take their message in mid-air
Sphere after sphere into the papal heaven.

The altar of the Hebrews is a house,
No relic but a place, Sinai itself,
Not holy ground but factual holiness
Wherein the living god is resident.
Our scrolls are volumes of the thundered law
Sabbath by sabbath wound by hand to read.

He knows Al-Eloah to whom the Arab
Barefooted falls on sands, on table roofs,
In latticed alleys underneath the egg
On wide mosaics, when the crier shrills.
O profitable curse, most sacred rug,
Your book is blindness and your sword is rust.

And Judenhetze is the course of time;

We were rebellious, all but Abraham,
And skulked like Jonah, angry at the gourd.
Our days are captives in the minds of kings,
We stand in tens disjointed on the world
Grieving the ribbon of a coast we hated.

Some choose the ethics of belief beyond
Even particular election. Some
In bland memorial churches modify
The architecture of the state, and heaven
Disfranchised watches, caput mortuum,
The human substance eating, voting, smiling.

The Jew has no bedecked magnificat
But sits in stricken ashes after death,
Refusing grace; his grave is flowerless,
He gutters in the tallow of his name.
At Rome the multiplying tapers sing
Life endless in the history of art.

And Zion womanless refuses grace
To the first woman as to Magdalene,
But half-remembers Judith or Rahab,
The shrewd good heart of Esther honors still,
And weeps for almost sacred Ruth, but doubts
Either full harlotry or the faultless birth.

Our wine is wine, our bread is harvest bread
That feeds the body and is not the body.
Our blessing is to wine but not the blood
Nor to sangreal the sacred dish. We bless
The whiteness of the dish and bless the water
And are not anthropaphagous to him.

The immanent son then came as one of us
And stood against the ark. We have no prophets,
Our scholars are afraid. There have been friars,
Great healers, poets. The stars were terrible.
At the Sadducee court he touched our panic;
We were bertayed to sacrifice this man.

We live my virtue of philosophy,

Past love, and have our devious reward.
For faith he gave us land and took the land,
Thinking us exiles of all humankind.
Our name is yet the identity of God
That storms the falling altar of the world.

DEBATE WITH THE RABBI

Howard Nemerov

You've lost your religion, the Rabbi said.
    It wasn't much to keep, said I.
You should affirm the spirit, said he,
And the communal solidarity.
    I don't feel so solid, I said.

We are the people of the Book, the Rabbi said.
    Not of the phone book, said I.
Ours is a great tradition, said he,
And a wonderful history.
    But history's over, I said.

We Jews are creative people, the Rabbi said.
    Make something, then, said I.
In science and in art, said he,
Violinists and physicists have we.
    Fiddle and physic indeed, I said.

Stubborn and stiff-necked man! the Rabbi cried.
    The pain you give me, said I.
Instead of bowing down, said he,
You go on in your obstinacy.
    We Jews are that way, I replied.

THE SOUL OF THE INDIAN

Charles A. Eastman

The original attitude of the American Indian toward the Eternal, the "Great Mystery" that surrounds and embraces us, was as simple as it was exalted. To him it was the supreme conception, bringing with it the fullest measure of joy and satisfaction possible in this life.

The worship of the "Great Mystery" was silent, solitary, free from all self-seeking. It was silent, because all speech is of necessity feeble and imperfect; therefore the souls of my ancestors ascended to God in wordless adoration. It was solitary, because they believed that He is nearer to us in solitude, and there were no priests authorized to come between a man and his Maker. None might exhort or confess or in any way meddle with the religious experience of another. Among us all men were created sons of God and stood erect, as conscious of their divinity. Our faith might not be formulated in creeds, nor forced upon any who were unwilling to receive it; hence there was no preaching, proselyting, nor persecution, neither were there any scoffers or atheists.

There were no temples or shrines among us save those of nature. Being a natural man, the Indian was intensely poetical. He would deem it sacrilege to build a house for Him who may be met face to face in the mysterious, shadowy aisles of the primeval forest, or on the sunlit bosom of virgin prairies, upon dizzy spires and pinnacles of naked rock, and yonder in the jeweled vault of the night sky! He who enrobes Himself in filmy veils of cloud, there on the rim of the visible world where our Great-Grandfather Sun kindles his evening campfire, He who rides upon the rigorous wind of the north, or breathes forth His spirit upon aromatic southern airs, whose

war-canoe is launched upon majestic rivers and inland seas—
He needs no lesser cathedral!

That solitary communion with the Unseen which was the
highest expression of our religious life is partly described in
the word *hambeday*, literally "mysterious feeling," which has
been variously translated "fasting" and "dreaming." It may
better be interpreted as "consciousness of the divine."

The first *hambeday*, or religious retreat, marked an epoch
in the life of the youth, which may be compared to that of
confirmation or conversion in Christian experience. Having
first prepared himself by means of the purifying vapor-bath,
and cast off as far as possible all human or fleshly influences,
the young man sought out the noblest height, the most commanding summit in all the surrounding region. Knowing that
God sets no value upon material things, he took with him no
offerings or sacrifices other than symbolic objects, such as
paints and tobacco. Wishing to appear before Him in all
humility, he wore no clothing save his mocassins and breech-
clout. At the solemn hour of sunrise or sunset he took up his
position, overlooking the glories of earth and facing the "Great
Mystery," and there he remained, naked, erect, silent, and mo-
tionless, exposed to the elements and forces of His arming, for
a night and a day to two days and nights, but rarely longer.
Sometimes he would chant a hymn without words, or offer the
ceremonial "filled pipe." In this holy trance or ecstasy the Indian mystic found his highest happiness and the motive power
of his existence.

When he returned to the camp, he must remain at a distance until he had again entered the vapor-bath and prepared
himself for intercourse with his fellows. Of the vision or sign
vouchsafed to him he did not speak, unless it had included
some commission which must be publicly fulfilled. Sometimes
an old man, standing upon the brink of eternity, might reveal
to a chosen few the oracle of his long-past youth.

The native American has been generally despised by his
white conquerors for his poverty and simplicity. They forget,
perhaps, that his religion forbade the accumulation of wealth
and the enjoyment of luxury. To him, as to other single-
minded men in every age and race, from Diogenes to the
brothers of Saint Francis, from the Montanists to the Shakers,
the love of possessions has appeared a snare, and the burdens
of a complex society a source of needless peril and temptation.

Furthermore, it was the rule of his life to share the fruits of his skill and success with his less fortunate brothers. Thus he kept his spirit free from the clog of pride, cupidity, or envy, and carried out, as he believed, the divine decree—a matter profoundly important to him.

It was not, then, wholly from ignorance or improvidence that he failed to establish permanent towns and to develop a material civilization. To the untutored sage, the concentration of population was the prolific mother of all evils, moral no less than physical. He argued that food is good, while surfeit kills; that love is good, but lust destroys; and not less dreaded than the pestilence following upon crowded and unsanitary dwellings was the loss of spiritual power inseparable from too close contact with one's fellow-men. All who have lived much out of doors know that there is a magnetic and nervous force that accumulates in solitude and that is quickly dissipated by life in a crowd; and even his enemies have recognized the fact that for a certain innate power and self-poise, wholly independent of circumstances, the American Indian is unsurpassed among men.

The red man divided mind into two parts,—the spiritual mind and the physical mind. The first is pure spirit, concerned only with the essence of things, and it was this he sought to strengthen by spiritual prayer, during which the body is subdued by fasting and hardship. In this type of prayer there was no beseeching of favor or help. All matters of personal or selfish concern, as success in hunting or warfare, relief from sickness, or the sparing of a beloved life, were definitely relegated to the plane of the lower or material mind, and all ceremonies, charms, or incantations designed to secure a benefit or to avert a danger, were recognized as emanating from the physical self.

The rites of this physical worship again, were wholly symbolic, and the Indian no more worshiped the Sun than the Christian adores the Cross. The Sun and the Earth, by an obvious parable, holding scarcely more of poetic metaphor than of scientific truth, were in his view the parents of all organic life. From the Sun, as the universal father, proceeds the quickening principle in nature, and in the patient and fruitful womb of our mother, the Earth, are hidden embryos of plants and men. Therefore our reverence and love for them was really an imaginative extension of our love for our immediate parents, and with this sentiment of filial piety was joined a willingness to appeal to them, as to a father, for such good gifts as we may desire. This is the material or physical prayer.

The elements and majestic forces in nature, Lightning, Wind, Water, Fire, and Frost, were regarded with awe as spiritual powers, but always secondary and intermediate in character. We believed that the spirit pervades all creation and that every creature possesses a soul in some degree, though not necessarily a soul conscious of itself. The tree, the waterfall, the grizzly bear, each is an embodied Force, and as such an object of reverence.

The Indian loved to come into sympathy and spiritual communion with his brothers of the animal kingdom, whose inarticulate souls had for him something of the sinless purity that we attribute to the innocent and irresponsible child. He had faith in their instincts, as in a mysterious wisdom given from above; and while he humbly accepted the supposedly voluntary sacrifice of their bodies to preserve his own, he paid homage to their spirits in prescribed prayers and offerings.

In every religion there is an element of the supernatural, varying with the influence of pure reason over its devotees. The Indian was a logical and clear thinker upon matters within the scope of his understanding, but he had not yet charted the vast field of nature or expressed her wonders in terms of science. With his limited knowledge of cause and effect, he saw miracles on every hand,—the miracle of life in seed and egg, the miracle of death in lightning flash and in the swelling deep! Nothing of the marvelous could astonish him; as that a beast should speak, or the sun stand still. The virgin birth would appear scarcely more miraculous than is the birth of every child that comes into the world, or the miracle of the loaves and fishes excite more wonder than the harvest that springs from a single ear of corn.

Who may condemn his superstition? Surely not the devout Catholic, or even Protestant missionary, who teaches Bible miracles as literal fact! The logical man must either deny all miracles or none, and our American Indian myths and hero stories are perhaps, in themselves, quite as credible as those of the Hebrews of old. If we are of the modern type of mind, that sees in natural law a majesty and grandeur far more impressive than any solitary infraction of it could possibly be, let us not forget that, after all, science has not explained everything. We have still to face the ultimate miracle,—the origin and principle of life! Here is the supreme mystery that is the essence of worship, without which there can be no religion, and in the presence of this mystery our attitude cannot be very unlike that of the natural philosopher, who beholds with awe the Divine in all creation.

It is simple truth that the Indian did not, so long as his native philosophy held sway over his mind, either envy or desire to imitate the splendid achievements of the white man. In his own thought he rose superior to them! He scorned them, even as a lofty spirit absorbed in its stern task rejects the soft beds, the luxurious food, the pleasure-worshiping dalliance of a rich neighbor. It was clear to him that virtue and happiness are independent of these things, if not incompatible with them.

There was undoubtedly much in primitive Christianity to appeal to this man, and Jesus' hard sayings to the rich and about the rich would have been entirely comprehensible to him. Yet the religion that is preached in our churches and practiced by our congregations, with its element of display and self-aggrandizement, its active proselytism, and its open contempt of all religions but its own, was for a long time extremely repellent. To his simple mind, the professionalism of the pulpit, the paid exhorter, the moneyed church, was an unspiritual and unedifying thing, and it was not until his spirit was broken and his moral and physical constitution undermined by trade, conquest, and strong drink, that Christian missionaries obtained any real hold upon him. Strange as it may seem, it is true that the proud pagan in his secret soul despised the good men who came to convert and to enlighten him!

Nor were its publicity and its Phariseeism the only elements in the alien religion that offended the red man. To him, it appeared shocking and almost incredible that there were among this people who claimed superiority many irreligious, who did not even pretend to profess the national faith. Not only did they not profess it, but they stooped so low as to insult their God with profane and sacrilegious speech! In our own tongue His name was not spoken aloud, even with utmost reverence, much less lightly or irreverently.

More than this, even in those white men who professed religion we found much inconsistency of conduct. They spoke much of spiritual things, while seeking only the material. They bought and sold everything: time, labor, personal independence, the love of woman, and even the ministrations of their holy faith! The lust for money, power, and conquest so characteristic of the Anglo-Saxon race did not escape moral condemnation at the hands of his untutored judge, nor did he fail to contrast this conspicuous trait of the dominant race with the spirit of the meek and lowly Jesus.

He might in time come to recognize that the drunkards and licentious among white men, with whom he too frequently came in contact, were condemned by the white man's religion as well, and must not be held to discredit it. But it was not so easy to overlook or to excuse national bad faith. When distinguished emissaries from the Father at Washington, some of them ministers of the gospel and even bishops, came to the Indian nations, and pledged to them in solemn treaty the national honor, with prayer and mention of their God; and when such treaties, so made, were promptly and shamelessly broken, is it strange that the action should arouse not only anger, but contempt? The historians of the white race admit that the Indian was never the first to repudiate his oath.

It is my personal belief, after thirty-five years' experience of it, that there is no such thing as "Christian civilization." I believe that Christianity and modern civilization are opposed and irreconcilable, and that the spirit of Christianity and of our ancient religion is essentially the same.

A NUN NO MORE

John Fante

My mother went to a high school which was run by the nuns. After she got through she wanted to be a nun too. My Grandma Toscana told me. But Grandma and the whole family didn't want her to become a nun. They told her it was all right for girls in other families to become nuns, but not their daughter. My mother's name was Regina Toscana and she was so holy the holiness lit up her eyes. She had a statue of Saint Teresa in her room, and when they kicked about her becoming a nun she stayed in her room day and night praying to Saint Teresa.

"Oh, beloved Saint Teresa!" she prayed. "Grant me the light to see the path thou hast made for me, that I might do thy holy bidding. Visit me with sanctifying grace in the name of our Blessed Mother and the Lord Jesus, amen!"

Some prayer. But it didn't do any good because Grandma Toscana still said nothing doing. She told my mother to cut out acting like a sick calf and get some sense. They all talked to her like that, Uncle Jim, Uncle Tony, and Grandma and Grandpa Toscana. They were Italian people and they didn't like the way she was acting, because Italians hate it when their women don't want to get married. They hate it and they think something is screwy somewhere. It is best for the Italian women to get married. Then the husband pays and the whole family saves money. And that was the way they talked to my mother.

Then my Uncle Tony got an idea. One night he brought a man named Pasquale Martello to the house. Uncle Tony introduced him to my mother, and he had a hunch she would go for him and maybe marry him and forget about the nun business. My mother was a honey and I know it, because we have some pictures and I can prove it.

Pasquale Martello owned a grocery store and he was lousy

with money, but otherwise he wasn't so hot for a girl like my mother. He sold fancy things in his store, like Parmesan cheese, salami, and a special kind of fancy garlic. He dressed real loud in green shirts with white stripes and red neckties. The only reason my mother went with him was on account of she was afraid of Uncle Tony, who raised hell if she didn't go out with him. Pretty soon Pasquale Martello got a crush on my mother and he tried to get her to marry him.

But he had so many bad habits that my mother got awfully tired of him pretty soon. For one thing, he ate too much fancy garlic and his breath was something fierce. He carried garlic around in a sack in his pockets and he used to toss it up in the air and catch it in his mouth the way you eat salted peanuts. He took my mother to different places, like Lakeside Park, and the dance, and to the movies. On account of that garlic you could smell him coming for miles. Every time they went to the movies people got up and found other seats. And my mother wanted to become a nun! It was very embarrassing for her. After the show they used to sit in front of the big stove in Grandma Toscana's parlor and talk. He was so dumb that my mother yawned right in his face and he never did catch on that she was hinting and wanted to go to bed. She had to tell him to go home or he would still be in that parlor, talking.

Every morning Uncle Tony asked the same question.

"Well, well! And when's the marriage going to be?"

"Never," my mother said. "There isn't going to be any marriage."

"Are you crazy?" Uncle Tony said. "That guys got money!"

"I'm sorry," she said. "My life is in another direction."

"Meaning?"

"My life is dedicated to the service of our Blessed Lady."

"My God!" Uncle Tony said. "Did you hear that one! I give up!"

"I'm sorry," my mother said. "I'm really sorry."

"*Sangue della madonna!*" Uncle Tony said. "And after all I've done for her! There's gratitude for you."

My mother went up to her room and stayed there all day, until Pasquale came that night. He always brought my grandmother something from the store, cheese mostly and sometimes tomato sauce in big cans, or Italian paste. Grandma Toscana liked him most on account of the Parmesan cheese, which was a dollar a pound in those days.

That night my mother told Pasquale it was too bad, but

he would have to find another girl because she did not love him. He was crazy about her, all right. He got down on his knees and kissed her hands, and he walked out of the house bawling. The next day he called Uncle Tony on the phone and told him my mother had given him the gate and wouldn't let him come around any more.

Uncle Tony got boiling mad. He ran home from work and raised hell with the whole family. When he came to my mother he shook his fist in her face and pushed her against the sidebord so hard it knocked the wind out of her.

"You crazy fool!" he hollered. "What good are you anyhow?"

"I'm sorry," she said.

"Good God!" he said. "Don't you know anything else but 'I'm sorry'?"

"I'm sorry," she said.

"Listen to her!" he yelled. "She's sorry!"

"But I am sorry," she said.

My Uncle Tony was in the grocery business too, but his store was a little one and he didn't sell Italian stuff, and he had it all figured out that when my mother and Pasquale got married he would merge his store with Pasquale's and they would all clean up. But Pasquale never came back to the house again. Before long he married a girl, and she wasn't an Italian either. She was an American and he didn't love her either. Grandma Toscana said it was a spite marriage. The Italians do that sometimes. A spite marriage is when you marry somebody else to get your real girl's goat and try to make her sorry she didn't marry you. But my mother wasn't sorry at all. The whole thing tickled her pink.

In North Denver is the Church of Saint Cecilia's. This was where my mother spent all of her time. It is across the street from the high school, an old red church without a lawn in front of it or anything, just the street, and not even a tree around. Once I went there for Christmas Mass with my mother. It was a long time after she got married. I mean, it had to be. The church is a big, sad church and the incense smells like my mother. It is a leery church. It scared me. I kept thinking I was not born and would never be born.

My mother knew all the nuns at Saint Cecilia's. She used to bum around with them, and they put her in charge of the altars and she decorated them with flowers. She washed and ironed the altar linen and things like that. It was more fun than getting married. She was there all afternoon, so that Uncle Jim or Uncle Tony had to come for her at supper time. Uncle Jim didn't mind because it was only a block away, but Uncle Tony raised hell. He thought church was a lot of boloney.

He said, "Instead of fooling around here all the time, why don't you stay home and help your mother?"

But my mother was a good worker and she told him to be careful what he said. She did all the washing and ironing around the house, and Grandma didn't have any kick coming, and once in a while she cooked the meals, but not often because she was not a good cook. She always did her work before she went to Saint Cecilia's. Her garden was in Grandma's back yard, and she grew peonies and roses for the altars. Uncle Tony told her to cut out the church stuff or he would wreck her garden.

"You go to the dickens!" she said.

Oh oh, that got him mad. Italian girls are not supposed to sass their big brothers. Uncle Tony wouldn't allow anything like that.

"By God, I'll show you!" he said.

He ran out to the coal shed and got the spade. Then he took off his sweater and spaded every flower in the garden to pieces. It hurt my mother. She stood on the back porch and it hurt her. She was crazy about her garden, and when she saw him hacking it up she hung on the door and almost fainted. Then she ran out and screamed and screamed. She fell on the ground and kicked with her feet and hit with her hands. It scared Uncle Tony. He called Grandma. She kept screaming. He tried to lift her. She screamed and kicked him.

She was very sick. They carried her upstairs and put her to bed. The doctor came. He said she was a very sick woman. For a long time he came every day. They had to have a nurse. For a year she was sick and nervous. Everybody in the house had to be quiet and walk on tiptoe. It cost a lot of money for doctor bills. My mother cried and cried night and day. They could stop her. Even the Sisters came, but they couldn't do anything. Finally Grandma Toscana called the priest. He gave her Holy Communion. Right away she felt better. Next day she was better than ever. Next day she was swell. Pretty soon she was able to get out of bed. Then she moved around more. All at once she was well again.

Grandma Toscana said it was a miracle. Uncle Tony felt like the devil. He told my mother how sorry he was, and he planted her a new garden. Everything was fine again. My mother liked the new garden better than ever, and Uncle Tony left her alone. Nobody bothered her any more.

She went on decorating the altars at Saint Cecilia's. Also she taught school. She went on retreats. A retreat is when you pray and meditate for three days without talking to anybody. Once she went on a retreat for six weeks. Whatever the nuns did, she did. She was crazy about them. All they ever did was wash clothes, decorate altars, scrub floors, and teach kids.

Before long, sure enough Uncle Tony started kicking again, but not like before. He was afraid my mother would get sick again. He even brought more men to the house. He brought Jack Mondi, who was the biggest bootlegger in North Denver. He isn't any more because he got shot, but he was important when Uncle Tony brought him to meet my mother. He scared the whole family stiff. Before sitting down, he always put his gun on the table. Every few minutes he jumped up and peeked out the front window. He brought gangsters with him, and they waited for him on the front porch. Even Uncle Tony didn't know it was going to be that scary, so he tried to get rid of Jack Mondi, but he didn't try very hard. He was afraid he would get hurt.

Once Jack Mondi came to the house drunk and he bit my mother on the cheek. It was the first time anything like that ever happened to her, and she got mad and hauled off and slapped him. The whole family held their breaths and waited for Jack Mondi to shoot them down. Uncle Tony made a sign to my mother to go easy and not make Jack mad. But my mother didn't think he was so tough. She told him to get out of the house and never come back. He did it too. He stuck his gun in his pocket and walked right out without saying a word. For a long time they thought he would come back and shoot the whole family, but he never came back again. Uncle Tony was so scared he even went to church. But Jack Mondi never showed up again. After he got killed they read about it in the papers. My mother went to his funeral and prayed for the repose of his soul. She was the only woman in the church besides Jack Mondi's mother. Which proves my mother was a good sport.

Another guy with a crush on my mother was Alfredo di

Posso. Uncle Tony brought him too. Whenever he found a guy he thought would make a good husband he brought him to dinner. There were others too, but I only know about Pasquale Martello, Jack Mondi, Alfredo di Posso, and a man named Murphy, but Murphy didn't cut much ice because he was Irish. Uncle Tony never did like the Irish.

Alfredo di Posso was a salesman for Lima beans. Once in a while Alfredo comes to our town, so I know him. He doesn't sell beans in cans or anything like that. He sells them by the carload. When he comes to our town he stops to see my mother. He is a swell guy, always laughing. He gives me money, usually four bits. When my mother met him, he didn't have a religion. She made him join the Catholic Church, but he made fun of it; he made fun of everything. My mother got tired of it. She told him she could never marry him.

When my mother was twenty-one everybody in North Denver knew she was going to be a nun. Her favorite order was the Sisters of Charity. You have to take the train to their convent in Kentucky. For a long time you study stuff. Then you become a real nun. They cut off your hair and you wear black dresses, and you can't get married or have fun. Your husband is Jesus. Anyway, that's what Sister Delphine told me.

It was all set. My mother was ready to go. Uncle Tony hated it and so did the rest, but they couldn't do anything. Grandpa was disappointed. He had a shoe shop on Osage Street. He liked nuns. He thought they were swell people, he even did their shoe work for nothing, but he couldn't see why his own daughter had to get mixed up in it.

He promised to send my mother to Colorado U. if she would forget it. My mother wouldn't hear of it because she thought Colorado U. was an awful place. Right now my mother knows a Catholic who doesn't believe in God. He went to Colorado U. He was all right until then. Now the Catholics in our town are off him for life. They even kicked him out of the Knights of Columbus because he made smart cracks. So my mother wouldn't go to a school like Colorado U. It was Kentucky or nothing.

All day long Uncle Tony yelled at her, calling her a dumb cluck and a stupe. She almost had another nervous breakdown. He followed her around the house, yelling at her trying to make her change her mind. Next door to Grandma Toscana's the Rocca people were building a new house. Uncle Tony had a big voice and he yelled so loud the bricklayers heard every word he hollowed. They used to stop work on the scaffold and listen to him.

One morning two months before she was to leave for Kentucky my mother was eating breakfast, and Uncle Tony started right in on the same old argument. She didn't have any sense. Weren't they treating her all right at home? She wanted to bury herself in a hole and forget all the fine things her family did for her. Didn't she get enough to eat and plenty of clothes to wear? Then what more did she want? Why did she have to be so selfish? Think of her poor mother getting old without her around. Why couldn't she think those things out and realize the mistake she was making?

My mother put her head down and started to cry.

One of the bricklayers was watching from the scaffold. He climbed down the ladder and walked over to the kitchen window. He was an Italian too, but not the ordinary kind. He had a red mustache for one thing, and red hair. He knocked on the screen and my mother looked up. Uncle Tony wanted to know what he wanted. The man had a trowel in his hand. He shook it in Uncle Tony's face.

"If you say another word to that girl I'll knock your head off!"

The minute my mother saw him something happened. Uncle Tony got so mad he went into the front room without speaking. My mother kept looking at the man with the trowel and the little red mustache. All at once they both started laughing. He went back to work, still laughing. At noon he sat on the scaffold looking down into the kitchen window. My mother could see him. He whistled. She laughed and came to the window. What he wanted was some salt for his sandwich. That was how it got started. The man was my father. Every day he laughed and asked for something. If it wasn't salt it was pepper, and my mother laughed and got it for him. Another time he asked for some fresh fruit to go with his lunch. One day he came to the window and laughed and asked if she had any wine. Then he wanted to know if she could cook. My mother laughed and laughed. Finally she told him not to bring his lunch any more but to come over and eat with her. He laughed and said sure. Two months later, instead of going to Kentucky, my mother came to our town and got married.

YONEKO'S EARTHQUAKE

Hisaye Yamamoto

Yoneko Hosoume became a free-thinker on the night of March 10, 1933, only a few months after her first actual recognition of God. Ten years old at the time, of course she had heard rumors about God all along, long before Marpo came. Her cousins who lived in the city were all Christians, living as they did right next door to a Baptist church exclusively for Japanese people. These city cousins, of whom there were several, had been baptized en masse, and were very proud of their condition. Yoneko was impressed when she heard of this and thereafter was given to referring to them as "my cousins, the Christians." She, too, yearned at times after Christianity, but she realized the absurdity of her whim, seeing that there was no Baptist church for Japanese in the rural community she lived in. Such a church would have been impractical, moreover, since Yoneko, her father, her mother, and her little brother Seigo, were the only Japanese thereabouts. They were the only ones, too, whose agriculture was so diverse as to include blackberries, cabbages, rhubarb, potatoes, cucumbers, onions, and canteloupes. The rest of the countryside there was like one vast orange grove.

Yoneko had entered her cousins' church once, but she could not recall the sacred occasion without mortification. It had been one day when the cousins had taken her and Seigo along with them to Sunday school. The church was a narrow, wooden building, mysterious-looking because of its unusual bluish-grey paint and its steeple, but the basement schoolroom inside had been disappointingly ordinary, with desks, a blackboard, and erasers. They had all sung "Let Us Gather at the River" in Japanese. This goes:

Mamonaku kanata no
Nagare no soba de
Tanoshiku ai-masho
Mata tomodachi to

Mamonaku ai-masho
Kirei-na, kirei-na kawa de
Tanoshiku ai-masho
Mata tomodachi to.

Yoneko had not known the words at all, but always clever in such situations, she had opened her mouth and grimaced nonchalantly to the rhythm. What with everyone else singing at the top of his lungs, no one had noticed that she was not making a peep. Then everyone had sat down again and the man had suggested, "Let us pray." Her cousins and the rest had promptly curled their arms on the desks to make nests for their heads, and Yoneko had done the same. But not Seigo. Because when the room had become so still that one was aware of the breathing, the creaking, and the chittering in the trees outside, Seigo, sitting with her, had suddenly flung his arm around her neck and said with concern, "Sis, what are you crying for? Don't cry." Even the man had laughed and Yoneko had been terribly ashamed that Seigo should thus disclose them to be interlopers. She had pinched him fiercely and he had begun to cry, so she had had to drag him outside, which was a fortunate move, because he had immediately wet his pants. But he had been only three then, so it was not very fair to expect dignity of him.

So it remained for Marpo to bring the word of God to Yoneko, Marpo with the face like brown leather, the thin moustache like Edmund Lowe's, and the rare, breathtaking smile like white gold. Marpo, who was twenty-seven years old, was a Filipino and his last name was lovely, something like Humming Wing, but no one ever ascertained the spelling of it. He ate principally rice, just as though he were Japanese, but he never sat down to the Hosoume table, because he lived in the bunk-house out by the barn and cooked on his own kerosene stove. Once Yoneko read somewhere that Filipinos trapped wild dogs, starved them for a time, then, feeding them mountains of rice, killed them at the peak of their bloatedness, thus insuring themselves meat ready to roast, stuffing and all, without further ado. This, the book said, was considered a delicacy. Unable to hide her disgust and her fascination, Yoneko went straightway to Marpo and asked, "Marpo, is it true that you eat dogs?", and he, flashing that smile, answered, "Don't be funny, honey!" This caused her no end of amusement, because it was a poem, and she completely forgot about the wild dogs.

Well, there seemed to be nothing Marpo could not do. Mr. Hosoume said Marpo was the best hired man he had ever had, and he said this often, because it was an irrefutable fact among Japanese in general that Filipinos in general were an indolent lot. Mr. Hosoume ascribed Marpo's industry to his having grown up in Hawaii, where there is known to be considerable Japanese influence. Marpo had gone to a missionary school there and he owned a Bible given him by one of his teachers. This had black leather covers that gave as easily as cloth, golden edges, and a slim purple ribbon for a marker. He always kept it on the little table by his bunk, which was not a bed with springs but a low, three-plank shelf with a mattress only. On the first page of the book, which was stiff and black, his teacher had written in large swirls of white ink, "As we draw near to God, He will draw near to us."

What, for instance, could Marpo do? Why, it would take an entire, leisurely evening to go into his accomplishments adequately, because there was not only Marpo the Christian and Marpo the best hired man, but Marpo the athlete, Marpo the musician (both instrumental and vocal), Marpo the artist, and Marpo the radio technician:

(1) As an athlete, Marpo owned a special pair of black shoes, equipped with sharp nails on the soles, which he kept in shape with the regular application of neatsfoot oil. Putting these on, he would dash down the dirt road to the highways, a distance of perhaps half a mile, and back again. When he first came to work for the Hosoumes, he undertook this sprint every evening before he went to get his supper but, as time went on, he referred to these shoes less and less and, in the end, when he left, he had not touched them for months. He also owned a muscle-builder sent him by Charles Atlas which, despite his unassuming size, he could stretch the length of his outspread arms; his teeth gritted then and his whole body became temporarily victim to a jerky vibration. (2) As an artist, Marpo painted larger-than-life water colors of his favorite movie stars, all of whom were women and all of whom were blonde, like Ann Harding and Jean Harlow, and tacked them up on his

walls. He also made for Yoneko a folding contraption of wood holding two pencils, one with lead and one without, with which she, too, could obtain double-sized likenesses of any picture she wished. It was a fragile instrument, however, and Seigo splintered it to pieces one day when Yoneko was away at school. He claimed he was only trying to copy Boob McNutt from the funny paper when it failed. (3) As a musician, Marpo owned a violin for which he had paid over one hundred dollars. He kept this in a case whose lining was red velvet, first wrapping it gently in a brilliant red silk scarf. This scarf, which weighed nothing, he tucked under his chin when he played, gathering it up delicately by the center and flicking it once to unfurl it— a gesture Yoneko prized. In addition to this, Marpo was a singer, with a soft tenor which came out in professional quavers and rolled r's when he applied a slight pressure to his Adam's apple with thumb and forefinger. His violin and vocal repertoire consisted of the same numbers, mostly hymns and Irish folk airs. He was especially addicted to "The Rose of Tralee" and the "Londonderry Air." (4) Finally, as a radio technician who had spent two previous winters at a specialists' school in the city, Marpo had put together a bulky table-size radio which brought in equal proportions of static and entertainment. He never got around to building a cabinet to house it and its innards of metal and glass remained public throughout its lifetime. This was just as well, for not a week passed without Marpo's deciding to solder one bit or another. Yoneko and Seigo became a part of the great listening audience with such fidelity that Mr. Hosoume began remarking the fact that they dwelt more with Marpo than with their own parents. He eventually took a serious view of the matter and bought the naked radio from Marpo, who thereupon put away his radio manuals and his soldering iron in the bottom of his steamer trunk and divided more time among his other interests.

However, Marpo's versatility was not revealed, as it is here, in a lump. Yoneko uncovered it fragment by fragment every day, by dint of unabashed questions, explorations among his possessions, and even silent observation, although this last was rare. In fact, she and Seigo visited with Marpo at least once a day and both of them regularly came away amazed with their findings. The most surprising thing was that Marpo was, after all this, a rather shy young man meek to the point of speechlessness in the presence of Mr. and Mrs. Hosoume. With Yoneko and Seigo, he was somewhat more self-confident and at ease.

It is not remembered now just how Yoneko and Marpo came to open their protracted discussion on religion. It is sufficient here to note that Yoneko was an ideal apostle, adoring Jesus, desiring Heaven, and fearing Hell. Once Marpo had enlightened her on these basics, Yoneko never questioned their truth. The questions she put up to him, therefore, sought neither proof of her exegeses nor balm for her doubts, but simply additional color to round out her mental images. For example, who did Marpo suppose was God's favorite movie star? Or, what sound did Jesus' laughter have (it must be like music, she added, nodding sagely, answering herself to her own satisfaction), and did Marpo suppose that God's sense of humor would have appreciated the delicious chant she had learned from friends at school today:

> *There ain't no bugs on us,*
> *There ain't no bugs on us,*
> *There may be bugs on the rest of you mugs,*
> *But there ain't no bugs on us.*

Or, did Marpo believe Jesus to have been exempt from stinging eyes when he shampooed that long, naturally wavy hair of his?

To shake such faith, there would have been required a most monstrous upheaval of some sort, and it might be said that this is just what happened. For early on the evening of March 10, 1933, a little after five o'clock this was, as Mrs. Hosoume was getting supper, as Marpo was finishing up in the fields alone because Mr. Hosoume had gone to order some chicken fertilizer, and as Yoneko and Seigo were listening to Skippy, a tremendous roar came out of nowhere and the Hosoume house began shuddering violently as though some giant had seized it in his two hands and was giving it a good shaking. Mrs. Housoume, who remembered similar, although milder experiences, from her childhood in Japan, screamed, *"Jishin, jishin!"* before she ran and grabbed Yoneko and Seigo each by a hand and dragged them outside with her. She took them as far as the middle of the rhubarb patch near the house, and there they all crouched, pressed together, watching the world about them rock and sway. In a few minutes, Marpo, stumbling in from the fields, joined them, saying, "Earthquake, earthquake!", and he gathered them all in his arms, as much to protect them as to support himself.

Mr. Hosoume came home later that evening in a stranger's car, with another stranger driving the family Reo. Pallid, trembling, his eyes wildly staring, he could have been mistaken for a drunkard, except that he was famous as a teetotaler. It seemed that he had been on the way home when the first jolt came, that the old green Reo had been kissed by a broken live wire dangling from a suddenly leaning pole. Mr. Hosoume, knowing that the end had come by electrocution, had begun to writhe and kick and this had been his salvation. His hands had flown from the wheel, the car had swerved into a ditch, freeing itself from the sputtering wire. Later, it was found that he was left permanently inhibited about driving automobiles and permanently incapable of considering electricity with calmness. He spent the larger part of his later life weakly, wandering about the house or fields and lying down frequently to rest because of splitting headaches and sudden dizzy spells.

So it was Marpo who went back into the house as Yoneko screamed, "No, Marpo, no!" and brought out the Hosoumes' kerosene stove, the food, the blankets, while Mr. Hosoume huddled on the ground near his family.

The earth trembled for days afterwards. The Hosoumes and Marpo Humming Wing lived during that time on a natural patch of Bermuda grass between the house and the rhubarb patch, remembering to take three meals a day and retire at night. Marpo ventured inside the house many times despite Yoneko's protests and reported the damage slight: a few dishes had been broken; a gallon jug of mayonnaise had fallen from the top pantry shelf and spattered the kitchen floor with yellow blobs and pieces of glass.

Yoneko was in constant terror during this experience. Immediately on learning what all the commotion was about, she began praying to God to end this violence. She entreated God, flattered Him, wheedled Him, commanded Him, but He did not listen to her at all—inexorably, the earth went on rumbling. After three solid hours of silent, desperate prayer, without any results whatsoever, Yoneko began to suspect that God was either powerless, callous, downright cruel, or nonexistent. In the murky night, under a strange moon wearing a pale ring of light, she decided upon the last as the most plausible theory.

"Ha," was one of the things she said tremulously to Marpo, when she was not begging him to stay out of the house, "you and your God!"

The others soon oriented themselves to the catastrophe with pilosophy, saying how fortunate they were to live in the country where the peril was less than in the city and going so far as to regard the period as a sort of vacation from work, with their enforced alfresco existence a sort of camping trip. They tried to bring Yoneko to partake of this pleasant outlook, but she, shivering with each new quiver, looked on them as dreamers who refused to see things as they really were. Indeed, Yoneko's reaction was so notable that the Hosoume household thereafter spoke of the event as "Yoneko's earthquake."

After the earth subsided and the mayonnaise was mopped off the kitchen floor, life returned to normal, except that Mr. Hosoume stayed at home most of the time. Sometimes, if he had a relatively painless day, he would have supper on the stove when Mrs. Hosoume came in from the fields. Mrs. Hosoume and Marpo did all the field labor now, except on certain overwhelming days when several Mexicans were hired to assist them. Marpo did most of the driving, too, and it was now he and Mrs. Hosoume who went into town on the weekly trip for groceries. In fact, Marpo became indispensable and both Mr. and Mrs. Hosoume often told each other how grateful they were for Marpo.

When summer vacation began and Yoneko stayed at home, too, she found the new arrangement rather inconvenient. Her father's presence cramped her style: for instance, once when her friends came over and it was decided to make fudge, he would not permit them, saying fudge used too much sugar and that sugar was not a plaything; once when they were playing paper dolls, he came along and stuck his finger up his nose and pretended he was going to rub some snot off onto the dolls. Things like that. So, on some days, she was very much annoyed with her father.

Therefore when her mother came home breathless from the fields one day and pushed a ring at her, a gold-colored ring with a tiny glasslike stone in it, saying "Look, Yoneko, I'm going to give you this ring. If your father asks where you got it, say you found it on the street," Yoneko was perplexed but delighted both by the unexpected gift and the chance to have some secret revenge on her father, and she said, certainly, she was willing to comply with her mother's request. Her mother went back to the fields then and Yoneko put the pretty ring on her middle finger, taking up the loose space with a bit of newspaper. It was similar to the rings found occasionally in boxes of Crackerjack, except that it appeared a bit more substantial.

Mr. Hosoume never asked about the ring: in fact, he never noticed she was wearing one. Yoneko thought he was about to, once, but he only reproved her for the flamingo nail polish she was wearing, which she had applied from a vial brought over by Yvonne Fournier, the French girl two orange groves away. "You look like a Filipino," Mr. Hosoume said sternly, for it was another irrefutable fact among Japanese in general that Filipinos in general were a gaudy lot. Mrs. Hosoume immediately came to her defense, saying that in Japan, if she remembered correctly, young girls did the same thing. In fact, she remembered having gone to elaborate lengths to tint her fingernails: she used to gather, she said, the petals of the red *tsubobana* or the purple *kogane* (which grows on the underside of stones), grind them well, mix them with some alum powder, then cook the mixture and leave it to stand overnight in an envelope of either persimmon or sugar potato leaves (both very strong leaves). The second night, just before going to bed, she used to obtain threads by ripping a palm leaf (because real thread was dear) and tightly bind the paste to her fingernails under shields of persimmion or sugar potato leaves. She would be helpless for the night, the fingertips bound so well that they were alternately numb or aching, but she would grit her teeth and tell herself that the discomfort indicated the success of the operation. In the morning, finally releasing her fingers, she would find the nails shining with a translucent, red-orange color.

Yoneko was fascinated, because she usually thought of her parents as having been adults all their lives. She thought that her mother must have been a beautiful child, with or without bright fingernails, because, though surely past thirty, she was even yet a beautiful person. When she herself was younger, she remembered, she had at times been so struck with her mother's appearance that she had dropped to her knees and mutely clasped her mother's legs in her arms. She had left off this habit as she learned to control her emotions, because at such times her mother had usually walked away, saying, "My, what a clinging child you are. You've got to learn to be a little more independent." She also remembered she had once heard someone comparing her mother to "a dewy, half-opened rosebud."

Mr. Hosoume, however, was irritated. "That's no excuse for Yoneko to begin using paint on her fingernails," he said. "She's only ten."

"Her Japanese age is eleven, and we weren't much older," Mrs. Hosoume said.

"Look," Mr. Hosoume said, "if you're going to contradict every piece of advice I give the children, they'll end up disobeying us both and doing what they very well please. Just because I'm ill just now is no reason for them to start being disrespectful."

"When have I ever contradicted you before?" Mrs. Hosoume said.

"Countless times," Mr. Hosoume said.

"Name one instance," Mrs. Hosoume said.

Certainly there had been times, but Mr. Hosoume could not happen to mention the one requested instance on the spot and he became quite angry. "That's quite enough of your insolence," he said. Since he was speaking in Japanese, his exact accusation was that she was *nama-iki*, which is a shade more revolting than being merely insolent.

"*Nama-iki, nama-iki?*" said Mrs. Hosoume. "How dare you? I'll have anyone calling me *nama-iki!*"

At that, Mr. Hosoume went up to where his wife was ironing and slapped her smartly on the face. It was the first time he had ever laid hands on her. Mrs. Hosoume was immobile for an instant, but she resumed her ironing as though nothing had happened, although she glanced over at Marpo, who happened to be in the room reading a newspaper. Yoneko and Seigo forgot they were listening to the radio and stared at their parents, thunderstruck.

"Hit me again," said Mrs. Hosoume quietly, as she ironed. "Hit me all you wish."

Mr. Hosoume was apparently about to, but Marpo stepped up and put his hand on Mr. Hosoume's shoulder. "The children are here," said Marpo, "the children."

"Mind your own business," said Mr. Hosoume in broken English. "Get out of here!"

Marpo left, and that was about all. Mrs. Hosoume went on ironing, Yoneko and Seigo turned back to the radio, and Mr.

Hosoume muttered that Marpo was beginning to forget his place. Now that he thought of it, he said, Marpo had been increasingly impudent towards him since his illness. He said just because he was temporarily an invalid was no reason for Marpo to start being disrespectful. He added that Marpo had better watch his step or that he might find himself jobless one of these fine days.

And something of the sort must have happened. Marpo was here one day and gone the next, without even saying goodbye to Yoneko and Seigo. That was also the day the Hosoume family went to the city on a weekday afternoon, which was most unusual. Mr. Hosoume, who now avoided driving as much as possible, handled the cumbersome Reo as though it were a nervous stallion, sitting on the edge of the seat and hugging the steering wheel. He drove very fast and about halfway to the city struck a beautiful collie which dashed out barking from someone's yard. The car jerked with the impact, but Mr. Hosoume drove right on and Yoneko, wanting suddenly to vomit, looked back and saw the collie lying very still at the side of the road.

When they arrived at the Japanese hospital, which was their destination, Mr. Hosoume cautioned Yoneko and Seigo to be exemplary children and wait patiently in the car. It seemed hours before he and Mrs. Hosoume returned, she walking with very small, slow steps and he assisting her. When Mrs. Hosoume got in the car, she leaned back and closed her eyes. Yoneko inquired as to the source of her distress, for she was obviously in pain, but she only answered that she was feeling a little under the weather and that the doctor had administered some necessarily astringent treatment. At that, Mr. Hosoume turned around and advised Yoneko and Seigo that they must tell no one of coming to the city on a weekday afternoon, absolutely no one, and Yoneko and Seigo readily assented. On the way home, they passed the place of the encounter with the collie, and Yoneko looked up and down the stretch of road but the dog was nowhere to be seen.

Not long after that, the Hosoumes got a new hired hand, an old Japanese man who wore his grey hair in a military cut and who, unlike Marpo, had no particular interests outside working, eating, sleeping, and playing an occasional game of *goh* with Mr. Hosoume. Before he came Yoneko and Seigo played sometimes in the empty bunkhouse and recalled Marpo's various charms together. Privately, Yoneko was wounded more than she would admit even to herself that Marpo should have subjected her to such an abrupt desertion. Whenever her indignation became too great to endure gracefully, she would console herself by telling Seigo that, after all, Marpo was a mere Filipino, an eater of wild dogs.

Seigo never knew about the disappointing new hired man, because he suddenly died in the night. He and Yoneko had spent the hot morning in the nearest orange grove, she driving him to distraction by repeating certain words he could not bear to hear: she had called him Serge, a name she had read somewhere, instead of Seigo; and she had chanted off the name of the tires they were rolling around like hoops as Goodrich Silver-TO-town, Goodrich Silver-TO-town, instead of Goodrich Silvertown. This had enraged him, and he had chased her around the trees most of the morning. Finally she had taunted him from several trees away by singing. "You're a Yellow-streaked Coward," which was one of several small songs she had composed. Seigo had suddenly grinned and shouted, "Sure!" and walked off, leaving her, as he intended, with a sense of emptiness. In the afternoon, they had perspired and followed the potato-digging machine and the Mexican workers, both hired for the day, around the field, delighting in unearthing marble-sized, smooth-skinned potatoes that both the machine and the men had missed. Then, in the middle of the night, Seigo began crying, complaining of a stomach ache. Mrs. Hosoume felt his head and sent her husband for the doctor, who smiled and said Seigo would be fine in the morning. He said it was doubtless the combination of green oranges, raw potatoes, and the July heat. But as soon as the doctor left, Seigo fell into a coma and a drop of red blood stood out on his underlip, where he had evidently bit it. Mr. Hosoume again fetched the doctor, who was this time very grave and wagged his head, saying several times, "It looks very bad." So Seigo died at the age of five.

Mrs. Hosoume was inconsolable and had swollen eyes in the morning for weeks afterwards. She now insisted on visiting the city relatives each Sunday, so that she could attend church services with them. One Sunday, she stood up and accepted Christ. It was through accompanying her mother to many of these services that Yoneko finally learned the Japanese words to "Let Us Gather at the River." Mrs. Hosoume also did not seem interested in discussing anything but God and Seigo. She was especially fond of reminding visitors how adorable Seigo had been as an infant, how she had been unable to refrain from dressing him as a little girl and fixing his hair in bangs until he was two. Mr. Hosoume was very gentle with her and when Yoneko accidentally caused her to giggle once, he nodded and said, "Yes, that's right, Yoneko, we must make your mother laugh and forget about Seigo." Yoneko herself did not think about Seigo at all. Whenever the thought of Seigo crossed her mind, she instantly began composing a new song, and this worked very well.

One evening, when the new hired man had been with them a while, Yoneko was helping her mother with the dishes when she found herself being examined with such peculiarly intent eyes that, with a start of guilt, she began searching in her mind for a possible crime she had lately committed. But Mrs. Hosoume only said, "Never kill a person, Yoneko, because if you do, God will take from you someone you love."

"Oh, that," said Yoneko quickly, "I don't believe in that, I don't believe in God." And her words tumbling pell-mell over one another, she went on eagerly to explain a few of her reasons why. If she neglected to mention the test she had given God during the earthquake, it was probably because she was a little upset. She had believed for a moment that her mother was going to ask about the ring (which, alas, she had lost already, somewhere in the flumes along the canteloupe patch).

IDENTITY

THE BADGES OF BELONGING

*Whence all this passion toward conformity
anyway?—diversity is the word.*

Ralph Ellison

"Whence all this passion toward conformity anyway?" the
hero of Ralph Ellison's *Invisible Man* demands. "Diversity
is the word." The invisible man, in reflecting upon his
varied experiences as a black man in America, uses color
as a metaphor of identity and concludes that the preservation of individual uniqueness is the preservation of America
itself.

Let man keep his many parts and you'll have no tyrant
states. Why, if they follow this conformity business they'll
end up by forcing me, an invisible man, to become white,
which is not a color but the lack of one. Must I strive
toward colorlessness? But seriously, and without snobbery,
think of what the world would lose if that should happen.
America is woven of many strands; I would recognize them
and let it so remain. It's "winner take nothing" that is the
great truth of our country or of any country. Life is to be
lived, not controlled; and humanity is won by continuing
to play in face of certain defeat. Our fate is to become one,
and yet many—This is not prophecy, but description. Thus
one of the greatest jokes in the world is the spectacle of the
whites escaping blackness and becoming blacker every day,
and the blacks striving toward whiteness, becoming quite

dull and gray. None of us seems to know who he is or where he's going.

Ellison expresses an idea central to American thought since the time of Emerson. The theme of self-reliance appears in the work of our greatest nineteenth-century authors, most of whom belong to the Anglo-Saxon tradition generally considered the "mainstream" of American life. These authors—Emerson, Thoreau, Whitman, Henry James, and others—speak vigorously of the need for individualism. Twentieth-century writers like Hemingway, Fitzgerald, and Faulkner express the same concern, although the theme now becomes a lament for the loss of self-reliance in the modern world.

As newcomers to America, ethnic authors respond directly to the need for individualism, making the idea central to their literature. The rediscovery of ethnic identity is one way to establish the writers' uniqueness in America. William Melvin Kelley makes a clear distinction between the white Anglo-Saxon tradition and that of the African; Muriel Rukeyser suggests the special identity that Jews must feel in the twentieth century; William Shannon writes of the distinctive heritage of the Irish, and John O'Hara of their special character in this country. As Americans seem to grow less varied and heterogeneous, less compelled by the idea of self-reliance, these writers insist more vigorously upon self-identity. For them selfhood begins with the knowledge of themselves as members, proud and articulate, of minority groups.

A POEM FOR BLACK HEARTS

LeRoi Jones

For Malcolm's eyes, when they broke
the face of some dumb white man. For
Malcolm's hands raised to bless us
all black and strong in his image
of ourselves, for Malcolm's words
fire darts, the victor's tireless
thrusts, words hung above the world
change as it may, he said it, and
for this he was killed, for saying,
and feeling, and being/change, all
collected hot in his heart, For Malcolm's
heart, raising us above our filthy cities,
for his stride, and his beat, and his address
to the grey monsters of the world, For Malcolm's
pleas for your dignity, black men, for your life,
black men, for the filling of your minds
with righteousness, For all of him dead and
gone and vanished from us, and all of him which
clings to our speech black god of our time.
For all of him, and all of yourself, look up,
black man, quit stuttering and shuffling, look up,
black man, quit whining and stooping, for all of him,
For Great Malcolm a prince of the earth, let nothing in us
    rest
until we avenge ourselves for his death, stupid animals
that killed him, let us never breathe a pure breath if
we fail, and white men call us faggots till the end of
the earth.

BLACK POWER

William Melvin Kelley

Is it still necessary to discuss the differences between the two peoples, African and European, who inhabit the United States?

I thought everybody accepted those differences. I thought that everybody knew the difference between James Brown and Elvis Presley, or Willie Mays and Mickey Mantle, or the waltz and the guaguanco, or the Temptations and the Beatles, or Leontyne Price and Joan Sutherland, or Duke Ellington and Aaron Copeland or even old Nat Turner and Mr. Jefferson Davis. And so I did not think we had to leaf back to Chapter One. But we do.

Please, sir, we are different, sir.

Our ancestors came from Africa, yours from Europe. Our ancestors did not want to come to the United States, yours did. Once we arrived in the United States, yes, we both worked— but separated from each other. We did not mix. You remained, essentially, a European people. We remained an African people.

We remained African because in Africa we had possessed a complex and highly-developed oral tradition. Knowledge—of the past, of the environment, artistic traditions, philosophy, myth, cuisine—was passed from one generation to the next, orally.

For the most part, we did not have written languages, books. You had books, libraries, where knowledge of the past, the environment, artistic traditions, philosophy, myth and even cuisine was boxed, packaged, stacked, catalogued, categorized, entombed and enshrined. In books. You must have money to get into such places, to study books, to buy books. Everybody cannot do it.

Many more people talk than write. Many more people hear and see than read. And we, those of us whose ancestors came from Africa, we had, still have, an oral tradition.

Unlike many immigrants, we did not suffer the shock of being separated, by English, from languages which were both oral and written. We were torn only from spoken cultures.

We missed the sounds of each of our languages, but the content, its meanings, stayed with us. An important aspect of our African cultures was the strong emphasis on Improvisation. Improvisation, in many different forms, is common to all of Africa.

In the United States, we improvised. An African, a grown man, taken in battle or kidnapped, marched to the coast in chains, forced onto a ship, carried across an ocean, unloaded, sold and told, finally, that he must pick somebody else's cotton, such a man had better improvise.

He did. We all did. We improvised on English. We improvised on Christianity. We improvised on European dress. We improvised on European instruments. We improvised on European games.

Orally. An African woman may have learned to cook her owner's dinner the way he liked it, but when she cooked her own food, she added a little pepper, as she had done in Africa. And that's the food she fed her children, or the African children she was feeding. And she taught the girls to cook that way, the old way. And those girls taught their girls. Orally. To our day.

We talked. We improvised. And our ancestors came from Africa. That is why you cannot compare James Brown to Elvis Presley, or the Temptations to the Beatles, or Duke Ellington to Aaron Copeland, or even the Black Power Movement to the Abolitionists and the Anarchists.

We are different.

ANGEL LEVINE

Bernard Malamud

Manischevitz, a tailor, in his fifty-first year suffered many reverses and indignities. Previously a man of comfortable means, he overnight lost all he had, when his establishment caught fire and, after a metal container of cleaning fluid exploded, burned to the ground. Although Manischevitz was insured against fire, damage suits by two customers who had been hurt in the flames deprived him of every penny he had collected. At almost the same time, his son, of much promise, was killed in the war, and his daughter, without so much as a word of warning, married a lout and disappeared with him as off the face of the earth. Thereafter Manischevitz was victimized by excruciating backaches and found himself unable to work even as a presser—the only kind of work available to him —for more than an hour or two daily, because beyond that the pain from standing became maddening. His Fanny, a good wife and mother, who had taken in washing and sewing, began before his eyes to waste away. Suffering shortness of breath, she at last became seriously ill and took to her bed. The doctor, a former customer of Manischevitz, who out of pity treated them, at first had difficulty diagnosing her ailment but later put it down as hardening of the arteries at an advanced stage. He took Manischevitz aside, prescribed complete rest for her, and in whispers gave him to know there was little hope.

Throughout his trials Manischevitz had remained somewhat stoic, almost unbelieving that all this had descended upon his head, as if it were happening, let us say, to an acquaintance or some distant relative; it was in sheer quantity of woe incomprehensible. It was also ridiculous, unjust, and because he had always been a religious man, it was in a way an affront to God.

Manischevitz believed this in all his suffering. When his burden had grown too crushingly heavy to be borne he prayed in his chair with shut hollow eyes: "My dear God, sweetheart, did I deserve that this should happen to me?" Then recognizing the worthlessness of it, he put aside the complaint and prayed humbly for assistance: "Give Fanny back her health, and to me for myself that I shouldn't feel pain in every step. Help now or tomorrow is too late. This I don't have to tell you." And Manischevitz wept.

Manischevitz's flat, which he had moved into after the disastrous fire, was a meager one, furnished with a few sticks of chairs, a table, and bed, in one of the poorer sections of the city. There were three rooms: a small, poorly-papered living room; an apology for a kitchen, with a wooden icebox; and the comparatively large bedroom where Fanny lay in a sagging secondhand bed, gasping for breath. The bedroom was the warmest room of the house and it was here, after his outburst to God, that Manischevitz, by the light of two small bulbs overhead, sat reading his Jewish newspaper. He was not truly reading, because his thoughts were everywhere; however the print offered a convenient resting place for his eyes, and a word or two, when he permitted himself to comprehend them, had the momentary effect of helping him forget his troubles. After a short while he discovered, to his surprise, that he was actively scanning the news, searching for an item of great interest to him. Exactly what he thought he would read he couldn't say—until he realized, with some astonishment, that he was expecting to discover something about himself. Manischevitz put his paper down and looked up with the distinct impression that someone had entered the apartment, though he could not remember having heard the sound of the door opening. He looked around: the room was very still, Fanny sleeping, for once, quietly. Half-frightened, he watched her until he was satisfied she wasn't dead; then, still disturbed by the thought of an unannounced visitor, he stumbled into the living room and there had the shock of his life, for at the table sat a Negro reading a newspaper he had folded up to fit into one hand.

"What do you want here?" Manischevitz asked in fright.

The Negro put down the paper and glanced up with a gentle expression. "Good evening." He seemed not to be sure of himself, as if he had got into the wrong house. He was a large man, bonily built, with a heavy head covered by a hard derby, which he made no attempt to remove. His eyes seemed sad, but his lips, above which he wore a slight mustache, sought to smile; he was not otherwise prepossessing. The cuffs of his sleeves, Manischevitz noted, were frayed to the lining and the dark suit was badly fitted. He had very large feet. Recovering from his fright, Manischevitz guessed he had left the door open and was being visited by a case worker from the Welfare Department—some came at night—for he had recently applied for relief. Therefore he lowered himself into a chair opposite the Negro, trying, before the man's uncertain smile, to feel comfortable. The former tailor sat stiffly but patiently at the table, waiting for the investigator to take out his pad and pencil and begin asking questions; but before long he became convinced the man intended to do nothing of the sort.

"Who are you?" Manischevitz at last asked uneasily.

"If I may, insofar as one is able to, identify myself, I bear the name of Alexander Levine."

In spite of all his troubles Manischevitz felt a smile growing on his lips. "You said Levine?" he politely inquired.

The Negro nodded. "That is exactly right."

Carrying the jest farther, Manischevitz asked, "You are maybe Jewish?"

"All my life I was, willingly."

The tailor hesitated. He had heard of black Jews but had never met one. It gave an unusual sensation.

Recognizing in afterthought something odd about the tense of Levine's remark, he said doubtfully, "You ain't Jewish anymore?"

Levine at this point removed his hat, revealing a very white part in his black hair, but quickly replaced it. He replied, "I have recently been disincarnated into an angel. As such, I offer you my humble assistance, if to offer is within my province and ability—in the best sense." He lowered his eyes in apology. "Which calls for added explanation: I am what I am granted to be, and at present the completion is in the future."

"What kind of angel is this?" Manischevitz gravely asked.

"A bona fide angel of God, within prescribed limitations," answered Levine, "not to be confused with the members of any particular sect, order, or organization here on earth operating under a similar name."

Manischevitz was thoroughly disturbed. He had been expecting something but not this. What sort of mockery was it—provided Levine was an angel—of a faithful servant who had from childhood lived in the synagogues, always concerned with the word of God?

To test Levine he asked, "Then where are your wings?"

The Negro blushed as well as he was able. Manischevitz understood this from his changed expression. "Under certain circumstances we lose privileges and prerogatives upon returning to earth, no matter what purpose, or endeavoring to assist whosoever."

"So tell me," Manischevitz said triumphantly, "how did you get here?"

"I was transmitted."

Still troubled, the tailor said, "If you are a Jew, say the blessing for bread."

Levine recited it in sonorous Hebrew.

Although moved by the familiar words Manischevitz still felt doubt that he was dealing with an angel.

"If you are an angel," he demanded somewhat angrily, "give me the proof."

Levine wet his lips. "Frankly, I cannot perform either miracles or near miracles, due to the fact that I am in a condition of probation. How long that will persist or even consist, I admit, depends on the outcome."

Manischevitz racked his brains for some means of causing Levine positively to reveal his true identity, when the Negro spoke again:

"It was given me to understand that both your wife and you require assistance of a salubrious nature?"

The tailor could not rid himself of the feeling that he was the butt of a jokester. Is this what a Jewish angel looks like? he asked himself. This I am not convinced.

He asked a last question. "So if God sends to me an angel, why a black? Why not a white that there are so many of them?"

"It was my turn to go next," Levine explained.

Manischevitz could not be persuaded. "I think you are a faker."

Levine slowly rose. His eyes showed disappointment and worry. "Mr. Manischevitz," he said tonelessly, "if you should desire me to be of assistance to you any time in the near future, or possibly before, I can be found"—he glanced at his fingernails—"in Harlem."

He was by then gone.

The next day Manischevitz felt some relief from his back-ache and was able to work four hours at pressing. The day after, he put in six hours; and the third day four again. Fanny sat up a little and asked for some halvah to suck. But on the fourth day the stabbing, breaking ache afflicted his back, and Fanny again lay supine, breathing with blue-lipped difficulty.

Manischevitz was profoundly disappointed at the return of his active pain and suffering. He had hoped for a longer interval of easement, long enough to have some thought other than of himself and his troubles. Day by day, hour by hour, minute after minute, he lived in pain, pain his only memory, questioning the necessity of it, inveighing against it, also, though with affection, against God. Why *so much*, Gottenyu? If He wanted to teach His servant a lesson for some reason, some cause—the nature of His nature—to teach him, say, for reasons of his weakness, his pride, perhaps, during his years of prosperity, his frequent neglect of God—to give him a little lesson, why then any of the tragedies that had happened to him, any *one* would have sufficed to chasten him. But *all together*— the loss of both his children, his means of livelihood, Fanny's health and his—that was too much to ask one frail-boned man to endure. Who, after all, was Manischevitz that he had been given so much to suffer? A tailor. Certainly not a man of talent. Upon him suffering was largely wasted. It went nowhere, into nothing: into more suffering. His pain did not earn him bread, nor fill the cracks in the wall, nor lift, in the middle of the night, the kitchen table; only lay upon him, sleepless, so sharply oppressively that he could many times have cried out yet not heard himself through this thickness of misery.

In this mood he gave no thought to Mr. Alexander Levine, but at moments when the pain waivered, slightly diminishing, he sometimes wondered if he had been mistaken to dismiss him. A black Jew and angel to boot—very hard to believe, but suppose he *had* been sent to succor him, and he, Manischevitz, was in his blindness too blind to comprehend? It was this thought that put him on the knife-point of agony.

Therefore the tailor, after much self-questioning and con-tinuing doubt, decided he would seek the self-styled angel in Harlem. Of course he had great difficulty, because he had not asked for specific directions, and movement was tedious to him. The subway took him to 116th Street, and from there he wandered in the dark world. It was vast and its lights lit nothing. Everywhere were shadows, often moving. Manischevitz hobbled along with the aid of a cane, and not knowing where to seek in the blackened tenement buildings, look fruitlessly through store windows. In the stores he saw people and *everybody* was black. It was an amazing thing to observe. When he was too tired, too unhappy to go farther, Manischevitz stopped in front of a tailor's store. Out of familiarity with the appearance of it, with some sadness he entered. The tailor, an old skinny Negro with a mop of woolly gray hair, was sitting cross-legged on his workbench, sewing a pair of full-dress pants that had a razor slit all the way down the seat.

"You'll excuse me, please, gentleman," said Manischevitz, admiring the tailor's deft, thimbled fingerwork, "but you know maybe somebody by the name Alexander Levine?"

The tailor, who Manischevitz thought, seemed a little antagonistic to him, scratched his scalp.

"Cain't say I ever heard dat name."

"Alex-ander Lev-ine," Manischevitz repeated it.

The man shook his head. "Cain't say I heared."

About to depart, Manischevitz remembered to say: "He is an angel, maybe."

"Oh *him*," said the tailor clucking. "He hang out in dat honky tonk down here a ways." He pointed with his skinny finger and returned to the pants.

Manischevitz crossed the street against a red light and was almost run down by a taxi. On the block after the next, the sixth store from the corner was a cabaret, and the name in sparkling lights was Bella's. Ashamed to go in, Manischevitz gazed through the neon-lit window, and when the dancing couples had parted and drifted away, he discovered at a table on the side, towards the rear, Levine.

He was sitting alone, a cigarette butt hanging from the corner of his mouth, playing solitaire with a dirty pack of cards, and Manischevitz felt a touch of pity for him, for Levine had deteriorated in appearance. His derby was dented and had a gray smudge on the side. His ill-fitting suit was shabbier, as if he had been sleeping in it. His shoes and trouser cuffs were muddy, and his face was covered with an impenetrable stubble the color of licorice. Manischevitz, though deeply disappointed, was about to enter, when a big-breasted Negress in a purple evening gown appeared before Levine's table, and with much laughter through many white teeth, broke into a vigorous shimmy. Levine looked straight at Manischevitz with a haunted expression, but the tailor was too paralyzed to move or acknowledge it. As Bella's gyrations continued, Levine rose, his eyes lit in excitement. She embraced him with vigor, both his hands clasped around her big restless buttocks and they tangoed together across the floor, loudly applauded by the noisy customers. She seemed to have lifted Levine off his feet and his large shoes hung limp as they danced. They slid past the windows where Manischevitz, white-faced, stood staring in. Levine winked slyly and the tailor left for home.

Fanny lay at death's door. Through shrunken lips she muttered concerning her childhood, the sorrows of the marriage bed, the loss of her children, yet wept to live. Manischevitz tried to not to listen, but even without ears he would have heard. It was not a gift. The doctor panted up the stairs, a broad but bland, unshaven man (it was Sunday) and soon shook his head. A day at most, or two. He left at once, not without pity, to spare himself Manischevitz's multiplied sorrow; the man who never stopped hurting. He would someday get him into a public home.

Manischevitz visited a synagogue and there spoke to God, but God had absented himself. The tailor searched his heart and found no hope. When she died he would live dead. He considered taking his life although he knew he wouldn't. Yet it was something to consider. Considering, you existed. He railed against God—Can you love a rock, a broom, an emptiness? Baring his chest, he smote the naked bones, cursing himself for having believed.

Asleep in a chair that afternoon, he dreamed of Levine. He was standing before a faded mirror, preening small decaying opalescent wings. "This means," mumbled Manischevitz, as he broke out of sleep, "that it is possible he could be an angel." Begging a neighbor lady to look in on Fanny and occasionally wet her lips with a few drops of water, he drew on his thin coat, gripped his walking stick, exchanged some pennies for a subway token and rode to Harlem. He knew this act was the last desperate one of his woe: to go without belief, seeking a black magician to restore his wife to invalidism. Yet if there was no choice, he did at least what was chosen.

He hobbled to Bella's but the place had changed hands. It was now, as he breathed, a synagogue in a store. In the front, towards him, were several rows of empty wooden benches. In the rear stood the Ark, its portals of rough wood covered with rainbows of sequins; under it a long table on which lay the sacred scroll unrolled, illuminated by the dim light from a bulb on a chain overhead. Around the table, as if frozen to it and the scroll, which they all touched with their fingers, sat four Negroes wearing skullcaps. Now as they read the Holy Word, Manischevitz could, through the plate glass window, hear the singsong chant of their voices. One of them was old, with a gray beard. One was bubble-eyed. One was hump-backed. The fourth was a boy, no older than thirteen. Their heads moved in rhythmic swaying. Touched by this sight from his childhood and youth, Manischevitz entered and stood silent in the rear.

"Neshoma," said bubble eyes, pointing to the word with a stubby finger. "Now what dat mean?"

"That's the word that means soul," said the boy. He wore glasses.

"Let's git on wid de commentary," said the old man.

"Ain't necessary," said the humpback. "Souls is immaterial substance. That's all. The soul is derived in that manner. The immateriality is derived from the substance, and they both, causally an' otherwise, derived from the soul. There can be no higher."

"That's the highest."

"Over de top."

"Wait a minute," said bubble eyes. "I don't see what is dat immaterial substance. How come de one gits hitched up to de odder?" He addressed the humpback.

"Ask me something hard. Because it is substanceless immateriality. It couldn't be closer together, like all the parts of the body under one skin—closer."

"Hear now," said the old man.

"All you done is switched de words."

"It's the primum mobile, the substanceless substance from which comes all things that were incepted in the idea—you, me and everything and body else."

"Now how did all dat happen? Make it sound simple."

"It de speerit,' said the old man. "On de face of de water moved de speerit. And at was good. It say so in de Book. From de speerit ariz de man."

"But now listen here. How come it become substance if it all de time a spirit?"

"God alone done dat."

"Holy! Holy! Praise His Name."

"But has dis spirit got some kind of a shade or color?" asked bubble eyes, deadpan.

"Man of course not. A spirit is a spirit."

"Then how come we is colored?" he said with a triumphant glare.

"Ain't got nothing to do wid dat."

"I still like to know."

"God put the spirit in all things," answered the boy. "He put it in the green leaves and the yellow flowers. He put it with the gold in the fishes and the blue in the sky. That's how come it came to us."

"Amen."

"Praise Lawd and utter loud His speechless name."

"Blow de bugle till it bust the sky."

They fell silent, intent upon the next word. Manischevitz approached them.

"You'll excuse me," he said. "I am looking for Alexander Levine. You know him maybe?"

"That's the angel," said the boy.

"Oh, *him*," snuffed bubble eyes.

"You'll find him at Bella's. It's the establishment right across the street," the humpback said.

Manischevitz said he was sorry that he could not stay, thanked them, and limped across the street. It was already night. The city was dark and he could barely find his way.

But Bella's was bursting with the blues. Through the window Manischevitz recognized the dancing crowd and among them sought Levine. He was sitting loose-lipped at Bella's side table. They were tippling from an almost empty whiskey fifth. Levine had shed his old clothes, wore a shiny new checkered suit, pearl-gray derby, cigar, and big, two- tone button shoes. To the tailor's dismay, a drunken look had settled upon his formerly dignified face. He leaned toward Bella, tickled her ear lobe with his pinky, while whispering words that sent her into gales of raucous laughter. She fondled his knee.

Manischevitz, girding himself, pushed open the door and was not welcomed.

"This place reserved."

"Beat it, pale puss."

"Exit, Yankel, Semitic trash."

But he moved towards the table where Levine sat, the crowd breaking before him as he hobbled forward.

"Mr. Levine," he spoke in a trembly voice. "Is here Mani-schevitz."

Levine glared blearily. "Speak yo' piece, son."

Manischevitz shuddered. His back plagued him. Cold trem-ors tormented his crooked legs. He looked around, everybody was all ears.

"You'll excuse me. I would like to talk to you in a private place."

"Speak, Ah is a private pusson."

Bella laughed piercingly. "Stop it, boy, you killin' me."

Manischevitz, no end disturbed, considered fleeing but Levine addressed him:

"Kindly state the pu'pose of yo' communication with yo's truly."

The tailor wet cracked lips. "You are Jewish. This I am sure."

Levine rose, nostrils flaring. "Anythin' else yo' got to say?"

Manischevitz's tongue lay like stone.

"Spak now or fo'ever hold off."

Tears blinded the tailor's eyes. Was ever man so tried? Should he say he believed a half-drunken Negro to be an angel?

The silence slowly petrified.

Manischevitz was recalling scenes of his youth as a wheel in his mind whirred: believe, do not, yes, no, yes, no. The pointer pointed to yes, to between yes and no, to no, no it was yes. He sighed. It moved but one had still to make a choice.

"I think you are an angel from God." He said it in a broken voice, thinking, If you said it it was said. If you believed it you must say it. If you believed, you believed.

The hush broke. Everybody talked but the music began and they went on dancing. Bella, grown bored, picked up the cards and dealt herself a hand.

Levine burst into tears. "How you have humiliated me."

Manischevitz apologized.

"Wait'll I freshen up." Levine went to the men's room and returned in his old clothes.

No one said goodbye as they left.

They rode to the flat via subway. As they walked up the stairs Manischevitz pointed with his cane at his door.

"That's all been taken care of," Levine said. "You best go in while I take off."

Disappointed that it was so soon over but torn by curiosity, Manischevitz followed the angel up three flights to the roof. When he got there the door was already padlocked.

Luckily he could see through a small broken window. He heard an odd noise, as though of a whirring of wings, and when he strained for a wider view, could have sworn he saw a dark figure borne aloft on a pair of magnificent black wings.

A feather drifted down. Manischevitz gasped as it turned white, but it was only snowing.

He rushed downstairs. In the flat Fanny wielded a dust mop under the bed and then upon the cobwebs on the wall.

"A wonderful thing, Fanny," Manischevitz said. "Believe me, there are Jews everywhere."

HOW MUCH ARE WE AMERICAN?

Muriel Rukeyser

How much are we American? Not knowing
those other lands, being
blood wrung from your bone, our pioneers,
we call kindred to you, we claim links, speaking
your tongue, although we pass, shaking
your dream with revolution since we must.
By these roads shall we come upon our country.
Pillowed upon this birthright, we may wake
strong for such treason, brave with your fallen dust.

O, we are afflicted with these present evils,
they press between the mirror and our eyes,
obscuring your loaned mouths and borrowed hair.
We focus on our times, destroying you, fathers
in the long ground : you have given strange birth
to us who turn against you in our blood
needing to move in our integrity, accomplices
of life in revolution, though the past
be sweet with your tall shadows, and although
we turn from treasons, we shall accomplish these.

TO BE A JEW IN THE
TWENTIETH CENTURY

. . .

To be a Jew in the twentieth century
Is to be offered a gift. If you refuse,
Wishing to be invisible, you choose
Death of the spirit, the stone insanity.
Accepting, take full life. Full agonies:
Your evening deep in labyrinthine blood
Of those who resist, fail, and resist; and God
Reduced to a hostage among hostages.

The gift is torment. Not alone the still
Torture, isolation; or torture of the flesh.
That may come also. But the accepting wish,
The whole and fertile spirit as guarantee
For every human freedom, suffering to be free,
Daring to live for the impossible.

THE REFUGEES

from Fourth Elegy

And the child sitting alone planning her hope:
I want to write for my race. But what race will you speak,
being American? I want to write for the living.
But the young grow more around us every day.
They show new faces, they come from far, they live
occupied with escape, freeze in the passes, sail
early in the morning. A few arrive to help.
        Mother, those were not angels, they were knights.

. . .

The age of the masked and the alone begins.
It is the children's voyage must be done
before the refugees come home again.

They are the children. They have their games.
They made a circle on a map of time,
skipping they entered it, laughing lifted the agate.
I will get you an orange cat, and a pig called Tangerine.—
They leave their games, and pass.

It will take a bell-ringing god tremendous imagined
        descending
for the healing of hell.

A line of birds, a line of gods. Of bells.
And all the birds have settled on their shadows.
And down the shadowed street a line of children.
You can make out the child ahead of you.

It turns with a gesture that asks for a soft answer.
It sees the smaller child ahead of it.
The child ahead of it turns. Now, in the close-up
faces throw shadow off. It is yourself
walks down this street at five-year intervals,
seeing yourself diminishing ahead,
five years younger, and five years younger, and young,
until the farthest infant has a face
ready to grow into any child in the world.

      They take to boats. The shipwreck of New York. . . .
         They are the strong. They see the enemy.
         They dream the relaxed heart, coming again
            to power,
        the struggle, the Milk-Tree of Children's Paradise.

. . .

Through epidemics of injuries, Madrid, Shanghai,
Vienna, Barcelona, all cities of contagion,
issue survivors from the surf of the age.
Free to be very hungry and very lonely.
And in the countries of the mind, Cut off at the knee. Cut
    off at the armpit. Cut off at the throat.
Free to reclaim the world and sow a legend,
to make the adjustments never made,
repair the promises broken and the promise kept.
They blame their lives, lie on our wishes with their eyes
    our own,
to say and to remember and avenge. A lullaby for a
    believing child.

A TURNING WIND

from Fifth Elegy

Knowing the shape of the country. Knowing the midway
    travels of
migrant fanatics, living that life, up with the dawn and
moving as long as the light lasts, and when the sun is
    falling to wait, still standing;

and when the black has come, at last lie down, too tired to
turn to each other, feeling only the land's demand under
    them.
Shape that exists not as permanent quality, but varies with
    even the movement of bone.

Even in skeletons, it depends on the choices of action.
A definite plan is visible. We are either free-moving or
fixed to some ground. The shape has no meaning
    outside of the function.

Fixed to Europe, the distant, adjacent, we lived, with the
    land-
promise of life of our own. Course down the East —
    frontiers
meet you at every turn — the headlights find them, the
    plain's, and the solar cities'

recurrent centers. And at the middle of the great world the
    wind
answers the shape of the country, a turning traveller
follows the hinge-line of coast, the first indefinite
    axis of symmetry

torn off from sympathy with the past and planted,
a primitive streak prefiguring the west, an ideal
which had to be modified for stability,
     to make it work.

•

These are the ritual years, whose lore is names of shapes,
Grabtown, Cockade Alley, Skid Row where jobless live,
their emblem a hitch-hiker with lips basted together,
     and marvel rivers,

the flooded James, a double rainbow standing over
     Richmond,
the remnant sky above the Cape Fear River, blue stain on
     red water,
the Waccamaw with its bone-trees, Piscataqua's rich mouth,
     red Sound and flesh of sand . . .

     . . .

And this shape, this meaning that promises seasonal joy,
whose form is unquietness and yet the seeker of rest,
whose travelling hunger has range enough, its root
     grips through the world.

The austere fire-world of night : Gary or Bethlehem,
in sacred stacks of flame — or stainless morning,
anti-sunlight of lakes' reflection, matchlight on face,
     the thorny light of fireworks

lighting a way for the shape, this country of celebrations
deep in a passage of rebirth . . .
· · · · · · · · · · · · · Masterpieces of happiness arrive,
     alive again in another land,

remembering pain, faces of suffering, but they know
     growth,
go through the world, hunger and rest desiring life.
Mountains are spines to their conquest, these wrecked
     houses (vines spiral the pillars)

are leaning their splintered sides on tornadoes, lifted
    careening
in wheels, in whirlwind, in a spool of power
drawing a spiral on the sun, drawing a sign of
    strength on the mountains,

following charts of the moving constellations.
Charts of the country of all visions, imperishable

stars of our old dream : process, which having neither
    sorrow nor joy

remains as promise, the embryo in the fire.
The tilted cities of America, fields of metal,
the seamless wheatfields, the current of cities running
    below our wings

promise that knowledge of systems which may bless.
May permit knowledge of self, a lover's wish for conversion
until the time when the dead lake rises in light,
the shape is organized in travelling space;
this hope of travel, to find the place again,
rest in the triumph of the reconceived,
lie down again together face to face.

22 MILES...

Josue A. Gonzalez

From 22 I see my first 8 weren't.
  Around the 9th, I was called "meskin".
    By the 10th, I knew and believed I was.
      I found out what it meant to know, to believe . .
        before my 13th.

Through brown eyes, seeing only brown colors and feeling
only brown feelings . . . I saw . . . I felt . . . I hated . . .
I cried . . . I tried . . . I didn't understand during these 4.
      I rested by just giving up.

While, on the side . . . I realized I BELIEVED in
  white as pretty,
    my being governor,
      blond blue eyed baby Jesus,
        cokes and hamburgers,
          equality for all regardless of race, creed, or color,
          Mr. Williams, our banker.
        I had to!
      That was all I had.
  Beans and Communism were bad.
            Past the weeds, atop the hill, I looked back.

Pretty people, combed and squeaky clean, on arrowlike
      roads.
Pregnant girls, ragged brats, swarthy machos, rosary beads,
and friends waddle clumsily over and across hills, each
      other,

mud, cold, and woods on caliche ruts.
At the 19th mile, I fought blindly at everything and
    anything.
Not knowing, Not caring about WHY, WHEN, or FOR
    WHAT.
  I fought. And fought.
    By the 21st, I was tired and tried.

                        But now. . . . .
I've been told that I am dangerous.
That is because I am good at not being a Mexican.
That is because I know now that I have been cheated.
That is because I hate circumstances and love choices.

    You know . . . chorizo tacos y tortillas ARE good, even
        at school.
  Speaking Spanish is a talent.
Being Mexican IS as good as Rainbo bread.
And without looking back, I know that there are still too
    many . . .
  brown babies,
    pregnant girls,
      old 25 year-old women,
        drunks,
          who should have lived but didn't,
            on those caliche ruts.

        It is tragic that my problems during these past 21
            miles
        were/are/might be . . .
          looking into blue eyes,
            wanting to touch a gringita,
          ashamed of being Mexican,
        believing I could not make it at college,
      pretending that I liked my side of town,

      remembering the Alamo,
    speaking Spanish in school bathrooms only,
  and knowing that Mexico's prostitutes like Americans
        better.

At 22, my problems are still the same but now I know
    I am your
problem.
That farm boys, Mexicans and Negro boys are in Vietnam
    is but one
thing I think about:
                Crystal City, Texas 78839
                The migrant worker;
                The good gringo:

Staying Mexican enough;
Helping;
Looking at the world from the back of a truck.

The stoop labor with high school rings on their fingers;
The Anglo cemetery,
Joe the different Mexican,

                Damn.
                Damn.
                Damn.

NOW THAT THE BUFFALO'S GONE

Buffy Sainte-Marie

1. Can you remember the times
   That you held your head high
   And told all your friends of your Indian claims
   Proud good lady and proud good man.
   Your great, great grandfather from Indian blood sprang,
   And you feel in your heart for these ones.

2. Oh it's written in books and in songs
   That we've been mistreated and wronged
   Well, over and over I hear the same words from you,
   Good lady, from you good man.
   Well listen to me—if you care where we stand,
   And you feel you're a part of these ones.

3. When a war between nations is lost
   The loser we know pays the cost
   But even when Germany fell to your hands
   Consider dear lady, consider dear man.
   You left them their pride and you left them their land
   And what have you done to these ones?

4. Has a change come about Uncle Sam
   Or are you still taking our land
   A treaty forever George Washington signed he did,
   Dear lady, he did, dear man
   And the treaty's being broken by Kinzua Dam
   And what will you do for these ones?

5. Oh it's all in the past you can say
   But it's still going on till today

The government now wants the Iriquois land
That of the Seneca and the Cheyenne
It's here and it's now you must help us, dear man
Now that the buffalo's gone.

THE RETURN TO THE SOURCE

Jo Pagano

When the letter came telling of my grandfather's death my father was downtown, at work, at the market. I was the first to see the letter. It stuck up out of the mailbox, an oblong, somewhat crumpled enveloped with a black border, postmarked from Italy and inscribed with a painful, cramped, old-fashioned handwriting. I took it upstairs, in the living room, where my mother was cleaning house.

"There's a letter here for the old man," I said, concealing it against my side. She looked at me expectantly, waiting for me to hand it to her. She had a dust towel wrapped around her head, and she was holding a rag in one hand. "It's from Italy," I said. "I'm afraid it's bad news."

"What is it?" she asked, looking at me fearsomely. I held it out.

"*Oh, come voglio fà!*" she moaned in terror, dropping the rag. She would not take the letter. She looked at the black border with dread-filled eyes.

"You'd better open it," I suggested, gently, painfully aware of the horror that any indication of death arouses in the aging.

She looked at me dumbly, then took the letter from my hand with repugnance. "It must be his father," she muttered. She sank down in the nearest chair and held the letter this way and that, looking at the writing, fearing to open it. "What shall we do?" she asked me in Italian.

"You'd better open it," I suggested again.

But the letter was for him! she protested, looking at it with morbid fascination. I told her that she had better open it anyhow; it was better that she break the news to my father herself before he saw the letter. "Do you think so?" she asked, looking at me timidly. She stared at the letter for a few moments, then started to open it. Her wrinkled fingers were trembling so much she could not hold the paper between them. Suddenly she dropped it. "I can't!" she said. "I'm afraid."

I picked the envelope up and took out the letter. It was from my father's sister, back in the Old Country. My grandfather had died peacefully in his sleep, at the age of eighty-six, in the town in which he had been born.

"*Povero vecchio*, poor old fellow," muttered my mother, her eyes filling with tears. She took the letter from my hand and read it over again to herself, laboriously, for her vision was failing: she had to hold it away from her, and she pursed her faded lips and squinted her eyes and muttered the words half-aloud.

"*Povero vecchio!*" she said again when she had finished, clucking her tongue and shaking her head; and getting up suddenly, she hobbled to the phone to call my sister Rose. She was no longer crying, and she dialed the number with the breathless excitement of one who has bad news to convey. "Yes, the old man, his father . . . isn't it a shame? The poor old fellow! Yes, in his sleep. . . . You and Frank had better come over. . . ."

This done with, she promptly called the Maccaluccis. Afterwards, we debated whether I should go downtown in the car and get my father. It seemed inconsiderate that we should allow him to come home, as on any ordinary day, on the streetcar; but on the other hand, if I were to go after him he would want to know what was the matter. In the end we decided to wait, staving off for as long as possible the breaking of the painful news.

Towards five o'clock my sister and her husband came over from their macaroni factory, and a little later Mrs. Maccalucci arrived. Meanwhile, my mother had called my brother Vincent, who lived across the city, and also my other sister, Marguerite. The market closed at six, and it was usually around a quarter of seven or so before my father got home; long before that time, the entire family was gathered together in our house, with the dutiful solemnity which a death in the family inspires.

It was the first time since Christmas that we had all—with the exception of Carl, who was in New York,—been gathered together at once. My sisters and Mrs. Maccalucci helped my mother prepare dinner in the kitchen; my brother and brothers-in-law and I sat in the living room. We did not, however, discuss the event which was the reason for our foregathering—our grandfather was too remote from us for his death to have any immediate interest; we sat and talked about our personal affairs. Occasionally my mother poked her head in and bade us not to talk so loud; once, when I snapped on the radio, she reprimanded me sharply. "What's the matter with you? You ought to know better than to turn on the radio tonight!"

At last we heard the click of the door opening downstairs, and my father's heavy tread. We all stopped talking and looked at each other. My mother came in from the kitchen, wiping her hands on her apron, her eyes filling with automatic tears; behind her stood my sisters and Mrs. Maccalucci with solemn faces. We all stared expectantly at the door through which my father would enter. His heavy steps became louder, and then the door clicked and opened and he came in, his massive body and florid head seeming at once to fill the room and to dwarf the rest of us. He glanced surprisedly at us and at the white dinner table, with its gleaming silver and the gold-rimmed wine goblets we used for "formal" occasions.

"What's the occasion?" he said jocularly in his booming, guttural voice; and then he saw my mother weeping.

"What's the matter?" he asked with quick apprehension. "What is it?"

None of us answered for a moment, and then my mother told him of the letter. He did not speak, nor did his face change expression. He stood there looking at her, and when she had finished he asked her quietly for the letter.

"Give it to him, Robert," she said to me.

I got the envelope from the mantel and handed it to him. He took the letter out and put on his glasses and read it slowly. "*Povero padre*, poor papa . . ." he muttered, and suddenly his eyes filled with tears. He looked up at us, dumbly, from over his glasses. My mother touched his arm consolingly and started to speak. He did not listen to her; he looked at the table.

"And what is this, a party?" he asked angrily in Italian. He stood looking at us for a moment, then turned sharply and went into his room.

He did not leave his room the rest of the evening. When, later that night, I passed my parents' bedroom on the way to my own room, I could hear him sobbing.

For a long time it hung on our living-room wall, our only picture of my grandfather: a photograph taken many years before, on the occasion of his only visit to this country; a big squarish picture, showing him and his five sons, each of them holding a stein of beer aloft; a picture of curiously modern design, the heads ranged circularly upon the page, the arms at stiff right angles, the steins placed like points in a modernistic abstract composition—this picture I always loved to look at, it had such a curious feeling of finality to it, as family groups always do seem to have somehow. Here was the endless wheel of life, father and sons, the old and the young: one saw the generations that had lived and spun their destinies before them, one felt the generations that were to come. Of the last, I was one; I was the product of these, I and my brothers; some day, perhaps, our own children would look upon similar portraits of their own fathers, and, so looking, would they not feel something of the mystery and portent of life, of the wheel that spun endlessly, of the beginnings and the endings, the fulfillment and the source?

A family is like a universe. Each of its members is a planet around which a thousand stars revolve. For a long time, in the early years, in the years of childhood and adolescence, one does not think of this: one grows into life like a quivering tentacle, and neither the beginning nor the end has much interest, for one does not think about them. Myself, for example, born in America, brought up in the schools and the streets of the New World, creating a life and being created by it— what knew I of Italy? A country built like a deformed shoe depending from maps of Europe pored over in musty schoolrooms; a name, a flavor, a language which my people spoke; what reality was there in all this, what remembrance? Later one thinks; one puts pieces together, like solving a puzzle; one sees a design grow beneath one's preoccupied fingers; but is it true? Is this, then, really the source?

Once we returned, my father and mother and I. I was very young then, no more than eight or nine. It was the only time I ever saw my grandfather. After his death I thought of this returning. So remote, it seemed; such a long, a very long time ago. How many years had passed, how many lives had I and my parents not lived since then! Now I was grown and my mother and father were aging; my grandfather was dead. And this past, this continuous flow of life that was like a river— sometime in the not too distant future it would flow over us also and we would join, in the category of the nonexistent, that old man who had himself, with the many others, swelled the tide and now lay at rest at last, in the earth of his beloved homeland, beneath the fair Italian sky.

I say that I saw my grandfather, but did I ever really see him? The eyes of childhood are large, but their vision is very small. He was an old man already when we made that trip to Italy, nearly seventy he must have been, sparse, withered, and small, with a cackling laugh and bright little eyes that were like brilliant black beads; that much at least I remember. Other things I remember also: trains; the towering buildings of New York; the magical boat with its corridors and stairways and decks and rails; the great billowing sweep of the ocean, so blue, so glasslike, beneath the limitless sky; the Bay of Naples and the streets of Naples—fragments all of them, pieces of a childish puzzle which older fingers seek to resolve. What did that child really see? That was a real and tangible world into which he entered, that summer so many years ago; but what, what? The mind is like a series of rooms, some of them closed forever, or almost forever; one seeks to unlock these chambers, one fumbles for the key; one sits, as I sat on a certain evening in our living room after my grandfather's death, and looks at a picture, and tries to remember.

I was not yet born when that picture was taken. My grandfather had come to this country to see his sons again, whom he had not seen for so many years; and of this visit my father had many stories to tell us. To begin with, my grandfather's train arrived early, and since he did not speak English he had to wait on the station platform for several hours, not understanding why his sons were not there to meet him; when my father and one of his brothers did arrive, he did not recognize them and refused to believe they were really his sons, thinking, perhaps, that they were some New World crooks trying to take advantage of him, knowing he was a foreigner. My father always roared when he told of this incident, of the two huge men (my father and his brothers all weighed above two hundred pounds) bent above the wary, gray-headed little man with his cackling laugh and toothless mouth, trying to convince him that he was really their father. He was at last persuaded of the genuineness of my uncle, but steadfastly refused to accept my father, who, being the youngest of his sons, was the most remote from his memory. It was not, indeed, until my father reminded him of an incident of his childhood that he would believe they were not trying to play a joke on him; he then cried out: "*Eh, Luigi, mio figlio, mio bambino,* my son, my baby!" and laughing and crying, he kissed him and hugged him and then, dancing nimbly up and down on the station platform, he pretended to spank my father's impressive posterior.

Looking at the picture of my grandfather surrounded by his sons, I remembered this incident; I remembered also other stories my father had to tell of my grandfather's visit: of how, though he had not a tooth left in his mouth, he would eat only the dry crust of bread, refusing the soft inner, the *mollica,* content so long as he had a glass of wine to dip it into. I remembered also my father's favorite story of his father, of how, when he sought to present him with a going-away present of a cane as a mark of filial respect and devotion, my grandfather refused it, saying, with a sly chuckle and a twinkle of his black eyes: "But people are liable to think I am old!" These fragmentary pictures of him were much more vivid than my own recollections, for being stories told to me by my father they had the literary advantage of form and a frame; my own memories were too nebulous and obscure, too clouded over by the fogs of distance and time. For a long time I sat there, looking at the picture on the wall, trying to remember; there was something related to that trip we had taken to Italy which I wanted, without quite knowing what it was, to remember, something which seemed pregnant with meaning and which all of my mind was striving to recapture. But what? What was it?

At last, in impatience, I got up and went into the kitchen, where my father was eating his dinner.

At this time in his life my father was past sixty, but he looked, aside from his white hair, no more than forty-five: his eyes were clear, his complexion smooth and ruddy, he had all his own teeth (aside from a glint of gold in the back of his mouth when he laughed); he had still the magnificent physique which he had gotten from his mother—who was a pretty big woman, you bet. Whenever people complimented him on his youthful appearance and his abundance of good health (as people were always doing) he would invariably give credit to the two factors in his life which he claimed were indispensable to health and longevity: hard work, and a good stomach. That breadth of shoulder, those bulging biceps and knotted forearms which even now hoisted sixty-pound crates of lettuce and celery as easily as though they were sacks of feathers—these were his inheritance from the coal mines of his youth. As for his stomach—surely that organ in his case was made of cast iron? No ordinary stomach of mortal flesh and tissue could possibly digest, as his digested, platters of peppers hot enough to singe the lining off the intestines of less fortunates; and who but a man of iron could take, as he could take, a slice of raw steak from the meat my mother would be preparing of a Saturday night for the Sunday dinner and, sprinkling it lavishly with salt and pepper, gulp it down with great relish and then go promptly to bed—and this after a hard day's work at the market? *"Buona salute!"* as he himself would say.

I sat down at the table opposite him and poured myself a glass of wine. He was having a light repast of spaghetti, meat balls, salad, and wine—no hot peppers, because for a couple of days his stomach had not been feeling so goddam' good. In the corner, next the stove, my mother was shelling some peas. She had a big pan in her lap and her nimble fingers, which could never stand being idle, were cracking the green cylinders open happily: *plink plink,* went the peas into the pan; *plink,* then *plink!* I lit a cigarette and took a sip of the wine and looked at my father across the table.

"Do you remember that time you and I and Mamma went to Italy?" I asked.

He looked up at me from over his plate, questioningly, and with something of the suspicion which a blunt and straightforward man feels for those of more devious ways.

"Sure," he said, wiping his moustache; "what about it?"

"I've been thinking about that trip ever since Grandpa died," I told him. "I've been trying to remember things that happened, but it's been so long ago I can't remember very much about it. How did we happen to go?"

He paused in his eating and looked at me, chewing slowly, a little surprised, perhaps, at my questioning. "Well," he said, scratching his head, struggling to anticipate what it was I wished to know, and to find the answer to it—

"We went for the trip," broke in my mother. "Don't you remember, Robert? I bought you a new Bust' Brown suit, said she, smiling happily; and to my father, in Italian: "Don't you remember how cute he looked?" He grunted and lifted a forkful of spaghetti to his mouth. "I remember so well," said my mother. "That was when we sold out the store in Salt Lake. . ."

But, of course! something inside of me exclaimed in recognition. Salt Lake, where I had spent my childhood; the store (that was before my father had the saloon)—a smell of salami and dried olives, the dark space beneath the counter where I had played at being a storekeeper; the dusty, sun-spilled street outside. . . .

"Oh, yes," I said to my mother. "I remember. I used to play back of the counter, isn't that right?"

"But yes!" said my mother, smiling her old-woman's smile and nodding her head in recollection. "Do you remember when you pulled the flour barrel down on top of you?"

My father looked up and laughed. "That'sa right," he said. He looked at my mother with a curious expression. "By God, that'sa long time ago," he said softly.

She nodded her head. "Yes," she said. "Yes. . . ." She picked up a pea and opened it abstractedly; my father returned to his spaghetti.

"But this trip, now," I said.

"Oh, yes," said my mother. "The trip."

After nearly thirty years in this country, over twenty of which they had been married, over twenty of which they had worked hard, brought into the world five children, and raised themselves up from the status of a poor immigrant coal miner and his bride to prosperous and solid members of the great middle classes—after all of this my mother and father had decided to visit again their native land, to rest, to travel, to see once more the familiar but almost forgotten scenes of their childhood. My sisters were both married, my oldest brother, Lou, was away from home, my other brother was working and old enough to take care of himself; hence it was I, the baby (Carl was not yet born), whom they decided to take with them. Most of these details I now, nearly twenty years later, learned for the first time, in answer to questions. But Lou now,

I would ask my mother. Where was he? And Vincent? And what about Rose and Marguerite, were they married then? And the store. How did you happen to sell it? Well, look, how long had you and Papa been married then?

What did I want from them? What, what? Sometimes they themselves would look at me quizzically, as though to ask that question of me; and could I have answered? One digs, sometimes, without knowing what it is one wishes to excavate, without, indeed, having any foreknowledge of what one's spade will eventually unearth. But there was something in all of this I wished to grasp, some essence, some meaning. Now, in the decline of their lives, my mother and father sat before me in our kitchen, the kitchen of their later years, the last of the kitchens they would ever know together: the big man with his ponderous shoulders and massive head, the little woman with her wrinkled face and bitter mouth; what of this life they had lived together, this inner life that had been their dream and of which I, one product of it, knew, at the last, nothing? A handful of pictures—the pictures of their wedding, snapshots, family groups: these were all that remained of the forty years they had spent together, these, and memories, those memories which I saw mirrored in their eyes when they referred to something that had happened long ago, those memories which I myself possessed of other times. Now, sitting in our kitchen, retracing step by step that trip we had taken so long ago, they remembered—and I, I also remembered.

The town in which my father was born was a small village three or four hours by train from Naples. It was set in the midst of a rich agricultural district, and it was necessary to walk, or ride by horse and cart, another five miles in order to get to the village after alighting from the train. Here my father's family had lived for generations. His father, and father's fathers before him, back to the fifth or sixth generation, had been sextons in the local church—an honorary position, and one in which the family took great pride. The village itself was a relic of feudal days: most of the three or four hundred inhabitants, at the time of my father's birth, were pitifully poor, living under a condition of what amounted to serfdom in allegiance to the grand *Signori,* who owned the land and the vineyards and who were themselves, no doubt, descendants of feudal barons. Of his boyhood in his native village my father in later years had many stories to tell us: of the poverty, the back-breaking work in the fields for a few pennies a day, the condition of almost hopeless economic slavery. All day long from morning until nightfall he and his brothers, along with the other peasants, worked in the fields, with only a piece of hard black bread (baked once a week in communal ovens) to sustain them; here, beneath the hot Italian sun, they tilled the fields and gathered the grapes, but always with a dream in their hearts, the dream of some day escaping to America.

Now, after nearly thirty years, my father was returning home. It is not difficult to conceive the emotions he must have experienced upon revisiting, by the standards of the villagers a rich man, the town in which he had been born. He was as rich as the richest man in town, and more: he, the sexton's son, had become himself a grand *Signore,* with a business and property and money in America; what was more, his person had attached to itself the glamour of the traveler from far places. Of all this I, of course, at that time understood nothing. We were visiting the town where my father was born, back in "Yurrup" (itself as vague a place in my imagination as darkest Africa); I remember being struck by how small everything looked, and lethargic: the primitive stone houses, the profound quietness, a quietness that seemed to emanate from the very dust of the roads. Young as I was (and I have never forgotten it), I felt very strongly this sensation of life being at pause, as though the flow of living had been caught in a pool and remained forever stagnating. If I had been older, the term I should have thought of to describe this sensation would perhaps have been "resignation"; the village and the inhabitants of the village, the very earth itself, seemed resigned to a way of living that had continued too long to admit of change. Then, it seemed to me only to be very quiet, profoundly, almost fearfully so: the hum of the insects at night, the bark of a dog, the murmur of human voices—each sound, magnified against the intense stillness, set my heart beating wildly and I longed with a fierce, almost panic-stricken desire for the familiar noise of America, the clang of streetcars, the hum of machines, all the raucous clatter that was for me associated with home.

And what did my father feel? Standing in a doorway looking down a road, embracing some childhood's friend he had not seen for thirty years, sleeping in the house where he was born, smelling the familiar yet long-forgotten odor of the earth his childish bare feet had trod—what did he feel?

I remember he wept when he embraced his aging father and sister; indeed, I remember that for the first couple of days he wept a great deal.

We were, of course, received like visiting royalty by what few inhabitants of the village remained. I say "what few" because in the thirty years my father had been away the inhabitants had dwindled to less than half the number occupying the town when my father was a boy. Most of the peasants (at least those of my father's generation) had like my father and his brothers emigrated to America; others had moved to the cities of Italy, to Naples and Florence and Milan and Rome, in quest of the fortune which my own father and his brothers had sought in America. As a result of these emigrations a great many changes had taken place, the most arresting of which was the alteration in the fortunes of the great landowners. So many of the peasants had gone away there were not enough to work the fields at a profit, and the vineyards had in large part shriveled from disuse. Besides this, most of the remaining villagers had, with money sent to them by sons or relatives who had found success in America, bought little portions of land for themselves from their former employers, so that they had become independent of the *Signori*, who in turn, as a result of all these upheavals, had become, some of them, as poor as the poorest inhabitant.

Every day there were visitors at my grandfather's house, to see "Francesco Simone's son, who had just returned from America"; they would come in, sometimes in groups of five and ten at a time, dressed in the picturesque garb of the Italian peasant (the women in their stitched skirts and aprons, with their earrings and chains and bracelets of gold, the men in the simple, hardy attire of the farmer); they would greet us with solemn deference, even awe, and sit at the rough table and ply my father with questions. And was it really true that every house in America had a stove? And was it really true that every man was equal, and could be "king" if he wanted to? And was it really true that every house had its own water closet? (These, from people who had lived their lives under the most rigid kind of class distinction, in houses so poor that they cooked in pots suspended within rude fireplaces, with neither plumbing nor toilets other than the crude backhouses which one saw in the early morning with both men and women waiting their turn, each after the other.) At my father's answers they looked at each other and shook their heads incredulously and exclaimed aloud; they would ask the same questions over and over, as though to relish again the delight of the magical answers. My father beamed and expanded and talked incessantly; my mother sat complacently and stroked my hair and nodded her head from time to time in agreement.

We were given dinner after dinner. Each of my grandfather's friends had a "party" for us in his house, one after the other; they prepared huge meals (for which they probably had to pay for months to come, in personal denial); the wine flowed, and the guitars spun their lilting music into the night, and we heard over and over again the songs and the dances of Italy (to which my mother and father listened, sometimes, with tears in their eyes). These, the entertainments given us by the simple villagers; but the high light of our sojourn was a visit to the *palazzo* of Don Carlo Metroni Salvatelli, the patriarchal aristocrat and landowner for whom my father had worked as a boy.

That we should be summoned to pay a visit to this gentleman was considered by my father to be the highest of all possible honors, for not even the thirty years he had spent in America had completely eradicated that sense of class distinction and what may be termed tribal loyalty which had been so deeply ingrained in him during his childhood. For though he might now be a rich and respected man and, in America, one whose life had no relation to the world which revolved around this village, nevertheless once he had set foot in the town of his birth the old relationships automatically sprang into existence. That the old aristocrat should summon him was therefore a great honor, and even my mother was impressed.

Don Carlo lived in a great stone house on a hill overlooking the village; there was a wall around it, I remember, and a great many fig and chestnut trees. We made the journey by horse and cart, my mother and father, my grandfather, and myself. Curiously enough, my grandfather, who had been somewhat in awe of his impressive son and daughter-in-law, became, once the invitation was brought to us, himself officiously paternal. For while his son might be this distinguished "personage" to whom he could not but pay a certain deference, that element of impressiveness belonged to America and the life my father lived there; over here, in relation to Don Carlo, he was simply one of the lowborn villagers, and this fact must be impressed upon him—and by whom else but his own father? "Now be careful of your manners!" he said over and over again on our way to the old aristocratic's *palazzo*, scowling at my father warningly. "Don't forget who you are; he must think well of you. He must think well of you!"

He was apparently terribly afraid that my father would not give a good impression to Don Carlo; perhaps this very success of his son's, of which he unquestionably was proud, seemed to him in some obscure manner disrespectful to Don Carlo, as though my father had wrongfully exceeded his natural destiny, the destiny which nature had designed for him in relation to the old aristocrat. "Don't forget yourself, now," he kept saying, looking anxiously at my father out of his brilliant black eyes; "remember always who you are, and do not speak unless you are spoken to."

We were admitted by an ancient woman servant and led to a kind of patio, where Don Carlo was seated at a table reading. Everything about the house gave indication of genteel poverty—the worn furniture, the peeling walls, the threadbare curtains; indeed, I remember stumbling over a crack in the stone floor of the entrance hall. Don Carlo himself looked a thousand years old, a lean, sparse, withered man, with a skin like yellow parchment and amazingly long hands covered with dull gold rings. Unlike my father's and grandfather's, his eyes were blue, and I remember that they looked like a sudden glimpse of the sky, they were so striking in his gaunt face with its thin, toothless mouth, its aquiline nose and bushy black eyebrows, its narrow forehead sweeping into a shock of fleecy white hair that reached almost to his shoulders.

We were all, with the exception of Don Carlo, painfully ill-at-ease: my father and grandfather stood awkwardly and held their hats and shuffled their feet. "But sit down!" said Don Carlo, smiling charmingly; and, calling to his servant, he ordered that wine be brought.

"So!" he said, after the wine had been poured. "Tell me about yourself, and America."

He treated my father as an equal; indeed, there was even a certain deference in his manner. And my father? He expanded, his chest swelled, his tongue and voice waxed warmer and warmer. Story after story he told of America and his own adventures there—so much so that once or twice my mother looked at him in embarrassment. Don Carlo nodded his head and chuckled indulgently, toying with his rings; but as the time wore on he no longer nodded his head and he no longer chuckled: he sat and twisted his rings and looked out of his ancient blue eyes at my father with an expression of—what? What? How to describe it? Alas, it is so long ago it is difficult to remember; do time and the imagination trick me into thinking it was wistfulness—and envy?

But all of a sudden—I do not know for what reason—my father stopped short in his speech; he seemed all at once to become self-conscious and uncomfortable. It was as though he had become aware for the first time of the old aristocrat's eyes on him, and his own eyes shifted uncertainly, and his face colored slightly. There was a moment of silence.

"Well!" said Don Carlo. "You have gone far and done much. Here, we are too old to go anywhere, and there is no longer anything to be done. We wait for death, and that is all."

Now, nearly twenty years later, seated in the kitchen with my mother and father, I remembered this incident, and remembering it I knew dimly what is was I had been trying to recapture from that return my mother and father and I had made to our source. But how to express it? There are emotions and ideas so subtle and complex it is difficult to capture them in words. Life and death, the old and the young; the life and death of towns, cities, countries, of people and of classes, of customs and of creeds—death always, and life always, the one feeding from the other endlessly. Once I had seen it, so poignantly I have never forgotten it: the old aristocrat there in his crumbling house and decaying civilization, knowing within himself, inevitably, the last downward revolutions of the wheel of his life; the young man of the earth who was my father, knowing within himself, with equal inevitability, the upward revolution of his own destiny; wheels within wheels. For a moment they had met, and crossed.

THE AMERICAN IRISH

William Shannon

For those who left, Ireland was a bundle of memories.

It was cutting peat on a rainy morning, gathering in the hay on long, warm August days, going to the spa for the fair. It was the picture of grandma churning butter by the door or making bread by the open hearth. It was the memory of Father coming home drawn and exhausted from a long day in the fields. ("I'm as tired as if I'd been drawing stones.") It was going to school on cold winter mornings, mind and feet racing with the knowledge that old Mrs. Boland would warm your hands very well with a stinging application of her cane. It was overhearing the old men around the fire, talking of British foreclosures and chewing over political gossip months old. Later on, it was coming home from country dances over dark roads and remembering uneasily the familiar stories of ghosts and fairies. The political gossip and the fairy stories alike were almost indistinguishable in their awesomeness and unreality.

There were many Irelands, of course, but this is the one the country people knew, and most of those who came to America were country people. For them the brilliant world of Anglo-Irish Dublin, of O'Connell and later of Parnell, of Tom Moore and later of Yeats and Lady Gregory, scarcely existed. The Ireland of the "Celtic twilight," the country which in the early Middle Ages sent saints and scholars wandering to the farthest reaches of Christendom, the country in which monks and minstrels made Gaelic a living language, this, too, was a lost land. For most country people who emigrated to America, the Gaelic language lived on only in tag words and old sayings. Only people in tiny scattered enclaves and an occasional schoolmaster could speak whole sentences in the ancient language. The country people regarded the Gaelic-speaking few, such as the fishermen of the Isles of Aran among whom Synge went to live, as unusual and, indeed, almost freakish persons. Still another Ireland is the land of the faith, the most devoutly and uniformly Catholic country in the modern world. But the ordinary country people, living in the circumscribed routines of farm and village for whom a ten-mile trip was a long journey, never realized there was anything unique about their religious affiliation or their devotion. Going to Church and partaking of the Sacraments were as natural and expected a part of life as milking the cow or gathering the hay. Only later, in America, would this become distinctive, a fact to reflect upon and boast about, a source of national chauvinism.

The life of the Irish people was simple and stripped down. And it was much the same background whether the immigrant came in 1840 or 1920. The surface of life changed greatly in those years, but the traditional rhythms of village life by which the country people lived were slow to change. The farm, the old people, the Church, the fair, the raising of potatoes, hay, and cattle, the cutting of turf, the talk of going to America and of those who had gone, the talk of fairies and magic, the inadequate school, the hardness of life, these things did not change during the ninety years in which the Irish came to America.

Irish life in America begins from a sharp and tragic rejection. To "come out" to the new country meant thrusting behind the old, usually forever, unless in a few instances success brought enough money to visit the old country once more. Even then, however, many who could financially afford the return visit to Ireland never made the trip. It would be a journey back in more than one sense, a journey back into the house of their father, into the womb of old memories and long-forgotten sadnesses. To return would be to reconsider the crucial decision that it was no use to reconsider. The pleasures of nostalgia would not be worth the pain.

Why did they leave and what did they seek?

The answer is that most did not leave willingly. They were hurled out, driven by forces larger and more complex than they could fully understand or cope with. They made the decision to go, of course; the responsibility was theirs and they could not deny it (least of all to themselves in the later and the harder years), but the range of choice was narrow. To the question What did they seek? the answer is the same for them as for all men. They sought a door that would open and give them access to hope.

Irish country life was not unrelievedly drab and hard; the races, the visits to the pub, the outdoor sports, the country dances and other entertainments did much to soften the rigors of existence. But they could not suffice in the sick, tormented society of nineteenth and early twentieth century Ireland. The young, spared to life by the mysterious drop in infant mortality, pressed upon their elders. Young men in their twenties saw ahead bleak years of waiting for a farm of their own, and were plagued by frustration and fears of unfulfillment. The girls, seeing marriage and motherhood delayed by impersonal economic considerations and the dreary calculations of the matchmaker, feared that their best years would slip by, empty and barren. Since parents wanted to keep the family and land system on an even keel, they usually married off their daughters strictly in order of age. Irish folklore is full of sad stories of the pretty young girls who could not marry until their plain-faced older sister was wed. Many an Irish girl decided she would rather join relatives in an overcrowded tenement in Chicago or wash dishes for three dollars a week in "cold roast Boston" than live out her life in an unequal race with those old gypsy men, time and fate. ("I had to go," the mother said to her son; "there was nothing for me in the old country.") Older men and women, squeezed or displaced altogether by the exactions of the landlord or by land consolidations, decided in middle life it was not, after all, too late for them to take the great gamble. And, at times of famine, whole families from infants to grandparents in desperation made the journey.

So it was that in their various ways they decided to leave. Their deep feelings about the familiar village and the gently sloping fields were overborne by the fact of failure and the fear of further defeat. Ireland was beautiful and damned. There was no life for them there. They had to go.

WELL, MY FATHER WAS
AN ARMENIAN, YES

John V. Hagopian

Joe Christmas, Faulkner's fleeing hero in *Light of August,* was lucky. He had no identity, no sure knowledge of his father or his race. Since he had no Negro pigmentation, he could—at least bodily—choose to be whatever he wished. Two neatly crystallized alternatives were available to him in the social stereotypes of Southern White and Negro, each of which involved clearly defined values, rights, privileges, and obligations. Condemned to freedom, he longed for definition. The taunt of the old Negro gardener tortured him: "You don't know what you are. And more than that, you won't ever know. You'll live and you'll die and you won't ever know." The excess of freedom drove him berserk, and his fierce assaults on life culminated in a violence that gave him an identity simultaneously with his death.

I have said that Joe Christmas was lucky. Perhaps this is not necessarily true. But consider how enviable his freedom to choose might seem to a man imprisoned by two half-worlds that don't merge, two vaguely defined identities neither of which he can fully accept. This is the condition of the so-called Armenian-American, that freakish, two-fronted beast whose cousins are the Jewish-American, the Polish-American, the Greek-American and all the other hyphenated creatures who, so long as they wear the tragicomic mask of double identity, can only stalk the fringes of respectability in any country.

I write this while serving as a Professor of American Studies in a German university. It is impossible to be certain whether Germans are more race-conscious toward me than Americans were, since I am inside the experiment, not outside looking in. After all, in any country, foreigners with a poor command of the language and with strange, deeply-ingrained social habits are always conspicuously outsiders. The fact that they are not immediately accepted must not necessarily be interpreted in racial terms.

Be that as it may, my own problem in racial identity has been heightened in recent months by two different reactions of Germans who meet me for the first time: (1) "Ah, Professor Hagopian, you are an American, yes?" and (2) "Ah, Professor Hagopian, you are an Armenian, yes?" I have developed subtle evasions to these questions. To the first question I always reply, "I am an American *citizen*, yes," or "I was *born* in America, yes." To the second, "Well, my father was Armenian, yes."

Similar evasions of the religious question are not always possible here. Since church contributions are deducted from wages, the German Tax Card bluntly asks, "Are you Catholic or Protestant?" When I said, "Neither," the official at the village Rathaus was quite distressed. On American forms I always wrote "Nondenominational," because it sounded like a religion and avoided a lot of fuss. For "Color?" I sometimes wrote "Flesh" or "Blue," which sometimes caused a fuss but, strangely enough, often didn't

My evasiveness concerning "Armenian" or "American" is not a sign of cowardice, but of doubt, of uncertainty, of flux. I have too much identity and not enough identity, and I write about it here not out of a belief that it is unique, but because I am certain it is shared by millions of hyphenated beings who are also distressed and don't know what it is that distresses them. Psychologists, semanticists, and makers of electric computers all agree that the first step toward solving a problem is defining it.

I grew up in the late 20's and the 30's in a slum called Delray near the waterfront on the southwest side of Detroit. Except among ourselves-themselves, Armenians in Delray, unlike those in ritzier Highland Park, were simply more foreigners to be crammed into the giant maws of the automobile factories. To most people, especially to the dominant white Anglo-Saxon Protestant minority, best represented by landlords, bosses, and school teachers, Armenians were not different from the Hunkies, Polacks, and Wops, and only slightly different from the sub-minority of all sub-minorities, the Niggers. It is curious, though, that I cannot recall any special term of abuse for Armenians—

only recently have I heard the term "Rug-beaters," which does not seem to be widespread.

To some people, who remembered contributing pennies in school for "the starving Armenians" just after World War I, we-they were objects of special pity and were a bit more gently treated. To a discriminating few, Armenians were known as a good, Christian people, martyrs to the Turks, and founders of the first national Christian church.

Today, of course, though this general pattern still prevails, the starving Armenians are an ancient memory and enough Armenians have achieved prominence in the arts, sciences, and in the entertainment world to make us-them distinguishable from the *lumpenproletariat*. Or to put it another way, they-we have assimilated so successfully as to be indistinguishable from the *lumpenbourgeoisie*. Even in the slum community in which I was raised there remain very few Armenians. Delray is now inhabited mostly by Negroes.

But in the old days the Armenians of Delray, like the Poles of Znaniecki's *Polish Peasant in America*, clung tenaciously to the Old World ways of life. After an anonymous day's labor in the factories, the men would go home to plates of *wewfti* (on Sundays *sheesh-kebab*) and *dolma* and *pilaf* with —if they could afford the expensive ingredients—*katah* or *bakhlava* for dessert. Then they would gather in colorful coffee houses on Solvay Street to play pinochle or *tavli* and drink *rakhi*. There were Armenian stores, Armenian churches, Armenian schools, and Armenian recreation centers, and occasionally an Armenian film or play in a rented hall.

But to the Armenians of that time and that place, there was no such thing as a *lumpen*-Armenian. One had to commit himself to being a particular kind of Armenian, and the variety was dazzling: Russian-Armenian or Turkish-Armenian, Armenians from specific villages, Greek-Orthodox Armenians and Apostolic Armenians. If three Armenians met on a street corner, nine political parties might be represented. I cannot recall what all the issues were, but I remember the terms *Bolshevik*, *Tashnag*, and *Ramgavar* being hurled about with great emotion, and I have the dim image of a smoke-filled coffee house rattling to furious shouting, table-slamming, and first-waving over the issue of an Armenian archbishop who was stabbed to death at his altar in New York, a sort of local Thomas à Becket.

But whatever kind of Armenian a man was, he was not an Armenian-American; he was simply an Armenian in America. On high religious holidays even many of the Bolshevik Armenians attended mass, officiated over by a black-bearded, berobed, blazing-eyed priest in the incense-reeking St. Sarkis Apostolic Church. At election time politicians sweated for the Armenian vote at *sheesh-kebab* picnics in smelly White House Park. The world of the Armenian was a highly-charged, and emotional daily experience, and it was a world he wanted desperately to bequeath to his children.

But the poor children! We were torn in half by the conflicting demands of our Armenian homes and our American environment. On Saturdays we were herded to the one-room Armenian school above a coffee-house, where a dumpling of a new immigrant tried to teach us grammar. But the texts were as musty as her pedagogy, and we resisted fiercely, longing to be playing baseball or to be watching "Tarzan of the Apes" at the Delray Theater.

Today, knowing how much a knowledge of Armenian is valued by my linguist colleagues and having observed the respect that command of an exotic language begets among intellectuals (remember the store-keeper in Saroyan's "My Name is Aram"), I wish I had attended more faithfully.

Our high-school dating aroused anxiety and desperation in our parents. "I want you should grow up marry nice Armenian gel," my father admonished, even though I was miserably certain that *nobody* would ever want to marry me. I watched the fear of intercultural marriage produce crisis after crisis in the families of my friends, until the war ripped us out of our hot-house Armenian environments, and flung us into the heterogenerous cultural maelstrom of the armed services.

The question that still puzzles me is: just what is it that our fathers wanted us to preserve? And just what is it that my German acquaintances want to know when they ask, "Ah, Professor Hagopian, you are Armenian, yes?" Is it language? In itself, command of the Armenian language means nothing, especially to the Germans I know. Any person of normal intelligence and linguistic aptitude, like Byron, could learn it. A scholar of the Indo-European languages might work at the riddle of the uniqueness of Armenian; or a structural linguist might use Armenian, as he might use Kirghis or Hopi, as a body of utterances for the analysis of phonemes.

But why, except for purely scientific, linguistic reasons, learn Armenian? Any Armenian born and raised in America already has in English a perfectly efficient and natural medium of communication. Immigration has long since ceased and he is unlikely ever to encounter a native Armenian who didn't understand English. Are there, perhaps, cultural values available only through a command of Armenian? Except for theological scholars, it would seem not—and they would have to learn Old Armenian, which is as far removed from modern Armenian as Anglo-Saxon is from modern English.

With a command of German one could read Goethe or Kafka; with Russian, Tolstoy or Dostoievski; with French, Molière or Camus—even with Old Norse one could read the Sagas. But what is there to read in Armenian? Nor is there any especially valuable audience to be gained in learning how to write Armenian.

Is there any special religious significance in being an Armenian? Except for a vague identification with Christianity, few Armenians of my acquaintance seem to think so. The Apostolic Church may be uniquely Armenian, but no Armenian I have ever met has been able to tell me exactly what doctrines or rituals distinguish it from the Eastern Orthodox Church to which most Christians (including Armenians) of Eastern Mediterranean origin subscribe. Does one genuflect on entering the Apostolic Church? Is there a "power and glory" clause in the Lord's Prayer? Does one cross oneself to the right or to the left? To an atheist like myself none of these questions matter much, but neither do they matter to most Armenians outside of Jerusalem and Yerevan—nor to those people who ask, "Ah, Professor Hagopian, you are an Armenian, yes?"

Is a reverence for Armenian history important to being an Armenian? Perhaps. I sometimes enjoy startling my friends with tid bits such as, "Did you know that it was the Armenians who stopped the eastward march of Pompey the Great?" And "Did you know that under Tigranes the Armenians had one of the largest empires in the Near East?" But, let's face it: these are footnotes to history, not very important parts of any grand design. I have known serious scholars of Near Eastern history who have not felt obliged to pay much attention to the Armenians.

In the broad aspects of cultural history, Armenians have played no significant part. No Armenian ever invented a cal-

endar, codified the laws, founded biology, produced great
sculpture or painting, invented the telephone, or fashioned a
mushroom-shaped cloud. Most Armenians who have accomplished something worthy of note have done so as members
of some other culture—for example, Mikoyan and Khachatourian in Russia, and Saroyan and Hovhanes in the United
States. Objectively viewed, the historical importance of the
Armenians seems rather small. Only a perverse and irrational
chauvinist can believe otherwise.

Perhaps my scales of measurement have been too grand,
too cosmic. Is there not some simpler human value to being an
Armenian—the sharing of pleasant customs, enjoying the tastes
of special foods, singing certain songs, and dancing certain
dances? Surely it is a natural and understandable desire of
human beings to belong to a group. Isn't it reassuring, com-
forting to know that all one needs to do to gain the hospitality
and friendly disposition of a family or a community is to produce the password of a surname ending in *-ian* or *-ouni,* to
smack one's lips over *kewfti,* to raise one's voice in "Mair Hair-
enig," or stomp one's feet in the circle dance? I suppose the
honest answer is that if one truly truly enjoys such activities he
should seek out others who share his joy.

However, outside of Armenia there are more ways and
more people through which one can enhance life. And an
ugly problem looms up when those who insist on being Armenians cramp and squeeze themselves to remain within the ab-
straction "Armenian," or who expect special favors or unearned
preferential treatment simply because they have so cramped
and squeezed themselves. I wonder how many ham actors with
Armenian names wanted Rouben Mamoulian to get them into
the movies, how many Armenian graduates of correspondence
schools wanted to become electrical engineers with Sarkis
Tarzian, how many Armenian matrons aspiring to authorship
plagued Saroyan to get them published. Let me be blunt about
it: whenever a man seeks a wife or a job or an honor—or
merely publication in *Ararat*—simply on the ground that he is
Armenian, he is betraying his humanity.

At one time I found the coercions of my family and community—and the curiosity or hostility of the Anglo-Saxon
community—so troublesome that I contemplated changing my
name. I was fed up with the automatic assumption of Armenians that I would welcome their daughters as marriage part-

ners; I was fed up with the necessity of spelling my name a hundred times a week to students, store clerks, and secretaries; I was fed up with explaining that I really didn't like the sad romanticism of William Saroyan and that I had had enough of Khachatourian's "Sabre Dance." For several months I worked under the name of John Haig and found respite from the old irritations. But new ones arose. I had to explain that the name was *Haig*—"Haig as in Scotch, not Hague!" And it was awkward when I met old friends. Furthermore, I felt like an imposter, and so I went back to being John Hagopian, patiently informing others that, yes, it was an Armenian name; no, I didn't think Arlene Francis was charming; yes, Akim Tamiroff was a ham.

As an Armenian I have been dunned for Armenian causes, have spent hours at dull funerals and weddings of Armenians, have been cheated by Armenians at poker, have been privy to government secrets by Armenian members of the CIA, and have been harbored an Armenian fugitive from the law. My Armenian name has involved me in many fascinating situations, pleasant and unpleasant, but never in anything as unpleasant as the time Antranik Havgitian came to Ann Arbor. I have, of course, changed the name.

One spring day in 1956, I came home from the university and my wife said cheerily, "A friend of yours is coming to dinner."

"Really? Who?"

"He said his name was Antranik Havgitian."

"Antranik Havgitian? Never heard of him!"

My wife then explained that a man had telephoned, introduced himself as an Armenian friend, and—my wife being hospitable—had been invited to stuffed cabbage and *pilaf*.

Havgitian arrived promptly. He had rich, slicked-down hair, hooked nose, huge brown eyes bridged by black brows, shiny teeth—the perfect grinning stereotype, a swarthy genie right out of the lamp. Completely self-assured, he introduced himself. In eloquent, heavily-accented English, he explained that he had come from Teheran four years before to work on a Ph.D. in mathematics, had recently passed his exams, and was touring the country before settling down to a teaching job in Tennessee. How had he happened to telephone my wife? Simple. He had thumbed through the faculty directory until he found an Armenian name. "All right," I thought, "here is this monster stuffing himself at my table. He'll be fed and gone soon. Then I can read the kids their bedtime story and work at grading papers."

My Armenian friend had other plans. For hours he reverberated the air with his virtues—how, when he solved an especially difficult math problem, he wept with joy at the beauty of the intricate design; how when he was moody, he cheered himself by writing poems:

> Oh Persian moon above the arched trees,
> Look at me praying on my knees
> Answer my call for immortal love,
> You Persian moon shining on above.

Then suddenly he grew silent and hung his head. My wife and I exchanged puzzled glances. We waited, but Havgitian sat there immersed in tremendous gloom. Finally I ventured the question, "Antranik, what's the matter?"

He sighed, paused, rolled up his moody brown eyes, and said, "I do not wish to go back to Teheran."

And then it came out that his student's visa was soon to expire, but he had come to love the rivers and mountains of our great land and felt destined for a career at the great American University of Tennessee. The only way he could remain in America was to marry an American citizen.

"Well, surely a handsome chap like you should have no trouble managing that," I said.

"No," he said. "I have no trouble like that. There is in particular this one beautiful girl—just a little bit skinny— who loves me and I love her and my heart could break in pieces!"

"Doesn't she want to marry you?"

"Oh, yes, very much."

"Well, then, what's the problem?"

"She is American."

This astounded me, I had thought that was precisely what he wanted, but it developed that he didn't believe in "mixed" marriages (he made no apologies to my wife) and, besides, he had promised his dear mother on her death bed that he would marry only an Armenian. In fact, his tour of the country was in search of an Armenian-American girl who would marry him.

"Do you have any sisters?" he asked.

"Yes, but they're all married."

He sighed. "Do you know any nice, single Armenian girls?"

"No," I said abruptly, my patience running out.

"I wonder," he said, "if you would let me use your telephone book."

"Certainly," I said, hoping he had another appointment.

He took the book, opened it to the first listings under "A" and began running his fingernail down the columns. We sat silently as he scanned column after column. Finally he said, "Ah, here is one. May I use your telephone?"

I listened in amazement as he purred through a practiced spiel and clinched an immediate appointment with a Miss Anush Derderian. Off he went in a great hurry.

Around midnight, I jotted the last C— on a paper and yawned, then started at the sound of the electric doorbell. It was Havgitian. In tears. He rushed in and collapsed on the sofa.

"For God's sake, man, what's the matter?"

"She won't marry me!"

"She won't . . . ? But what the hell did you expect?"

"Oh, she is beautiful—a little fat, but beautiful. And smart, very smart, a medical student. She plays the piano, too —she played for me. Like me, she harmonizes science and art. She's perfect! My mother would be so happy! But she won't marry me." And he heaved with sobs.

"Of course she won't marry you, you idiot! You can't walk in on a strange girl out of the blue and propose marriage."

"Ah, but she is an Armenian girl, no stranger to another Armenian. Like you! But she is proud. The only reason she wouldn't marry me is that she heard I had proposed to her sister yesterday in Detroit." And he fell to sobbing again.

The moral of this story may not be perfectly clear. I don't know precisely what "being an Armenian" means to others or what it is supposed to mean to me. After all, I am not quite sure what it means to be an American, and that, after all, is my experiential if not my genetic background. Furthermore, as Professor of American Studies in a German university, being an American is part of my present professional responsibility. But even more difficult is the fact that I am only just beginning to discover what it means to be John Hagopian. Perhaps I'll never fully discover that—or, even worse, I may discover it (like Joe Christmas) when there is no time left to be John Hagopian.

Of course, the process of discovering oneself is contextually bound. It will always be shaped by the specific people, places, and things that one directly or indirectly experiences. One can and should exert his will as conscientiously and intelligently as he can to shape those experiences in such a way as to develop the maximum of his potential vitality. To set up arbitrary limits, to say, "I define myself as an Armenian (or American, or Baluba) and therefore I will experience and value only people, places, and things Armenian (or American, or Baluba)," is to cripple oneself.

Of course, even the crippled can live good lives. A man in a strait-jacket can scratch his nose—he need only rub it against a wall. But it's certainly more rewarding to have one's arms free, to get at the itch more accurately and scratch more satisfyingly.

PREJUDICE

ETHNIC CONFLICTS

*The price of hating other human beings is
loving oneself less.*

Eldridge Cleaver

Immigrants have rarely discovered immediate freedom and
equality in America. They find themselves, most often, in
the slums of large cities—the Irish in Boston; the Orientals
in San Francisco; the Jews, Negroes, Puerto Ricans, and
Italians in New York—forced to work at underpaid jobs.
Only through a tenacious will and determination are the
children able to join the mainstrea mof American life.
between the majority culture and a specific minority. Leslie
Fiedler points to this kind of conflict in "Negro and Jew:
Encounter in America." He suggests that hatred for one
minority is almost always linked to hatred for others and
that this hatred is really for one's own ethnic origins, and
finally for oneself. Self-hatred can even extend to the members of one's own minority group, as a first generation of
immigrants regards the second with contempt. The literature of ethnic groups is, in many ways, a record of how
immigrants struggle against the prejudices imposed upon
them from without and within.

The varieties of racial prejudice in America are too
many and complex to define in this brief space, but some
examples are suggested in the following works: the black-

white conflict in Countee Cullen's "Incident," Ralph Ellison's "Battle Royal," and Mari Evans' "Alarm Clock"; the
prejudices inflicted upon Orientals in Toshio Mori's "Slant-
Eyed Americans" and Jose Garcia Villa's poetry; and the
abuse suffered by the Indian in N. Scott Momaday's "The
Well."

SPEECH TO THE COURT*

Bartolomeo Vanzetti

It is seven years that we are in jail.
What we have suffered during those years no human
  tongue can say.
And yet you see me before you, not trembling, not
  ashamed, not in fear.
But I would not wish to a dog or to a snake
  to the most low and misfortunate creature on this
  earth,
I would not wish to any of them what I have had to suffer
  for thing I am not guilty of.
But my conviction is that I have suffer for thing I am
  guilty of.
I am suffering because I am a radical
  And indeed, I am a radical.
I am suffering because I was an Italian
  And indeed, I am an Italian.

But, if it had not been for these thing
I might have live out my life
Talking at street corners to scorning men.

---

* Nicola Sacco and Bartolomeo Vanzetti were Italian immigrants who
became active Socialists during the early twentieth-century. In 1920 they
were indicted for the murder of a shop foreman in a New England town.
The trial lingered for seven years, but the two men were finally convicted
and executed in spite of only circumstantial evidence and another man's
confession to the crime. Their death elicited great protest from Americans
who believed that the conviction was based on prejudice against immigrants and radicals.
  This statement is a poetic rendering of Bartolomeo Vanzetti's final
speech to the Court, before the Judge pronounced sentence, and the last
letter Vanzetti wrote to his son.

I might have die—unknown, unmarked, a failure.
This suffering is our career and our triumph.
Never in our full life could we hope to do such work
    for tolerance, for justice, for man's understanding
    of man
As now we do by accident.

Our words, our lives, our pains—nothing.
The taking of our lives, the lives of a good shoemaker
    and a poor fish peddler—
All.
That last moment belong to us
That agony is OUR triumph.

INCIDENT

Countee Cullen
For Eric Walrond

Once riding in old Baltimore,
   Heart-filled, head-filled with glee,
I saw a Baltimorean
   Keep looking straight at me.

Now I was eight and very small,
   And he was no whit bigger,
And so I smiled, but he poked out
   His tongue, and called me, "Nigger."

I saw the whole of Baltimore
   From May until December;
Of all the things that happened there
   That's all that I remember.

BATTLE ROYAL

Ralph Ellison

It goes a long way back, some twenty years. All my life I had been looking for something, and everywhere I turned someone tried to tell me what it was. I accepted their answers too, though they were often in contradiction and even self-contradictory. I was naïve. I was looking for myself and asking everyone except myself questions which I, and only I, could answer. It took me a long time and much painful boomerang-ing of my expectations to achieve a realization everyone else appears to have been born with: That I am nobody but myself. But first I had to discover that I am an invisible man!

And yet I am no freak of nature, nor of history. I was in the cards, other things having been equal (or unequal) eighty-five years ago. I am not ashamed of my grandparents for having been slaves. I am only ashamed of myself for having at one time been ashamed. About eighty-five years ago they were told that they were free, united with others of our country in everything pertaining to the common good, and, in everything social, separate like the fingers of the hand. And they believed it. They exulted in it. They stayed in their place, worked hard, and brought up my father to do the same. But my grandfather is the one. He was an odd old guy, my grandfather, and I am told I take after him. It was he who caused the trouble. On his deathbed he called my father to him and said, "Son, after I'm gone I want you to keep up the good fight. I never told you, but our life is a war and I have been a traitor all my born days, a spy in the enemy's country ever since I give up my gun back in the Reconstruction. Live with your head in the lion's mouth. I want you to overcome 'em with yeses, undermine 'em with grins, agree 'em to death and de-

struction, let 'em swoller you till they vomit or bust wide open."
They thought the old man had gone out of his mind. He had
been the meekest of men. The younger children were rushed
from the room, the shades drawn and the flame of the lamp
turned so low that it sputtered on the wick like the old man's
breathing. "Learn it to the younguns," he whispered fiercely;
then he died.

But my folks were more alarmed over his last words than
over his dying. It was as though he had not died at all, his
words caused so much anxiety. I was warned emphatically to
forget what he had said and, indeed, this is the first time it has
been mentioned outside the family circle. It had a tremendous
effect upon me, however. I could never be sure of what he
meant. Grandfather had been a quiet old man who never made
any trouble, yet on his deathbed he had called himself a traitor
and a spy, and he had spoken of his meekness as a dangerous
activity. It became a constant puzzle which lay unanswered in
the back of my mind. And whenever things went well for me
I remembered my grandfather and felt guilty and uncomfortable. It was as though I was carrying out his advice in spite of
myself. And to make it worse, everyone loved me for it. I was
praised by the most lily-white men of the town. I was considered an example of desirable conduct—just as my grandfather
had been. And what puzzled me was that the old man had
defined it as *treachery*. When I was praised for my conduct I
felt a guilt that in some way I was doing something that was
really against the wishes of the white folks, that if they had
understood they would have desired me to act just the opposite,
that I should have been sulky and mean, and that that really
would have been what they wanted, even though they were
fooled and thought they wanted me to act as I did. It made
me afraid that some day they would look upon me as a traitor
and I would be lost. Still I was more afraid to act any other
way because they didn't like that at all. The old man's words
were like a curse. On my graduation day I delivered an oration
in which I showed that humility was the secret, indeed, the
very essence of progress. (Not that I believed this—how could
I, remembering my grandfather?—I only believed that it
worked.) It was a great success. Everyone praised me and I
was invited to give the speech at a gathering of the town's
leading white citizens. It was a triumph for our whole community.

It was in the main ballroom of the leading hotel. When I got there I discovered that it was on the occasion of a smoker, and I was told that since I was to be there anyway I might as well take part in the battle royal to be fought by some of my schoolmates as part of the entertainment. The battle royal came first.

All of the town's big shots were there in their tuxedoes, wolfing down the buffet foods, drinking beer and whiskey and smoking black cigars. It was a large room with a high ceiling. Chairs were arranged in neat rows around three sides of a portable boxing ring. The fourth side was clear, revealing a gleaming space of polished floor. I had some misgivings over the battle royal, by the way. Not from a distaste for fighting, but because I didn't care too much for the other fellows who were to take part. They were tough guys who seemed to have no grandfather's curse worrying their minds. No one could mistake their toughness. And besides, I suspected that fighting a battle royal might detract from the dignity of my speech. In those pre-invisible days I visualized myself as a potential Booker T. Washington. But the other fellows didn't care too much for me either, and there were nine of them. I felt superior to them in my way, and I didn't like the manner in which we were all crowded together into the servants' elevator. Nor did they like my being there. In fact, as the warmly lighted floors flashed past the elevator we had words over the fact that I, by taking part in the fight, had knocked one of their friends out of a night's work.

We were led out of the elevator through a rococo hall into an anteroom and told to get into our fighting togs. Each of us was issued a pair of boxing gloves and ushered out into the big mirrored hall, which we entered looking cautiously about us and whispering, lest we might accidentally be heard above the noise of the room. It was foggy with cigar smoke. And already the whiskey was taking effect. I was shocked to see some of the most important men of the town quite tipsy. They were all there—bankers, lawyers, judges, doctors, fire chiefs, teachers, merchants. Even one of the more fashionable pastors. Something we could not see was going on up front. A clarinet was vibrating sensuously and the men were standing up and moving eagerly forward. We were a small tight group, clustered together, our bare upper bodies touching and shining with anticipatory sweat; while up front the big shots were becoming increasingly excited over something we still could not see. Suddenly I heard the school superintendent, who had told me to come, yell, "Bring up the shines, gentlemen! Bring up the little shines!"

We were rushed up to the front of the ballroom, where it smelled even more strongly of tobacco and whiskey. Then we were pushed into place. I almost wet my pants. A sea of faces, some hostile, some amused, ringed around us, and in the center, facing us, stood a magnificent blonde—stark naked. There was dead silence. I felt a blast of cold air chill me. I tried to back away, but they were behind me and around me. Some of the boys stood with lowered heads, trembling. I felt a wave of irrational guilt and fear. My teeth chattered, my skin turned to goose flesh, my knees knocked. Yet I was strongly attracted and looked in spite of myself. Had the price of looking been blindness, I would have looked. The hair was yellow like that of a circus kewpie doll, the face heavily powdered and rouged, as though to form an abstract mask, the eyes hollow and smeared with a cool blue, the color of a baboon's butt. I felt a desire to spit upon her as my eyes brushed slowly over her body. Her breasts were firm and round as the domes of East Indian temples, and I stood so close as to see the fine skin texture and beads of pearly perspiration glistening like dew around the pink and erected buds of her nipples. I wanted at one and the same time to run from the room, to sink through the floor, or to go to her and cover her from my eyes and the eyes of the others with my body; to feel the soft thighs, to caress her and destroy her, to love her and murder her, to hide from her, and yet to stroke where below the small American flag tattooed upon her belly her thighs formed a capital V. I had a notion that of all in the room she saw only me with her impersonal eyes.

And then she began to dance, a slow sensuous movement; the smoke of a hundred cigars clinging to her like the thinnest of veils. She seemed like a fair bird-girl girdled in veils calling to me from the angry surface of some gray and threatening sea. I was transported. Then I became aware of the clarinet playing and the big shots yelling at us. Some threatened us if we looked and others if we did not. On my right I saw one boy faint. And now a man grabbed a silver pitcher from a table and stepped close as he dashed ice water upon him and stood him up and forced two of us to support him as his head hung

and moans issued from his thick bluish lips. Another boy began
to plead to go home. He was the largest of the group, wearing
dark red fighting trunks much too small to conceal the erection
which projected from him as though in answer to the insinuat-
ing low-registered moaning of the clarinet. He tried to hide
himself with his boxing gloves.

And all the while the blonde continued dancing, smiling
faintly at the big shots who watched her with fascination, and
faintly smiling at our fear. I noticed a certain merchant who
followed her hungrily, his lips loose and drooling. He was a
large man who wore diamond studs in a shirtfront which
swelled with the ample paunch underneath, and each time the
blonde swayed her undulating hips he ran his hand through the
thin hair of his bald head and, with his arms upheld, his pos-
ture clumsy like that of an intoxicated panda, wound his belly
in a slow and obscene grind. This creature was completely hyp-
notized. The music had quickened. As the dancer flung herself
about with a detached expression on her face, the men began
reaching out to touch her. I could see their beefy fingers sink
into the soft flesh. Some of the others tried to stop them and
she began to move around the floor in graceful circles, as they
gave chase, slipping and sliding over the polished floor. It was
mad. Chairs went crashing, drinks were spilt, as they ran
laughing and howling after her. They caught her just as she
reached a door, raised her from the floor, and tossed her as
college boys are tossed at a hazing, and above her red, fixed-
smiling lips I saw the terror and disgust in her eyes, almost
like my own terror and that which I saw in some of the other
boys. As I watched, they tossed her twice and her soft breasts
seemed to flatten against the air and her legs flung wildly as
she spun. Some of the more sober ones helped her to escape.
And I started off the floor, heading for the anteroom with the
rest of the boys.

Some were still crying and in hysteria. But as we tried to
leave we were stopped and ordered to get into the ring. There
was nothing to do but what we were told. All ten of us climbed
under the ropes and allowed ourselves to be blindfolded with
broad bands of white cloth. One of the men seemed to feel a
bit sympathetic and tried to cheer us up as we stood with our
backs against the ropes. Some of us tried to grin. "See that boy
over there?" one of the men said. "I want you to run across
at the bell and give it to him right in the belly. If you don't

get him, I'm going to get you. I don't like his looks." Each of us was told the same. The blindfolds were put on. Yet even then I had been going over my speech. In my mind each word was as bright as flame. I felt the cloth pressed into place, and frowned so that it would be loosened when I relaxed.

But now I felt sudden fit of blind terror. I was unused to darkness. It was as though I had suddenly found myself in a dark room filled with poisonous cotton mouths. I could hear the bleary voices yelling insistently for the battle royal to begin.

"Get going in there!"

"Let me at that big nigger!"

I strained to pick up the school superintendent's voice, as though to squeeze some security out of that slightly more familiar sound.

"Let me at those black sonsabitches!" someone yelled.

"No, Jackson, no!" another voice yelled. "Here, somebody, help me hold Jack."

"I want to get at that ginger-colored nigger. Tear him limb from limb," the first voice yelled.

I stood against the ropes trembling. For in those days I was what they called ginger-colored, and he sounded as though he might crunch me between his teeth like a crisp ginger cookie.

Quite a struggle was going on. Chairs were being kicked about and I could hear voices grunting as with a terrific effort. I wanted to see, to see more desperately than ever before. But the blindfold was as tight as a thick skin-puckering scab and when I raised my gloved hands to push the layers of white aside a voice yelled, "Oh, no you don't, black bastard! Leave that alone!"

"Ring the bell before Jackson kills him a coon!" someone boomed in the sudden silence. And I heard the bell clang and the sound of the feet scuffling forward.

A glove smacked against my head. I pivoted, striking out stiffly as someone went past, and felt the jar ripple along the length of my arm to my shoulder. Then it seemed as though all nine of the boys had turned upon me at once. Blows pounded me from all sides while I struck out as best I could. So many blows landed upon me that I wondered if I were not the only blindfolded fighter in the ring, or if the man called Jackson hadn't succeeded in getting me after all.

Blindfolded, I could no longer control my motions. I had no dignity. I stumbled about like a baby or a drunken man. The smoke had become thicker and with each new blow it seemed to sear and further restrict my lungs. My saliva became like hot bitter glue. A glove connected with my head, filling my mouth with warm blood. It was everywhere. I could not tell if the moisture I felt upon my body was sweat or blood. A blow landed hard against the nape of my neck. I felt myself going over, my head hitting the floor. Streaks of blue light filled the black world behind the blindfold. I lay prone, pretending that I was knocked out, but felt myself seized by hands and yanked to my feet. "Get going, black boy! Mix it up!" My arms were like lead, my head smarting from blows. I managed to feel my way to the ropes and held on, trying to catch my breath. A glove landed in my mid-section and I went over again, feeling as though the smoke had become a knife jabbed into my guts. Pushed this way and that by the legs milling around me, I finally pulled erect and discovered that I could see the black, sweat-washed forms weaving in the smoky-blue atmosphere like drunken dancers weaving to the rapid drum-like thuds of blows.

Everyone fought hysterically. It was complete anarchy. Everybody fought everybody else. No group fought together for long. Two, three, four, fought one, then turned to fight each other, were themselves attacked. Blows landed below the belt and in the kidney, with the gloves open as well as closed, and with my eye partly opened now there was not so much terror. I moved carefully, avoiding blows, although not too many to attract attention, fighting from group to group. The boys groped about like blind, cautious crabs crouching to protect their mid-sections, their heads pulled in short against their shoulders, their arms stretched nervously before them, with their fists testing the smoke-filled air like the knobbed feelers of hypersensitive snails. In one corner I glimpsed a boy violently punching the air and heard him scream in pain as he smashed his hand against a ring post. For a second I saw him bent over holding his hand, then going down as a blow caught his unprotected head. I played one group against the other, slipping in and throwing a punch then stepping out of range while pushing the others into the melee to take the blows blindly aimed at me. The smoke was agonizing and there were no rounds, no bells at three minute intervals to relieve our exhaustion. The room spun round me, a swirl of lights, smoke, sweating bodies surrounded by tense white faces. I bled from both nose and mouth, the blood spattering upon my chest.

The men kept yelling, "Slug him, black boy! Knock his guts out!"

"Uppercut him! Kill him! Kill that big boy!"

Taking a fake fall, I saw a boy going down heavily beside me as though we were felled by a single blow, saw a sneaker-clad foot shoot into his groin as the two who had knocked him down stumbled upon him. I rolled out of range, feeling a twinge of nausea.

The harder we fought the more threatening the men became. And yet, I had begun to worry about my speech again. How would it go? Would they recognize my ability? What would they give me?

I was fighting automatically when suddenly I noticed that one after another of the boys was leaving the ring. I was surprised, filled with panic, as though I had been left alone with an unknown danger. Then I understood. The boys had arranged it among themselves. It was the custom for the two men left in the ring to slug it out for the winner's prize. I discovered this too late. When the bell sounded two men in tuxedoes leaped into the ring and removed the blindfold. I found myself facing Tatlock, the biggest of the gang. I felt sick at my stomach. Hardly had the bell stopped ringing in my ears than it clanged again and I saw him moving swiftly toward me. Thinking of nothing else to do I hit him smash on the nose. He kept coming, bringing the rank sharp violence of stale sweat. His face was a black blank of a face, only his eyes alive—with hate of me and aglow with a feverish terror from what had happened to us all. I became anxious. I wanted to deliver my speech and he came at me as though he meant to beat it out of me. I smashed him again and again, taking his blows as they came. Then on a sudden impulse I struck him lightly and as we clinched, I whispered, "Fake like I knocked you out, you can have the prize."

"I'll break your behind," he whispered hoarsely.

"For *them*?"

"For *me*, sonofabitch!"

They were yelling for us to break it up and Tatlock spun me half around with a blow, and as a joggled camera sweeps in a reeling scene, I saw the howling red faces crouching tense beneath the cloud of blue-gray smoke. For a moment the world wavered, unraveled, flowed, then my head cleared and Tatlock bounced before me. That fluttering shadow before my eyes was his jabbing left hand. Then falling forward, my head against his damp shoulder, I whispered,

"I'll make it five dollars more."

"Go to hell."

But his muscles relaxed a trifle beneath my pressure and I breathed, "Seven?"

"Give it to your ma," he said, ripping me beneath the heart.

And while I still held him I butted him and moved away. I felt myself bombarded with punches. I fought back with hopeless desperation. I wanted to deliver my speech more than anything else in the world, because I felt that only these men could judge truly my ability, and now this stupid clown was ruining my chances. I began fighting carefully now, moving in to punch him and out again with my greater speed. A lucky blow to his chin and I had him going too—until I heard a loud voice yell, "I got my money on the big boy."

Hearing this, I almost dropped my guard. I was confused: Should I try to win against the voice out there? Would not this go against my speech, and was not this a moment for humility, for nonresistance? A blow to my head as I danced about sent my right eye popping like a jack-in-the-box and settled my dilemma. The room went red as I fell. It was a dream fall, my body languid and fastidious as to where to land, until the floor became impatient and smashed up to meet me. A moment later I came to. An hypnotic voice said FIVE emphatically. And I lay there, hazily watching a dark red spot of my own blood shaping itself into a butterfly, glistening and soaking into the soiled gray world of the canvas.

When the voice drawled TEN I was lifted up and dragged to a chair. I sat dazed. My eye pained and swelled with each throb of my pounding heart and I wondered if now I would be allowed to speak. I was wringing wet, my mouth still bleeding. We were grouped along the wall now. The other boys ignored me as they congratulated Tatlock and speculated as to how much they would be paid. One boy whimpered over his smashed hand. Looking up front, I saw attendants in white jackets rolling the portable ring away and placing a small square rug in the vacant space surrounded by chairs. Perhaps, I thought, I will stand on the rug to deliver my speech.

Then the M.C. called to us, "Come on up here boys and get your money."

We ran forward to where the men laughed and talked in their chairs, waiting. Everyone seemed friendly now.

"There it is on the rug," the man said. I saw a rug covered with coins of all dimensions and a few crumpled bills. But what excited me, scattered here and there, were the gold pieces.

"Boys, it's all yours," the man said. "You get all you grab."

"Thats' right, Sambo," a blond man said, winking at me confidentially.

I trembled with excitement, forgetting my pain. I would get the gold and the bills, I thought. I would use both hands. I would throw my body against the boys nearest me to block them from the gold.

"Get down around the rug now," the man commanded, "and don't anyone touch it until I give the signal."

"This ought to be good," I heard.

As told, we got around the square rug on our knees. Slowly the man raised his freckled hand as we followed it upward with our eyes.

I heard, "These niggers look like they're about to pray!"

Then, "Ready," the man said. "Go!"

I lunged for a yellow coin lying on the blue design of the carpet, touching it and sending a surprised shriek to join those rising around me. I tried frantically to remove my hand but could not let go. A hot, violent force tore through my body, shaking me like a wet rat. The rug was electrified. The hair bristled up on my head as I shook myself free. My muscles jumped, my nerves jangled, writhed. But I saw that this was not stopping the other boys. Laughing in fear and embarrassment, some were holding back and scooping up the coins knocked off by painful contortions of the others. The men roared above us as we struggled.

"Pick it up, goddamnit, pick it up!" someone called like a bass-voiced parrot. "Go on, get it!"

I crawled rapidly around the floor, picking up the coins, trying to avoid the coppers and to get greenbacks and the gold. Ignoring the shock by laughing, as I brushed the coins off quickly, I discovered that I could contain the electricity—a contradiction, but it works. Then the men began to push us onto the rug. Laughing embarrassedly, we struggled out of their hands and kept after the coins. We were all wet and slippery and hard to hold. Suddenly I saw a boy lifted into the air, glistening with sweat like a circus seal, and dropped, his wet back landing flush upon the charged rug, heard him yell and saw him literally dance upon his back, his elbows beating a frenzied tattoo upon the floor, his muscles twitching like the flesh of a horse stung by many flies. When he finally rolled off, his face was gray and no one stopped him when he ran from the floor amid booming laughter.

"Get the money," the M.C. called. "That's good hard American cash!"

And we snatched and grabbed, snatched and grabbed. I was careful not to come too close to the rug now, and when I felt the hot whiskey breath descend upon me like a cloud of foul air I reached out and grabbed the leg of a chair. It was occupied and I held on desperately.

"Leggo, nigger! Leggo!"

The huge face wavered down to mine as he tried to push me free. But my body was slippery and he was too drunk. It was Mr. Colcord, who owned a chain of movie houses and "entertainment palaces." Each time he grabbed me I slipped out of his hands. It became a real struggle. I feared the rug more than I did the drunk, so I held on, surprising myself for a moment by trying to topple *him* upon the rug. It was such an enormous idea that I found myself actually carrying it out. I tried not to be obvious, yet when I grabbed his leg, trying to tumble him out of the chair, he raised up roaring with laughter and, looking at me with soberness dead in the eye, kicked me viciously in the chest. The chair leg flew out of my hand and I felt myself going and rolled. It was as though I had rolled through a bed of hot coals. It seemed a whole century would pass before I would roll free, a century in which I was seared through the deepest levels of my body to the fearful breath within me and the breath seared and heated to the point of explosion. It'll all be over in a flash, I thought as I rolled clear. It'll all be over in a flash.

But not yet, the men on the other side were waiting, red faces swollen as though from apoplexy as they bent forward in their chairs. Seeing their fingers coming toward me I rolled

away as a fumbled football rolls off the receiver's fingertips,
back into the coals. That time I luckily sent the rug sliding out
of place and heard the coins ringing against the floor and the
boys scuffling to pick them up and the M.C. calling, "All right,
boys, that's all. Go get dressed and get your money."

I was limp as a dish rag. My back felt as though it had
been beaten with wires.

When we had dressed the M.C. came in and gave us
each five dollars, except Tatlock, who got ten for being last in
the ring. Then he told us to leave. I was not to get a chance
to deliver my speech, I thought. I was going out into the dim
alley in despair when I was stopped and told to go back. I
returned to the ballroom, where the men were pushing back
their chairs and gathering in groups to talk.

The M.C. knocked on a table for quiet. "Gentlemen," he
said, "we almost forgot an important part of the program. A
most serious part, gentlemen. This boy was brought here to
deliver a speech which he made at his graduation yesterday . . ."

"Bravo!"

I'm told that he is the smartest boy we've got out there
in Greenwood. I'm told that he knows more big words than a
pocket-sized dictionary."

Much applause and laughter.

"So now, gentlemen, I want you to give him your attention."

There was still laughter as I faced them, my mouth dry,
my eye throbbing. I began slowly, but evidently my throat was
tense, because they began shouting, "Louder! Louder!"

"We of the younger generation extol the wisdom of that
great leader and educator," I shouted, "who first spoke these
flaming words of wisdom: 'A ship lost at sea for many days
suddenly sighted a friendly vessel. From the mast of the
unfortunate vessel was seen a signal: "Water, water; we die
of thirst!" The answer from the friendly vessel came back:
"Cast down your bucket where you are." The captain of the
distressed vessel, at last heeding the injunction, cast down his
bucket, and it came up full of fresh sparkling water from the
mouth of the Amazon River.' And like him I say, and in his
words, 'To those of my race who depend upon bettering their
condition in a foreign land, or who underestimate the importance of cultivating friendly relations with the Southern white

man, who is his next-door neighbor, I would say: "Cast down your bucket where you are"—cast it down in making friends in every manly way of the people of all races by whom we are surrounded . . .'"

I spoke automatically and with such fervor that I did not realize that the men were still talking and laughing until my dry mouth, filling up with blood from the cut, almost strangled me. I coughed, wanting to stop and go to one of the tall brass, sand-filled spittoons to relieve myself, but a few of the men, especially the superintendent, were listening and I was afraid. So I gulped it down, blood, saliva and all, and continued. (What powers of endurance I had during those days! What enthusiasm! What a belief in the rightness of things!) I spoke even louder in spite of the pain. But still they talked and still they laughed, as though deaf with cotton in dirty ears. So I spoke with greater emotional emphasis. I closed my ears and swallowed blood until I was nauseated. The speech seemed a hundred times as long as before, but I could not leave out a single word. All had to be said, each memorized nuance considered, rendered. Nor was that all. Whenever I uttered a word of three or more syllables a group of voices would yell for me to repeat it. I used the phrase "social responsibility" and they yelled:

"What's that word you say, boy?"

"Social responsibility," I said.

"What?"

"Social . . ."

"Louder."

". . . responsibility."

"More!"

"Respon—"

"Repeat!"

"—sibility."

The room filled with the uproar of laughter until, no doubt, distracted by having to gulp down my blood, I made a mistake and yelled a phrase I had often seen denounced in newspaper editorials, heard debated in private.

"Social . . ."

"What?" they yelled.

". . . equality—"

The laughter hung smokelike in the sudden stillness. I opened my eyes, puzzled. Sounds of displeasure filled the room.

The M.C. rushed forward. They shouted hostile phrases at me. But I did not understand.

A small dry mustached man in the front row blared out, "Say that slowly, son!"

"What sir?

"What you just said!"

"Social responsibility, sir," I said.

"You weren't being smart, were you, boy?" he said, not unkindly.

"No, sir!"

"You sure that about 'equality' was a mistake?"

"Oh, yes, sir," I said. "I was swallowing blood."

"Well, you had better speak more slowly so we can understand. We mean to do right by you, but you've got to know your place at all times. All right, now, go on with your speech."

I was afraid. I wanted to leave but I wanted also to speak and I was afraid they'd snatch me down.

"Thank you, sir," I said, beginning where I had left off, and having them ignore me as before.

Yet when I finished there was a thunderous applause. I was surprised to see the superintendent come forth with a package wrapped in white tissue paper, and, gesturing for quiet, address the men.

"Gentlemen, you see that I did not overpraise this boy. He makes a good speech and some day he'll lead his people in the proper paths. And I don't have to tell you that that is important in these days and times. This is a good, smart boy, and so to encourage him in the right direction, in the name of the Board of Education I wish to present him a prize in the form of this . . ."

He paused, removing the tissue paper and revealing a gleaming calfskin brief case.

". . . in the form of this first-class article from Shad Whitmore's shop."

"Boy," he said, addressing me, "take this prize and keep it well. Consider it a badge of office. Prize it. Keep developing as you are and some day it will be filled with important papers that will help shape the destiny of your people."

I was so moved that I could hardly express my thanks. A rope of bloody saliva forming a shape like an undiscovered continent drooled upon the leather and I wiped it quickly away. I felt an importance that I had never dreamed.

"Open it and see what's inside," I was told.

My fingers a-tremble, I complied, smelling the fresh leather and finding an official-looking document inside. It was a scholarship to the state college for Negroes. My eyes filled with tears and I ran awkwardly off the floor.

I was overjoyed; I did not even mind when I discovered that the gold pieces I had scrambled for were brass pocket tokens advertising a certain make of automobile.

When I reached home everyone was excited. Next day the neighbors came to congratulate me. I even felt safe from grandfather, whose deathbed curse usually spoiled my triumphs. I stood beneath his photograph with my brief case in hand and smiled triumphantly into his stolid black peasant's face. It was a face that fascinated me. The eyes seemed to follow everywhere I went.

That night I dreamed I was at a circus with him and that he refused to laugh at the clowns no matter what they did. Then later he told me to open my brief case and read what was inside and I did, finding an official envelope stamped with the state seal; and inside the envelope I found another and another, endlessly, and I thought I would fall of weariness. "Them's years," he said. "Now open that one." And I did and in it I found an engraved document containing a short message in letters of gold. "Read it," my grandfather said. "Out loud."

"To Whom It May Concern," I intoned. "Keep This Nigger-Boy Running."

I awoke with the old man's laughter ringing in my ears.

(It was a dream I was to remember and dream again for many years after. But at that time I had no insight into its meaning. First I had to attend college.)

THE ALARM CLOCK

Mari Evans

Alarm clock
sure sound
loud
this mornin'

remind me of the time
I sat down
in a drug store
with my mind
a way far off

until the girl
and she was small
it seems to me
with yellow hair
a hangin'
smiled up and said
'I'm sorry but
we don't serve
you people
here'
and I woke up
quick
like I did this mornin'
when the
alarm
went off

It don't do
to wake up
quick

NEGRO AND JEW:
ENCOUNTER IN AMERICA

Leslie Fiedler

I have never read anything by James Baldwin which has not moved me. Both his novel, *Go Tell It on the Mountain,* and his recent collection of essays possess a passion and a lyricism quite unlooked for in another book about "the Negro." There is no securer or more soporific refuge from the realities of Negro-white conflict than most of the writing on the subject; and the greatest tribute one can pay to Baldwin is to state unequivocally that he does not contribute to that pious bedtime literature. Since I am impelled to take off from, and in certain respects to amend what he has to say about the relations of Negro and Jew to each other and to America, I feel his honesty as a challenge. To write with less involvement or risk of pain would be an offense.

I am moved to begin with Baldwin's title. Unlike the Negro, the Jew is apt to feel himself not a "native son" but a sojourner in America. I do not mean that he cannot by assimilation and adaptation become as American as anyone else, merely that he knows he can only achieve that end by accepting a role which he has played no part in creating. The Jew is, by and large, a late-comer in the United States; and when he begins to arrive in significant numbers toward the end of the nineteenth century, he and America are already set in their respective ways; theirs is a marriage of the middle-aged. The guilts and repressions, the boasts and regrets of America are already formulated when he debarks, waiting for him. Their genesis goes back to an experience he does not share; and he himself is determined by quite other experiences—

twice determined, in fact: by the dim pre-history of *Eretz Yisrael* and by the living memory of Exile.

Indeed, the Jew may already have been determined a third time, by the impact of the Enlightenment, perhaps even in the form of anarchism or socialism. Whatever the shape of his own life, the Jew comes to America with a history, the memory of a world he cannot afford to and does not want to deny. But the Negro arrives without a past, out of nowhere—that is to say, out of a world he is afraid to remember, perhaps could not even formulate to himself in the language he has been forced to learn. Before America, there is for him simply nothing; and America itself, white America, scarcely exists until he is present. Whatever the fate of the Jew in America, he knows he has not helped forge the conscience of the country. He may give a special flavor to New York or Hollywood, even to one or more of the arts in recent days; but he does not exist for the American imagination at those deep levels where awareness is determined. The encounter with the Jew is irrelevant to America's self-consciousness.

Nowhere in all of American literature is there a sentence bearing on the Jew with the terrible resonance of Benito Cereno's cry in Melville's story, "It is the Negro!" This is an exclamation of terror, to be sure; but it is also a statement of fact: the black man is the root of our guilt and fear and pain. Similarly, in Whitman's "Song of Myself," where the United States found in the mid-nineteenth century a lyric voice, the Negro is evoked in all his suffering: "I am the hounded slave, I wince at the bite of dogs, Hell and despair are upon me . . ." but there is no Jew. No more than he can forget he was a slave can the Negro forget that he was the occasion, whatever the cause, of a war which set white American against white American and created a bitterness we have not yet ceased to feel. It is the historical fact of the Civil War, not specifically alluded to in Baldwin's book, which gives special sanction to his grim vaunt: "The time has come to realize that the interracial drama acted out on the American Continent has not only created a new black man, it has created a new white man, too. . . . One of the things that distinguishes Americans from other people is that no other people has ever been so deeply involved in the lives of black men. . . ." Certainly, none has witnessed its white citizens killing each other over the question of their relation to the blacks. Yet at the time of the Civil War, the single Jewish member of my own family by marriage or blood who was in this country (and I suspect this is not untypical) was called on to mount guard on the roof of a Fifth Avenue shop during the draft riots in New York. Baldwin's boast is one no Jew could make; and "Thank God for that!" one is tempted to add, for the Negro, insofar as he considers himself responsible for that war and all it sums up that is dark and ambiguous in the American experience, must endure a sense of guilt of which we are free.

Indeed, superficially at least, the history of the Jew in America is singularly free of guilt on either hand. We represent, rather disconcertingly, the major instance in America of an ethnic minority redeemed rather than exploited or dispossessed. Other foreign groups, the Italians or Scandinavians, for instance, were also welcomed in the time of the great immigrations; but they did not arrive like the Jews, on a dead run, universally branded and harried. Only the Irish can be compared with us in the urgency of their flight. We fled to the Golden Door not merely from poverty and hunger, but impelled by an absolute rejection and the threat of extinction; and it is, therefore, no accident that the lines on the Statue of Liberty: "Give me your tired, your poor, your huddled masses yearning to breathe free . . ." were written by a Jew. They are sentimental enough, to be sure; but they could at least be inscribed by one of our people without the destructive irony that would have undercut them had they been written by a Negro.

The Jews have prospered in the United States, the single Western country never to have had a real ghetto, as they have nowhere else in the world. Even the niggling social snobbery, the occasional outbursts of violence against us can be understood, without extraordinary injustice to the facts, as hangovers from the European experience we have all fled, remnants of debased religion and ancient terror that we have not yet sloughed off. The American, who must wince when the Negro is mentioned, thinking of the slave ships; stutter when the Indian is brought up, remembering the theft of the land; and squirm when the Japanese are touched on, recalling the concentration camps of the last war—can cite the Jews with pride. We are (it is fashionable to forget this now, but salutory to recall) the boast of the United States, as the Negroes are its shame; and it is across the barrier of this discrepancy that our two peoples confront each other. The Negro boasts grimly that he has helped shape with terror the American spirit; we admit shamefacedly that we have profited by its generosity. It is no good showing our minor wounds, on the one hand; or insisting, on the other, upon the squalor and brutality of the Africa out of which the Negro was kidnapped; the guilt of Isaac toward Ishmael can not be so easily dispelled.

The problem, however, is more complicated than that; the relationship of Negro and Jew to America involves their relationship to Europe; for America, transmuted as it is, remains still somehow the Europe it thought to flee. But Europe is "the West"—that is to say, Christendom in decay. What, then, is the relationship of the Jew to the Christian world he invented and rejected; and how does it compare with the relation to that world of the Negroes—that is, of the last heathen to be converted by force? We are strangers both, outsiders in some senses forever, but we are outsiders with a difference.

America is for the Negro a way into the West, a gateway to Europe—and not only for the young colored writers and students and artists, like Baldwin himself, whom one sees sitting in the cafés of Paris and Rome, sustained by awards from our large Foundations. They are merely the vanguard, the symbolic representatives of their whole people. The Jew, conversely, is the gateway into Europe for America; for he has carried with him, almost against his will, his own history, two thousand years of which is European. The anti-American Frenchman or Italian condemning our culture and its representatives will brush aside the names of certain writers and thinkers offered in our defense, protesting, "But he's a *Jew*," meaning, of course, a European, not really an American. And there is a kind of miserable half-truth in the rejoinder.

Certainly, no young Jewish-American writer (*returning* to Europe, after all) can feel what Baldwin does confronting a group of ignorant Europeans in a remote Swiss village, "the most illiterate among them is related in a way I am not to Dante, Shakespeare, Michelangelo . . . the Cathedral of Chartres says to them which it cannot say to me. . . ." Alien as the Jew may feel himself, he is an alien with a culture ambiguously related to that which informs all the monuments of European art. It is not merely that people of our blood, whether converts to Christianity or skeptics or orthodox believers, have been inextricably involved in the making of the European mind: Leone Ebreo, Maimonides, Montaigne and Spinoza and Marx— perhaps even St. John of the Cross and Christopher Columbus; but that we have haunted the mind of Europe for two thousand years as the black man has haunted that of America for two hundred. Standing before the cathedrals that make Baldwin feel a stranger, we remember that here a spokesman of our people was dragooned into debating the incarnation; there, every Sunday, the elders of the ghetto were forced to listen to a sermon on the destruction of the Temple. Walk down into the Forum, and there is the arch of Titus; enter the palace of the Dukes of Urbino, and there is Uccello's painting of the Jew burning the bleeding host; open Shakespeare, and there is Shylock.

But even this, of course, is by no means all. The Jew is bound to Europe not only by ties of guilt and mutual hatred, and he lives in its imagination not only as the sinister usurer and defiler of altars. The images of all it most aspires to and reveres are also Jewish images: the David and Moses of Michelangelo, the Virgin of Dante—the very figure of the Christian God are collaborations of our mind and theirs. Before the Cathedral at Chartres, the Jew cannot help thinking, wryly, ironically or bitterly: this is our gift to the barbarians. And this the barbarians cannot deny. The boast of that Church most deeply rooted in the history of Europe is "Abraham is our father. Spiritually we are Semites." The West may, in occasional spasms, try to cast us out; but it cannot without spiritual self-castration deny its own Jewishness. The Jew is the father of Europe (irksome as that relationship may sometimes seem on both sides); the Negro only an adopted child. If Christendom denies us, it diminishes itself; but if we reject the West, we reject not our legend, only a historical interruption of it. We are what we always were—ourselves. The Negro, on the other hand, cannot endure alienation from the West; for once he steps outside of it, he steps outside of culture—not into Africa, to which he cannot return, but into nothing. The cases of Liberia and modern Israel make the point vividly: a homeland urged on the American Negro and (by and large) rejected, versus one denied the Jew, but fought for and, against ridiculous odds, achieved. Similarly, the Negro is the prisoner of his face in a way the Jew is not. The freedom of the Jew is no mere matter of plastic surgery and nose-shortening; this would be a vanity as pointless as the Negro's skin bleaches and hair-straighteners. A generation or two in America, however, and the Jew is born with a new face. A blond and snub-nosed little boy looks out of the Barton's Pesach ad in *The New York Times,* crying, "Happy Passover, Grandma!" and it is hard to tell him from the pink Protestant image of "Dick" in the school primers. But no Negro dares imagine his child with such a face. This, too, lies between the Jew and Negro in America: the realization that for one (whether he finally choose it or not) there is always a way out, by emigration or assimilation; for the other there is no exit.

Both Negro and Jew exist for the Western world, as I have already suggested, not only in history but also in the timeless limbo of the psyche—that is, as archetypes, symbolic figures presumably representing the characters and fates of alien peoples, but actually projecting aspects of the white Christian mind itself. It is the confusion between these legendary projections (necessary to the psychological well-being of Europe and America) and actual living men called by the same labels which makes the elimination of race prejudice a problem beyond the scope of mere economic and social measures.

The differences between the archetypes of Negro and Jew are especially illuminating. They begin with the fact, which we have noticed earlier, that the myth of the Jew is a European inheritance, or, perhaps better, a persistence; while the myth of the Negro is a product of the American experience and of a crisis in the American mind. The image of the usurer and bad father with a knife that lies behind Shylock existed long before even the dream of America; indeed, it represents a distortion of our own myths of Jacob and Abraham in alien and hostile minds. The evil Jews of American writers like Fitzgerald, Pound or Cummings are no more than refurbishings of the original symbolic figure out of the Middle Ages; for there is, in the world of the imagination, no American Jew. The key Archetypes of the Negro, however, are purely American: Aunt Jemima and Uncle Tom, those insipid and infuriating but (as Mr. Baldwin justly observes) inescapable images that, still in the best American tradition, belong really to childhood. From Uncle Tom, in particular, there descend such important characters of our literature as Mark Twain's Nigger Jim and Faulkner's Lucas Beauchamp, who symbolically grant the white man forgiveness in the name of their whole race, redeem him by enduring the worst he can inflict.

It is intriguing that the chief literary archetypes of the Jew are frankly villains and figures of terror, while the myth of the Negro as it takes flesh in our classic novels is more often than not the symbol of a reconciliation more hoped-for than real, a love that transcends guilt. It is the noblest American sentimentality. By the same token, the counterimages of Jew and Negro in the "enlightened" fiction of the most recent past differ equally from each other but in reverse: the conciliator has been transformed into the murderer, the murderer into the conciliator; that is, Uncle Tom has become Bigger Thomas, while the Jew's daughter who lured Hugh of Lincoln to his death has been transformed into Marjorie Morningstar.

The Negro, however, whether thought of as killer or pious slave, has always represented for the American imagination the primitive and the instinctive, the life of impulse whether directed toward good or ill. The Jew, on the other hand, stands symbolically for the uses and abuses of intelligence, for icy legalism or equally cold vengefulness. They represent the polar opposition of law and lawlessness, the eternal father and the eternal child, who is also, according to the Romantic poets, "father of the man." In Freudian terminology, the one can be said to stand for the superego, the other the id, though both are felt, like the peoples with whom they are identified, as *other* by the white, Gentile ego.

Toward id and superego alike, the American, with his double inheritance of Romanticism and Puritanism, has a divided attitude; and this ambivalence is transferred to the symbolic Negro and Jew. The black man is associated with the primitive and the forest, with the "natural," which Americans like to think of as their element. But the Devil was called in Massachusetts the "Black Man," too; and what we label nowadays the unconscious had earlier no other name than the "satanic." The heart is another symbol for the same "natural" for which the Negro comes to stand, but so are the genitals; and if the Negro comes into classic fiction as a source of pity and love, he lurks in the back of the popular mind always as the rapist—the projection of the white man's own "dark" sensuality which he can neither suppress nor justify.

No Christian, however, can without calling Jehova the Devil (and even this was tried long ago and condemned as a heresy) think of the Jews as wholly satanic; recalcitrant or rejected, they are still God's people. The final Puritan equivalent of the id is Satan, but that of the superego is God: and this is why no good Protestant American can, whatever the presumable Gospel justification, hate the Jew (who stands forever on Sinai, the Tables in his hand), without a sneaking suspicion that he is also hating God.

Perhaps this explains, too, why a certain kind of Romantic anti-Puritanism, which aims at setting traditional morality on its head and prefers whim to law, ends with a violent and sentimental espousal of the dark-skinned peoples and a complementary hatred of the Jews. D. H. Lawrence is one example of this tendency; but its clearest exponent is, as one would expect, an American. For Sherwood Anderson, the Negro in his *Dark Laughter*, his visceral, impulsive joy in life, represents a positive pole, while the Jew, cerebral, talkative, melancholy, the enemy of his own sexuality, stands for all that is negative and reprehensible in modern life.

Yet despite the many spectacular differences between the history and status of Negroes and Jews, between the ways in which they have come to America and the ways in which the American imagination uses them—they are somehow bound together and condemned to a common fate, not less real for being so hard to define. "Prejudice against Negroes and Jews" —it is a phrase that comes naturally and inevitably; and for all its banality, it contains a truth. As far as economic and professional opportunities are concerned there is no comparison between the status of Negroes and Jews; but in a certain kind of social exclusion, in the *quality* of that exclusion rather than its degree (for it is much more severe in the case of the Negro), they are one. Similarly though not equally, both peoples are bound by restrictions that determine where they can live, what clubs and fraternities they can join, what hotels they can enter and finally (and this is the crux, though we are often driven to deny its importance for what seem good strategic reasons) *whom they can marry.*

There are no other white ethnic groups against whom such thoroughgoing exclusions are practiced; for there is no other group which is felt, viscerally not rationally, as so completely alien, so totally other. Though none of our state laws against miscegenation apply, as far as I am aware, to Jews, every Jew knows that the spoken and occasionally printed injunction "For White Only" may exclude him. There is at work everywhere in the United States, the Protestant-North European tendency to think of all Mediterranean peoples as more black than white, Dagos and Gypsies, swarthy fiddlers and actors, not to be trusted with women; but only in respect to the Jews among those peoples is there the true primitive fear of the *contamination of blood*. Historically, the Jew has been rejected on two grounds, for his religion and for his "race"; but in America in recent years the decay of piety into interfaith good will has rendered the former more and more negligible. The last irrational grounds of our exclusion are not very different from those which surround the Negro with horror: we are taboo peoples, both of us. The secret of our fraternity lies in the barbarous depths of the white, Gentile heart; and it is that shared secret which makes us aware of how we resemble each other and are mutually different from the Irish, the Poles or the Yugoslavs, discriminated against only for comparatively *rational* reasons: because they have arrived here later than other groups and now displace them in jobs, etc.

To be so alike and so different; different in ourselves and alike only in the complicated fear we stir in the hearts of our neighbors, this is what exacerbates our relations with each other. Surely the Negro cannot relish (for all his sentimental desire to think of himself metaphorically as Israel, "Let my people go . . .") this improbable and unwanted yoking any more than the Jew; and yet even physically our people have been thrust together. It is in the big cities of the industrial North, in New York or Philadelphia or Chicago or Detroit, that the Negro and the Jew confront each other and that their inner relationship is translated into a spatial one. The "emancipated" Negro fleeing poverty and the South, and the "emancipated" Jew fleeing exclusion and Europe, become neighbors; and their proximity serves to remind both that neither is quite "emancipated" after all. In America, to be sure, the ultimate ghetto (there is no way of avoiding the word, which gives its name to Baldwin's chief essay on the subject I am treating, "The Harlem Ghetto") is reserved for Negroes. Jews inhabit at one remove or another the region between it and the neighborhoods which mean real belonging, except for the marginal Jewish merchant who finds himself inside the Negro quarter, forced to squeeze his colored customers for his precarious livelihood and to bear the immediate brunt of their hatred for all white men.

It doesn't matter how much newer and richer are the homes which the Jews attain in their flight toward the tonier suburbs and how shabby the dwellings they leave to the Negroes always behind them, five years away or twenty or thirty; and they can never lose the sense of being merely a buffer between the blacks and the "real" whites. Insofar as they are aware of their undeniable economic superiority to the Negroes, middle-class Jews are likely to despise them for lagging behind at the same time that they resent them for pressing so close. It is not an easy relationship.

Most Jews have, I think, little sense of how the Negroes regard them specifically as Jews. They are likely to assume to begin with that Negroes are incapable of making subtle distinctions between whites and whites; and they are, moreover, accustomed to look for anti-Semitism chiefly from people who are, or whom the Jews believe to be, socially more secure than themselves. And so they are easily taken in by the affable play-acting of the Negroes, from whom they believe they have no cause to expect hatred. Jews, more often than not, take it for granted that the Negroes are grateful to them for the historical accident of their never having been the masters of black slaves; and they are shocked at the sort of black anti-Semitism which Baldwin describes: "But just as society must have a scapegoat, so hatred must have a symbol. Georgia has the Negro. Harlem has the Jew."

But why should the Negro hate the Jew? As far as he is aware, the Jew does not hate the Negro—at least not as much as the Gentiles do! To be sure, most Jews are conscious that the Negro is their lightning rod, that he occupies a ghetto which might otherwise be theirs and bears the pogroms which might otherwise be directed at them. But no Jew has ordained these ghettos, and if the owner of a Negro tenement happens to be a Jew, after all, he must live! In any court of law, the Jew would be declared innocent of major complicity in the oppression of the Negro in America. What if he sometimes bamboozles or overcharges a colored customer, or refuses to sell his house to the first Negro to try to enter a neighborhood? He and his ancestors have never owned a slave or participated in a lynching or impregnated Negro women while worrying publicly about miscegenation. Almost alone among Americans, the Jew seems to have no reason to feel guilt toward the Negro; and this is, though Baldwin makes no point of it, a matter of great importance.

Yet it is not true that the Jew feels no guilt toward the Negro; he merely believes that he *should* feel none, and is baffled when he does. There is no reason, the Jew tells himself, why he should be expected to be more liberal than any other Americans in regard to such problems as fair employment codes and desegregation; and yet I am sure that most Jews are. On the record and at the polls, they are the Negroes' friends; and if the overwhelming majority of them would object to their daughters' marrying Negroes, they would object with hardly less violence to their marrying *goyim*. If we discriminate against Ham in this regard, we discriminate also against Japheth. Some Jews, to be sure, adopt the anti-Negro attitudes of their neighbors in an excess of assimilationist zeal, as a way of demonstrating by the all-American quality of their hatred that they, too, are "white." There is, however, also a particularly Jewish distrust of the black man, buried deep in our own tradition. Are we not told in the Torah itself that the offspring of Ham will be cursed: "A servant of servants shall he be unto his brethren."

There is no use quibbling about it; though he does not oppress the Negro, the Jew does hate him with a double though muted hatred: for being at once too like himself and too like the *goyim*—for resembling what the Jew most resents in his own situation and also what he most despises in the whole non-Jewish world. The Jew sees in the Negro a carefree and improvident life-style, that he has also observed and envied a little, all around him, but which he feels he could not afford (even if, improbably, he could approve) in his rejection and devotion to God. Yet though the Negro is also poor and rejected and pious, he is able to laugh overloud and drink overmuch, to take marriage lightly and money without seriousness, to buy spangles at the expense of food, to despise thrift and sobriety and to be so utterly a fool that one is *forced* into taking financial advantage of him. Real or legendary, this Negro the Jew finds or thinks he finds in his run-down, slovenly house; and he considers him no more admirable at worship than at play, jerking and howling and writhing on the floor in a final degradation of the alien Evangelical tradition.

Perhaps the Jew cannot be taken to task for despising improvidence and superstition. And yet he knows that somehow he has failed an obligation that he does not quite understand, failed his own history of persecution and oppression by not managing to—to do *what*? What he might have performed he can never really say, some bold revolutionary blow for emancipation, some superhuman act of love. So he cries out, if he is disturbed enough, against segregation to a group of his friends who are also against segregation, or he writes a letter to the papers, or makes a contribution to the NAACP. And, after all, what else can he do? What else can *I* do?

At least it is necessary to say "I" and pass on from safe generalizations about what the abstract "Jew" thinks about the abstract "Negro," generalizations from which it is possible to be secretly exempting oneself all the time. Even at the cost of some pain, it is necessary to say what "this Jew," what *I* feel on these matters in my own quite unstatistical flesh.

I can begin by saying, in the teeth of the usual defensive cliché, that none of my best friends is black. I have known many Negroes in my life and have talked to some, chiefly comrades in one radical party or another, far enough into the night to have some notion of the distrust we would have had to overcome, the masks we would have had to penetrate, to discover our real selves, much less become real friends. I cannot see how that gap could be closed without genuine passion; and my only passionate relation to a Negro I do not even remember, but take on trust from stories of my mother. When I was little more than a year old, I was taken care of by a black girl, whom I loved so deeply, caressing and kissing her black skin in a way which horrified my family, that she was fired. I assume that I was desolate for a little while; I do not really recall, and my mother never carried her account that far.

My only other conection with a Negro that involves any tenderness comes at a much later date. I was thirteen or fourteen, working at my first job in a shoe store, and more than a little scared at the cynicism and worldliness of the other "boys" (some of whom were as old as sixteen!), much less the salesmen and the hose girls. My only friend in the store, the only one who never mocked me, intentionally or unwittingly, was the colored porter. We would eat our lunches together in the basement out of paper bags, while all the others were off at cafeterias or lunch counters. He would speak to me gravely and without condescension about life—mostly sex, of course, which he thought the salesmen made too much of in their boastful anecdotes and I was over-impressed with in my callow innocence. After we finished eating, I would retouch the crude sketch of a gigantic, naked woman that someone had roughed out on one of the cellar walls, while he leaned back and criticized my efforts. Before we went upstairs to work again, he would help me push a pile of empty hose boxes in front of our private mural.

In retrospect, it seems to me that I found in this Negro porter, quite in accord with the best American traditions, my own Nigger Jim or Sam Fathers—but with what a difference! Urban Jew that I was, I had no nighttime Mississippi for the encounter, no disappearing virgin forest—only the half-lit cellar with the noise of the city traffic rumbling dimly above and the rustling of rats in the trashbin. It was not, however, a relationship with a person, but with a type.

Aside from these, my early encounters with Negroes were casual and public. There was, of course, the colored tenor who could sing "*Eli, Eli*" in Yiddish and was therefore in great demand at all Jewish events as a curiosity, a freak. What his fellow Negroes thought of him God only knows! I can remember the old women shaking their heads incredulously as he sang, and the kids afterwards arguing about whether one could really be both black and a Jew. Beyond this, there were the Negro customers in the shoe store and in my father's pharmacy. The shoe-store customers fell into two classes: ignorant working girls and old servants with broad, horny heels and monstrous bunions, who could be sold practically anything (even extra arch-supports for their rubbers!); and middle-class Negro women from the suburbs whom we hated for assuming, quite correctly, that we were trying to put something over on them. My father's customers I would see less frequently; his drugstore was in a distant and disreputable part of the city, with a Mission for repentant drunks on one side and a factory across the street. I would visit him occasionally, taking along a "hot meal" that had grown rather cold on the long streetcar ride, and watch him wait on the Negroes who made up a large part of his trade and whom he supplied with asafoetida to charm off the "misery," hair-straightener and large boxes of candy tied with even larger pink ribbons.

Last of all, there were the maids—which is to say, the kind of part-time help that would appear at my grandmother's house or ours when we were prosperous enough to afford it. I think it was a long time before it entered my head that a maid might not be a Negro, or a healthy young Negro woman not a maid. In conversations between my grandmother and my mother, the girl who helped us was always referred to simply as "the *schwarze*," which did not really mean "Negro," nor, God forbid, "nigger," but only "servant." After a while, we settled down to one *schwarze*, Hattie, who was an ardent disciple of Father Divine, and would dance abandonedly in one corner of the kitchen when the spirit moved her or preach at us in the name of peace. It pleased my mother, I know, to be called "Miz Lillie" in an unfamiliar style handed down from plantation days and reminiscent of movies about the South; and she would certainly roar with laughter when Hattie clowned and grimaced and played the darkie for all she was worth. When I was adolescent and very earnest on the Negro question, I would rush out of the house sometimes, equally furious with Hattie for her play-acting and my own family for lapping it up and laughing at the display with winks and condescension.

Things have changed a good deal since I was a kid; and when I return now to the city where I was born, there are not only colored cops on the corners, but in the stores, even the biggest ones, colored salesgirls as well as customers, black salesgirls who do not hesitate to be as insolent as the white ones. Indeed, when my grandmother was dying and I came back to see her for the last time, I found not only Hattie, quite old but spry enough to caper on seeing me as absurdly as she knew was expected, but also a Negro nurse. The nurse was a follower of Father Divine, too, but this was her only bond with Hattie; for she was not only a "professional woman," but a West Indian, very light-skinned, and spoke a painfully refined brand of British English. She insisted on having a papaya every day for lunch, presumably to keep her origins clear in the minds of everyone; but she was kind and patient all the same, though she slipped away, quietly but firmly, a few hours before my grandmother's death. "It's coming," she whispered to my mother in the kitchen. "I'm sorry, but its against my principles to stay in a house of death."

Despite my lack of intimacy with Negroes, I have possessed from my earliest childhood very strong theoretical opinions on the question of their rights. The first book I ever bought for myself with my own money (I was eight) was *Uncle Tom's Cabin*, which I read over and over, weeping in secret, and making vows to myself that I would work always (imagining, of course, a heroic stand against the ignorant multitude) until the last vestiges of racial inequality were wiped out. Needless to say, no heroic exploits followed, though I have a vivid memory of myself at twelve, shouting and pounding the table until I grew red-faced in an argument with the rabbi of the chief Reform temple of our city. I can still remember his face, unspeakably moderate (either he looked like the late Senator Taft or I have remade his remembered face into that image), nodding at me disapprovingly, while my family, acutely embarrassed, tried to signal silence from behind his back. His apology for discrimination was certainly one of the spiritual scandals that drove me in despair from the bourgeois Jewish community. The poor Orthodox Jews did not, it seemed to me, even know there was a Negro problem: while the richer, Reformed ones had, for all their "liberalism," surrendered to Gentile conformism.

If the first impulse that took me as a young man into the radical movement was a desire to be delivered of the disabilities of being a Jew, the second was the counterdesire to be delivered of the guilt of the discriminations practiced by Jews in their efforts to free themselves from those disabilities. Only in the Marxist scheme for remaking society could I then see the possibility of winning my freedom rather than buying it at the expense of somebody else—particularly of the Negro. Besides, I thought that one could discover in the Movement a society in which already Negro and white were living together on the basis of true equality. Did not white girls and Negro boys dance together at their social evenings? Were they not even lovers without special recrimination or horror? I soon became uncomfortably aware, however, that the radical movement was plagued by the same inability as bourgeois society to treat the Negroes as more than instances of their color. Turning this inability upside down helped very little.

That the girls chose Negroes as boy friends *because* they were Negroes, or that the top leadership (who were, it happened, Jews once more) appointed Negro organizers not in spite of their color but because of it—and that they would, when their directives changed, hurry them out of sight—all this became distressingly clear. That one could not call a sonofabitch a sonofabitch if he happened to be black, that a comrade who was sullen, uncooperative and undependable was immune to blame because he was colored—this became unendurable. The fear of being labeled a "white chauvinist" is as disabling as that of being called a "nigger-lover"; and to be barred a priori from hating someone is as debasing as being forbidden a priori to love him.

It is not, finally, a question of the Marxian movement failing its own dream, the dream of an assimilated Jew not above calling a political opponent a "Jew-nigger." Such a failure could be an accident of history, reparable under changed circumstances. The fatal flaw of all such approaches is that they begin with self-congratulation: permitting us to set ourselves apart from the guilty others and to think of ourselves as immune to the indignity and hatred which are the very condition of the coexistence of white and black in America. Only with the recognition of our own implication can we start to be delivered: not to fight for Negro rights as if we were detached liberators from another planet, but to know that those rights must be granted to ease us of the burden of our own guilt.

Of all my own experiences, the one which seems to me now central to an understanding of my problem, a real clue to the nature of Negro-Jewish relations, is that of merely *walking to school*. For some six months, when I was in the ninth grade, I went to what was called "The Annex," an aging, standardly dismal primary-school building used to catch the overflow from one of our high schools. It stood in a neighborhood largely inhabited by Negroes, though there were still Jewish delicatessens and kosher poultry slaughterers among the "race record" shops; and one of the streets was lined throughout the day with pushcarts, among which Yiddish was the commonest language spoken. The sons of butchers and the few trapped Jewish property owners left in the area seemed to become almost as often as not gangsters (one especially successful one, I recall, ran a free soup kitchen all through the Depression); and a standard way of proving ones toughness was "nigger-smashing." This sport involved cruising a side street at a high rate of speed, catching a lonely Negro, beating the hell out of him and getting back into the car and away before his friends could gather to retaliate. I remember that one of the local figures associated, in kids' legend at least, with "nigger-smashing" was himself called "Niggy" because of his kinky hair and thick lips, features not so uncommon among Jews, after all.

I had to walk to school through those streets, and it was not long before I was repeating to my friends what was quickly whispered to me: that it was not safe for either a white boy or for a colored one to walk there alone. It was a strange enough feeling to pass even in packs through so black a neighborhood to one's totally white class; for though the grade school was predominantly Negro, there was not a single colored student in my ninth-grade room. Especially on the warm days in late spring, when everyone was out on his stoop or sidewalk, in shirt sleeves or undershirt, one had a sense of an immense, brooding hostility. The fattest and most placid-looking woman leaning out of her window or the knot of yelling kids who parted to let one pass could suddenly seem a threat. It was like entering the territory of a recently subdued enemy, still too weary and disorganized for resistance but not for hatred. And saying to oneself, "I am a friend of the Negro people. I am on your side," didn't help a bit. It would have been absurd to cry it aloud, though sometimes the temptation was great; for in such a context, it would seem as false to the mouth that spoke it as to the ear that heard.

The sense of entering an alien country was exaggerated during my first month in school by the barricades which blocked off the streets just past the last plush Jewish apartment house and on the verge of that real ghetto. A smallpox epidemic had spread through the crowded, filthy living quarters of the Negroes, and only those with business in the neighborhood were permitted to enter, though even they were snatched up and rudely vaccinated on the spot. After a while, the sense of poverty and dirt, the dark faces looking out of the windows and the fear of the most dreadful of diseases blended into one; and even a kid going to school had the sense that he was entering not a place but a condition, that he was confronting the sickness and terror of his own soul made manifest.

Once toward the end of my endless term there, I was walking with my mother down the same street I followed daily to school. We were after something special, who knows, hot pastrami, maybe, or onion rolls or a fresh-killed chicken; when suddenly and quite casually she pointed to one of those drab, alien houses from which I had shrunk day after day, saying, "I was born there." It is the familiar pattern of the decay of urban neighborhoods; when the Jews are ready to go and it no longer pays to patch and paint, the Negroes are permitted to move in. The street where I myself was born is now almost all Negro, as is my high school; and the neighborhood where I lived until I was married is now surrounded. But at that moment beside my mother, I heard behind her familiar voice another which prompted it: the voice of a mild, horrified, old Gentile lady over her tea: "First the Jews, then the Negroes . . ." But this is also the voice of T. S. Eliot, "And the jew squats on the window sill, the owner . . ."

Emancipated and liberal, I could scarcely shake off my resentment and rage; for I saw the comedy and pathos of our plight, how *we* looked to the *goyish* eye at the very moment we were looking at the Negro: the first symptom of a disease, as inexorable as age itself, which eventually reduces newly seeded lawns and newly painted houses to baked gray mud and scabby boards. I could feel the Jew's special rancor at the Negro for permitting himself visibly to become (there is no question of the justice of such a notion, only of its force) the image, the proof of the alien squalor that the white, Gentile imagination finds also in the Jew. "As he to me," the Jew thinks helplessly, "so *I* to *them!*" And the "them" refers to the Gentiles already in the new, restricted addition to which the Jew will eventually come, by hard work and with much heart-burning, only to find the Gentiles gone and the Negro still at his heels.

For the Jew, the Negro is his shadow, his improbable caricature, whom he hates only at the price of hating himself; and he learns quickly (unless he allows rage to blind him) that for this reason his own human dignity depends not only theoretically but in terrible actuality upon that of the Negro. No Jew can selflessly dedicate himself to the fight for the equality of the Negro; when he pretends that he is not also fighting for himself, he is pretending that he is indistinguishable from a *goy.*

SLANT-EYED AMERICANS

Toshio Mori

My mother was commenting on the fine California weather. It was Sunday noon, December 7. We were having our lunch, and I had the radio going. "Let's take the afternoon off and go to the city," I said to Mother.

"All right. We shall go," she said dreamily. "Ah, four months ago my boy left Hayward to join the army, and a fine send-off he had. Our good friends—ah, I shall never forget the day of his departure."

"We'll visit some of our friends in Oakland and then take in a movie," I said. "Care to come along, Papa?"

Father shook his head. "No, I'll stay home and take it easy."

"That's his heaven," Mother commented. "To stay home, read the papers over and over, and smoke his Bull Durham."

I laughed. Suddenly the musical program was cut off as a special announcement came over the air: At 7:25 a.m. this morning a squadron of Japanese bombing planes attacked Pearl Harbor. The battle is still in progress.

"What's this? Listen to the announcement," I cried, going to the radio.

Abruptly the announcement stopped and the musicale continued.

"What is it?" Mother asked. "What has happened?"

"The radio reports that the Japanese planes attacked Hawaii this morning," I said incredulously. "It couldn't be true."

"It must be a mistake. Couldn't it have been a part of a play?" asked Mother.

I dialed other stations. Several minutes later one of the stations confirmed the bulletin.

"It must be true," Father said quietly.

I said, "Japan has declared war on the United States and Great Britain."

The room became quiet but for the special bulletin coming in every now and then.

"It cannot be true, yet it must be so," Father said over and over.

"Can it be one of those programs scaring the people about invasion?" Mother asked me.

"No, I'm sure this is a news report," I replied.

Mother's last ray of hope paled and her eyes became dull. "Why did it have to happen? The common people in Japan don't want war, and we don't want war. Here the people are peace-loving. Why cannot the peoples of the earth live together peacefully?"

"Since Japan declared war on the United States it'll mean that you parents of American citizens have become enemy aliens," I said.

"Enemy aliens," my mother whispered.

Night came but sleep did not come. We sat up late in the night hoping against hope that some good news would come, retracting the news of vicious attack and open hostilities.

"This is very bad for the people with Japanese faces," I said.

Father slowly shook his head.

"What shall we do?" asked Mother.

"What can we do?" Father said helplessly.

At the flower market next morning the growers were present but the buyers were scarce. The place looked empty and deserted. "Our business is shot to pieces," one of the boys said.

"Who'll buy flowers now?" another called.

Don Haley, the seedsman, came over looking bewildered. "I suppose you don't need seeds now."

We shook our heads.

"It looks bad," I said. "Will it affect your business?"

"Flower seed sale will drop but the vegetable seeds will move quicker," Don said. "I think I'll have to put more time on the vegetable seeds."

Nobu Hiramatsu who had been thinking of building another greenhouse joined us. He had plans to grow more carnations and expand his business.

"What's going to happen to your plans, Nobu?" asked one of the boys.

"Nothing. I'm going to sit tight and see how the things turn out," he said.

"Flowers and war don't go together," Don said. "You cannot concentrate too much on beauty when destruction is going about you."

"Sure, pretty soon we'll raise vegetables instead of flowers," Grasselli said.

A moment later the market opened and we went back to the tables to sell our flowers. Several buyers came in and purchased a little. The flowers didn't move at all. Just as I was about to leave the place I met Tom Yamashita, the Nisei gardener with a future.

"What are you doing here, Tom? What's the matter with your work?" I asked as I noticed his pale face.

"I was too sick with yesterday's news so I didn't work," he said. "This is the end. I am done for."

"No, you're not. Buck up, Tom," I cried. "You have a good future, don't lose hope."

"Sometimes I feel all right. You are an American, I tell myself. Devote your energy and life to the American way of life. Long before this my mind was made up to become a true American. This morning my Caucasian American friends sympathized with me. I felt good and was grateful. Our opportunity has come to express ourselves and act. We are Americans in thought and action. I felt like leaping to work. Then I got sick again because I got to thinking that Japan was the country that attacked the United States. I wanted to bury myself for shame."

I put my hand on his shoulder. "We all feel the same way, Tom. We're human so we flounder around awhile when an unexpected and big problem confronts us, but now that situation has to be passed by. We can't live in the same stage long. We have to move along, face the reality no matter what's in store for us."

Tom stood silently.

"Let's go to my house and take the afternoon off," I suggested. "We'll face a new world tomorrow morning with boldness and strength. What do you say, Tom?"

"All right," Tom agreed.

At home Mother was anxiously waiting for me. When

she saw Tom with me her eyes brightened. Tom Yamashita was a favorite of my mother's.

"Look, a telegram from Kazuo!" she cried to me, holding up an envelope. "Read it and tell me what he says."

I tore it open and read. "He wants us to send $45 for train fare. He has a good chance for a furlough."

Mother fairly leaped in the air with the news. She had not seen my brother for four months. "How wonderful! This can happen only in America."

Suddenly she noticed Tom looking glum, and pushed him in the house. "Cheer up, Tom. This is no time for young folks to despair. Roll up your sleeves and get to work. America needs you."

Tom smiled for the first time and looked at me.

"See, Tom?" I said. "She's quick to recover. Yesterday she was wilted, and she's seventy-three."

"Tom, did you go to your gardens today?" she asked him.

"No."

"Why not?" she asked, and then added quickly. "You young men should work hard all the more, keeping up the normal routine of life. You ought to know, Tom, that if everybody dropped their work everything would go to seed. Who's going to take care of the gardens if you won't?"

Tom kept still.

Mother poured tea and brought the cookies. "Don't worry about your old folks. We have stayed here to belong to the American way of life. Time will tell our true purpose. We remained in America for permanence—not for temporary convenience. We common people need not fear."

"I guess you are right," Tom agreed.

"And America is right. She cannot fail. Her principles will stand the test of time and tyranny. Someday aggression will be outlawed by all nations."

Mother left the room to prepare the dinner. Tom got up and began to walk up and down the room. Several times he looked out the window and watched the wind blow over the field.

"Yes, if the gardens are ruined I'll rebuild them," he said. "I'll take charge of every garden in the city. All the gardens of America for that matter. I'll rebuild them as fast as the enemies wreck them. We'll have nature on our side and you cannot crush nature."

I smiled and nodded. "Good for you! Tomorrow we'll get up early in the morning and work, sweat, and create. Let's shake on it."

We solemnly shook hands, and by the grip of his fingers I knew he was ready to lay down his life for America and for his gardens.

"No word from him yet," Mother said worriedly. "He should have arrived yesterday. What's happened to him?"

It was eight in the evening, and we had had no word from my brother for several days.

"He's not coming home tonight. It's too late now," I said. "He should have arrived in Oakland this morning at the latest."

Our work had piled up and we had to work late into the night. There were still some pompons to bunch. Faintly the phone rang in the house.

"The phone!" cried Mother excitedly. "It's Kazuo, sure enough."

In the flurry of several minutes I answered the phone, greeted my brother, and was on my way to San Leandro to drive him home. On the way I tried to think of the many things I wanted to say. From the moment I spotted him waiting on the corner I could not say the thing I wanted to. I took his bag and he got in the car, and for some time we did not say anything. Then I asked him how the weather had been in Texas and how he had been.

"We were wating for you since yesterday," I said. "Mother is home getting the supper ready. You haven't eaten yet, have you?"

He shook his head. "The train was late getting into Los Angeles. We were eight hours behind time and I should have reached San Francisco this morning around eight."

Reaching home it was the same way. Mother could not say anything. "We have nothing special tonight, wish we had something good."

"Anything would do, Mama," my brother said.

Father sat in the room reading the papers but his eyes were over the sheet and his hands were trembling. Mother scurried about getting his supper ready. I sat across the table from my brother, and in the silence which was action I watched the wave of emotions in the room. My brother was aware of it too. He sat there without a word, but I knew he understood.

Not many years ago he was the baby of the family, having never been away from home. Now he was on his own, his quiet confidence actually making him appear larger. Keep up the fire, that was his company's motto. It was evident that he was a soldier. He had gone beyond life and death matter, where the true soldiers of war or peace must travel, and had returned.

For five short days we went about our daily task, picking and bunching the flowers for Christmas, eating heavy meals, and visiting the intimates. It was as if we were waiting for the hour of his departure, the time being so short. Every minute was crowded with privacy, friends, and nursery work. Too soon the time for his train came but the family had little to talk.

"Kazuo, don't worry about home or me," Mother said as we rode into town.

"Take care of yourself," my brother told her.

At the 16th Street Station Mother's close friend was waiting for us. She came to bid my brother good-bye. We had fifteen minutes to wait. My brother bought a copy of *The Coast* to see if his cartoons were in.

"Are you in this month's issue?" I asked.

"I haven't seen it yet," he said, leafing the pages. "Yes, I'm in. Here it is."

"Good!" I said. "Keep trying hard. Someday peace will come, and when you return laughter will reign once again."

My mother showed his cartoon to her friend. The train came in and we got up. It was a long one. We rushed to the Los Angeles-bound coach.

Mother's friend shook hands with my brother. "Give your best to America. Our people's honor depend on you Nisei soldiers."

My brother nodded and then glanced at Mother. For a moment her eyes twinkled and she nodded. He waved good-bye from the platform. Once inside the train we lost him. When the train began to move my mother cried, "Why doesn't he pull up the shades and look out? Others are doing it."

We stood and watched until the last of the train was lost in the night of darkness.

THE COUNTRY
THAT IS MY COUNTRY

Jose Garcia Villa

The country that is my country

Is not of this hemisphere, nor of any
Other: is neither west nor east:
Nor is it on the north or south:

    I reject the littleness of the compass.

Is not the Philippines:
Nor America: nor Spain nor Hungary:
Nor is it any other country.
                      I disclaim
Nations, tribes, peoples, flags:
I disclaim the Filipino,
The American, the Yugoslavian,
The Swede—all separations,
Divisions, distinctions.
                      I disclaim
The countryman, the patriot,
The talker of countries.

    I claim the Fellowman:
    The Human Being: the Man.

    Only thus do I claim you:
    Only thus can I belong to you:
    And only thus can you belong to me.

Go from me, you patriots:
Go from me who would have me babble
Of love for my nation!

> *I have no such love:*

> *I am the patriot of no country:*
> *I patriotise no nation—*
> *I patriotise Man, the Human Being.*

The country that is my country
Is in no geography:
Is in no mouth:

> *Is in the heart.*

The country that is my country

> *Is Earth: its men.*
> *Is Sky: the love within their hearts.*
> *Is the Sky beyond the Sky: the One.*

A BRIEF HISTORY
OF ANY COUNTRY

And there shall be many birds.
As it is seen.
How many seasons, how many languages
do you please to observe.
Make them three.
If in the end it was as in the beginning
there is really no end.
It can be said agreeably.
How many races to propagate
Make them few.
That is to say, how are you.
I cannot pray well.
I cannot even talk.
Do you doubt now about patriots.
They die for their country.
They die so comfortably.
I will not die for the country.
I will die for myself.
If your country is my country
what a country.
Let my mother-in-law in.

A BRIEF HISTORY
OF THE PHILIPPINES

How many islands. I refer you
to the census.
Truly a divine archipelago.
Magellan had a word for it
it is lost now.
Yet speak well of Magellan
he found the land.
For whom.
For Spain for Aguinaldo for America
for Quezon.
For all lovely patriots.
Do not forget the unpatriots though.
They also die, though not so
comfortably.
In any history also do not forget
the mango. Divine fruit.
We are not without brains
therefore forget not the great
university at Padre Faura.
Forget not our preachers
they are my little dears.
Remember also Rizal Day.
Rizal had his day but *they* had it
at Bagumbayan.
Today, well, what finer than
the missions.
Independencing in America.
Truly a divine archipelago
sending such divine missions.
I forgot the lanzon. Nice

little fruit.

And now while you are remembering all these please also to remember me your poor historian.

LINES AGAINST A LOVED AMERICAN POET AFTER HEARING AN IRISH ONE'S NICKNAME

John Logan

When Munson was in Paris Harold Crane
Sent him twenty bucks for one of Joyce's
Dirty books. What did *Ulysses* do for him
If he could only write while he was young,
Or felt he couldn't stand to face the boy
And woman in the aging man. Oh,
I know he lived an adolescent hell
Hurt by a candy merchant father
Who made his son wheel it in a cart—
A pimp who got a fortune from the itch
For sweets, which is like the itch for love
He didn't give. The dirty bum. The dirty
Father. What can you say? He was a dog.
He had his son's day. In the night the boy
Would stand beside his sleeping mother's bed.
Puzzled. Didn't know what the hell. Who does?
Who does. Still it takes particular heart
Not to eat the fondant of the sea,
That winking merchant attractive to any body.
Easy admirers have lied. A man
Cannot be a poet if he died.
They hold in them the feeling of the living.
I learn little, but he learns less from "Germs
Choice" crying in the wilderness.

THINGS IN COMMON

May Swenson

We have a good relationship, the elevator boy and I.
I can always be cheerful with him.
We make jokes. We both belong to the TGIF Club.
No matter how artificial and stiff I've had to be in the
    office,
seems like I can be natural with *him*.
We have basic things in common—
the weather, baseball, hangovers,
the superiority of Friday over Monday.

It's true I make it a point to be pleasant to him. Why?
Honest, its because I really like him.
Individually, I mean.
There's something about him—relaxed and balanced
like a dancer or a cat—
as if he knows who he is and where he's at.
At least he knows how to act like that.
Wish I could say the same for myself.

I like his looks, his manner, his red shirt,
the smooth panther shape to his head and neck.
I like it that he knows I don't mean to flirt—
even though I really like him.
I feel he knows I know the score.
It's all in the gleam of his eyes,
the white of his teeth, when he slides back the door
and says, "TGIF, Ma'am, have a nice weekend."

He's strong muscled, good looking—could be 35—
though with his cap off he's 50, I suppose.

So am I. Hope he thinks I look younger too.
I want him to like it that my eyes are blue—
I want him to really like me.
We look straight at each other when we say goodnight.
Is he thinking it's only an accident I'm white?
"TGIF," we say. "Have a nice weekend."

That's the way it's been so far.
We have a good relationship, just the two of us
and the little stool on which he never sits, in the car.
Fridays I work late. I'm the last one down.
Been, let's see, 11 years now. . .
These days I hug the newspaper to me so the headlines
    won't show.
Why he never has a paper I don't know.
Probably not supposed to read in the elevator.

Lately I've asked myself why don't I say:
"What do you think of the mess down South, Willie?
Or for that matter, right here in D.C.?"
Wish I dared ask him. Or that he'd find a way to put it to
    me.
I'd like to say bluntly, "Willie, will there be war?"
Neither of us has been able to say it so far.
Will I dare, someday? I doubt it . . . Not *me*, to *him*. . . .
"Thank God It's Friday," we say. "Have a nice weekend."

AMERICA IS IN THE HEART

Carlos Bulosan

It was now the year of the great hatred: the lives of Filipinos were cheaper than those of dogs. They were forcibly shoved off the streets when they showed resistance. The sentiment against them was accelerated by the marriage of a Filipino and a girl of the Caucasian race in Pasadena. The case was tried in court and many technicalities were brought in with it to degrade the lineage and character of the Filipino people.

Prior to the *Rolden vs. The United States* case, Filipinos were considered Mongolians. Since there is a law which forbids the marriage between members of the Mongolian and Caucasian races, those who hated Filipinos wanted them to be included in this discriminatory legislation. Anthropologists and other experts maintained that the Filipinos are not Mongolians, but members of the Malayan race. It was then a simple thing for the state legislature to pass a law forbidding marriage between members of the Malayan and Caucasian races. This action was followed by neighboring states until, when the war with Japan broke out in 1941, New Mexico was the nearest place to the Pacific Coast where Filipino soldiers could marry Caucasian women.

This was the condition in California when José and I arrived in San Diego. I was still unaware of the vast social implications of the discrimination against Filipinos, and my ignorance had innocently brought me to the attention of white Americans. In San Diego, where I tried to get a job, I was beaten upon several occasions by restaurant and hotel proprietors. I put the blame on certain Filipinos who had behaved badly in America, who had instigated hate and discontent among their friends and followers. This misconception was generated by a confused personal reaction to dynamic social forces, but my hunger for the truth had inevitably led me to take an historical attitude. I was to understand and interpret this chaos from a collective point of view, because it was pervasive and universal.

From San Diego, José and I traveled by freight train to the south. We were told, when we reached the little desert town of Calipatria, that local whites were hunting Filipinos at night with shotguns. A countryman offered to take us in his loading truck to Brawley, but we decided it was too dangerous. We walked to Holtville where we found a Japanese farmer who hired us to pick winter peas.

It was cold at night and when morning came the fog was so thick it was tangible. But it was a safe place and it was far from the surveillance of vigilantes. Then from nearby El Centro, the center of Filipino population in the Imperial Valley, news came that a Filipino labor organizer had been found dead in a ditch.

I wanted to leave Holtville, but José insisted that we work through the season. I worked but made myself inconspicuous. At night I slept with a long knife under my pillow. My ears became sensitive to sounds and even my sense of smell was sharpened. I knew when rabbits were mating between the rows of peas. I knew when night birds were feasting in the melon patches.

One day a Filipino came to Holtville with his American wife and their child. It was blazing noon and the child was hungry. The strangers went to a little restaurant and sat down at a table. When they were refused service, they stayed on, hoping for some consideration. But it was no use. Bewildered, they walked outside; suddenly the child began to cry with hunger. The Filipino went back to the restaurant and asked if he could buy a bottle of milk for his child.

"It is only for my baby," he said humbly.

The proprietor came out from behind the counter. "For *your* baby?" he shouted.

"Yes, sir," said the Filipino.

The proprietor pushed him violently outside. "If you say *that* again in my place, I'll bash in your head!" he shouted aloud so that he would attract attention. "You goddamn brown monkeys have your nerve, marrying our women. Now get out of this town!"

"I love my wife and my child," said the Filipino desperately.

"*Goddamn* you!" The white man struck the Filipino viciously between the eyes with his fist.

Years of degradation came into the Filipino's face. All the fears of his life were here—in the white hand against his face. Was there no place where he could escape? Crouching like a leopard, he hurled his whole weight upon the white man, knocking him down instantly. He seized a stone the size of his fist and began smashing it into the man's face. Then the white men in the restaurant seized the small Filipino, beating him unconscious with pieces of wood and with their fists.

He lay inert on the road. When two deputy sheriffs came to take him away, he looked tearfully back at his wife and child.

I was about to go to bed when I heard unfamiliar noises outside. Quickly I reached for José's hand and whispered to him to dress. José followed me through the back door and down a narrow irrigation ditch. We crept on our bellies until we reached a wide field of tall peas, then we began running away from the town. We had not gone far when we saw our bunkhouse burning.

We walked all the cold, dark night toward Calexico. The next morning we met a Filipino driving a jalopy.

"Hop in, Pinoys!" he said. "I'm going to Bakersfield. I'm on my way to the vineyards."

I ran for the car, my heart singing with relief. In the car, José went to sleep at once.

"My name is Frank," said the driver. "It is getting hot in Imperial Valley, so I'm running away. I hope to find work in the grape fields."

It was the end of spring. Soon the grapevines would be loaded with fruit. The jalopy squeaked and groaned, and once when we were entering Los Angeles, it stalled for hours. Frank tinkered and cooed over it, as though the machine were a baby.

I wanted to find my brother Macario, but my companions were in a hurry. In Riverside the jalopy stalled again. José ran to the nearest orange grove. In San Bernardino, where we had stopped to eat pears, José took the wheel and drove all through the night to Bakersfield.

We found a place on a large form owned by a man named

Arakelian. Hundreds of Filipinos were arriving from Salinas and Santa Maria, so we improvised makeshift beds under the trees. Japanese workers were also arriving from San Francisco, but they were housed in another section of the farm. I did not discover until some years afterward that this tactic was the only way in which the farmers could forestall any possible alliance between the Filipinos and the Japanese.

Some weeks after our work had begun rumors of trouble reached our camp. Then, on the other side of town, a Filipino labor camp was burned. My fellow workers could not explain it to me. I understood it to be a racial issue, because everywhere I went I saw white men attacking Filipinos. It was but natural for me to hate and fear the white man.

I was nailing some boards on a broken crate when Frank came running into the vineyard.

"Our camp is attacked by white men!" he said. "Let's run for our lives!"

"I'm going back to Los Angeles," José said.

"Let's go to Fresno," I insisted.

We jumped into Frank's jalopy and started down the dirt road toward the highway. In Fresno the old car skidded into a ditch, and when we had lifted it back to the highway, it would not run any more. Frank went to a garage and sold it. I told my companions that we could take the freight train to Stockton. I knew that the figs were about ready to be picked in Lodi.

We ran to the freight yards, only to discover that all the boxcars were loaded. I climbed to the top of a car that was full of crates and my companions followed me. The train was already moving when I saw four detectives with blackjacks climbing up the cars. I shouted to my companions to hide. I ran to the trap door of an icebox, watching where the detectives were going.

José was running when they spotted him. He jumped to the other car and hid behind a trap door, but two more detectives came from the other end and grabbed him. José struggled violently and freed himself, rolling on his stomach away from his captors. On his feet again, he tried to jump to the car ahead, but his feet slipped and he fell, shouting to us for help. I saw his hands clawing frantically in the air before he disappeared.

I jumped out first. Frank followed me, falling upon the cinders almost simultaneously. Then we were running to José. I thought at first he was dead. One foot was cut off cleanly, but half of the other was still hanging. Frank lifted José and told him to tie my handkerchief around his foot. We carried him to the ditch.

"Hold his leg," Frank said, opening a knife.

"Right." I gripped the bleeding leg with all my might, but when Frank put the sharp blade on it, I turned my face away.

José jerked and moaned, then passed out. Frank chewed some tobacco and spread it on the stump to keep the blood from flowing. Then we ran to the highway and tried to hail a car, but the motorists looked at us with scorn and spat into the wind. Then an old man came along in a Ford truck and drove us to the county hospital, where a kind doctor and two nurses assured us that they would do their best for him.

Walking down the marble stairway of the hospital, I began to wonder at the paradox of America. José's tragedy was brought about by railroad detectives, yet he had done no harm of any consequence to the company. On the highway, again, motorists had refused to take a dying man. And yet in this hospital, among white people—Americans like those who had denied us—we had found refuge and tolerance. Why was America so kind and yet so cruel? Was there no way to simplifying things in this continent so that suffering would be minimized? Was there no common denominator on which we could all meet? I was angry and confused, and wondered if I would ever understand this paradox.

We went to the hospital the following morning. José was pale but gay.

"I guess this is the end of my journey with you fellows," he said.

"For a while," Frank said. "You will be well again. We will meet you again somewhere. You will see!"

"I sent a telegram to your brother," I said. "He will be here tomorrow."

"We've got to go now," Frank said.

"We have a long way to go," I said.

"You are right," José said.

"Good-bye till we meet again," Frank said, taking José's hand affectionately.

I looked back sadly. It was another farewell. How many others had I met in my journey? Where were they now? It was like going to war with other soldiers; some survived death but could not survive life. Could I forget all the horror and pain? Could I survive life?

I walked silently beside Frank to the highway. I was tired and exhausted and hungry. Frank and I had given all our money to José. We walked several miles out of town and took the first freight train going north. I did not care where we were going so long as it was away from Bakersfield. I shrank from tragedy, and I was afraid of death. My fear of death made me love life dearly.

We jumped off in Fresno where Filipinos told us that trouble was brewing. Frank wanted to proceed to Alaska for the fishing season, but I told him that conditions there were intolerable. The east was still an unexplored world, so we agreed to take a freight train to Chicago.

When we arrived in Idaho, I changed my plans. The pea fields decided me. Why go to an unknown city where there was no work? Here in this little town of Moscow were peas waiting and ready to be picked. So Frank and I worked for three weeks picking peas. But his heart was already in Chicago. He could not work any more.

I took him to the bus station and gave him a little of my money. I hate slow partings. I patted him on the back and left. I met some Mexican families on their way to the beet fields in Wyoming. I rode on a truck with them as far as Cheyenne, where they stopped off to work for a month.

I went to town and walked around the premises of the Plains Hotel, hoping to see some workers there who might have come from Binalonan. I tried to locate them by peering through the windows, but gave up when some women looked at me suspiciously. I was too dirty to go inside. And I was afraid. My fear was the product of my early poverty, but it was also the nebulous force that drove me frantically toward my goal.

I caught a freight train that landed me in Billings, Montana. The beet season was in full swing. Mexicans from Texas and New Mexico were everywhere; their jalopies and makeshift tents dotted the highways. There were also Filipinos from California and Washington. Some of them had just come back from the fish canneries in Alaska.

I went to Helena and found a camp of Filipino migratory workers. I decided to live and work with them, hoping to put my life in order. I had been fleeing from state to state, but now I hoped to gather the threads of my life together. Was there no end to this flight? I sharpened my cutting knife and joined my crew. I did not know that I was becoming a part of another tragedy.

The leader of our crew was a small Filipino called Pete. He walked lightly like a ball. When he was thinking, which he seldom did, he moved his head from side to side like a cart. He had a common-law wife, a young Mexican girl who was always flirting with the other men. I do not know what tribe he came from in the Philippines because he spoke several dialects fluently.

Every Saturday night the men rushed to town and came home at dawn, filling the house with the smell of whiskey and strong soap. Once I went with them and found out that they played pool in a Mexican place and bought cheap whiskey in a whorehouse where they went when the poolroom closed at midnight.

I was distracted by Myra, Pete's wife. She was careless with herself, in a house where she was the only girl. I noticed that she was always going to town with Poco, a tubercular Filipino who loved nice clothes and dancing. One afternoon when it was my turn to cook, I saw Myra come to the kitchen with her suitcase.

"I'm going now," she said to Pete, looking at the other men who were eating at the table.

Pete was at the far end of the table, his bare feet curling around the legs of the chair. He stopped the hand with the ball of rice in mid-air and leaped to the floor. Then he placed the rice carefully on the edge of his plate.

"Are you going with Poco?" Pete asked.

"Yes," Myra said.

"You can't go with him," he said.

"You are not married to me," she said, picking up her suitcase.

Pete grabbed her with one hand and struck her with the other. Then he dragged her to the parlor like a sack of beets, beating her with his fists when she screamed for Poco. Myra's lover was waiting in a car in the yard. Pete pulled off Myra's shoes and started beating the soles of her feet with a baseball bat, shouting curses at her and calling her obscene names.

I could not stand it any longer. I stopped washing the dishes, grabbed a butcher knife and ran into the parlor where they were. But Alfred, Poco's cousin, leaped from the table and grabbed me. I struggled violently with him, but he was much stronger than I. He struck me at the base of my skull and the knife went flying across the room. It struck a pot in the sink.

When I regained consciousness, I heard Myra moaning. Pete was still beating her.

"So you want to run away!" he kept saying. "I will show you who is going to run away!"

I got up on my knees and crawled to a bench. Pete threw Myra on the floor and went back to his plate. Alfred grabbed Pete's neck and hit him on the bridge of his nose with brass knuckles. Pete fell on the floor like a log and did not get up for minutes. When he regained consciousness, Alfred was sitting in the car with Poco. Pete resumed eating silently, but the blood kept coming out of his nose. He stopped eating and bathed his nose in the sink. Then he went to the parlor and began washing and bandaging Myra's feet.

I gathered the plates and continued washing. I heard Myra laughing and giggling softly. She was in bed with Pete.

"I won't do it again, honey," she kept saying.

"Will you be good now?" Pete asked her.

"I love you, darling," she said, laughing. "I love you! I love you!"

I cursed her under my breath. What kind of a girl was she? I cursed him, too. Pete bounced suddenly into the kitchen, rolling from side to side. I did not look at him. He was preparing something for Myra to eat. Then he carried the plates to her bed, walking lightly like a cat. I looked up from the sink. He was feeding her with a spoon, holding her head with one hand. Myra reached for Pete's neck and kissed him.

Suddenly Poco came into the house and started shooting at them. I ran out of the house terrified, shouting to Alfred. But he opened the door and told me to jump into the car. Poco showed his face at the door.

"Run away, Alfred!" he shouted to his cousin. "Run away and don't come back! I will kill them! Go now!"

Alfred hesitated for a moment; carefully he put the key in the lock and shifted the gear. Then we were driving furiously down the dirt road.

"The damn fool," Alfred wept. "That damn fool is going to be hanged—and all for a prostitute!"

I grabbed the front seat for fear I would fall out when we turned a corner. I could tell by the stars in the wheeling sky that we were driving west. I was going back to the beginning of my life in America. I was going back to start all over again.

THE WELL

N. Scott Momaday

She was old the first time he had seen her, and drunk. She had screamed at him some unintelligible curse from the doorway of her shack when, as a child, he had herded the sheep nearby. And he had run away, hard, until he came to a clump of mesquite on the bank of an arroyo. There he caught his breath and waited for the part fox dog to close the flock and follow. Later, when the sheep had filed into the arroyo and from the bank he could see them all, he dropped a piece of dried meat to the part fox dog. But the dog had quivered and laid back its ears. Slowly it backed away and crouched, not looking at Hobson, not looking at anything, but listening. Then Hobson heard. He knew even then that it was only the wind, but it was a stranger sound than any he had ever known. And at the same time he saw the hole in the ground where the wind dipped, struck, and rose. It was larger than a rabbit hole and partly concealed by the choke cherry which grew beside it. The moan of the wind grew loud. It filled him with dread. For the rest of his life it would be for him the particular sound of anguish.

He had returned on a Tuesday. On the following Monday the Jicarilla fiesta began at Stone Lake. The tents, pitched on the near hills, were white as wool in the sunlight. Riders in bright shirts and hats, their boots spurred and taped white around the insteps, rode among them, along the edge of the water, to and from the corrals: slim Utes and Apaches, Navajos in denim and velveteen. The bartenders clustered about the dance ground draping bright rugs, exchanging baskets and pottery, flashing the silver on their wrists and fingers. The children milled around the refreshment stalls or raced among the tourists, laughing and yelling. The timbered slopes to the north were russet and, beyond them, the dark peaks towered, sheer and shining.

Hobson had drunk heavily and gone the morning without food. When he arrived at the lake nausea began to overcome him. He walked across the road and up the hill to the Quintana tent. He sat at the table and Josie Quintana gave him posole and coffee. They did not talk. When he had eaten he became sleepy, and he went outside and lay down under a wagon. He tried to remember how Josie had looked twelve years before. He no longer knew her. He no longer knew anything of these people. For a time he fixed his eyes on the landscape, but it too had changed. His homeland lay dim and dark in his memory, and there only. He slept.

He awoke to the cold and the sound of the drums. It was dark. He could see the gray shapes of people moving about. Below him and across the road, the dancers circled the fires slowly, their feet shuffling almost imperceptibly. The chant of the singers was low, rolling, and monotonous. He wedged himself into one of the rings and tried to take up the chant. Deeper than the drone of a waterfall, and as incessant, it made pure sound of the dark. He closed his eyes, and shapes almost familiar to him took form against the lids. He was a long time in the dance.

Startled by the hand on his shoulder, he whirled blinking.

"Hey, c'mon. I show you something," Levi said. He was dead drunk, and he enunciated slowly, carefully, laboring with his tongue. "C'mon," he repeated and pulled at Hobson's arm. His eyes were glazed and half-closed in the firelight. Minute beads of sweat glistened on his nose, and spittle oozed from the corner of his mouth. His lower lip hung wet and purple, even as he spoke.

Hobson supported him as they made their way from the dance ground. It was painfully cold away from the fires. There was a moon and the night was bright, but a bank of black clouds was rising in the west. As they neared the corrals Hobson could hear voices. He asked who was there.

"C'mon, I show you damn funny something." said Levi. He began to laugh. He nulled Hobson in and out among the wagons and along the fence. They turned a corner and Hobson saw the outline of two men standing close together and weaving as they made exaggerated gestures and shouted. Lying on the ground at their feet was the old woman Munoz, writhing and screaming. She struggled to free her skirts from their boot heels. Her head jerked and her little arms flailed against their legs. The men were convulsed with laughter.

"Wheee Ha! See? See?" Levi squirmed in his glee. "See? I told you, no? We got ol' wooman Munoz. She been to her wheesky well!" He stumbled and fell against the fence. Leaning there too weak to move, he wheezed and watched. Hobson gaped. He recognized Ruben Vicenti. The other man was a Ute whom he had never seen before. He was short and thick, without a neck, and his arms reached barely to the hips. He held a bottle ad wore a rodeo harness to which there was affixed the numeral 4.

The old woman Munoz gasped. Hobson suddenly wanted to retch. He had never seen her at close quarters. Her dress was torn from one shoulder. It hung loose from the other, exposing half of her chest. The sallow skin of her arms sagged from bones which bore no flesh. The little hands were gnarled and hideous, grown curved into claws. Thrashing like a thong, the exposed breast was shrivelled and elongated. Her legs, kicking against and ripping her ancient dress, were incredibly thin and huge-jointed. The little humped back, angular and grotesque, heaved and twisted in spasms. The long white hair was matted with damp and dirt. It swung round her head in a blur of motion until it fell in a pale tangle at the old woman's face. And she was suddenly still and silent. They looked at her. Their laughter stopped. *Dead. She is dead,* Hobson thought. *Oh God they have killed her.* He wanted to walk or run, move, but his limbs were leaden. Slowly the old woman Munoz turned on her side and raised her head. One of the claws parted the hair from her face and she peered at him. Even under the mask of white dust the little face was deeply furrowed about the toothless mouth and along the hollow jowls. Thin streams of blood trickled from either corner of the mouth, giving the chin the appearance of a hinge. There were no lips. The eyes were the centers of round shadows, large and black as the sockets of a skull. But the ugliness of the eyes rent the shadows with the wild gleam of the old woman's hatred.

"Bastards," she rasped. "You will be in hell." It was little more than a whisper. Still she looked only at him. They watched as she struggled to sit up. At last she was upright, and only then did she look away from him.

"Give me a drink, huh?" The hatred was spent of its sound, and the voice was pitiful.

Number 4 saw his chance to restore the scene, which, when the old woman stopped fighting, had given way to fear and perplexity. He moved over her and shouted: "Ha! You want some wheesky, huh? Here!" He tilted the bottle above her. It spilled over her face. She reached for it, but he held it beyond her reach, spilling it again. The whisky fell in her hair and eyes, and her tongue wagged to take it in. He continued to shout. "Ol' wooman, why don't you go to the wheesky well? huh?" She began to sob softly, almost inaudibly. It was not the response he wanted. He began to feel himself betrayed. "WHEESKY WELL, OL' WOOMAN!" The whisky was gone. "Aw, c'mon, ol' wooman. Call me names, huh?" She only sobbed. He looked at the others. Their faces were blank. "Gotdammit!" he said, and his chin began to quiver. He stepped back and wedged his boot into the dirt. He kicked with all the might of the short and massive leg. The earth flew against the old woman and she cringed.

Number 4's fall was entire. He seemed for a long moment horizontal in the air. The impact was unbroken; it was absorbed by the whole of his back surface. Throughout, the pudgy arms were outspread and the stricken face expressed a kind of overstated amazement. He grunted like a pig. The old woman Munoz blinked. She raised her hand and pointed a finger at him. Then, in a satire of decorum, she placed the hand over her mouth and cackled. "Eeeeee heh heh heh heh." There was no mirth in it, only derision.

Number 4 rose. There was pure rage in his red eyes, and the certain vision of having been made a particular fool.

"You weech," he said. "You gotdamned weech!"

"Leave her alone. She is sick," Hobson said.

Number 4 looked at him.

"She is sick," Hobson repeated. "Old and sick."

The old woman Munoz lay still for a long time after the three men had gone. Hobson watched her. Her back swelled and fell with breathing, but she made no sound. She had stopped crying.

"Old woman," he said after a time, "wait for me. I will be back."

She did not move or answer. He went to the Quintana

tent and got a blanket. He made a fire near where the old woman lay and put the blanket over her.

"It is cold," he said.

"It is cold," she repeated, and she sat up.

He sat beside her and opened his hands to the fire. For a time they were silent, listening to the chant and the drums. The moon moved upward in the sky and shone in a long bright line on the lake, but half of the sky was black now. He could see her without looking at her, out of the corner of his eye. She smelt of liquor and old age.

The chanting grew faint and no one came to their fire. It began to grow light on the line of the hills. He had dozed. The old woman Munoz was looking at him. The fire had burned away and only the embers remained.

"Are you cold, grandmother?"

"Whisky," she said softly. "I want whisky."

"You must go home, old woman. You will be sick."

"Whisky. You gimmie whisky, huh?"

"I have no whisky," he said.

"Hey, we go to the whisky well, okay?"

"No," he said. 'There is no whisky well. It was a lie. They were making fun of you."

"Those bastards don't know nothing! You come with me. I will show you where is the whisky well."

He watched her as she made ready to stand. His throat was dry and he was numb with cold. His mind had begun to turn on him. He got to his feet and helped her.

"Yes, old woman," he said. "Yes, the well. Take me to the whisky well."

They walked along the corrals. The chanting had died away. The narrow horizon before them had become a pale and brilliant rose, and it began to rain.

As they were about to turn the last corral Number 4 stepped in front of them. Hobson saw the low gray arc as the blade flashed across the old woman's middle. The blow spun her into the fence. He caught her before she could fall and heard the footsteps fade in the distance. His eyes were wide and he saw the poles of the fence. They were gray and smooth where the bark had been stripped away and the sun had dried and burned them. He laid the old woman down.

He walked south until he came to the arroyo. He stood on the edge and looked at the sky. The bright jagged line between the hills and the dark clouds was almost gone, but he could see one patch of pure color where there was a saddle on the skyline. There, like a small pool of water, was eternity. As he looked at it he thought he heard the first wind of the morning But it was only a ruse of the silence. There was no wind. There was only the windless rain.

THE COMMUNITY

FACES IN THE CROWD

*You followed the ship whose hopeful ones
dreamed of a golden trip to a golden city.*

Joe Papaleo

Minorities in America initially establish their communities
in the ghettoes of large cities. By insulating themselves
from the dominant American society, ethnic groups ease
the adjustment of the immigrant and, at the same time,
render American society diverse and varied. In the most
vivid fashion, minorities testify to the rich pluralism of
America, to its image as a nation of nations.

Ethnic writers often lament the conditions of their
community—the poverty, insularity, and parochialism of
their ghetto childhood. But their connection with a minority
community, however filled with deprivation, gives their
work its particular significance and individuality. Through
the eyes of the black man, the Jew, or the Puerto Rican, the
writer explores the dangers of a society in which there are
no ethnic, and therefore no human, differences. At a time
when technocracy threatens the individual, his sense of
himself in relation to his community is of special consequence. The following stories and poems suggest the heterogeneous quality of the city, that part of America which is
the home of ethnic writers.

BEYOND THE MELTING POT

Nathan Glazer and Daniel P. Moynihan

In 1660 William Kieft, the Dutch governor of New Netherland, remarked to the French Jesuit Isaac Jogues that there were eighteen languages spoken at or near Fort Amsterdam at the tip of Manhattan Island. There still are: not necessarily the same languages, but at least as many; nor has the number ever declined in the intervening three centuries. This is an essential fact of New York: a merchant metropolis with an extraordinarily heterogeneous population. The first shipload of settlers sent out by the Dutch was made up largely of French-speaking Protestants. British, Germans, Finns, Jews, Swedes, Africans, Italians, Irish followed, beginning a stream that has never yet stopped.

The consequences of this confusion, soon to be compounded by the enormous size of the city itself, have been many. Not least has been the virtual impossibility ever of describing New York City or even the state in simple terms. By preference, but also in some degree by necessity, America has turned elsewhere for its images and traditions. Colonial America is preserved for us in terms of the Doric simplicity of New England, or the pastoral symmetry of the Virginia countryside. Even Philadelphia is manageable. But who can summon an image of eighteenth-century New York that will hold still in the mind? A third of the battles of the Revolution were fought on New York soil, but Bunker Hill and Yorktown come easiest to memory, as do Paul Revere and Patrick Henry.

History, or perhaps historians, keep passing New York by. During the Civil War "New York [State] provided the greatest number of soldiers, the greatest quantity of supplies, and the largest amount of money. In addition, New York's citizens paid the most taxes, bought the greatest number of war bonds, and gave the most to relief organizations." Yet it is recalled as a war between Yankees and Southerners. The Union preserved, the American mind roams westward with the cowboys, returning, if at all, to the Main Streets of the Midwest. The only New York image that has permanently impressed itself on the national mind is that of Wall Street—a street on which nobody lives. Paris may be France, London may be England, but New York, we continue to reassure ourselves, is *not* America.

But, of course, it *is* America: not all of America, or even most, but surely the most important single part. As time passes, the nation comes more under the influence of the city—consider the effect of television in the past fifteen years. As time passes, the nation comes more to resemble the city: urban, heterogeneous, materialist, tough; also, perhaps, ungovernable, except that somehow it is governed, and not so badly, and wtih a considerable measure of democracy.

With all this, our feeling for the city is at best remote. Even New Yorkers seem to avoid too direct an involvement. The taverns of the West Side of New York boast tunes as old and as good as many gleaned in Appalachian hollows, but when the latter-day folk singers of Morrisania and Greenpoint take to the night clubs, they give forth with "Barbree Allen" and the "Ballad of the Boll Weevil." Even the sociologists, wedded to complexity and eager for fresh subjects, have tended to shy away from the city. Chicago has been far more thoroughly studied, in part because of the accident of the existence of a great department of sociology at the University of Chicago. But it is no accident that a department of equal distinction at Columbia University during the 1940's and 1950's had almost nothing to do with New York. Big as it was, Chicago still offered a structure and scale that could be more easily comprehended.

When magazines on occasion devote issues to San Francisco or Chicago or Houston, and publish pictures of well-dressed and distinguished people in elegant settings, and tell us that these are the important people in this city, it is easy to believe them. When the same magazines get to New York and do the same, the informed reader cannot help but think they are indulging in a game. True, there *must* be important people in New York, but are they this banker, this publisher, this playwright, this society leader? The head of a huge corporation or financial complex in Chicago or Pittsburgh or Boston does play an important role in his city. He will be a central figure in a great movement to reform city government or rebuild the city center. In New York, the man who heads an institution or corporation of equal size is only one of many. The men who can sit around a table and settle things in smaller cities would here fill an auditorium. Indeed, in New York one can fill an auditorium with people of many kinds, who in other cities can sit around a room—high school principals, or educational reformers and thinkers and leaders, police captains and experts on crime and law enforcement, housing project managers and experts on housing and urban renewal, hospital directors and specialists in any field of medicine, directors of societies that help the poor and organizations that raise money from the rich, professors of sociology and owners of art galleries.

Of course there are important people in New York. But they have been men like Robert Moses, who has no equivalent in any other city in the United States, and whose major virtue was that he was well enough connected with enough of the centers of power to get something done, to get things moving. Everyone was so astonished at this fact that for a long time it hardly mattered that what he was getting done on a scale appropriate to the city's size was brutal and ugly, and only exacerbated its problems. The Rockefellers are also important in New York City. Perhaps only their combination of wealth and energy and political skill makes it possible for them to approximate the role that the Mellons play in Pittsburgh. But really there is no comparison. The Mellons can be a moving force in remaking the center of Pittsburgh, and in reshaping the image of that city. But all the wealth and skill of the Rockefellers, wedded to the power of Robert Moses, produce a smaller impact on New York. Robert Wagner, the mayor of New York, is an important man. He probably has never met, and never consults, men who in cities of a million or two million people would be movers of city affairs.

We must begin with this image of the city. New York is more than ten times as large as San Francisco, and twice as large as Chicago, but this does not suggest how much more complicated it is. For in the affairs of men, twice as large means four or eight times as complicated. Twice as large means that the man on top is perhaps four or eight times away from what happens on the bottom. But attempts at calculation understate the complexity. When you have 24,000 policemen in a city, it not only means that you need a few additional levels of authorities to deal with them—those over hundreds, and five hundreds, and thousands, and five thousands—but it also means (for example) that there are enough Jewish or Negro policemen to form an organization. And they too can fill a hall.

The interweaving of complexity that necessarily follows from its size with the complexity added by the origins of its population, drawn from a staggering number of countries and from every race, makes New York one of the most difficult cities in the world to understand, and helps us understand why so few books try in any serious way to understand it.

Ideally, if we are to describe one aspect of a city, in this case its ethnic groups, we should begin by spreading out as a background something about the city as a whole. We should speak about its politics, its economic life, its culture, its social life, its history. But none of these aspects of the city can be adequately described or explained except by reference to its ethnic groups.

Consider the politics of New York. Major changes are now taking place in the city. The power of the regular Democratic party—the "machine"—to name its candidates has been broken. In 1961 Mayor Robert F. Wagner, having been denied the nomination, ran in opposition to the regular party, and won. To explain what happened, we have to say that he won with the support of lower-class Negro and Puerto Rican voters, and middle-class Jewish voters who together were enough to overcome the opposition of Italian, Irish, and white Protestant middle-class and upper-working-class voters. One could describe his victory and the political transition now underway in the city without using ethnic labels, but one could barely explain it. For in New York City ethnicity and class and religion are inevitably tied to each other. The votes of the poor and the well-to-do cannot be understood without looking into the question of who the poor and the well-to-do are, without examining their ethnic background.

Similarly, to describe the economy of New York fully, one would have to point out that it is dominated at its peak (the banks, insurance companies, utilities, big corporation offices) by white Protestants, with Irish Catholics and Jews playing somewhat similar roles. In wholesale and retail commerce,

Jews predominate. White-collar workers are largely Irish and Italian if they work for big organizations, and Jewish if they work for smaller ones. The city's working class is, on its upper levels, Irish, Italian, and Jewish; on its lower levels, Negro and Puerto Rican. Other ethnic groups are found scattered everywhere, but concentrated generally in a few economic specialties.

Despite all this, it remains something of a question just what role the ethnic groups play in the development of New York economy. New York is affected by the growth of suburbia, where it is easier to locate plants and shopping centers, and where the middle class prefers to live—and presumably this would be happening no matter what ethnic groups made up the city. New York is affected by the growth of the Far West and Southwest, for more and more productive and commercial facilities are located in those areas. New York is affected by the power of unions in old centers, just as Detroit and New England are, and this encourages some plants to move away. Its original growth was touched off presumably by the fact that it was the terminus of the best level route to the Midwest, both in the canal era and the railroad era, and that it has the best natural port on the Northeastern Seaboard. These factors are quite independent of the nature of its population.

But there are other elements in the relationship between the population of New York and the economic development of New York. New York is now plagued by low wages in manufacturing. In the years since the end of the Second World War, the city has declined, relative to other cities, in the wages paid in manufacturing industries. This is a very complicated matter. Yet it must be of some significance that its manufacturing wages have fallen at a time when it has had a vast influx of relatively unskilled and untrained manufacturing labor. If through some historical accident the immigrants of the period 1946–1960 had been of the same level of education and training as the refugee German and Austrian Jews of 1933–1940, might not the economic history of the city have been different? Clearly, the main lines of the economic history of New York have been fixed by great factors that are quite independent of the nature of the population. Yet obvious as this is, there are important connections between what a people are, or what they have been made by history and experience, and their economic fate, and as economists now become more and more involved in considering the development of people of widely different cultures, they may learn things that will throw more light on the economic development of New York.

New York's culture is what it is presumably because it is the cultural capital of the richest and most important nation in the world. If America's culture is important, New York's culture must be important, and this would be true even if New York were all Anglo-Saxon and Protestant. And yet, the fact that the city is one-quarter Jewish, and one-sixth Italian, and one-seventh Negro—this also plays some part in the cultural history of New York. Ethnic identity is an element in all equations.

The census of 1960 showed that 19 per cent of the populalation of the city were still foreign-born whites, 28 per cent were children of foreign-born whites, another 14 per cent were Negro, 8 per cent were of Puerto Rican birth or parentage. Unquestionably, a great majority of the rest (31 per cent) were the grandchildren and great-grandchildren of immigrants, and still thought of themselves, on some occasions and for some purposes, as German, Irish, Italian, Jewish, or whatnot, as well as of course Americans.

Of the foreign-stock population (immigrants and their children), 859,000 were born in Italy or were the children of Italian immigrants; 564,000 were from the U.S.S.R. (these are mostly Jews); 389,000 from Poland (these too are mostly Jews); 324,000 from Germany; 312,000 from Ireland; 220,000 from Austria; 175,000 from Great Britain; almost 100,000 from Hungary; more than 50,000 from Greece, Czechoslovakia, Rumania, and Canada; more than 25,000 from Yugoslavia, around 10,000 from the Netherlands, Denmark, Finland, and Switzerland; more than 5,000 from Portugal and Mexico. There were more than a million Negroes, and more than 50,000 of other races, mostly Chinese and Japanese. From almost every country in the world there are enough people in the city to make up communities of thousands and tens of thousands with organizations, churches, a language, some distinctive culture.

Let us introduce some order into this huge buzzing confusion. The best way to do so is historically. English stock has apparently never been in a clear majority in New York City. In 1775 one-half of the white population of the state was of English origin, but this proportion was probably lower in New York

City, with its Dutch and other non-English groups, and with its large Negro population. After the Revolution and the resumption of immigration, English and Scottish immigrants as well as migrants from New England and upstate New York probably maintained the British-descent group as the largest in the city through the first half of the nineteenth century.

In the 1840's Irish and Germans, who had of course been present in the city in some numbers before this time, began to enter in much larger numbers, and soon became dominant. By 1855 the Irish-born made up 28 per cent of the city, the German-born 16 per cent of the city; with their children they certainly formed a majority of the city, and they maintained this dominance until the end of the century. In 1890 Irish-born and German-born and their children made up 52 per cent of the population of New York and Brooklyn (then separate cities).

In the 1880's Jews and Italians began to come in large numbers (there were of course sizable communities of both groups in the city before this time), and this heavy immigration continued until 1924, and on a reduced scale after that.

The Negroes began to enter the city in great numbers after World War I, the Puerto Ricans after World War II.

Thus six great groups have entered the city two by two, in subsequent epochs; and to these we must add as a seventh group the "old stock," or the "white Anglo-Saxon Protestants." The two terms are of course not identical, but the overlap among those they comprise is great. The "old stock" includes those New Yorkers who descend from families that were here before the Revolution. They were largely of English, Scottish, and Welsh origin, but also included Dutch, French, and other settlers from Northwestern Europe. It has been relatively easy for later immigrants of the same ethnic and religious background—from Canada and from Europe—to assimilate to this "old stock" group if they were in occupations of high status and of at least moderate affluence.

What is the relative size of these seven groups in the city today? For all except the Negroes and the Puerto Ricans, who are listed separately in the census, it is difficult to give more than a very general guess. The accepted religious breakdown of the city population, based on sample surveys and estimates by various religious groups, indicates that less than a quarter of the population is Protestant, and more than half of that is

Negro. The white Protestants of course include many of German, Scandinavian, Czech, and Hungarian origins. It is thus not likely that more than about one-twentieth of the population of the city is "old stock," or "WASP." Public opinion polls which ask for "national origin" suggest that about a tenth of the population is Irish, another tenth German. The same sources suggest that about a sixth is Italian. Jewish organizations estimate that one-quarter of the population is Jewish. The census reports that Negroes form 14 per cent of the population, Puerto Ricans 8 per cent. We have accounted for about 90 per cent of the population of the city. . . . These figures, aside from being inexact (except for Puerto Rican and Negro), also assume that everyone in the city can be neatly assigned to an ethnic category. Of course this in large measure myth; many of the people in the city, as in the nation, have parents and grandparents of two or three or four groups.

Despite the immigration laws, old groups grow and new groups form in the city. Thus, Batista and Castro, as well as the growing size of the Spanish-speaking population, have encouraged the growth of a large Cuban community of 50,000. For despite the stringent immigration laws, the United States is still the chief country of immigration in the world, and 2,500,000 were able to enter this country as immigrants between 1950–1959. Very large numbers of these immigrants settle in New York and its region, where large communities of their compatriots make life easier and pleasanter. Buried in this vast population of the city are new groups (such as 18,000 Israelis) that in any other city would be marked and receive attention. In New York their coffee shops and bars and meeting places and political disputes and amusements and problems are of interest only to themselves. Only when an immigrant group reaches the enormous size of the Puerto Ricans does it become a subject of interest, attention, and concern.

New York cannot be read out of America because of its heterogeneity; but it is true its heterogeneity is to some extent extreme, even among the heterogeneous cities of the Northeast. The cities of the South, except for the presence of Negroes, are far more homogeneous. They are largely inhabited by white Protestants whose ancestors came from the British Isles. The cities of the Great Plain—from Indianapolis to Kansas City— are also somewhat less mixed. Their largest ethnic element is generally German; and Germans have also found it easiest to assimilate to the white Anglo-Saxon Protestant culture that is still the norm in American life. The cities of the Far West, too, are in their ethnic aspect somewhat different from the cities of the Northeast. Their populations, if we trace them back far enough, are as diverse as the populations of Northeastern cities. But these immigrants have come from the East, Midwest, and South of the United States, rather than from Europe. This second immigration to the Far West has made them more alike. If you ask people there, 'Where did you come from?," the answer is Illinois or Iowa, Oklahoma or New York. In the Northeast, the answer is more likely to be Germany or Sweden, Russia or Italy. In terms of immediate origins, the populations of Far Western cities consist of Iowans and Illinoisans and New Yorkers, rather than Germans, Jews, and Italians.

But now what does it mean for New York that most of its population is composed of people who think of themselves— at least at some times, for some purposes—as Jews, Italians, Negroes, Germans, Irishmen, Puerto Ricans? Is New York different, because of this fact, from London, Paris, Moscow, Tokyo?

Do we not, in every great city, meet people from all over the world? We do; but we should not confuse the heterogeneity of most of the great cities of the world with that of New York. The classic heterogeneity of great cities has been limited to the elite part of the population. It is the small numbers of the wealthy and exceptional who represent in those other cities the variety of the countries of the world, not, as in the United States, the masses. This for the most part is still true of the great cities of Europe, even though large numbers of Irishmen and colored people now form part of the working class of London, large numbers of Algerians part of the working class of Paris. Those with very special skills and talents have always been drawn from all over the world into its great cities. Thus, the specialized trading peoples—Phoenicians, Syrians, Greeks, Jews—have formed, for thousands of years, part of the specialized commercial and trading classes of the Mediterranean cities. And even today, trade with foreign countries is still in large measure carried on by nationals of the countries involved, who have special knowledge of language and conditions and local laws and regulations. There is also to be found in all great cities the diplomatic corps, now enormously swollen by international agencies of all sorts. There are the people involved in cultural and artistic activities, who may be of any part of the world. These elites, commercial, political, cultural, today give such cities as London, Paris, and Tokyo an international flavor. It is these people we think of when we say that people from all over the world flock to its great cities; they do; but they are relatively few in numbers.

The heterogeneity of New York is of the masses—numbers so great that Negroes are not exotic, as they are in Paris, Puerto Ricans not glamorous representatives of Latin American culture, as they might be in London, Italians not rare representatives of a great nation, as they are in Tokyo. Here the numbers of each group are so great, so steady and heavy a presence, that it takes an effort of mind to see that all these group names describe a double aspect: those one sees around one, and those in some other country, on some other continent, with a different culture.

Admittedly, even this heterogeneity of the masses is not unique to the cities of the United States. The cities of Canada and Latin America have also drawn their populations from varied groups (though none equals New York in its variety). Even in the great cities of the past one could find sizable differences among the masses. In Athens one might presumably find countrymen from every deme, in Paris workers from every province. There was probably a tendency for them to cluster together. Even though all spoke the same language, they spoke different dialects. Even though they were all of the same religion, they may have preferred to worship among friends and relatives. Even though they all participated in some forms of a growing national culture, they must have preferred their own provincial specialties in food, folk music, and dancing.

But in New York the masses that make up the city have come not from different provinces but different countries. Their languages have been mutually unintelligible, their religion radically different, their family structures, values, ideals, cultural patterns have been as distinct as those of the Irish and the Southern Negro, of urban Jews and peasant Italians.

This is the way it was, but will it be relevant for New York City much longer? The foreign-language press declines rapidly in circulation; the old immigrant quarters now hold only some of the old-timers. The immigrant societies play little role in the city's politics. The American descendants of immigrants diverge markedly from the people of the old country. American descendants of Germans seem no more committed to the unity of Germany and the defense of Berlin than other Americans, the foreign policy of the American Irish seems to have nothing in common any more with the foreign policy of a neutral Eire, and the political outlook and culture of Americans of Italian descent seem to have little in common with what one can see in Italy. (New Italian movies exploring the limits of modern sensibility are as incomprehensible to Italian immigrants as to other immigrants.) And perhaps the Jewish commitment to Israel is best explained by the recency of the establishment of the state and the permanent danger surrounding it. American culture seems to be as attractive to the children of immigrants as the descendants of pioneers (and indeed, as attractive to Indonesians or Russians as to Americans). The powerful assimilatory influences of American society operate on all who come into it, making the children of immigrants and even immigrants themselves a very different people from those they left behind. In what sense, then, can we put immigrants, their children, their grandchildren, and even further descendants into one group and speak of, for example, "the" Irish? Must we not speak of the middle-class Irish and the working-class Irish, the big-city Irish and the small-town Irish, the recent immigrants and the second and third and fourth generation, the Democrats and the Republicans; and when we do, is there any content left to the group name?

Perhaps the meaning of ethnic labels will yet be erased in America. But it has not yet worked out this way in New York. It is true that immigrants to this country were rapidly transformed, in comparison with immigrants to other countries, that they lost their language and altered their culture. It was reasonable to believe that a new American type would emerge, a new nationality in which it would be a matter of indifference whether a man was of Anglo-Saxon or German or Italian or Jewish origin, and in which indeed, because of the diffusion of populations through all parts of the country and all levels of the social order, and because of the consequent close contact and intermarriage, it would be impossible to make such distinctions. This may still be the most likely result in the long run. After all, in 1960 almost half of New York City's population was still foreign-born or the children of foreign-born. Yet it is also true that it is forty years since the end of mass immigration, and new processes, scarcely visible when our chief concern was with the great masses of immigrants and the problems of their "Americanization," now emerge to surprise us. The initial notion of an American melting pot did not, it seems, quite grasp what would happen in America. At least it did not grasp what would happen in the short run, and since this short run encompasses at least the length of a normal lifetime, it is not something we can ignore.

It is true that language and culture are very largely lost in the first and second generations, and this makes the dream of "cultural pluralism"—of a new Italy or Germany or Ireland in America, a League of Nations established in the New World —as unlikely as the hope of a "melting pot." But as the groups were transformed by influences in American society, stripped of their original attributes, they were recreated as something new, but still as identifiable groups. Concretely, persons think of themselves as members of that group, with that name; they are thought of by others as members of that group, with that name; and most significantly, they are linked to other members of the group by new attributes that the original immigrants would never have recognized as identifying their group, but which nevertheless serve to mark them off, by more than simply name and association, in the third generation and even beyond.

The assimilating power of American society and culture operated on immigrant groups in different ways, to make them, it is true, something they had not been, but still something distinct and identifiable. The impact of assimilating trends on the groups is different in part because the groups are different —Catholic peasants from Southern Italy were affected differently, in the same city and the same time, from urbanized Jewish workers and merchants from Eastern Europe. We cannot even begin to indicate how various were the characteristics of family structure, religion, economic experience and attitudes, educational experience and attitudes, political outlook that differentiated groups from such different backgrounds. Obviously, some American influences worked on them in common and with the same effects. But their differences meant they were open to different parts of American experience, interpreted it in different ways, used it for different ends. In the third generation, the descendants of the immigrants confronted each other, and knew they were both Americans, in the same dress, with the same language, using the same artifacts, troubled by the same things, but they voted differently, had different ideas about education and sex, and were still, in many essential ways, as different from one another as their grandfathers had been.

The initial attributes of the groups provided only one reason why their transformations did not make them all into the same thing. There was another reason—and that was the nature of American society itself, which could not, or did not, assimilate the immigrant groups fully or in equal degree. Or perhaps the nature of human society in general. It is only the experience of the strange and foreign that teaches us how provincial we are. A hundred thousand Negroes have been enough to change the traditional British policy of free immigration from the colonies and dominions. Japan finds it impossible to incorporate into the body of its society anyone who does not look Japanese, or even the Koreans, indistinguishable very often in appearance and language from Japanese. And we shall test the racial attitudes of the Russians only when there are more than a few Negroes passing through as curiosities; certainly the inability of Russians to get over anti-Semitism does not suggest they are any different from the rest of mankind. In any case, the word "American" was an unambiguous reference to nationality only when it was applied to a relatively homogeneous social body consisting of immigrants from the British Isles, with relatively small numbers from nearby European countries. When the numbers of those not of British origin began to rise, the word "American" became a far more complicated thing. Legally, it meant a citizen. Socially, it lost its identifying power, and when you asked a man what he was (in the United States), "American" was not the answer you were looking for. In the United States it became a slogan, a political gesture, sometimes an evasion, but not a matter-of-course, concrete social description of a person. Just as in certain languages a word cannot stand alone but needs some particle to indicate its function, so in the United States the word "American" does not stand by itself. If it does, it bears the additional meaning of patriot, "authentic" American, critic and opponent of "foreign" ideologies.

The original Americans became "old" Americans, or "old stock," or "white Anglo-Saxon Protestants," or some other identification which indicated they were not immigrants or descendants of recent immigrants. These original Americans already had a frame in their minds, which became a frame in reality, that placed and ordered those who came after them. Those who were like them could easily join them. It was important to be white, of British origin, and Protestant. If one was all three, then even if one was an immigrant, one was really not an immigrant, or not for long.

Thus, even before it knew what an Italian or Jew or an Irishman was like, the American mind had a place for the category, high or low, depending on color, on religion, on how close the group was felt to be to the Anglo-Saxon center. There were peculiarities in this placing. Why, for example, were the Germans placed higher than the Irish? There was of course an interplay to some extent between what the group actually was and where it was placed, and, since the German immigrants were less impoverished than the Irish and somewhat more competent craftsmen and farmers, this undoubtedly affected the old American's image of them. Then ideology came in to emphasize the common links between Englishmen and Germans, who, even though they spoke different languages, were said to be really closer to each other than the old Americans were to the English-speaking, but Catholic and Celtic, Irish. If a group's first representatives were cultured and educated, those who came after might benefit, unless they were so numerous as to destroy the first image. Thus, German Jews who arrived in the 1840's and 1850's benefited from their own characteristics and their link with Germans, until they were overwhelmed by the large number of East European Jewish immigrants after 1880. A new wave of German Jewish immigrants, in the 1930's, could not, regardless of culture and education, escape the low position of being "Jewish."

The ethnic group in American society became not a survival from the age of mass immigration but a new social form. One could not predict from its first arrival what it might become or, indeed, whom it might contain. The group is not a purely biological phenomenon. The Irish of today do not consist of those who are descended from Irish immigrants. Were we to follow the history of the germ plasm alone—if we could —we should find that many in the group really came from other groups, and that many who should be in the group are in other groups. The Protestants among them, and those who do not bear distinctively Irish names, may now consider themselves, and be generally considered, as much "old American" as anyone else. The Irish-named offspring of German or Jewish or Italian mothers often find that willy-nilly they have become Irish. It is even harder for the Jewish-named offspring of mixed marriages to escape from the Jewish group; neither Jews nor non-Jews will let them rest in ambiguity.

Parts of the group are cut off, other elements join the group as allies. Under certain circumstances, strange as it may appear, it is an advantage to be able to take on a group name, even of a low order, if it can be made to fit, and if it gives one certain advantages. It is better in Oakland, California, to be a Mexican than an Indian, and so some of the few Indians call themselves, at certain times, for certain occasions, "Mexicans." In the forming of ethnic groups subtle distinctions are overridden; there is an advantage to belonging to a big group, even if it is looked down upon. West Indian Negroes achieve important political positions, as representatives of Negroes; Spaniards and Latin Americans become the representatives of Puerto Ricans; German Jews rose to Congress from districts dominated by East European Jews.

Ethnic groups then, even after distinctive language, customs, and culture are lost, as they largely were in the second generation, and even more fully in the third generation, are continually recreated by new experiences in America. The mere existence of a name itself is perhaps sufficient to form group character in new situations, for the name associates an individual, who actually can be anything, with a certain past, country, race. But as a matter of fact, someone who is Irish or Jewish or Italian generally has other traits than the mere existence of the name that associates him with other people attached to the group. A man is connected to his group by ties of family and friendship. But he is also connected by ties of *interest*. The ethnic groups in New York are also *interest groups*.

This is perhaps the single most important fact about ethnic groups in New York City. When one speaks of the Negroes and Puerto Ricans, one also means unorganized and unskilled workers, who hold poorly paying jobs in the laundries, hotels, restaurants, small factories or who are on relief. When one says Jews, one also means small shopkeepers, professionals, better-paid skilled workers in the garment industries. When one says Italians, one also means homeowners in Staten Island, the North Bronx, Brooklyn, and Queens.

If state legislation threatens to make it more difficult to get relief, this is headline news in the Puerto Rican press— for the group is affected—and news of much less importance to the rest of the press. The interplay between rational economic interests and the other interests or attitudes that stem out of group history makes for an incredibly complex political and social situation. Consider the local laws against discrimination in housing. Certain groups that face discrimination want such laws—Negroes, Puerto Ricans, and Jews. Jews meet little discrimination in housing in New York but have an established ideological commitment to all anti-discrimination laws. Apartment-house owners are against any restriction of their freedom or anything that might affect their profits. In New York, this group is also largely Jewish, but it is inhibited in pushing strongly against such laws by its connections with the Jewish community. Private homeowners see this as a threat to their homogenous neighborhoods. These are largely German, Irish, and Italian. The ethnic background of the homeowners links them to communities with a history of anti-Negro feelings. The Irish and Italian immigrants have both at different times competed directly with Negro labor.

In the analysis then of the conflict over anti-discrimination laws, "rational" economic interests and the "irrational" or at any rate noneconomic interests and attitudes tied up with one's own group are inextricably mixed together. If the rational interests did not operate, some of the older groups would by now be much weaker than they are. The informal and formal social groupings that make up these communities are strengthened by the fact that Jews can talk about the garment business, Irish about politics and the civil service, Italians about the state of the trucking or contracting or vegetable business.

In addition to the links of interest, family and fellowfeeling bind the ethnic group. There is satisfaction in being with those who are like oneself. The ethnic group is something of an extended family or tribe. And aside from ties of feeling and interest, there are concrete ties of organization. Certain types of immigrant social organization have declined, but others have been as ingenious in remolding and recreating themselves as the group itself. The city is often spoken of as the place of anonymity, of the breakdown of some kind of preexisting social order. The ethnic group, as Oscar Handlin has pointed out, served to create a new form of order. Those who came in with some kind of disadvantage, created by a different language, a different religion, a different race, found both comfort and material support in creating various kinds of organizations. American social services grew up in large part to aid incoming immigrant groups. Many of these were limited to a single religious or ethnic group. Ethnic groups set up hospitals, old people's homes, loan funds, charitable organizations, as well as churches and cultural organizations. The initial need for a separate set of welfare and health institutions became weaker as the group became more prosperous and as the government took over these functions, but the organizations nevertheless continued. New York organizational life today is in large measure lived within ethnic bounds. These organizations generally have religious names, for it is more acceptable that welfare and health institutions should cater to religious than to ethnic communities. But of course religion institutions are generally closely linked to a distinct ethnic group. The Jewish (religious) organizations are Jewish (ethnic), Catholic are generally Irish or Italian, now with the Puerto Ricans as important clients; the Protestant organizations are white Protestant—which means generally old American, with a smaller German wing —in leadership, with Negroes as their chief clients.

Thus many elements—history, family and feeling, interest, formal organizational life—operate to keep much of New York life channeled within the bounds of the ethnic group. Obviously, the rigidity of this channeling of social life varies from group to group. For the Puerto Ricans, a recent immigrant group with a small middle class and speaking a foreign language, the ethnic group serves as the setting for almost all social life. For Negroes too, because of discrimination and poverty, most social life is limited to the group itself. Jews and Italians are still to some extent recent immigrants, and despite the growing middle-class character of the Jewish group, social life for both is generally limited to other members of the group. But what about the Irish and the Germans?

Probably, many individuals who by descent "belong" to one of these older groups go through a good part of their lives with no special consciousness of the fact. It may be only under very special circumstances that one becomes aware of the matter at all—such as if one wants to run for public office. The political realm, indeed, is least willing to consider such matters a purely private affair. Consciousness of one's ethnic background may be intermittent. It is only on occasion that someone may think of or be reminded of his background, and perhaps become self-conscious about the pattern formed by his family, his friends, his job, his interests. Obviously, this ethnic aspect of a man's life is more important if he is part of one group than if he is part of another; if he is Negro, he can scarcely escape it, and if he is of German origin, little will remind him of it.

Conceivably the fact that one's origins can become only a memory suggests the general direction for ethnic groups in the United States—toward assimilation and absorption into a homogeneous American mass. And yet, as we suggested earlier, it is hard to see in the New York of the 1960's just how this comes about. Time alone does not dissolve the groups if they are not close to the Anglo-Saxon center. Color marks off a group, regardless of time; and perhaps most significantly, the "majority" group, to which assimilation should occur, has taken on the color of an ethnic group, too. To what does one assimilate in modern America? The "American" in abstract does not exist, though some sections of the country, such as the Far West, come closer to realizing him than does New York City. There are test cases of such assimilation in the past. The old Scotch-Irish group, an important ethnic group of the early nineteenth century, is now for the most part simply old American, "old stock." Old Dutch families have become part of the upper class of New York. But these test cases merely reveal to us how partial was the power of the old American type to assimilate—it assimilated its ethnic cousins.

There is also, in New York, a nonethnic city. There are the fields that draw talent from all over the country and all over the world. There are the areas, such as Greenwich Village, where those so collected congregate. On Broadway, in the radio and television industry, in the art world, in all the spheres of culture, mass or high, one finds the same mixture that one finds in every country. Those involved in these intense and absorbing pursuits would find the city described in these pages strange. Another area of mixture is politics. It is true that political life itself emphasizes the ethnic character of the city, with its balanced tickets and its special appeals. But this is in large part an objective part of the business, just as the Jewish plays on Broadway are part of the business. For those in the field itself, there is more contact across the ethnic lines, and the ethnic lines themselves mean less, than in other areas of the city's life.

How does one write about such groups? If one believes, as the authors of this book do, that the distinctions are important, and that they consist of more than the amusing differences of accent and taste in food and drink, then it is no simple matter to decide how to describe and analyze this aspect of American reality. For it has been common to speak about the ethnic groups in terms of either blame or praise.

It is understandable that as foreigners flooded American cities all the ills of the cities were laid on their shoulders. It is also understandable that the children of the immigrants (and they had the help of many other Americans) should have defended themselves. They had become part of America; they spoke the language, fought in the wars, paid the taxes, were as patriotic as those who could count more generations in the country—and just as they had become Americanized and good citizens, others would. There is no way of discounting the polemical impact of anything written on this question. How many and of what kind to let into this country is a permanent and important question of American public life. It is also a permanent question in American life what attitudes to take in matters of public welfare, public education, housing—toward increasing numbers of Negroes in American cities. This is a matter that involves the chance for happiness of many Americans, and mobilizes the deep and irrational passions of many others. On such issues, most people will simply have to use arguments and facts and ideas as weapons, and will not be able to use them for enlightenment. Even scholarship is generally enlisted in the cause, on one side or another. And yet beyond personal interest and personal commitment, it is possible to view this entire fascinating spectacle of the ethnic variety of the American city and to consider what it means.

KEEP ON PUSHING*
(HARLEM RIOTS/SUMMER/1964)

David Henderson

Lenox Avenue is a big street
The sidewalks are extra wide—three and four times the
    size of a regular Fifth Avenue or East 34th Street
    sidewalk—and must be so to contain the
unemployed vigiling Negro males, the picket lines
and police barricades.
Police Commissioner Murphy can
muster five hundred cops in fifteen minutes.
He can summon extra
tear gas bombs, guns, ammunition
within a single call
to a certain general alarm.
For Harlem
reinforcements come from the Bronx
just over the three-borough Bridge.
    a shot   a cry   a rumor
can muster five hundred Negroes
from idle and strategic street corners
    bars   stoops   hallways   windows
Keep on pushing.
I walk Harlem
I see police eight per square block
crude mathematics
eight to one
eight for one

---

* *The title taken from a recent hit recording (Summer, '69) by the
famous rhythm & blues trio, Curtis Mayfield and The Impressions.*

I see the store owners and keepers—all white
and I see the white police force
The white police in the white helmets
and the white proprietors in their white shirts
talk together and
look around.
    I see Negro handymen put to work because of the
    riots
boarding up smashed storefronts
They use sparkling new nails
The boards are mostly fresh-hewn pine
and smell rank fresh.
The pine boards are the nearest Leonx Avenue will ever
have to trees.
    Phalanxes of police
march   up   and   down
They are dispatchedandgathered   helmet heads
Bobbingwhiteblack and blue.
They walk around—squadroned & platooned.
groups of   six   eight   twelve.
Even in a group
the sparse Negro cop walks alone
or with a singular
talkative
white buddy.
            keep on pushing
        Am I in the 1940's?
        Am I in Asia? Batista's Havana?
where is Uncle Sam's Army? The Allied Forces
when are we going to have the plebescite?

III

I walk and the children playing frail games seem
like no other children anywhere
they seem unpopular   foreign
as if in the midst of New York existed
a cryptic and closed society.
        Am I in Korea?
I keep expecting to see
companies of camouflage-khakied Marines
the Eighth Army
Red Crosses—a giant convoy

through the narrow peopled streets
jeeps with granite-faced generals colonels
marching grim champions of the free world
Trucks dispensing Hershey Bars and Pall Malls
Medical equipment
nurses doctors drugs serums to treat
The diseased and the maimed
and from the Harlem River
Blasting whistles horns
volleying fire bombs against the clouds
the 7th fleet
            but the prowling Plymouths
        and helmeted outlaws from Queens
        persist
                Keep On A' Pushing

IV

I see plump pale butchers pose with their signs:
    "Hog Maws 4 pounds for 1 dollar"
"Pigs ears 7 pounds for 1 dollar"
"Neck Bones Chitterlings 6 pounds for 1"
Nightclubs, liquor stores bars 3, 4 & 5 to one block
3 & 4 shots for one dollar
I see police eight to one
        in its entirety Harlem's 2nd Law of Thermodynamics
            Helmet to barehead
            nightsticks bullets to barehead
            black reinforced shoes to sneaker
Am I in Korea?

V

At night Harlem sings and dances
and as Jimmy Breslin of the *Herald Tribune* says
they also pour their whiskey on one another's heads.
They dog and slop in the bars
The children monkey in front of Zero's Record Chamber
on 116th and Lenox
They mash potatoes and madison at the Dawn Casino,
Renaissance Ballroom, Rockland Palace, and the Fifth
        Avenue

Armory on 141st and the Harlem River
    Come out of your windows
dancehalls, bars and grills Monkey Dog in the streets
like Martha and the Vandellas
Dog for NBC
The *Daily News* and the *Christian Science Monitor*
Dog for Adlai Stevenson
And shimmy a bit
for 'the boys upstate'
        'cause you got soul
        Everybody knows . . .
        Keep on Pushin'

VI

This twilight
I sit in Baron's Fish & Chip Shack
Alfonso (the counterman) talks of ammunition
and violence   The *Journal American* in my lap
headlines promised 'exclusive battle photos'
by a daring photographer they call Mel Findlestein
through him they insure "The Face Of Violence—The
    most striking Close-ups"
WWRL the radio station that serves
the Negro community
tools along on its rhythm and blues vehicle
The colorful unison announcers
declare themselves "The most soulful station in the nation"
Then the lecture series on democracy comes on
The announcer Professor Robert Scalapino for this series
    doesn't sound soulful.
        (eight to one he's white, representing manage-
        ment)
We Negroes are usually warned of the evils of Communism
and the fruits of democracy, but this evening he tells us
that in this troubled time we must keep our heads
and our law
and our order
he says violence only hurts (and he emphasizes hurts)
    the cause of freedom and dignity. He urges the
    troubled
restless residents of Harlem and Bedford-Stuyvesant to
    stay

in their homes, mark an end to the tragic and sense-
    less violence
a pause
then he concludes
and a rousing mixed chorus ends with
        "And the home of the brave."
Alfonso didn't acknowledge the majestic harmony
he hears it every hour on the hour.
The rhythm and blues returns
a flaming bottle bursts on Seventh Avenue
and shimmies fire across the white divider line
helmets
and faces white as the white fluorescence of the street
bob by   BLACK
Prowl cars speeding wilding wheeling
the looney tune of the modulating de-modulating sirens
climb the tenements window by window.
Harlem moves on an automatic platform.
The red fish lights swirl the gleaming storefronts
there will be no Passover this night
and then the gunfire high
in the air   death static
        over everything
ripped glass
shards   sirens   gunfire
down towards 116th
        Then Jocko scenes radio WWRL
late at night he hustles wine: Italian Swiss Colony Port
sherry and muscatel. Gypsy Rose and Hombre "The man's
Adult western drink,"
but by day and evening
his raiment for Harlem's head is different
zealous Jocko coos forward
his tongue baroque-sinister
snakes like fire "Headache?   —Take Aspirin"
        "Tension?
                . . . . take *Compoz!*"
    Keep on a' pushin'
    Someway somehow
    I know we can make it
    with just a little bit of soul.

CITY OF HARLEM

LeRoi Jones

In a very real sense, Harlem is the capital of Black America. And America has always been divided into black and white, and the substance of the division is social, economic, and cultural. But even the name Harlem, now, means simply Negroes (even though some other peoples live there too). The identification is international as well: even in Belize, the capital of predominantly Negro British Honduras, there are vendors who decorate their carts with flowers and the names or pictures of Negro culture heroes associated with Harlem like Sugar Ray Robinson. Some of the vendors even wear t-shirts that say "Harlem, U.S.A.," and they speak about it as a black Paris. In Havana a young Afro-Cuban begged me to tell him about the "big leg ladies" of Lenox Avenue, hoping, too, that I could provide some way for him to get to that mystic and romantic place.

There are, I suppose, contained within the central mythology of Harlem, almost as many versions of its glamour, and its despair, as there are places with people to make them up. (In one meaning of the name, Harlem is simply a place white cab drivers will not go.) And Harlem means not only Negroes, but, of course, whatever other associations one might connect with them. So in one breath Harlem will be the pleasure-happy center of the universe, full of loud, hippy mamas in electric colors and their fast, slick-head papas, all of them twisting and grinning in the streets in a kind of existential joyousness that never permits of sadness or responsibility. But in another breath this same place will be the gathering place for every crippling human vice, and the black men there simply victims of their own peculiar kind of sloth and childishness. But perhaps these are not such different versions after all; chances are both these stereotypes come from the same kinds of minds.

But Harlem, as it is, as it exists for its people, as an actual place where actual humans live—that is a very different thing. Though, to be sure, Harlem is a place—a city really—where almost anything any person could think of to say goes on, probably does go on, or has gone on, but like any other city, it must escape *any* blank generalization simply because it is alive, and changing each second with each breath any of its citizens take.

When Africans first got to New York, or New Amsterdam as the Dutch called it, they lived in the farthest downtown portions of the city, near what is now called The Bowery. Later, they shifted, and were shifted, as their numbers grew, to the section known as Greenwich Village. The Civil War Draft Riots in 1863 accounted for the next move by New York's growing Negro population.

After this violence (a few million dollars' worth of property was destroyed, and a Negro orphanage was burned to the ground) a great many Negroes moved across the river into Brooklyn. But many others moved farther uptown to an area just above what was known as Hell's Kitchen. The new Negro ghetto was known as Black Bohemia, and later, after the success of an all black regiment in the Spanish-American was, this section was called San Juan Hill. And even in the twenties when most Negroes had made their move even further uptown to Harlem, San Juan Hill was still a teeming branch office of black night life.

Three sections along the east side of Manhattan, The Tenderloin, Black Bohemia, and San Juan Hill or The Jungle featured all kinds of "sporting houses," cabarets, "dancing classes," afterhours gin mills, as well as the Gumbo Suppers, Fish Fries, Egg Nog Parties, Chitterlin' Struts, and Pigfoot Hops, before the Negroes moved still farther uptown.

The actual move into what is now Harlem was caused by quite a few factors, but there are a few that were particularly important as catalysts. First, locally, there were more race riots around the turn of the century between the white poor (as always) and the Negroes. Also, the Black Bohemia section was by now extremely overcrowded, swelled as it was by the influx of Negroes from all over the city. The section was a notorious red light district (but then there have only been two occupations a black woman could go into in America without too much trouble: the other was domestic help) and the over-crowding made worse by the moral squalor that poverty encourages meant that the growing local black population had to go somewhere. The immigrant groups living on both sides of the black ghetto fought in the streets to keep their own ghettoes autonomous and pure, and the Negro had to go elsewhere.

At this time, just about the turn of the century, Harlem (an area which the first Africans had helped connect with the rest of the Dutch city by clearing a narrow road—Broadway—up into the woods of Nieuw Haarlem) was still a kind of semi-suburban area, populated, for the most part, by many of the city's wealthiest families. The elaborate estates of the eighteenth century, built by men like Alexander Hamilton and Roger Morris, were still being lived in, but by the descendants of wealthy merchants. (The Hamilton house still stands near Morningside Heights, as an historic landmark called The Grange. The Morris house, which was once lived in by Aaron Burr, is known as The Jumel House, and it still stands at the northern part of Harlem, near the Polo Grounds, as a museum run by the D.A.R. George Washington used it as his head-quarters for a while during the Revolutionary War.) So there was still the quiet elegance of the nineteenth century brown-stones and spacious apartment buildings, the wide drives, rolling greens, and huge-trunked trees.

What made the area open up to Negroes was the progress that America has always been proud of—an elevated railway went up in the nineties, and the very rich left immediately and the near rich very soon after. Saint Philips Church, after having its old site bought up by a railroad company, bought a large piece of property, with large apartment buildings, in the center of Harlem, and, baby, the panic was on. Rich and famous Negroes moved into the vacated luxury houses very soon after, including the area now known as "Strivers Row," which was made up of almost one hundred brick mansions designed by Stanford White. The panic was definitely on—but still only locally.

What really turned that quiet suburb into "Black Paris," was the coming of the First World War and the mass exodus of Negroes from the South to large urban centers. At the turn of the century most Negroes still lived in the South and were agricultural laborers, but the entrance of America into the

War, and the desperate call for cheap unskilled labor, served to start thousands of Negroes scrambling North. The flow of immigrants from Europe had all but ceased by 1914, and the industrialists knew immediately where to turn. They even sent recruiters down into the South to entice the Negroes north. In 1900 the Negro population of New York City was 60,000; by 1920 it was 152,467; by 1930 it was 327,706. And most of these moved, of course, uptown.

It was this mass exodus during the early part of the century that was responsible for most of the black cities of the North—the huge Negro sections of New York, Chicago, Philadelphia, Detroit, etc. It was also responsible for what these sections would very shortly become, as the masses of Southern Negroes piled into their new Jordans, thinking to have a go at an innocent America.

The twenties are legend because they mark America's sudden insane entrance into the 20th century. The war had brought about a certain internationalism and prosperity (even, relatively speaking, for Negroes). During the twenties Harlem was the mecca of the good time and in many ways even came to symbolize the era called the Jazz Age. Delirious white people made the trip uptown to hear Negro musicians and singers, and watch Negro dancers, and even Negro intellectuals. It was, I suppose, the black man's debut into the most sophisticated part of America. The old darkies of the plantation were suddenly all over the North, and making a whole lot of noise.

There were nightclubs in Harlem that catered only to white audiences, but with the best Negro entertainers. White intellectuals made frequent trips to Harlem, not only to find out about a newly emerging black America, but to party with an international set of swinging bodies. It was the era of Ellington at The Cotton Club for the sensual, and The New Negro for the intellectual. Everyone spoke optimistically of the Negro Renaissance, and The New Negro, as if, somehow, the old Negro wasn't good enough. Harlem sparkled then, at least externally, and it took the depression to dull that sparkle, and the long lines of unemployed Negroes and the longer lines at the soup kitchens and bread queues brought reality down hard on old and New Negroes alike. So the tourist trade diminished, and colorful Harlem became just a social liability for the white man, and an open air jail for the black.

The cold depression thirties, coupled with the decay of old

buildings and ancient neighborhoods, and, of course, the seeming inability of the "free enterprise" system to provide either jobs or hope for a great many black people in the city of Harlem, have served to make this city another kind of symbol. For many Negroes, whether they live in Harlem or not, the city is simply a symbol of naked oppression. You can walk along 125th Street any evening and meet about one hundred uniformed policemen, who are there, someone will tell you, to protect the people from themselves.

For many Negroes Harlem is a place one escapes from, and lives in shame about for the rest of his life. But this is one of the weirdest things about the American experience, that it can oppress a man, almost suck his life away, and then make him so ashamed that he was among the oppressed, rather than the oppressors, that he will never offer any protest.

The legitimate cultural tradition of the Negro in Harlem (and America) is one of wild happiness, usually at some black man's own invention—of speech, of dress, of gait, the sudden twist of a musical phrase, the warmness or hurt of someone's voice. But that culture is also one of hatred and despair. Harlem must contain all of this and be capable of producing all of these emotions.

People line the streets in summer—on the corners or hanging out the windows—or head for other streets in winter. Vendors go by slowly . . . and crowds of people from movies or church. (Saturday afternoons, warm or cold, 125th is jammed with shoppers and walkers, and the record stores scream through loudspeakers at the street.) Young girls, doctors, pimps, detectives, preachers, drummers, accountants, gamblers, labor organizers, postmen, wives, Muslims, junkies, the employed, and the unemployed: all going someplace—an endless stream of Americans, whose singularity in America is that they are black and can never honestly enter into the lunatic asylum of white America.

Harlem for this reason is a community of nonconformists, since any black American, simply by virtue of his blackness, is weird, a nonconformist in this society. A community of nonconformists, not an artist's colony—though blind "ministers" still wander sometimes along 137th Street, whispering along the strings of their guitars—but a colony of old-line Americans who can hold out, even if it is a great deal of the time in misery and ignorance, but still hold out, against the hypocrisy and sterility of big-time America, and still try to make their own lives, simply because of their color, but by now, not so simply, because that color now does serve to identify people in America whose feelings about it are not broadcast every day on television.

CRUZ MOVES TO A HOUSING PROJECT

Oscar Lewis

The social worker told me it would be a good idea to get the children out of La Esmeralda because there's so much delinquency there. Moving here to the housing project was practically her idea; she insisted and insisted. Finally one day she came to me and said, "Tomorrow you have to move to the *caserío* in Villa Hermosa." I didn't want to upset her because she's been good to me, so I said *O.K.*

You should have seen this place when I moved in. It was spilling over with garbage and smelling of shit, pure shit. Imagine, when the social worker opened the door that first day, a breeze, happened to blow her way. She stepped back and said, "Wait, I can't go in. This is barbarous." I had to go outside with her. I tell you, the people who lived here before me were dirtier than the dirtiest pigs. When I moved out of my little room in La Esmeralda, I scrubbed it so clean you could have eaten off the floor. Whoever moved in could see that a decent person had lived there. And then I came here and found this pigsty, and the place looked so big I felt too little and weak to get it clean. So, fool that I am, instead of sending out for a mop and getting right down to work. I just stood in a corner and cried. I locked the door and stayed in all day, weeping. I cried floods.

And this place isn't like La Esmeralda, you know, where there's so much liveliness and noise and something is always going on. Here you never see any movement on the street, not one little domino or card game or anything. The place is dead. People act as if they're angry or in mourning. Either they don't know how to live or they're afraid to. And yet it's full of shameless good-for-nothings. It's true what the proverb says, "May God deliver me from quiet places; I can defend myself in the wild ones."

Everything was so strange to me when I first moved here that I was scared to death. I hated to go out because it's hard to find your way back to this place even if you know the address. The first couple of times I got lost and I didn't dare ask anybody the way for fear they would fall on me and beat me. If anyone knocked on my door I thought four times before deciding to open it. Then when I did, I took a knife along. But I'm not like that any more. I've made my decision: if someone wants to kill me, let him. I can't live shut in like that. And if anybody interferes with me it will be the worse for them. I have a couple of tricks up my sleeve and can really fuck things up for anybody when I want to.

After a few days I finally started cleaning up the place. I scrubbed the floors and put everything in order. I even painted the whole apartment, although I had to fight tooth and nail with the man in charge of the buildings in order to get the paint. That old man wanted to get something from me in return, but I wouldn't give it to him. I never have been attracted to old men.

The apartment is a good one. I have a living room, bedroom, kitchen, porch and my own private bathroom. That's something I never had in La Esmeralda. I clean it every morning and when the children use it I go and pull the chain right away.

I never had a kitchen sink in La Esmeralda either, and here I have a brand-new one. It's easy to wash the dishes in these double sinks because they're so wide and comfortable. The only trouble is the water, because sometimes it goes off, and the electricity too—three times since I've been here.

I still don't have an icebox or refrigerator, but the stove here is the first electric one I've ever had in my life. I didn't know how to light it the day I moved in. I tried everything I could think of, backward and forward. Luckily, the social worker came in and she turned it on for me, but even so I didn't learn and Nanda had to show me again that afternoon. She has worked for rich people so long that she knows all those things. I really miss my own litle kerosene stove, but Nanda wanted it, so what could I do? She's my *mamá,* and if she hankered after a star I would climb up to Heaven to get it for her if I could.

The main advantage of the electric stove is that when I have a lot of work to do and it gets to be ten or eleven o'clock, I just turn on the stove and have lunch ready in no time. In La Esmeralda I had to wait for the kerosene to light up well before I could even start to cook. And this stove doesn't smoke and leave soot all over the place, either. Still, if the power fails again or is cut off because I don't pay my bill, the kids will just have to go hungry. I won't even be able to heat a cup of milk for them. In La Esmeralda, whenever I didn't have a quarter to buy a full gallon of kerosene, I got ten cents' worth. But who's going to sell you five or ten cents' worth of electricity?

I haven't seen any rats here, just one tiny little mouse. There's no lack of company anywhere, I guess; rats in La Esmeralda and lots of little cockroaches here.

This apartment is so big that I don't have to knock myself out keeping it in order. And there's plenty of room for my junk. I even have closets here, and lots of shelves. I have so many shelves and so few dishes that I have to put a dish here and a dish there just to keep each shelf from being completely empty. All the counters and things are no use at all to me, because I just cook a bit of oatmeal for the children and let them sit anywhere to eat it since I have no dishes with which to set a table. Half of my plates broke on the way from La Esmeralda. I guess they wanted to stay back there where they weren't so lonely.

Here even my saints cry! They look so sad. They think I am punishing them. This house is so big I had to separate the saints and hang them up in different places just to cover the empty walls. In La Esmeralda I kept them all together to form a little altar, and I lit candles for them. They helped me there but here I ask until I'm tired of asking and they don't help me at all. They are punishing me.

In La Esmeralda I never seemed to need as many things as here. I think it is because we all had about the same, so we didn't need any more. But here, when you go to other people's apartments and see all their things! It's not that I'm jealous. God forbid! I don't want anyone to have less than they have. It's only that I would like to have things of my own too.

What does bother me is the way people here come into my apartment and furnish the place with their mouths. They start saying, "Oh, here's where the set of furniture should go; you need a TV in that corner, and this one is just right for a record player." And so on. I bite my tongue to keep from swearing at them because, damn it, I have a good taste too. I know a TV set would look fine in that corner, but if I don't have the money to buy one, how can I put it there? That's what I like about La Esmeralda—if people there could help someone they did; if not, they kept their mouths shut.

I really would like a TV, though, because they don't have public sets here, the way they do in La Esmeralda. I filled in some blanks for that program, *Queen for a Day*, to see if I can get one as a gift. Even if you aren't chosen Queen, those people give you what you ask for. It was Fernanda's idea, and she's so lucky that maybe I will get it. If I do, then at least I could spend the holidays looking at TV. And the children might stay home instead of wandering around the neighborhood so much.

The traffic here really scares me. That's the main reason I don't like this place. Cars scud by like clouds in a high wind, and I'm telling you, I'm always afraid a car will hit the children. If something should happen to my little penguins I'd go mad. I swear I would. Here there is plenty of room to run around indoors, but my kids are little devils, and when I bring them in through the front door, they slip out again by climbing over the porch railing. Back in La Esmeralda, where our house was so small, they had to play out in the street whenever people came over, but there were no cars to worry about.

Maybe I was better off in La Esmeralda. You certainly have to pay for the comforts you have here! Listen, I'm jittery, really nervous, because if you fail to pay the rent even once here, the following month you're thrown out. I hardly ever got behind on my payments in La Esmeralda, but if I did, I knew that they wouldn't put me out on the street. It's true that my rent is only six-fifty a month here while I paid eight dollars in La Esmeralda, but there I didn't have a water bill and I paid only one-fifty a month for electricity. Here I have already had to pay three-fifty for electricity, and if I use more than the minimum they allow for water I'll have to pay for that too. And I do so much washing!

It's a fact that as long as I lived in La Esmeralda I could always scare up some money, but here I'm always broke. I've gone for as long as two days without eating here. I don't play the races any more. I can't afford to. And I can't sell *bolita* numbers here because several cops live in this *caserío* and the place is full of detectives. Only tne other day I almost sold a number to one of them, but luckily I was warned in time. I don't want to be arrested for anything in the world, not because I'm scared of being in jail but because of the children.

Since I can't sell numbers here, I sell Avon cosmetics. I like the pretty sets of china they give away and I'm trying to sell a lot so that they'll give me one. But there's hardly any profit in it for me.

In La Esmeralda I could get an old man now and then to give me five dollars for sleeping with him. But here I haven't found anything like that at all. The truth is, if a man comes here and tries to strike up a conversation I usually slam the door in his face. So, well, I have this beautiful, clean apartment, but what good does it do me? Where am I to get money? I can't dig for it.

In La Esmeralda we used to buy things cheap from thieves. They stole from people who lived far away, in Santurce or Río Piedras, and then they came to La Esmeralda through one of the side entrances to sell. And who the hell is going to go looking for his things down there? Not a chance! You hardly ever saw a rich person in La Esmeralda. We didn't like them and we scared them off. But so far as I can tell, these dopes around here always steal from the *blanquitos*, the rich people, nearby. Suppose one of them took it into his head to take a look around here for his missing things? What then?

Since I've been living here I'm worse off than I have ever been before, because now I realize all the things I lack, and besides, there are so many rich people around, who always want everything for themselves. In La Esmeralda you can bum a nickel from anyone. But with these people, the more they have, the more they want. It's everything for themselves. If you ask them for work, they'll find something for you to do fast enough, but when it's time to pay, you'd think it hurt them to pull a dollar out of their pocket.

Listen, to get a few beans from some people who live in a house near here I had to help pick and shell them. People here are real hard and stingy. What's worse, they take advantage of you. The other day I ironed all day long for a woman and all I got for it was two dollars and my dinner. I felt like throwing the money in her face but I just calmly took it. At another lady's house near here I cooked, washed the dishes, even scrubbed the floor, and for all that she just gave me one of her old dresses, which I can't even wear because it's too big for me.

Right now, I don't have a cent. The lady next door lets me charge the food for breakfast at her husband's *kiosco*, the yellow one out there. She's become so fond of me, you can't imagine. Her husband won't sell on credit to anybody, but there's nothing impossible for the person who is really interested in helping you out. She trusts me, so she lets me write down what I take and I keep the account myself.

I buy most of my food at the Villa Hermosa Grocery. It's a long way from here and I have to walk it on foot every time I need something. It's a supermarket, so they don't give credit, but everything is cheaper there, much cheaper. A can of tomato sauce costs seven cents there and ten cents in La Esmeralda. Ten pounds of rice cost a dollar and a quarter in La Esmeralda and ninety-nine cents here. The small bottles of King Pine that cost fifteen cents each in La Esmeralda are two for a quarter here.

The minute Chuito landed in Villa Hermosa he started turning up his nose at everything he used to eat in La Esmeralda, even rice and beans. He must have smelled out the fact that this is a rich neighborhood. I don't know what to do with this little penguin of mine. It is harder to feed him than to buy the food. And he gets sick here more often because it's a cold place. What he needs is the sea air.

One day he was feeling fine and then during the night he was burning up with fever. I thought he was going to die. By two o'clock in the morning he couldn't talk any more and there I was, all alone, not knowing what to do. I looked at the saints and fell on my knees. "Oh, my God, oh, my saints, if you save my child I'll repay you with a Mass on my knees, holding my son in my arms. I'll have an evangelical service here in my house and I'll have a seance, too. But you must save my child. That's what you're there for."

I left Anita and Angelito asleep here and took my little boy to the hospital at that hour of the night. When the doctor saw him, he undressed him quickly and examined him and called the other doctors and they began to whisper. I said to myself, "My God, my son is dying."

They gave him an injection and put him in an oxygen tent and then they said to me, "*Senora*, we're sorry but the child must stay. You may go now."

"Fuck your mother. She's going, not I. I don't leave so long as my son remains." I was getting angry with the saints until I heard my boy say, "Crucita." Then I thought, "Ah, the saints are answering my prayers. Now he won't die. This is a miracle!"

At six o'clock in the morning I went home because if the children woke up and found themselves alone they would yell like a couple of street vendors. I called my *papá* at that hour to come and take care of Anita and Angelito until Chuito got better. I was afraid to call *papá* but he came right away and took them to his house.

I went back to the hospital and didn't leave any more. They told me that the baby needed blood and that I would have to pay for it. I thought, "Pay! Just try to get it out of me. I don't have even one cent." I was dying of hunger all the time I was there. I sent a message to Nanda and she had a peso and went and spent it on a toy for Chuito instead of giving it to me for food. I was furious with her.

Finally they let me take the baby home but my heart sank when they told me that he was sick in the chest. Oh, my God and saints! My poor little son is going to be an invalid when he grows up. Do you know what they told me to do? To keep separate the dishes he eats from, as though he were infected! But I'm not doing any separating for anyone! In this house no one is afraid of anything!

I'm supposed to feed him well on milk with chocolate, and eggs. They told me that If I wanted to keep him with me I had to feed him well. But what food did I have to give him? Even if I dropped dead I had nothing to give him. But for my son I'd go out hustling even if it means getting pregnant. At least it would solve things for the moment.

The baby is much better now, thank God, and I am fulfilling my promises. On Sunday the Pentecosts came and had a service here. But they told me that I had to get rid of the saints. I'd make *them* get out before I'd throw out my saints. These saints cost me a lot of money. They're the only things here that have any value, and when I'm hard up I can sell one without any trouble at all.

El Welfare still gives me food, but not always, and I don't like most of the things they give. That long-grain rice doesn't taste like anything. It's like eating hay. The meat they give has fat on top and it comes in a can and it's real dark. They say it's corned beef, but I don't know. The same goes for that powdered milk. Who could drink the stuff? In La Esmeralda I saved until I was really hard up and then I sold it to anybody who was willing to shell out a quarter for it to feed it to their animals, or something. But I do not dare do that here because it's Federal Government food and it's against the law to sell it. I could get into trouble that way in a place like this, where I don't know anybody. I might try to sell that stuff to a detective without realizing who he was and I'd land in jail.

I haven't been to La Esmeralda often since I moved here, because I can't afford it. Every trip costs forty cents, twenty cents each way. I want to pay up all my debts in La Esmeralda so that I can hold my head high and proud when I go there. I want people to think I've bettered myself because one can't get screwed all one's life. Even now when I visit, still owing money as I do, I put on my best clothes and always try to carry a little cash. I do this so that Emilio's aunt Minerva won't get the idea I'm starving or anything. She really suffers when she sees me in La Esmeralda and I do all that just to bother her. I dress up the kids real nice and take them to call on everybody but her.

When I first moved out of La Esmeralda, nobody knew that I was leaving, in the first place because it made me sad and in the second place because that old Minerva had gone around telling everybody she hoped I'd clear out. She even said it to my face. I'd yell back at her, "What right do you have to say that? Did you buy La Esmeralda or something?"

Another reason why I hardly ever go to La Esmeralda is because Emilio spies on me. He has come after me in the *caserío* just the way he did in La Esmeralda, though not as often. He likes to use the shower in my new apartment when he comes. When I start home after visiting La Esmeralda, he goes into his car and drives along behind me, offering to give me a lift. But listen I wouldn't get into that car even if I had to walk all the way from San Juan to Villa Hermosa. I put a curse on that car, such a tremendous curse that I'm just waiting to see it strike. I did it one day when Anita had asthma and I had no money to take her to the hospital. I happened to glance out of the window and I saw Emilio stretched out in his car, relaxed as could be, as if he deserved nothing but the best. I let go and yelled at the top of my lungs, "I hope to God someday you'll wear that car as a hat. I hope it turns to dust, with you all fucked up inside it." Now I can't ride in the car because I'm afraid the curse will come true at a time when both of us are in it.

You can't imagine how lonely I feel here. I have friends but they're sort of artificial, pasted-on friends. I couldn't confide in them at all. For example, I got pregnant a little while ago and I had to have an abortion. I nearly went crazy thinking about it. Having a baby is nothing, it's the burden you have afterward, especially with a cowardly husband like mine who takes the easiest way out, denying that the child is his. So there I was, pregnant, and you know I was ashamed. I was already out of La Esmeralda, see? Well, I know that my womb is weak, so I took two doses of Epsom salts with quinine and out came the kid. You can't imagine how unpleasant that is. In La Esmeralda you can tell everybody about it and that sort of eases your heart. But here I didn't tell anybody. These girls I know here are mere children, and something like that—*ay, bendito!*

But to tell you the truth, I don't know what they call a *senorita* here in Villa Hermosa. The way it is in La Esmeralda, a girl and boy fall in love. For a few months they control themselves. Then they can't any more, and the boy does what he has to do to the girl. The hole is bigger than the full moon, and that's that. They tell everybody, and become husband and wife in the eyes of all the world. There's no trying to hide it. But here you see girls, who by rights should have a couple of kids at least, trying to keep from being found out. They call themselves *senoritas* but they'll go to a hotel with their sweetheart and let him stick his prick into every hole in their body except the right one. And they'll suck his prick and he'll come right in her mouth or over her thighs. The girls do all that and then they're so brazen as to come out of that hotel claiming they're still *senoritas*. It's plain shameless.

There are some policemen here who make love like this to some girls I know. Well, the policeman who did it to my friend Mimí told me that if I loaned him my bed for a little while he would give me three pesos. As that money wouldn't be bad at all and as he wasn't going to do it to me, I rented him the bed and grabbed the three pesos. Let them go screw! They locked themselves in the bedroom for a little while and then they went away. It was none of my business. If they didn't do it here they would go and do it somewhere else. And she didn't lose her virginity or anything here. So my hands are clean.

Sometimes I want to go back to La Esmeralda to live and

other times I don't. It's not that I miss my family so much. On
the contrary, relatives can be very bothersome. But you do need
them in case you get sick because then you can dump the children on them. Sometimes I cry for loneliness here. Sometimes
I'm bored to death. There's more neighborliness in La Esmeralda. I was used to having good friends stop by my house all
the time. I haven't seen much of this neighborhood because I
never go out. There's a Catholic church near by but I've never
been there. And I haven't been to the movies once since I've
been living here. In La Esmeralda I used to go now and then.
And in La Esmeralda, when nothing else was going on, you
could at least hear the sea.

In La Esmeralda nobody ever made fun of my lameness.
On the contrary, it was an advantage because everyone went
out of his way to help me: "Let me help the lame girl. Let
me buy *bolita* numbers from Lame Cruz, because cripples bring
luck." But it isn't like that here, where people just laugh. That's
why I'd like to live in La Esmeralda again or have Nanda move
in here with me.

The social worker told me that I could have an operation
to fix my back. Imagine, I'd have to go to the doctor and to the
hospital. Who could I leave my little baby crows with? And suppose what they do is take my guts out in order to make me look
right? But still, now that I live in a place like Villa Hermosa,
I would like to have an operation to make me straight.

THE PRISONER'S BENCH

Arturo Giovanitti

Through here all wrecks of the tempestuous mains
    Of life have washed away the tides of time.
Tatters of flesh and souls, furies and pains,
    Horrors and passions awful or sublime,
All passed here to their doom. Nothing remains
    Of all the tasteless dregs of sin and crime
But stains of tears, and stains of blood and stains
    Of the inn's vomit and the brothel's grime.

And now we, too, must sit here, Joe. Don't dust
These boards on which our wretched brothers fell,
They are clean, there's no reason for disgust.
For the fat millionaire's revolting stench
Is not here, nor the preacher's saintly smell.
And the judge never sat upon this bench.

TO A BENCH IN
MULBERRY PARK

Well, after many a year,
I see thou art still here,
Old bench, old haven of my roaming days;
And like a canopy
On royal beds, on thee
Its green pavilion still the maple sprays.

They were not sweet, indeed,
Those dreary days of need
When I, each night, would wonder here alone
Whether the dawn would hail
Another thief in jail
Or at the morgue another corpse unknown.

They were, indeed, so crude,
Those days of solitude
When hunger grinned at madness' stony stare.—
Recall not that again,
For love has come since then
And youth has won the battle with despair.

Those songs instead evoke
That sobs and tears did choke,
And that young faith no tempest could destroy;
Recall the tunes I knew,
The dreams each morning slew,
And those that since fulfilled their task of joy.

When every roar and sound
The heartless city drowned

Into the surging ocean of the night,
To me alone would drift,
A rich and kingly gift,
The flotsam of its song for my delight.

From all these windows purred
The slumbers, and I heard,
Now and again, a cradling mother croon,
While from the roofs afar
Dropped from an old guitar
The sighs of some young lover to the moon.

Watching the clouds' odd race
In my ecstatic maze
Meseemed that thou into their sea didst soar,
And I went sailing by,
Young Orpheus of the sky,
Like a doge in a gorgeous bucentaur.

I dreamed and dreamed all night,
Young dreams, and frail and bright,
Like little buds that never grow to bloom,
Like silver clouds that pass,
Like crickets in the grass,
Like yellow fireflies twinkling in the gloom.

Yea, I was hungry—yet
Sometimes one can forget
And hungry stomachs often find a dole,
But the young days are fleet
When one can fill with sweet
And moonlit dreams the hunger of the soul.

Ah me! They're gone, those days,
And love for me now lays
A pillow full of lullabies to sleep;
But it is hard, alack!
That memories come back
Of days that were so sad when one can't weep.

Yet in my deepest heart
I feel a sudden smart

That I won't tell my love and she won't see—
Old bench, if some new wretch
His limbs on thee should stretch,
Be kind to him as thou hast been to me.

BEYOND DELINQUENCY

Gregory Corso

What can the Deathmonger bring—horror delayed?
    Health's fooly alibi:
Life a trivial sacrament spitting eternity?
Persistence betrays yesterday's doubt, there is no more
    ugliness
        nor ever was—What drills this compliment to Beauty?
Everyone is asleep, something like a cunning lullaby
    or a child's wreck dares—Fullness or failure,
        the allotment is perfect, Life, countenance of a drift
        a drowse, slow and sleep, a death, it cannot be
            Absolute
There is sorrow in eternity, call it heaven,
    Life does not deny the affinity—
What can sold-out Death even bring? Repentance lifts
    its cheap despair,
It cannot see children pause before tired men
    with untimed eyes—
This is not the bravo definite, Oh so remote the sustenance
How well I knew such sight—possessor of the hand to
    touch it
    Majesty with vast veins—

There is a gangwar which changes nothing,
    not all the stubborn reasons of youth
    can harbor at this stretched turn;
The Deather of the cub of the Royal Dukes perhaps knew
    the very rich meaninglessness of Life too;
Two-Thumb the holy terror from Red Hook
    broke his head with an unread book
    —chance to time their eyes

Life is many times accomplished, it cannot fail
    or be postponed;
The countless dying prompts more than Death
    —as in the distance
    The little light's approach becomes a train—

Heaven is sad, it is God who cries
    heavy like the seas—Not for Harlem or the Bronx
Nor something as old and forgotten
Hurtling the Acanthians against the Chalcidians
Here the Puerto Ricans of Life by no divine element
    but man's plastic sun
    outstand no history—
Pain is a sacred deliverance;
All that of Life can speed supreme, the angelical inpath
    in which hopeless delivery boys might
    pick and set their own hip elements
    as though the realm were a pasteboard—
Reason enough to hand them the sceptre
    and have them sit no less environed kings—

WRIT ON THE STEPS
OF PUERTO RICAN HARLEM

There's a truth limits man
A truth prevents his going any farther
The world is changing
The world *knows* it's changing
Heavy is the sorrow of the day
The old have the look of doom
The young mistake their fate in that look
This is truth
But it isn't *all* truth

Life has meaning
And I do not know the meaning
Even when I felt it were meaningless
I hoped and prayed and sought a meaning
It wasn't all frolic poesy
There were dues to pay
Summoning Death and God
I'd a wild dare to tackle Them
Death proved meaningless without Life
Yes the world is changing
But Death remains the same
It takes man away from Life
The only meaning he knows
And usually it is a sad business
This Death

I'd an innocence I'd a seriousness
I'd a humor save me from amateur philosophy
I am able to contradict my beliefs

RHAPSODY

Frank O'Hara

515 Madison Avenue
door to heaven? portal
stopped realities and eternal licentiousness
or at least the jungle of impossible eagerness
your marble is bronze and your lianas elevator cables
swinging from the myth of ascending
I would join
or declining the challenge of racial attractions
they zing on (into the lynch, dear friends)
while everywhere love is breathing draftily
like a doorway linking 53rd with 54th
the east-bound with the west-bound traffic by 8,000,000s
o midtown tunnels and the tunnels, too, of Holland

where is the summit where all aims are clear
the pin-point light upon a fear of lust
as agony's needlework grows up around the unicorn
and fences him for milk- and yoghurt-work
when I see Gianni I know he's thinking of John Ericson
playing the Rachmaninoff 2nd or Elizabeth Taylor
taking sleeping-pills and Jane thinks of Manderley
and Irkutsk while I cough lightly in the smog of desire
and my eyes water achingly imitating the true blue

a sight of Manahatta in the towering needle
multi-faceted insight of the fly in the stringless labyrinth
Canada plans a higher place than the Empire State Building
I am getting into a cab at 9th Street and 1st Avenue
and the Negro driver tells me about a $120 apartment

"where you can't walk across the floor after 10 at night
not even to pee, cause it keep them awake downstairs"
no, I don't like that "well, I didn't take it"
perfect in the hot humid morning on my way to work
a little supper-club conversation for the mill of the gods

you were there always and you know all about these things
as indifferent as an encyclopedia with your calm brown
    eyes
it isn't enough to smile when you run the gauntlet
you've got to spit like Niagara Falls on everybody or
Victoria Falls or at least the beautiful urban fountains of
    Madrid
as the Niger joins the Gulf of Guinea near the Menemsha
    Bar
that is what you learn in the early morning passing
    Madison Avenue
where you've never spent any time and stores eat up light

I have always wanted to be near it
though the day is long (and I don't mean Madison Avenue)
lying in a hammock on St. Mark's Place sorting my poems
in the rancid nourishment of this mountainous island
they are coming and we holy ones must go
is Tibet historically a part of China? as I historically
belong to the enormous bliss of American death

PERICLES ON 31st STREET

Harry Mark Petrakis

Louie Debella's bar was located on the corner of 31st Street and Dart Avenue, the last store in a group of five stores owned by Leonard Barsevick, who besides being a landlord operated the Lark Wholesale Clothing Company across the street.

My name is George. My last name is not important. I'm Louie Debella's bartender and I count myself a good bartender. I might mention a few of the quality places I have tended bar, but that has nothing to do with this story.

If I have learned anything from fifteen years of tending bar it is that a bartender cannot take sides with anything that goes on across the bar. He has got to be strictly nonpartisan. A cousin of mine in South Bend, also in the business, once tried to mediate an argument about Calvin Coolidge. Somebody hit him in the back of the head with a bottle of beer that was not yet empty, and besides needing stitches he got wet. Now when I am on the job I never take sides. That is, I never did until the episode of Pericles.

As I understand it this fellow Pericles was a Greek general and statesman who lived back in those Greek golden years you read about in the school history books. From all reports he was a pretty complete sort of guy who laid down a set of rules and was tough on everybody who did not read them right.

If you are wondering what a Greek who lived a couple of thousand years ago has got to do with this story, I guess it all started because the storekeepers in our row of stores gathered in the bar in the evening after they locked their doors for a glass of beer.

The first man in was usually Dan Ryan, who had the

butcher shop. Ryan was a heavy beer man and needed the head start on the others. A little later Olaf Johnson, who ran the Sunlight lunchroom, came in with Sol Reidman the tailor. Olaf had a huge belly that was impossible to keep under a coat. Sol liked nothing better than to tease Olaf about when the triplets were expected.

The last man in was Bernard Klioris, who had a little grocery next to Sol's tailor shop. Bernard usually got lost in the arguments, and swung back and forth like a kitchen door in a restaurant. He had a sad thin face and was not so bright, but among our patrons you could hardly tell.

Last Tuesday night after I had served Ryan his fourth beer, Olaf and Sol and Bernard came in together, with Olaf and Sol arguing as usual.

"She told me she was a Republican," Olaf said. "They want some lunk for Congress. I told her to come by you and get her petition signed."

Sol waggled his bald head indignantly. "Who gave you leave to advertise my business?" he said. "A man's politics is a sacred trust that belongs to him alone."

"She only had a petition, not a gun," Olaf said. "I knew you was a Republican so I sent her."

"How can anyone," Ryan said from the bar, "be in his right mind and still be a Republican?"

Sol waved a warning finger. "Be careful," he said. "You are stepping on the Constitution when you ridicule a man's politics."

"I read about the Constitution," Bernard said.

They lined up at the bar. I poured them beer. All they ever drank was beer.

The door opened and Nick Simonakis came in. He was the vendor who took his stand at night on the corner of 31st and Dart. He had a glassed-in wagon that he pushed into place under the street lamp, and from the wagon he sold hot dogs and tamales and peanuts. Several times during the evening he locked up the wagon and came into the bar for a glass of wine. He would sit alone at a table to the side of the room, his dark eyes in his hollow-cheeked face glaring at the room from above the white handlebar mustache. Every now and then he would sip his wine and shake his head, making his thick white hair hang more disordered over his forehead.

Other men might have thought he was a little crazy because sometimes he sat there alone talking to himself, but like I said, I do not take sides. At other times he gave up muttering and loudly berated the drinkers of beer. "Only Turks would drink beer," he said, "when they could drink wine. One for the belly and the other for wisdom." He would sip his wine slowly, mocking their guzzling of beer, and the storekeepers would try to ignore him.

"The sun-ripened grapes," Simonakis said, "hanging until they become sweet. Then the trampling by the young maidens to extract the lovely juices. A ceremony of the earth."

"Beer don't just grow in barrels," Olaf said. "Good beer takes a lot of making."

The old man laughed softly as if he was amused. "You are a Turk," he said. "I excuse you because you think and talk like a Turk."

"Say, old man," Sol said. "Someone wants a bag of peanuts. You are losing business."

Simonakis looked at Sol with bright piercing eyes. "I will lose business," he said. "I am drinking my wine."

"He must be rich," Ryan said, 'and pushing business away. I wish I had gone into peddling peanuts myself."

"It is not a case of wealth," Simonakis said. "There is a time for labor and a time for leisure. A man must have time to sit and think. This made Greece great."

"Made who what?" Olaf asked with sarcasm.

The old man swept him with contempt. "In ancient Greece," he said coldly, "an elephant like you would have been packed on a mountaintop as bait for buzzards."

"Watch the language," Olaf said. "I don't have to take that stuff from an old goat like you."

"A land of ruined temples," Sol said, and he moved from the bar and carried his beer to a nearby table. "A land of philosophers without shoes."

"A land of men!" Simonakis spit out. "We gave the world learning and courage. We taught men how to live and how to die."

Ryan and Bernard and Olaf had followed Sol to the table, drawing their chairs.

"Would you mind, old man," Ryan said as he sat down, "leaving a little bit of credit to the Irish?"

"I give them credit," Simonakis said, "for inventing the wheelbarrow, and giving the world men to push it."

"Did you hear that!" Ryan said indignantly and looked fiercely at the old man.

The old man went on as if he had not heard. "A model of courage for the world," he said. "Leonidas with three hundred men holding the pass at Thermopylae against the Persian hordes. Themistocles destroying the great fleet of Xerxes at Salamis."

"That's history," Olaf said. "What have they done lately?"

Simonakis ignored him. He motioned to me and I took him the bottle of port. He raised the full glass and held it up and spoke in Greek to the wine as if performing some kind of ceremony. The men watched him and somebody laughed. Simonakis glared at them. "Laugh, barbarians," he said. "Laugh and forget your debt to Greece. Forget the golden age and the men like lions. Hide in your smoking cities and drown in your stinking beer."

"What a goat," Olaf said.

Sol shook his head sadly. "It is a pity to see a man ruined by drink," he said. "That wine he waves has soaked his head."

"Wheelbarrow indeed," Ryan said, and he glared back at the old man.

2

At that moment the front door opened and Leonard Barsevick, the landlord, walked in. He carried an air of elegance into the bar. Maybe because of his Homburg and the black chesterfield coat he wore.

The storekeepers greeted him in a respectful chorus. He waved his hand around like a politician at a beer rally and smiled broadly. "Evening, boys," he said. "Only got a minute but I couldn't pass by without stopping to buy a few of my tenants a beer. George, set up the drinks and mark it on my tab."

"Thank you, Mr. Barsevick," Olaf said. "You sure look like a million bucks tonight."

Barsevick laughed and looked pleased. "Got to keep up a front, Olaf," he said. "If a man in my position gets a spot on his suit he might as well give up."

"That's right, Mr. Barsevick," Ryan said. "A man in your position has got to keep up with the best and you sure do."

"Say, Mr. Barsevick," Bernard said. "You know the leak

in the roof at my store I spoke to you about last month. It hasn't been fixed yet and that rain the other night . . ."

"Wait a minute, Bernie," Barsevick laughed. "Not tonight. If I promised to fix it, I'm going to have it fixed. Leonard Barsevick is a man of his word. Ain't that right, boys?"

They all nodded and Olaf said, "Yes, sir," emphatically.

"But not tonight," Barsevick said. "Tonight I'm out for a little relaxation with a baby doll that looks like Jayne Mansfield." He made a suggestive noise with his mouth.

"You're sure a lucky man, Mr. Barsevick," Olaf said admiringly.

"Not luck at all, Olaf," Barsevick said, and his voice took on a tone of serious confidence. "It's perseverance and the ability to get along with people. I always say if I didn't know how to get along with people I wouldn't be where I am today."

"That's sure right, Mr. Barsevick," Ryan said. The others nodded agreement.

"Fine," Barsevick beamed. "All right, boys, drink up, and pass your best wishes to Leonard Barsevick for a successful evening." He winked broadly.

The storekeepers laughed and raised their glasses. Everybody toasted Barsevick but Simonakis. He sat scowling at the landlord from beneath his shaggy brows. Barsevick noticed him.

"You didn't give this gentleman a drink, George," he said. "What are you drinking, sir?"

"He ain't no gentleman," Olaf said. "He is a peanut peddler."

"An authority on wheelbarrows," Ryan said.

Simonakis cocked a thumb at Barsevick. "Hurry, landlord," he said, "your Mansfield is waiting."

Barsevick gave him a cool glance, but the old man just looked bored. Finally the landlord gave up and turned away, pulling on his suede gloves. He strode to the door cutting a fancy figure and waved grandly. "Good night, boys," he said.

The boys wished him good night. Simonakis belched.

3

On the following Thursday the notices came from Barsevick's bookkeeper announcing a fifteen per cent rent increase all along the block. All the storekeepers got a notice of the raise becoming effective with the expiration of their leases about a month away. Louie was so disturbed he called me down in the middle of the afternoon and took off early.

That night the storekeepers were a sad bunch. They sat around the table over their beer, looking like their visas had expired.

"I don't understand it," Ryan said. "Mr. Barsevick knows that business has not been good. Fifteen per cent at this time makes for an awful load."

"With license fees and the rest," Olaf said, "a lunchroom ain't hardly worth while. I was not making nothing before. With this increase it ain't going to get no better."

"Two hands to sew pants will not be enough," Sol said. "I must sew with four hands, all my own."

Bernard looked distressed. "Mr. Barsevick must have a good reason," he said.

"He's got expenses," Olaf said.

"He should have mine," Ryan said. "Beef is up six cents a pound again."

Simonakis came into the bar pulling off his gloves. He ignored the men as he walked by them to his table against the wall and signaled to me for his bottle of wine.

"I am going to buy a wagon," Olaf said loudly, "and sell peanuts and hot dogs on the street."

"You must first," Simonakis said, "have the wisdom to tell them apart."

Olaf flushed and started to get up. Sol shook him down. "No time for games with crazy men tonight," Sol said. "This matter is serious. We must organize a delegation to speak to Mr. Barsevick. It must be explained that this increase imposes a terrible burden on us at this time. Perhaps a little later."

"Shoot him," Simonakis said. He waved the glass I had just filled with dark wine.

"You mind your own business, peddler," Ryan said. "Nobody is talking to you."

"A Greek would shoot him," Simonakis said. "But you are toads."

"I get my rent raised," Olaf said, "and now I got to sit here and be insulted by a peanut peddler."

The front door opened and the room went quiet.

Barsevick closed the door softly behind him and walked over to the storekeepers' table and pulled up a chair and sat down like a sympathetic friend coming to share their grief.

I guess they were all as surprised as I was and for a long moment no one spoke and Barsevick looked solemnly from one to the other. "I hope you do not mind my butting in, boys," he said and he motioned to me. "George, bring the boys a round on me."

"Mr. Barsevick," Ryan said, "the boys and me were just discussing . . ."

Barsevick raised his hand gravely. "I know, Danny," he said. "I know what you are going to say. I want to go on record first as saying there is nobody any sorrier than Leonard Barsevick about this. That is why I am here. My bookkeeper said I did not have to come over tonight and talk to you. I told him I would not stand for that, that you boys were not just tenants, you were friends of mine."

"It is a lot of money, Mr. Barsevick," Olaf said. "I mean if we were making more, things might be different."

"I know that, Olaf," Barsevick said. "Believe me, if there was any other way I would jump at the chance. I said to Jack, my bookkeeper, 'Isn't there any other way?' I swear to you boys he said, 'Mr. Barsevick, if that rent is not increased it will be charity.'" I brought the tray of fresh beer and set the glasses around the table. "Not that I mind a little help to my friends," Barsevick said, "but it is not good business. I would be shamed before my competitors. 'There's Barsevick,' they would laugh, 'too soft to raise his tenants' rent.' They would put the screws on me and in no time at all I might be out of business."

Everybody was silent for a moment, probably examining the prospect of Leonard Barsevick put out of business because of his soft heart.

"We know you got expenses," Ryan said.

Barsevick shook his head mournfully. "You got no idea," he said. "I mean you boys got no idea. I am afraid sometimes for the whole economy. Costs cannot keep rising and still keep the country sound. Everything is going up. Believe me, boys, being a landlord and a businessman is hell."

"Shoot him," Simonakis said loudly.

Barsevick stopped talking and looked across the tables at the old man.

"He is a crazy man," Sol said. "That wine he drinks makes him talk to himself."

Barsevick turned back to the men but he was disturbed. He looked over at the old man once more like he was trying to understand and then started to get up. "I got to go now, boys," he said. "I'm working late tonight with my bookkeeper. If we see any other way to cut costs I will be glad to reconsider the matter of the increase. That is my promise to you boys as friends."

"We sure appreciate you stopping by, Mr. Barsevick," Ryan said. "We know there is many a landlord would not have bothered."

Barsevick shook his head vigorously. "Not Leonard Barsevick," he said. "Not even his worst enemy will say that Barsevick does not cut a straight corner when it comes to friends."

"We know that, Mr. Barsevick," Olaf said.

"We sure do," Bernard said.

"Shoot him," Simonakis said. "Shoot him before he gets away."

4

Barsevick whirled around and stared in some kind of shock at the old man. I guess he was trying very fast to figure out if the old man was serious.

"Don't pay him no mind, Mr. Barsevick," Olaf said. "He has been out in the rain too long."

"You are a demagogue." Simonakis spoke loudly to the landlord. "You wave your greedy fingers and tell them you are a friend. Aaaaaaaaa!" The old man smiled craftily. "I know your kind. In Athens they would tie you under a bull."

Barsevick stood there like rocks were being bounced off his head, his face turning a bright shade of red.

Sol motioned angrily at the old man. "Somebody wants a hot dog," he said. "You are losing business."

Simonakis looked at Sol for a moment with his mustache bristling, then looked at the others. "I have lost business," he said slowly. "You have lost courage."

A sound of hissing came from Barsevick, his red cheeks shaking off heat like a capped kettle trying to let off steam. "You goddam pig," he said huskily. "You unwashed old bum. You damn peddler of peanuts."

The old man would not give an inch. "You are a hypocrite," he said. "A hypocrite and a libertine. You live on the sweat of better men."

Barsevick's jaw was working furiously like he was trying to chew up the right words.

"Let me tell you," Simonakis said, and his voice took on a more moderate tone as if he were pleased to be able to pass information on to the landlord, "let me tell you how the hypocrite goes in the end. One day the people wake up. They know he is a liar and a thief. They pick up stones. They aim for his head." He pointed a big long finger at Barsevick and made a rattling sound rise from his throat. "What a mess a big head like yours would make."

Barsevick gasped and whirled to the men at the table. "He's threatening me," he shouted. "Did you hear him? Throw the old bastard out."

No one moved. I kept wiping glasses. A good bartender learns to keep working.

"Did you hear me!" Barsevick yelled. "Somebody throw him out."

"He is a crazy old man," Sol said. "He talks without meaning."

"Shut up!" Barsevick said. "You stick with him because you are no damn good either."

"I do not stick with him," Sol said, and he drew himself up hurt. "I am trying to be fair."

Barsevick turned to me. "George, throw him out!"

I kept wiping the glasses. "I am underpaid, Mr. Barsevick," I said. "My salary barely covers my work. Any extra service would be charity."

The old man took after him again. "Who likes you, landlord?" he said. "Be honest and speak truth before your tenants. Who likes you?"

"You shut up!" Barsevick shouted.

"I mean really likes you," Simonakis said. "I do not mean the poor girls you buy with your tainted money."

"I'll shut the old bastard up!" Barsevick hollered and started for the table against the wall.

Simonakis stood up and Barsevick stopped. The old man looked tall and menacing with his big hands and bright eyes and his white mustache standing out like a joyous challenge to battle. "You cannot shut up truth," Simonakis said. "And the truth is that you are a leech feeding on the labor of better men. You wish to become rich by making them poorer."

Barsevick stood a couple of tables away from the old man with his back bent a little waiting for a word to be raised in his defense. No one spoke and the old man stared at him with eyes like knives.

"You old bastard . . ." Barsevick said weakly.

Ryan made a sound clearing his throat. He wore a stern and studied look on his face. "Fifteen per cent is a steep raise," he said. "Right at this time when it is tough to make ends meet."

Barsevick whirled on him. "You keep out of this," he said. "You just mind your own business."

"I would say," Ryan said slowly, "fifteen per cent more rent to pay each month is my business."

"I'll make it twenty-five per cent," Barsevick shouted. "If you don't like it you can get out!"

"I have a lease," Ryan said quietly. He was looking at the landlord like he was seeing him for the first time.

"I will break it," Barsevick said. He looked angrily around at the other storekeepers. "I will break all your leases."

"I did not say nothing!" Bernard protested.

"The way of tyrants and thieves," Simonakis said. "All who oppose them suffer." He raised his head and fixed his eyes upon the ceiling. "O Pericles, lend us a stick so we may drive the tyrant from the market place."

"Stop calling me a tyrant," Barsevick fumed.

Simonakis kept his head raised praying to that guy Pericles.

"I'm going to put every one of you into the street," Barsevick said. "I'm going to teach you all not to be so damn smart."

Sol shook his head with measured contempt for the landlord on his face. "You will not put us out," he said. "First, you are too greedy for the rent. Second, you would not rent those leaking barns again without major repairs, and third . . ." He paused. "Third, I do not admire your personality."

"Amen," Bernard said. "My roof keeps leaking."

"O Pericles!" Simonakis suddenly cried out and everybody looked at him. "They are barbarians and not of Athens but they are honest men and need your help. Give them strength to destroy the common enemy. Lend them your courage to sweep out the tyrant."

"You are all crazy," Barsevick said and he looked driven and disordered. His tie was outside his coat and the Homburg perched lopsided over one ear.

"You are a tiger," Sol said. "Tell me what circus you live in and I will rent a cage to take you home."

"Do not be insulting," Ryan said to Sol. "You will hurt

the landlord's feelings. He cannot help he has got a head like a loin of pork."

"You ignorant bastards!" Barsevick shouted.

Ryan got up and came over to the bar. He stepped behind and pulled out the little sawed-off bat Louie kept under the counter. He winked at me. "I am just borrowing it," he said. "I want to put a new crease in the landlord's hat."

Simonakis came back from calling on Pericles. "Do not strike him," he said. "Stone him. Stone him as they stoned tyrants in Athens." He looked at the floor and around the room excitedly searching for stones.

Barsevick in full retreat began to edge toward the door. He opened his mouth to try and speak some final word of defiance but one look at the bat in Ryan's hands must have choked off his wind.

"Tyrant!" Simonakis shouted.

"Vulture!" Olaf said. "Stop and eat on me, and I'll grind some glass for your salad!"

"Greedy pig!" Ryan said, and he waved the bat. "You try and collect that rent and we all move out!"

"Judas!" Sol said. "Come to me only to sew your shroud!"

"Fix my leaking roof!" Bernard said.

With one last helpless wail, Barsevick stumbled out through the door.

For a long moment after the door closed nobody moved. Then Ryan handed me back the bat. I put it under the counter. Olaf started to the bar with his glass. Bernard came after him. Soon all were lined up at the bar. All except Simonakis, who had gone back to sit down at his table staring moodily into his glass of wine.

Ryan turned his back to the bar and looked across the tables at Simonakis. He looked at him for a long time and no one spoke. The old man kept staring at his wine. Ryan looked back helplessly at Olaf and Sol and they watched him struggling. Bernard looked dazed. I held a wet towel in my hands and forgot to wipe the bar. When Ryan finally turned back to Simonakis, you could see he had made up his mind. He spoke slowly and carefully.

"Mr. Simonakis," he said.

The old man raised his head scowling.

"Mr. Simonakis," Ryan said. "Will you be kind enough to join my friends and me in a drink?"

The old man stopped scowling. He nodded gravely and stood up tall and straight, his mustache curved in dignity, and came to the bar. Ryan moved aside to make a place for him.

I began to pour the beer.

"No, George," Ryan said. "We will have wine this trip."

"Yes, sir," I said.

I took down the bottle of port and filled a row of small glasses.

Ryan raised his glass and looked belligerently at the others. "To the glory of Greece," he said.

The rest of them raised their glasses.

"To Athens," Sol said.

"To Mr. Simonakis," Olaf said.

"Ditto," Bernard said.

I took down another wineglass. I poured myself some wine. They all looked at me. I did not care. I was abandoning a professional tradition of neutrality.

"To Pericles," I said.

Simonakis stroked his mustache and sipped his wine. The rest of us sipped right with him.

FLOWER DRUM SONG
Chin Y. Lee

To the casual tourists, Grant Avenue is Chinatown, just another colorful street in San Francisco; to the overseas Chinese, Grant Avenue is their showcase, their livelihood; to the refugees from the mainland, Grant Avenue is Canton. Although there are no pedicabs, no wooden slippers clip-clapping on the sidewalks, yet the strip of land is to the refugee the closest thing to a home town. The Chinese theatres, the porridge restaurants, the tea-houses, the newspapers, the food, the herbs . . . all provide an atmosphere that makes a refugee wonder whether he is really in a foreign land. And yet, in this familiar atmosphere, he struggles and faces many problems that are sometimes totally unfamiliar.

Wang Chi-yang was one of those who could not live any-where else in the United States but in San Francisco China-town. He was from central China, speaking only Hunan dialect, which neither a Northerner nor a Cantonese can understand. His working knowledge of the English language was limited to two words: "yes" and "no." And he seldom used "no," for when people talked to him in English or Cantonese, he didn't want to antagonize them unnecessarily since he had no idea what they were talking about. For that reason, he wasn't too popular in Chinatown; his "yes" had in fact antagonized many people. Once at a banquet, his Cantonese host claimed modestly that the food was poor and tasteless and begged his honorable guest's pardon, a customary polite remark to be refuted by the guests, and Wang Chi-yang, ignorant of the Cantonese dialect, nodded his head and said "yes" twice.

But Wang Chi-yang loved Chinatown. He lived comfortably in a two-story house three blocks away from Grant Avenue that he had bought four years ago, a house decorated with Chinese paintings and couplet scrolls, furnished with uncomfortable but expensive teakwood tables and chairs, and staffed with two servants and a cook whom he had brought from Hunan Province. The only "impure" elements in his household were his two sons, Wang Ta and Wang San, especially the latter, who had in four years learned to act like a cowboy and talk like the characters in a Spillane movie. At thirteen he had practically forgotten his Chinese.

Wang Ta, the elder son, was less of a rebel. Quiet and unhappy at twenty-eight, he was often embarrassed in his father's company. But he was reluctant to correct the old man's old habits and mistakes, for Wang Chi-yang was a stubborn man. In his house he was the "lord"; his words were the law. His servants still addressed him as Old Master Wang and worked for him seven days a week at ten dollars a month. They were loyal to him and respected him, although his stern looks, his drooping mustache, his large frame, his loose gown of blue satin, his constant cough, his unyielding demands and orders would have been very unpleasant to any servant hired in America. The only person who refused to be awed by him was Madam Tang, the widowed sister of his late wife. Madam Tang came often to give him advice. She regarded her sixty-three-year-old brother-in-law as extremely old-fashioned and backward. "Aiyoo, my sister's husband," she often said, "please put your money in the bank. And buy yourself a suit of Western dress. In this country you truly look like a stage actor in that satin gown."

But Madam Tang's advice went into Old Master Wang's one ear and promptly came out of the other. Not that Old Master Wang didn't trust the banks; he just couldn't compromise with the idea that one's money should be kept in strangers' hands. In China, his money had always been in the hands of his close friends, and it had always been safe even without a signature. And his friends had always brought him profit and interest twice a year and he had accepted them without a question. He believed that banks in this country would probably do the same, but in a bank everybody was a stranger. Money, in his opinion, was like one's wife; he just couldn't let a stranger keep it for him.

As for Western clothes, wearing them was out of the

question. He had always worn long gowns, silk gowns in the summer, satin gowns in the spring or autumn, fur gowns or cotton-padded gowns in the winter. It would be unthinkable for him to change into the Western clothes with only two or three buttons and an open collar. Furthermore, a piece of rag tied around one's neck seemed to him an outrage, besides being ugly and an indication of ill omen. He would never dream of tying one around his neck. The Communists in Hunan Province had tried to discard the long gown and make everybody wear the Lenin uniform, which, in his opinion, was more formal than the Western dress since it had more buttons and a closed collar. To him, even that was too much of an undesirable change; and it was one of the reasons why he had escaped the mainland of China five years ago. No, he would never wear anything but the long gown. He was going to die in it and be buried in it. And he didn't think that his long gown would bother anyone but his sister-in-law. He had often walked on Grant Avenue in it and nobody had paid much attention to him. Even the American tourists seemed to regard him as a natural phenomenon on Grant Avenue.

Old Master Wang loved to walk on Grant Avenue. Every other evening, after dinner, he walked down Jackson Street, turned south on Grant Avenue and strolled for six blocks until he reached Bush Street, then he crossed Grant and turned back. He regarded this section beyond Bush as no longer Chinatown but a foreign territory. At the border of Chinatown he stopped and looked at the brightly lighted Chinatown thoroughfare for a moment, at its skyline with the pagoda roofs, at the lantern-like street lights, the blinking neon signs of English and Chinese in red, blue, yellow and green. He looked at the cars which crawled endlessly into the heart of Chinatown, then he took a deep breath and started the journey back. The street was gay and noisy, and yet it had its tranquil quality, as no one seemed to be in a great hurry.

He strolled down the street and studied every poster and advertisement that was written in Chinese. During the New Year festivities he loved to read the orange couplet banners posted on the door of each shop. If he found the poetry on the banners well composed and the calligraphy having character and strength, he would read it aloud twice or thrice with his head shaking rhythmically in a scholarly manner, and then grade it. He graded all New Year poetic greetings on Grant Avenue, memorized the best ones and wrote them down when he came home.

He also enjoyed the articles displayed in the shop windows—the exquisitely carved furniture, the brass and earthenware bowls, the straw hats and bamboo baskets, the miniature trees, the lacquer, the silk, the tiny porcelain, the jade, the silk brocade of gold and lavender. . . . His great favorite was an intricately carved eight-foot tusk in a large gift store near California Street. He went in and inquired the price. The owner of the store, who spoke some Mandarin, managed to make him understand that it was a rare mastodon tusk that had been buried in Siberian ice centuries ago. The carvings, which told a story of a festival at an emperor's palace, took twenty-five years to complete. The price, therefore, was $15,-000.

For three weeks Old Master Wang stopped in front of the window, admired the tusk and wondered whether he should buy it. Finally he made up his mind. He could enjoy the tusk on Grant Avenue as much as he could enjoy it privately at his home; why should he own it? Besides, it would be an act of selfishness to deprive others of the pleasure of looking at it by removing it from Grant Avenue. He was glad of the decision; for four years now he had enjoyed the tusk every other evening as much as if it were his own.

He didn't find much pleasure walking on upper Grant Avenue, for it smelled too much of fowl and fish. When passing Washington Street, he would take a quick trip to the Buddhist church that was being constructed a block down, make a five-dollar donation and then return to Grant. He seldom went farther to Kearny, for he regarded it as a Filipino town and he had no desire to go there. He always walked past Grant on Jackson and went home through Stockton Street or Powell Street, avoiding the chicken and fish marts on upper Grant.

Back home, he always sat comfortably in his rattan chair and waited for Liu Lung, the deaf manservant, to bring him tea, water pipe and the four Chinese newspapers. He subscribed to all the Chinatown newspapers for many reasons, the main reason being to see if there was any political fight among the editors. He always followed an editorial war with great interest; occasionally he would take sides and write an anonymous letter to the one with whom he sided, praising his reasoning and his fluency of composition. He always read all the papers from page to page, including the advertisements. He had no strong political convictions. He disliked communism for one reason only, that it destroyed Chinese traditions and turned the Chinese social order upside down.

After he had enjoyed his tea, the water pipe and the four newspapers, he was ready for his ginseng soup. Liu Ma, the fat, talkative woman servant, who was Liu Lung's wife and Old Master Wang's information bureau, brought in the soup, eased the Old Master's cough by beating his shoulders with the palms of her hands for five minutes, and in the meantime supplied all the household information of the day. "The cook had a visitor today," she said confidentially in Hunan dialect. "A crooked-looking man. I did not know what they talked about, but they talked for a long time in the cook's bedroom."

Old Master Wang grunted. "Has Young Master Wang San studied his lessons in his room this evening?" he asked.

"Yes. I saw to it that he studied."

"Are you sure he went to school instead of a motion picture?" he asked.

"He came home with many books this evening," Liu Ma said. "And went straight to his room and studied."

Old Master Wang grunted. "Has Young Master Wang Ta come home yet?"

"No, not yet," said Liu Ma, then she lowered her voice and confided, "Old Master Wang, when I cleaned Young Master Wang Ta's room this morning, I found a woman's picture in his desk drawer. A picture with five colors, the very expensive kind. On it were some foreign words I did not understand. I told Liu Lung this morning, 'No wonder Young Master Wang Ta has always come home late recently.' "

Old Master Wang grunted. "What does this woman look like?" he asked.

"She is a foreigner," Liu Ma said emphatically.

Old Master Wang stiffened. "What? Are you sure?"

"She has silk-colored hair, blue eyes and a large nose. She is a foreigner."

"Ask Young Master Wang Ta to see me when he comes home."

"Yes, Old Master Wang," she said beating his shoulders more energetically. "Do you want to talk to the cook too? I suspected that visitor of his is a bad character. Perhaps the cook is trying to find another job again and the crooked-looking visitor is trying to help him."

"No, I don't want to talk to him," Old Master Wang said. "He is permitted to receive visitors. It is enough beating. You may go now."

After Liu Ma had gone, Wang Chi-yang thought more of the foreign woman in Wang Ta's drawer than he worried about the cook. He knew that the cook wouldn't leave him again. A year ago his cook had been lured away by a Cantonese cook who made three hundred dollars a month in a restaurant. But two months afterward his cook returned, saying that he had been unhappy working in a restaurant as an assistant. He didn't understand their dialect and he had been pushed around; furthermore, he couldn't save any money although he had made two hundred dollars a month. The chief cook, who gambled, had often borrowed money from him. Now he realized that he had really been very happy in the kitchen in the House of Wang, where he was the chief. And he had always saved at least ten dollars of his fifteen-dollar monthly pay and during the past three years he had saved almost five hundred dollars. But he had lost all of his savings at the gambling tables during the two months when he was making two hundred a month. With tears in his eyes he had begged Old Master Wang to take him back. Wang Chi-yang remembered the cook's predicament and was sure that he wouldn't be so foolish as to work elsewhere and try to make two hundred dollars a month again.

But the foreign woman in Wang Ta's drawer bothered him. He waited for Wang Ta to come home but his son did not come. When the old clock on the marble mantel struck twelve he went to bed: he tossed under the huge square mosquito net, unable to fall asleep. He had brought the mosquito net from China and had slept peacefully for twenty years under it. He would feel naked without it. But tonight he felt disturbed as though hundreds of mosquitoes had been humming in his net. Was Wang Ta in bed with that foreign woman in some cheap hotel room now? He thought of it and he shivered.

The next morning he got up as soon as the clock struck eight, had his ginseng soup and inquired about Wang Ta. Liu Ma told him that the Young Master had come back very late and had gone out again early this morning. Old Master Wang was relieved, but he was still slightly disturbed by the fact that the younger generation was not obedient any more. His son should have at least waited and come to see him as ordered. Feeling a bit crabbed he dismissed Liu Ma and attended his miniature garden beside his bed. The garden was built on a huge Kiangsi plate, with a magnificent emerald mountain rising high above the water. There were caverns, roads, bridges, paths, pagodas and a monastery in the garden, with tiny goldfish swimming about in the lake. He fed the fish, watered the moss and the miniature trees in the mountain. He felt better. The beauty of nature always cured him of his bad mood.

Then he went to his large red lacquered desk beside the window and practiced calligraphy for an hour. He wrote famous poetry on his fine rice paper with great care and deliberation, his head moving slightly with the brush. Then he wrote the poetry all over again in grass style, his brush flying swiftly and smoothly on the paper. He was not satisfied with his grass style. For practice' sake, he wrote casually some folklore sayings on top of it: "Tight lips catch no flies," "Waste no time quarreling with women," "Loud bark, no good dogs; loud talk, no wise man" . . .

Then he suddenly remembered it was Monday, the day for his weekly trip to the Bank of America on Grant Avenue, not to deposit money, but to have a hundred-dollar bill changed into small bills and silver. He put his stationery away, put on a black satin jacket over his long gown, took a brand new hundred-dollar bill from his locked iron trunk in the closet and went out.

The teller in the bank knew what he wanted and, with a smile, she changed the money for him without a question. He wrapped up the small bills and the change in his handkerchief, and with an anticipation of the pleasure of counting the money, he hurried home. Counting money had become almost a hobby to him, and he enjoyed it as much as he did attending his miniature garden. After he had counted the total sum, he sorted the bills according to their denominations, then sorted them once more according to their degree of newness, putting the brand-new ones on one pile, the newer ones on another and the old ones on a third. He treated the silver coins with more deliberation, taking pains to examine them under a magnifying glass to see which was the newest. He would spend the old ones first and the new ones later, as for the brand-new ones, he would save them in an exquisitely carved sandalwood box locked in one of his desk drawers. When he had nothing else to do, he would sometimes bring the box out and enjoy counting the shiny half dollars, quarters and dimes until their luster began to fade, then he would spend them to make room for other brand-new ones. He counted the money until Liu Lung, the deaf servant, came to his bedroom to announce his lunch.

After lunch he took a nap. He was awakened by an itch in his throat and he coughed. He had been coughing for years and now he even began to enjoy that too. So he lay in his bed and coughed mildly and sporadically for an hour or so, then he heard his sister-in-law's voice calling for Liu Lung.

"Has the Old Master waked up yet?" she shouted.

"Enh?"

"I said, has the Old Master wakened from his afternoon nap?" she shouted louder.

"Oh," said Liu Lung after a moment, "I don't know. I shall look."

"Go wake him, I have something important to tell him!"

Wang Chi-yang lay in his bed waiting for Liu Lung to come in to wake him. The servant shuffled in quietly, opened the square mosquito net and called him cautiously, as though afraid of startling him. Old Master Wang opened his eyes slowly and grunted. "What is it?" he asked.

"Madam Tang has come," Liu Lang said.

"Ask her to wait." He seldom asked his sister-in-law to come in to talk in his bedroom where he received most of his guests. He always received her in the large living room furnished with the uncomfortable straight-backed teakwood chairs which often discouraged the visitor from staying long. Madam Tang had advised him to buy a few sofas and some soft chairs; he had said "yes" many times, but never bought them. He disliked sofas; sitting on a sofa often made him feel as if he were sitting in the arms of a fat woman.

He struggled out of the bed, took his water pipe and went to the living room where Madam Tang was sitting on one of the tall hard chairs waiting, her bright-colored umbrella and black leather handbag properly placed in her lap. She was fifty, but looked a few years younger in her blue silk gown with the short sleeves. She used no make-up except a little lipstick, and her hair was combed back and tied into a little bun, neat and well-oiled. "My sister's husband," she said as soon as Wang Chi-yang came in, "I have something very important to tell you." And she opened her handbag and fished out a little newspaper clipping in English.

Wang Chi-yang sat down next to her and smoked his water pipe, knowing that there was nothing very important. "Here is a piece of news I cut off from a foreign paper," Madam Tang went on, brandishing the newspaper clipping importantly. "I shall read it to you and translate it for you. It will serve as a good warning and make you realize that my advice concerning your money is sound." She cleared her throat and, with difficulty and her individual pronunciation, she read the news aloud. " 'Lum Fong, manager of Sam Sung Café on Stockton Street, told the police how a well-dressed man came into the café, ordered a meal, and when it came time to pay, slipped Lum Fong at the cash register this penciled message: "Give me all the money. I have a gun." The Chinese went blank. "So sollee," he said, "I no savvee." "You monee," whispered the bandit, trying to make the manager understand. "You monee! I have gun, I have gun!" But the manager was still puzzled. "So sollee," he said. "No savvee." The bandit, frustrated, started for the door. "So sollee," Lum Fong called out. "Checkee please!" The thug paid eighty-five cents and left!' "

When she finished reading she looked at Old Master Wang significantly with her lips tightly pursed.

"A bandit robbed a Chinese restaurant on Stockton Street," Madam Tang said. "The bandit had a gun; he almost shot Lum Fong, the owner of the restaurant. Fortunately Lum Fong had only eighty-five cents on him. The bandit robbed the eighty-five cents and escaped." She paused for a moment for emphasis, then went on, "My sister's husband, I have always told you to put your money in the bank. You will regret one day when a bandit comes in with a gun and robs you of everything. This piece of news will serve you as a good warning. I hope you will consider my advice and do as I have repeatedly told you."

Old Master Wang grunted and smoked his water pipe. He was only slightly worried. Nobody knew that his money was locked in an iron trunk in the closet. If a bandit came in, he would just yield to him the contents of his sandalwood box. No, he was not going to let any strangers in the bank keep his money. Nevertheless he grunted and said to his sister-in-law, "I shall consider your advice, my wife's sister."

INTO THE
MAINSTREAM

AND OBLIVION

> *I think that what we really have to do is to create a country in which there are no minorities—for the first time in the history of the world.*
>
> James Baldwin

"A people that has lost its traditions is doomed!" cries the Reverend in Ole Rolvaag's *Their Father's God.* "If this process of leveling down, of making everybody alike by blotting out all racial traits, is allowed to continue, America is doomed to become the most impoverished land spiritually on the face of the earth."

This sentiment, uttered by a Norwegian-American, has been echoed by ethnic writers throughout the history of immigrants in America. In the 1940s, with the persecution of Jews in Europe and the rise of a national state in Palestine, American Jews became more self-conscious of their rich cultural heritage. In the 1950s and '60s, with the rise of independent nations in Africa and the Supreme Court decision of 1954, black Americans began to emphasize a concept of negritude that had the most serious social repercussions. As we enter the seventies, Indians and Puerto Ricans are also exhibiting a new awareness of their ethnic origins that expresses genuine doubt concerning the value of assimilation into the mainstream of American society.

The minorities of America have underscored one of the most serious problems of contemporary society: the dehumanization of the individual in a mass civilization. Ethnic writers refuse to sacrifice their heritage to a way of life that standardizes food and clothing, entertainment, leisure, and education. There is scarcely an important work of contemporary literature that does not confront this central issue of dehumanization. When seen from the point of view of ethnic authors who cling to their origins as one way to assert their humanity, the dangers of American technocracy become dramatically apparent.

INTO THE MAINSTREAM
AND OBLIVION

Julian Mayfield

Recently an African student, long resident in this country, con-
fessed to a group of his intimates that he did not trust the American Negro. "What will you do," he asked them, "in the unlikely
event that the United States becomes involved in a colonial war
in Africa?" The immediate answer was: "Man, we will shoot
you down like dogs." The remark prompted general laughter,
but, on reflection, it is not amusing.

The visiting student had sensed what his friends already
took for granted: that the contemporary American Negro is
faced with a most perplexing dilemma. He does not know who
he is or where his loyalties belong. Moreover, he has every right
to his confusion for he exists on a moving plateau that is rapidly shifting away from the candid oppression of the past
toward—what? The future of the American Negro is most often
depicted as an increasingly accelerated absorption into the
mainstream of American life where, presumably, he will find
happiness as a first-class citizen. This is perhaps the rosy view,
but it already has validity insofar as it represents the attitude
and aspiration of a majority of Negroes, especially those who
are called leaders.

Unfortunately—and one cannot see how it could have been
otherwise—the Negro writer has been unable to escape this
confusion. The AMSAC writers' conference demonstrated that
the Negro writer is having trouble squaring his art and his
sense of reality with the American dream. He, too, finds himself wondering who he is, an American or what? And if finally
the scholars convince him that he is indeed an American, he
asks if this condition must be the extent of his vision. He is all

too aware that in recent years a myth that was once accepted without question has shown signs of being discredited. This myth implied that if one could become a real American, he had achieved the best that world could offer.

The conference panel on social protest was especially interesting in regard to the advisability of the Negro's embracing the white American's literary values in exchange for those of his own that he now finds outmoded. Many of the speakers felt that social protest as we have known it, had outlived its usefulness. They knew, of course, that racial injustice still flourishes in our national life, but they felt that the moral climate has been established for the eventual breakdown of racism, and that they need not therefore employ their literary tools to attack it in the same old way, that is to say, directly and violently. To this participant it seemed that the younger writer was seeking a new way of defining himself. Grudgingly he admitted that his work in the past may have suffered artistically because of his preoccupation with the problem of being a Negro in the United States. Yet he seemed reluctant to leap head first into the nation's literary mainstream (a word that was heard repeatedly throughout the conference).

In this I believe the writers were being wiser than most of our church, civic, and political leaders, who are pushing with singular concentration toward one objective: integration. This is to be applauded and actively encouraged so long as integration is interpreted to mean the attainment of full citizenship rights in such areas as voting, housing, education, employment, and the like. But if, as the writers have reason to suspect, integration means completely identifying the Negro with the American image—that great-power face that the world knows and the Negro knows better—then the writer must not be judged too harshly for balking at the prospect.

Perhaps some of them had seen a recent film called *The Defiant Ones,* which attracted world-wide attention because of its graphic, symbolic depiction of American Negro-white relations. In the film a black convict and a white convict are chained to one another in a desperate bid for freedom. Each hates the other intensely, but both soon realize that if they are to find freedom they must cooperate for their mutual good. By the time their actual chains are removed, they have come to believe that they are bound together in a larger way—that their fates, their destinies, are intertwined—so much so that in the end, most remarkably (and, one hopes, not prophetically) the Negro foregoes his chance for freedom because his white comrade is too weak to escape.

The symbolism is obvious and, to one observer at least, disturbing in its implications. For it is not uncommon to hear nowadays that the American Negro and the white are forever bound together and must, perforce, pursue a common destiny. On the face of it this approach seems soundly based on common sense. Throughout his long, cruel history in this land, the Negro has been the most avid seeker of the American dream—most avid because for him its realization was often a matter of life and death. If he could but grasp the dream, he could walk in dignity without fear of the abuse heaped on him by a scornful white majority. So fervid has been his pursuit of the dream that in every war and regardless of the nature of the war, his leaders have offered up his sons, the strength of any race, saying, "Take our youth—take our youth and they will prove their worth as Americans."

But the dream has proved elusive, and there is reason to believe that for the Negro it never had a chance of realization. Now, because of a combination of international and domestic pressures, a social climate is being created wherein, at least in theory, he may win the trappings of freedom that other citizens already take for granted. One may suggest that during this period of transition the Negro would do well to consider if the best use of these trappings will be to align himself totally to the objectives of the dominant sections of the American nation. Just as an insurance company will not issue a policy without determining the life expectancy of the buyer, neither should the Negro—in this case the buyer—accept the policy before he determines if the company is solvent. If the dream he has chased for three centuries is now dying even for white Americans, he would be wise to consider alternative objectives. The urgency of our times demands a deeper and more critical approach from Negro leadership. This new approach is suggested by the Negro mother who, having lost one of her sons in the Korean adventures, was heard to remark: "I don't care if the army is integrated; next time I want to know what kind of war my boy is being taken to."

In the same sense the Negro writer is being gently nudged

toward a rather vague thing called "the mainstream of American literature." This trend also would seem to be based on common sense. But before plunging into it he owes it to the future of his art to analyze the contents of the American mainstream to determine the full significance of his commitment to it. He may decide that, though the music is sweet, he would rather play in another orchestra. Or, to place himself in the position of the black convict in *The Defiant Ones*, he may decide that he need not necessarily share the fate of his white companion who, after all, proffers the hand of friendship a little late. The Negro writer may conclude that his best salvation lies in escaping the narrow national orbit—artistic, cultural and political—and soaring into the space of more universal experience.

What are the principal characteristics of the mainstream of American literature? To this observer they are apathy and either a reluctance or a fear of writing about anything that matters. William Barrett in *The New York Times* (May 10, 1959) asserts that power, vitality and energy have been abundant in recent American writing, but concedes that "the writers have lacked a center somewhere, they have been without great and central themes."

The phenomenon of our era is the seeming lack of concern shown by American creative writers for the great questions facing the peoples of the world. The most important of these, and the most obvious, is the madness of war. There are other great issues that challenge us, but the American writer has turned his back on them. He deals with the foibles of suburban living, the junior executive, dope addiction, homosexuality, incest and divorce.

I am not suggesting that anyone (least of all the present writer) should sit down with the grand purpose of writing a novel against war. But I do mean to imply that writers of the mainstream, reflecting the attitude of the American people generally, seem determined not to become involved in any of the genuine fury, turmoil, and passion of life; and it is only such involvement that makes life worth living. Where, for instance, is the humor that once characterized our national literature, and what has happened to the American's ability, indeed his proclivity, to laugh at himself? A stultifying respectability hangs over the land, and that is always a sign of decline, for it inhibits the flowering of new ideas that lead to progress and cultural regeneration. In short, the literary mainstream seems to be running dangerously shallow.

It would be pleasant to report that Negro writers have been unaffected by the current literary atmosphere, but it would not be candid. If the AMSAC conference demonstrated any one thing, it was that Negro writers generally are uncertain about the path they should explore in seeking to illuminate the life of man. I say "generally," for the individual writer charts his own course and follows or changes it at will. But it is interesting that there was evident so little unity of approach. One would have thought that Negro writers, representing a tragic and unique experience in our national history, would be bound together by a dominant theme in their work. But if this is the case, it was not obvious at the conference, and such a theme is difficult to detect in recent novels and plays.

The advantage of the Negro writer, the factor that may keep his work above the vacuity of the American mainstream, is that for him the façade of the American way of life is always transparent. He sings the national anthem *sotto voce* and has trouble reconciling the "dream" to the reality he knows. If he feels American at all, it is only when he is on foreign soil and, peculiarly enough, often finds himself defending that which he hated at home. He walks the streets of his nation an alien, and yet he feels no bond to the continent of his ancestors. He is indeed the man without a country. And yet this very detachment may give him the insight of the stranger in the house, placing him in a better position to illuminate contemporary American life as few writers of the mainstream can. This alienation should serve also to make him more sensitive to philosophical and artistic influences that originate beyond our national cultural boundaries.

Finally, if the situation I have described is real, a tragic future is indicated for the American Negro people. Unlike most of the colored peoples of the earth, he has no land and cannot realistically aspire to supremacy in the environment that has been his home for three centuries. In his most optimistic moods —and this period is one of them—the best he can hope for is submersion in what is euphemistically called the American melting pot. Despite the vigorous efforts of Negro leaders and the international pressures on the United States, it seems unlikely that this submersion will occur to any large degree within the foreseeable future. The likelihood is that the Negro people will continue for several decades to occupy, to a diminishing degree, the position of the unwanted child who, having been brought for a visit, must remain for the rest of his life. This is a hard conclusion to draw, but if it has validity, it is better recognized than ignored.

THEIR FATHER'S GOD

Ole Rolvaag

The minister was tight-lipped and swarthy, stocky of build, with a head set firmly on a pair of broad shoulders; his beard was black and full; his hair combed back into a flowing pompadour; the eyes, cold and grey, examined carefully into things before pronouncing judgment. He had not been long in his present call and was seldom seen abroad except on occasional sick-calls or in response to an invitation such as to-night. His parishioners had not yet been able to make him out; all they could say with certainty was that his sermons were unusually well prepared, that he stoutly defended everything Norwegian, and that he was punctilious in the performance of his duties.

The dinner finished, Reverend Kaldahl went about thanking the hostess and all her family, shaking hands with each one. He talked long with Beret and was extravagant in his praise of her excellent dinner. After a while he came into the front room where the guests had gathered; those who smoked were already puffing their pipes. He smiled a refusal of the rocking-chair which the others had let stand for him, strode to the opposite wall, and stationed himself there with his arms folded over his chest.

When he entered, the talk in the room died down. He felt the men were waiting for him to strike the note of the conversation, and so he began telling about Christmas in Norway, slowly, trying to determine how his remarks were being received. He dwelt particularly on the Christmas customs of the country districts. By and by this led him into a discussion of how "the race" (he used the phrase often) had lived in olden times.

Tönseten could not restrain himself for long. Gosh! here was a subject worth discussing!

"Them vikings were boys you couldn't sniff at!" He struck his knee a profound slap. "Dandy fellows, I tell you!" His remark aroused laughter, and more so because of Tambour-Ola's quick rejoinder:

"If you, Syvert, had been living in those days, I'll bet you'd either have been a king or a pirate!"

The minister took his lead from Tönseten's remark:

"Fine men they were, some of them; daring and deed-hungry, unafraid to risk their lives on a great adventure. Yet we must not believe that the Norwegians of that day and age, taken as a whole, were any worthier than they are now. It is the sensational in their deeds, the things unheard of, that catch the eye as we now look back. But their deeds were, after all, the accomplishments of a meagre handful. The great mass of Norwegians stayed snugly at home with their porridge-bowls between their knees; that was as far as their vision carried them. That part of our race has always been in the great majority. The same holds true for us Norwegians in America. Here, too, the porridge-bowl type of viking predominates, and it is that kind that lends colour to all our life and activities." A bitterness had crept into his even voice; he had crossed his legs and was toying with his watch chain.

"So also with the Norwegians of that time; there were those in whom the urge to cope wth the greatest difficulties and to reach the last horizon could not be downed. They must sail the far seas. In the spring when the blue mountaintops lay goldening in the sun and fair winds set the surf singing, these men would hoist sail and set out down the lane of the fiord for the open unknown that tossed and rocked and gave promise of high adventure. For them there was no recourse; their urge was too strong, and they went. Likewise to-day. Among the hundreds of thousands of Norwegians in America there have been a few who have felt the old urge and have heeded it. They aren't many, but their deeds will live."

Now and then the minister glanced up; the grey eyes studied the faces of his listeners; in his even calmness was a warm glow:

"There is nothing in all history comparable to the deeds of our viking ancestors. Their expeditions, to be sure, show forbidding, gruesome aspects, and plenty of them, but I am convinced that never in all the world's history has man's courage spanned higher and overcome greater odds. If we claim relationship with them, we would do well to remember that fact."

It so happened that Peder was standing directly opposite him. Involuntarily the words leapt from his tongue:

"And what on earth did they accomplish?"

In silence Reverend Kaldahl fingered his chain. Moments passed before he looked up; a suppressed petulance disturbed the evenness of the voice:

"You have been entrusted with a rich inheritance, an inheritance built up through the ages. How much of it, what portion, are you trying to get? Isn't it your irrevocable duty to see how much of it you can preserve and hand down to those coming after you? *A people that has lost its traditions is doomed!*" The pronouncement bore the ring of the prophecy. He didn't wait for Peder to answer, but more calmly began describing the viking expeditions, tracing their journeys into the North Sea and out into the North Atlantic, from one group of islands to the other, from one colony to the next. Finally he came to Iceland, where he dwelt long. He told his small group of listeners of the world's oldest republic which soon could celebrate its one thousandth anniversary. Their own race it was who laid the foundation and who built upon it. They could do that because since time immemorial the spirit of democracy had glowed in the Norsemen's hearts. Rather than pay taxes to self-acclaimed rulers their old ancestors had chosen the pioneer's lot out on those inhospitable isles. The development the minister sketched stirred his own enthusiasm; he grew eager and spoke with power; the dark, bushy eyebrows arched under the tenseness that was upon him:

"We pride ourselves on our accomplishments in this country, and in a way we are justified. But we must not forget that all through the nineteenth century we have followed the crowd; we were not the leaders; it wasn't our people that blazed the trail. Not so in the ninth and tenth centuries. Compare the means of transportation then and now! Nor must we forget that at that time our race numbered less than 400,000 souls; when Cleng Pierson in 1825 set out from Stavanger we were more than a million. But in spite of this small number the Norsemen of old achieved deeds that will be remembered to the end of time. Why? I ask you. How did it come to pass?" The minister's voice was challenging, like that of a man who has been wronged and is demanding redress. "Those deeds were made possible simply because the men who performed them remained true to their traditions and went on building and achieving as their forefathers had done before them. What do we do to-day? We turn up our noses at the inheritance that has come down to us. We cast on the scrap heap the noblest traditions of our race. We set higher value on aping strange manners and customs than in guarding our God-given heritage. So wise have we become and so far-seeing! God's command to the Israelites means nothing to us. We are ashamed of the age-old speech of our forefathers. And we find it embarrassing to admit our Norwegian ancestry. Such an attitude can never, I tell you, *never* build a nation. Like dead timber we go into the building. We may harm, but we cannot be of much help!"

The unmistakable passion in the minister's words struck fire in those of his listeners that understood Norwegian, but with each one differently: Gjermund's lower lip had grown inordinately long; Peder's face was clamped shut and silent; Tambur-Ola's head was cocked, like that of one with an ear for pure tones, listening to a meadow lark singing out in the dusk; Tönseten puffed furiously; he had got up and was tugging at the belt line of his trousers. . . . Preacher or no preacher, by jimminy! I got to get a word in here! . . . Let's see now, which of the Olafs was it that fell in the battle at Svolder? . . . Let's see now? . . . Doheny, who had not the faintest notion of what the long harangue was about, had pulled his chair far into the corner and was dozing peacefully; Charley stayed in the kitchen with the girls. . . . Great sport teasing Nikoline and making her answer in English!

Peder broke the silence:

"We're Americans here!"

All sensed the hot challenge in the tone of his voice, and looked at Reverend Kaldahl.

"Yes, sir, so we are," he agreed, good-naturedly. "Seems to me I've heard that saying before. May I ask you, does the leopard change his spots by coming into new pastures?"

"I agree with Peder," said Gjermund, thoughtfully, before the other could answer. "As Norwegians we'd never get very far in this country."

Reverend Kaldahl bit his lips; the eyebrows crept closer together:

"And I maintain just the opposite. If we're to accomplish anything worth while, anything at all, we must do it as Norwegians. Otherwise we may meet the same fate as corn in too strong a sun. Look at the Jews, for example: Take away the contributions they have made to the world's civilization and you'd have a tremendous gap that time would never be able to fill. Did they make their contribution by selling their birthright and turning into Germans, Russians, and Poles? Or did they achieve greatly because they stubbornly refused to be dejewed? See what they have done in America! Are they as citizens inferior to us? Do they love this country less? Are they trying to establish a nation of their own? Empty nonsense! But they haven't ceased being Jews simply because they live here in America, and because they have adopted this country's language and become its citizens. Do you think their children will become less worthy Americans because they are being fostered in Jewish traits and traditions? Quite the contrary! If they, as individuals or as a group, owe any debt to America, the payment can only be made by their remaining Jews, and the same holds true for all nationalities that have come here. One thing I can see clearly: If this process of levelling down, of making everybody alike by blotting out all racial traits, is allowed to continue, America is doomed to become the most impoverished land spiritually on the face of the earth; out of our highly praised melting-pot will come a dull"—he paused to hunt for words—"a dull, smug complacency, barren of all creative thought and effort. Soon we will have reached the perfect democracy of barrenness. Gone will be the distinguishing traits given us by God; dead will be the hidden life of the heart which is nourished by tradition, the idioms of language, and our attitude to life. It is out of these elements that our character grows. I ask again, what will we have left? We Norwegians have now become so intelligent," he continued, scornfully, "that we let our children decide whether we should preserve our ancient tongue!"

Peder's reply burnt his throat:

"It would be folly to try to build up the different European nations over here. The foundation is new, the whole structure must be new, and so it shall be!"

"In that you're greatly mistaken," declared the minister, coldly. "The foundation is not quite as new as you think. If you dig deep enough and look around a little, you will find some good old timbers, materials that have been brought here from far away. Where did the Puritans come from? Mostly from eastern England. Was that mere accident? Not at all; there, too, cause and effect worked hand in hand. It was in that part of England that the Scandinavians, and not least the Norwegians, exerted their greatest influence. By nature the Puritans were nonconformists; an imposed system of worship was to them unthinkable; just as it was to your own forefathers. Suppose you look at this a little more closely: What did the framers of our Constitution have to work with? First and foremost two priceless documents which supplied the very groundsills for their structure, the *Magna Charta* and the *Bill of Rights*. Where do you suppose the basic principles set forth in these two documents came from? The seeds came from the Scandinavian peninsula, some directly to eastern England, others through Normandy, and still others, perhaps, by way of the Western Isles. There is no getting away from the fact that in no place on earth has the desire for liberty and individualism glowed brighter and more impelling than in the Scandinavian north. Read your people's history and see for yourself. This fable," continued the minister with quiet indignation, "that America more than any other nation is 'the land of the free' is only romantic schoolma'am nonsense." He looked searchingly at Peder. "Come over and see me some time. I have books that might interest you."

"Why don't we find these things in our school-books?" asked Peder, incredulously.

The minister became more sober:

"There are many, many things that don't get into your school-books. I venture to say that your teachers taught you that the Pilgrims came to America seeking religious liberty, or am I wrong?"

"What else could have brought them here?"

"I thought so! But that dogma is only part of the truth. From England the Pilgrims first went to Holland; there they enjoyed all the religious liberties they could ask. But those men were not fools; racial traditions were of vital importance to them. That's what eventually brought them to realize that if they remained in Holland their children would become Hollanders, and what was worse, they would soon lose their mother tongue. Rather than suffer such an irretrievable loss they made ready and sailed for New England."

"Can that be right?" asked Peder, dubiously.

"Right?" shouted Tönseten enthusiastically. "Why, them are the pure facts; I've read it many times myself!"

The minister had pulled out his watch. He glanced at it now and seemed terrified.

'Here I've stood talking away the time. I was to call on old David Johnson, who has been sick abed all through the holidays!" He went about the room shaking hands with all. To Peder he said: "Come over to see me as soon as you can. I'd like to have a talk with you. Bring your family."

Beret, sitting on a chair near the door in the kitchen, had followed the discussion from the beginning; she pressed fold upon fold in her apron; her eyes were wet, her hand toyed with the edge of her apron. An old saying came to her mind and she mumbled it to herself: "Now lettest Thou Thy servant depart in peace!" When the minister was ready to leave she hurried upstairs. Once last fall she had placed a ten-dollar bill in her Bible and there it had since remained; lately she had been using it for a bookmark; bringing the bill down with her now, she stuck it into the minister's hand with a request that he give it to the missions.

DAMIÁN SÁNCHEZ, G.I.

Emilio Díaz Valcárcel

Fifteen minutes after taking off his shirt, private Damián Sánchez had turned darker and drenched with perspiration.

"What a country!" When a man isn't shivering from the cold, he's choking to death from the heat."

The pick gleamed momentarily over his head and came down, stirring up tiny lumps of dry dirt.

The lieutenant walked up and down to inspect his men's work. A lieutenant is always a lieutenant, no matter if he's at the front or if, as now, he trains his men in a "rest area." His reddish face sweated profusely and his shirt was soaked under his armpits.

Damián Sánchez watched him and spoke in Spanish, so that the officer and the group of blond men digging at his side could not understand.

"When a man isn't shivering from cold, he is choking from heat."

The lieutenant wrinkled his brow and walked away. The soldiers watched Damián sullenly over their shoulders.

Trucks shook raspily along the nearby dirt road, leaving dense clouds of dust behind. The big dry leaves on the bushes were weighed down by a thick crust of dirt.

At night it would usually get cold. Then Damián used to take a little box he kept under his cot and, by the shaky light of a candle, he would read and reread his precious letters. Sometimes the other men—those now working at his side— wondered if he was sane. For in the shadows the dark face of the Puerto Rican could be just dimly seen wrinkled in a wide smile, his teeth gleaming in the flickering candlelight. That was the time when he would have been with Diana, over there, at a movie or under a tree, squeezing her and firing up her blood. Once the Americans had heard him call out that name—Diana—and they woke up startled for it was three in the morning and the one who had called out was the damned *Porto Rican* and you had to be on the lookout.

Damián rested the handle of the pick against his thigh and pulled out his canteen. The hot heavy water oozed down his throat; feeling nauseous, he spit in anger. He wiped his forehead with his thumb, bent his head forward, and let the trickle of sweat drop on the removed ground.

"A hundred miles from the Chinese and we dig! I'd like to . . . !"

He felt the stares of the others humming over his temples, and laughed impudently without looking at any of them.

"I'd like to . . . !" he repeated in a louder voice.

Had Kim Wan been there, everything would be different. Poor Kim Wan had served in the 65th Infantry Regiment for two years and had learned Spanish and would joke with the men about wanting to go to *Puertorro* to take the women away from the Puerto Ricans. Everybody in the 65th would laugh at his jokes because a Korean is a human being just like the others and, besides, they had taken a liking to him. Once, on White Horse Hill, Kim Wan had cleaned up a couple of *mongoles*, thus saving the lives of many guys from Borinquen. So good was he, that once he got Damián a cousin of his at a reduced rate. They had gone together along high hard trails that crossed the rice paddies, the native in front, Damián slipping and stumbling on the early November frost.

"Tchon, buena yangar*baw, two* dollar," Kim Wan told him.

And they sneaked into the first little shack of clay and straw. Going in, Damián felt the pleasant warmth that came under the heavy wooden floor. Some very nice young women smiled at him so broadly that their dark little eyes became even more slanted. The rest was easy; the small doll room, the mat on the floor, the body sculptured in fine porcelain, the fever of a lusty man who had been sleeping for six months among soldiers and stinks and curses.

Damián leaned forward and began to take out the earth with his trench shovel. The sun lit a blaze on his naked back. The light tortured his senses, sucked the weak plants dry, dug at the scorched earth of the bomb-torn hills, boiled over the rocks and the ruined military weapons. The few trees existent crawled pitifully and terribly silent toward the sky, their branches like bones and their leaves completely still, like metal. Bees and flies buzzed insanely for the lack of a breeze. Suffocating under the foliage, a kec-cori would pierce the air from time to time with his desolate cry.

Some thirty yards away, Damián saw one of the men turn ashen, crumple slowly and fall on his face. He wanted to run over to him, for even if he was an American he was in need of help, but the hard face of the lieutenant stopped him.

He then gathered new strength and swung the pick furiously at the ground. The earth was softer now and the hole reached his knees already.

Of course, in the 65th he had to work even harder. There every corporal was bucking for a sergeant's stripes and every sergeant wanted to become an officer's right arm by taking advantage of the men of lowest rank, offering them as "volunteers" for any hard or dangerous task. After sunset, however, he used to gather with his countrymen to tell them of his plans, and he spoke for quite some time about his girl Diana, who was as ardent as any *geisha,* and told them that when he went back to *Puertorro* he would buy a little Ford and no woman would then be safe on the highway. He talked a lot and listened a lot to guys from Utuado and Morovis and Mayagüez and Trujillo and San Juan. But the new colonel with the pock-marked nose did not like the color of the Puerto Ricans at all, nor the mustaches of the Puerto Ricans, and least of all the language of the Puerto Ricans. After a while, to make things worse, orders came from above, from very far away from the front, and the regiment was disbanded and the Puerto Ricans distributed— like individual packages—among different combat units. Damián, since then, became mute. Or almost mute. For they transferred good Kim Wan along with him, on the request of the Korean boy himself, and they had both ended in the same infantry company. His everyone was blond and none of them spoke Spanish. At night, scaring the shadows away, the Oriental and the Puerto Rican would mix Asiatic, English and Spanish terms and talk in a low tone.

"You say Puerto Rico, *tagzán yangarbó?*"

"Many, many."

"*Semo semo Kórea?*"

"No. *Más, más* . . . *Tagzán*, more, see? And like the ones you see in the movies."

"¿*Las has visto?*"

"¿*Qué?*"

"The *yangarbó* in movies."

"*Yo ir a Puerto Rico*, okaee?"

Their new tent-mates growled at them. Damián always heard them mutter the same thing: "God-damn bastard, shut up." He already understood the curses and bit his lips, not knowing how to reply. Kim Wan knew some English but preferred to speak Spanish even if he had to suffer the tantrums of the Americans.

Damián Sánchez leaned forward again to dig with his trench shovel. He felt exhausted; the hard work under the beating sun, the frustration of his natural wish to express himself not by sign language, created a deadening confusion in him. If only Kim Wan were with him! Damián reproached himself in silence for what had happened that night. But hadn't he been perfectly right in acting as he did?

With a grimy handkerchief he wiped his forehead, his neck and his armpits. Right in front of him, objects expanded and contracted and spun around.

Damián had drunk at least eight cans of beer on that Saturday night. Kim Wan was sitting at his side on the cot and his own hiccups made him shake from time to time; his slanted eyes watched unseeingly the group of men who, horselaughing and shouting drunkenly, were playing dice. Some of them pushed each other, falling all over the cots, or lay drunk on the floor, or fought over a drink of whiskey. Damián was quiet because it was Saturday night and he could not forget. Diana might be dancing at that very minute, not even remembering him. He bent over and pulled a little box from under his cot. When he straigtened up, Kim Wan saw the tin can in his hand and asked, "Chop chop?"

"*Sí. Pasteles . . . pasteles criollos*, number one. Mamá sends, *mamasan*, see?"

The other nodded jerkily.

"Good?" he asked.

"*Echosoomnidá.*"

The Korean came closer and looked at the can. Damián took an opener out of his pocket and began to tear away the top. Kim Wan could hardly wait to taste the *pasteles*.

The other men had stopped playing games and they now watched the two friends in silence. They stood in a group at the end of the tent with an air of resignation, as if forced to tolerate some nonsense.

"Look at 'em," said one of them at last. "They look like a damn couple of lovers."

Kim Wan knew that a joke was going around and he smiled uneasily. Damián thought he understood. He sensed the eyes nailed on him, and his movements became as heavy as those of a child before an exacting teacher. The Korean, in order to break the silence, asked, "*Buena?*"

Damián tightened his jaw and did not say anything. He took out his mess kit and emptied half of the *pasteles* in it, which he then handed to Kim Wan. The other soldiers came closer, staggering, and looked on with tight lips. One of them moved forward, exclaiming, "Jesus! What the hell is this?"

They laughed raucously even though they didn't seem to want to do so. Damián fixed each one with cold attention, as if he were figuring out the best way to mow them down. He stared at the tin and began to eat without appetite, but firmly. One of them came close to Kim Wan, who did not dare to eat, and, practically putting his finger in the kit, asked, "Tell me, porky, what the hell is this?"

Kim Wan was shaking. He thought he'd make a joke in order to soften up the intruders, and said in halting English, "Don't know . . . It . . . looks like shit . . ."

Damián saw his home and his island and Diana and his people outraged, nothing else. He jumped on the Korean, hitting his face cruelly with the tin can, sobbing crazily. He straightened up and kicked all around and bit arms and in turn was beaten all over. Before he passed out, he managed to shout frenziedly, "*Gringos maricones,* you are the shit!"

It seemed that the sun would never go down; it dehydrated the soldiers to the bone. An airplane passed over noisily—its shadow ran swiftly over the men and climbed the nearby brown hill. An odor of resin filled the valley, pinching nostrils anxious for air.

Damián sat on the edge of the foxhole, which now came up to his belt, and took off one of his boots. A stone had cut his heel.

"I shouldn't have hit him. The poor kid is in the hospital and only God knows whether he'll lose his eye. And me with a court martial probably . . ."

A whistle blew, making him raise his eyes. While he put his boot on, he thought of Diana and his parents and his island. Then he got up, put on his shirt, picked up his tools, thought again about Diana, and moved wearily toward the group of men who had already begun to fall into formation.

THIS COUNTRY WAS
A LOT BETTER OFF
WHEN THE INDIANS
WERE RUNNING IT

Vine Deloria , Jr.

On November 9, 1969, a contingent of American Indians, led by Adam Nordwall, a Chippewa from Minnesota, and Richard Oakes, a Mohawk from New York, landed on Alcatraz Island in San Francisco Bay and claimed the 13-acre rock "by right of discovery." The island had been abandoned six and a half years ago, and although there had been various suggestions concerning its disposal nothing had been done to make use of the land. Since there are Federal treaties giving some tribes the right to abandoned Federal property within a tribe's original territory, the Indians of the Bay area felt that they could lay claim to the island.

For nearly a year the United Bay Area Council of American Indians, a confederation of urban Indian organizations, had been talking about submitting a bid for the island to use it as a West Coast Indian cultural center and vocational training headquarters. Then, on Nov. 1, the San Francisco American Indian Center burned down. The center had served an estimated 30,000 Indians in the immediate area and was the focus of activities of the urban Indian community. It became a matter of urgency after that and, as Adam Nordwall said, "it was GO." Another landing, on Nov. 20, by nearly 100 Indians in a swift midnight raid secured the island.

The new inhabitants have made "the Rock" a focal point symbolic of Indian people. Under extreme difficulty they have worked to begin repairing sanitary facilities and buildings. The population has been largely transient, many people have stopped by, looked the situation over for a few days, then gone home, unwilling to put in the tedious work necessary to make the island support a viable community.

The Alcatraz news stories are somewhat shocking to non-Indians. It is difficult for most Americans to comprehend that there still exists a living community of nearly one million Indians in this country. For many people, Indians have become a species of movie actor periodically dispatched to the Happy Hunting Grounds by John Wayne on the "Late, Late Show." Yet there are some 315 Indian tribal groups in 26 states still functioning as quasi-sovereign nations under treaty status; they range from the mammoth Navajo tribe of some 132,000 with 16 million acres of land to tiny Mission Creek of California with 15 people and a tiny parcel of property. There are over half a million Indians in the cities alone, with the largest concentrations in San Francisco, Los Angeles, Minneapolis and Chicago.

The take-over of Alcatraz is to many Indian people a demonstration of pride in being Indian and a dignified, yet humorous, protest against current conditions existing on the reservations and in the cities. It is this special pride and dignity, the determination to judge life according to one's own values, and the unconquerable conviction that the tribes will not die that has always characterized Indian people as I have known them.

I was born in Martin, a border town on the Pine Ridge Indian Reservation in South Dakota, in the midst of the Depression. My father was an Indian missionary who served 18 chapels on the eastern half of the reservation. In 1934, when I was 1, the Indian Reorganization Act was passed, allowing Indian tribes full rights of self-government for the first time since the late eighteen-sixties. Ever since those days, when the Sioux had agreed to forsake the life of the hunter for that of the farmer, they had been systematically deprived of any voice in decisions affecting their lives and property. Tribal ceremonies and religious practices were forbidden. The reservation was fully controlled by men in Washington, most of whom had never visited a reservation and felt no urge to do so.

The first years on the rsservations were extremely hard for the Sioux. Kept confined behind fences they were almost wholly dependent upon Government rations for their food supply. Many died of hunger and malnutrition. Game was scarce and few were allowed to have weapons for fear of another Indian war. In some years there was practically no food available. Other years rations were withheld until the men agreed to farm the tiny pieces of land each family had been given. In desperation many families were forced to eat stray dogs and cats to keep alive.

By World War I, however, many of the Sioux families had developed prosperous ranches. Then the Government stepped in, sold the Indians' cattle for wartime needs, and after the war leased the grazing land to whites, creating wealthy white ranchers and destitute Indian landlords.

With the passage of the Indian Reorganization Act, native ceremonies and practices were given full recognition by Federal authorities. My earliest memories are of trips along dusty roads to Kyle, a small settlement in the heart of the reservation, to attend the dances. Ancient men, veterans of battles even then considered footnotes to the settlement of the West, brought their costumes out of hiding and walked about the grounds gathering the honors they had earned half a century before. They danced as if the intervening 50 years had been a lost weekend from which they had fully recovered. I remember best Dewey Beard, then in his late 80's and a survivor of the Little Big Horn. Even at that late date Dewey was hesitant to speak of the battle for fear of reprisal. There was no doubt, as one watched the people's expressions, that the Sioux had survived their greatest ordeal and were ready to face whatever the future might bring.

In those days the reservation was isolated and unsettled. Dirt roads held the few mail routes together. One could easily get lost in the wild back country as roads turned into cowpaths without so much as a backward glance. Remote settlements such as Buzzard Basin and Cuny Table were nearly inaccessible. In the spring every bridge on the reservation would be washed out with the first rain and would remain out until late summer. But few people cared. Most of the reservation people, traveling by team and wagon, merely forded the creeks and continued their journey, almost contemptuous of the need for roads and bridges.

The most memorable event of my early childhood was visiting Wounded Knee where 200 Sioux, including women and children, were slaughtered in 1890 by troopers of the Seventh Cavalry in what is believed to have been a delayed act of vengeance for Custer's defeat. The people were simply lined up and shot down much as was allegedly done, according to newspaper reports, at Songmy. The wounded were left to die in a three-day Dakota blizzard, and when the soldiers returned to the scene after the storm some were still alive and were saved. The massacre was vividly etched in the minds of many of the older reservation people, but it was difficult to find anyone who wanted to talk about it.

Many times, over the years, my father would point out survivors of the massacre, and people on the reservation always went out of their way to help them. For a long time there was a bill in Congress to pay indemnities to the survivors, but the War Department always insisted that it had been a "battle" to stamp out the Ghost Dance religion among the Sioux. This does not, however, explain bayoneted Indian women and children found miles from the scene of the incident.

Strangely enough, the Depression was good for Indian reservations, particularly for the people at Pine Ridge. Since their lands had been leased to non-Indians by the Bureau of Indian Affairs, they had only a small rent check and the contempt of those who leased their lands to show for their ownership. But the Federal programs devised to solve the national economic crisis were also made available to Indian people, and there was work available for the first time in the history of the reservations.

The Civilian Conservation Corps set up a camp on the reservation and many Indians were hired under the program. In the canyons north of Allen, S. D., a beautiful buffalo pasture was built by the C.C.C., and the whole area was transformed into a recreation wonderland. Indians would come from miles around to see the buffalo and leave with a strange look in their eyes. Many times I stood silently watching while old men talked to the buffalo about the old days. They would conclude by singing a song before respectfully departing, their eyes filled with tears and their minds occupied with the memories of other times and places. It was difficult to determine who was the captive—the buffalo fenced in or the Indian fenced out.

While the rest of America suffered from the temporary deprivation of its luxuries, Indian people had a period of prosperity, as it were. Paychecks were regular. Small cattle herds were started, cars were purchased, new clothes and necessities became available. To a people who had struggled along on $50 cash income per year, the C.C.C. was the greatest program ever to come along. The Sioux had climbed from absolute deprivation to mere poverty, and this was the best time the reservation ever had.

World War II ended this temporary prosperity. The C.C.C. camps were closed; reservation programs were cut to the bone and social services became virtually nonexistent; "Victory gardens" were suddenly the style, and people began to be aware that a great war was being waged overseas.

The war dispersed the reservation people as nothing ever had. Every day, it seemed, we would be bidding farewell to families as they headed west to work in the defense plants on the Coast.

A great number of Sioux people went west and many of the Sioux on Alcatraz today are their children and relatives. There may now be as many Sioux in California as there are on the reservations in South Dakota because of the great war-time migration.

Those who stayed on the reservation had the war brought directly to their doorstep when they were notified that their sons had to go across the seas and fight. Busloads of Sioux boys left the reservation for parts unknown. In many cases even the trip to nearby Martin was a new experience for them, let alone training in Texas, California or Colorado. There were always going-away ceremonies conducted by the older people who admonished the boys to uphold the old tribal traditions and not to fear death. It was not death they feared but living with an unknown people in a distant place.

I was always disappointed with the Government's way of handling Indian servicemen. Indians were simply lost in the shuffle of 3 million men in uniform. Many boys came home on furlough and feared to return. They were not cowards in any sense of the word but the loneliness and boredom of stateside duty was crushing their spirits. They spent months without seeing another Indian. If the Government had recruited all-Indian outfits it would have easily solved this problem and also had the best fighting units in the world at its disposal. I often wonder what an all-Sioux or Apache company, painted and singing its songs, would have done to the morale of élite German panzer units.

After the war Indian veterans straggled back to the reservations and tried to pick up their lives. It was very difficult for them to resume a life of poverty after having seen the affluent outside world. Some spent a few days with the old folks and then left again for the big cities. Over the years they have emerged as leaders of the urban Indian movement. Many of their children are the nationalists of today who are adamant about keeping the reservations they have visited only on vacations. Other veterans stayed on the reservations and entered tribal politics.

The reservations radically changed after the war. During the Depression there were about five telephones in Martin. If there was a call for you, the man at the hardware store had to come down to your house and get you to answer it. A couple of years after the war a complete dial system was installed that extended to most of the smaller communities on the reservation. Families that had been hundreds of miles from any form of communication were now only minutes away from a telephone.

Roads were built connecting the major communities of the Pine Ridge country. No longer did it take hours to go from one place to another. With these kinds of roads everyone had to have a car. The team and wagon vanished, except for those families who lived at various "camps" in inaccessible canyons pretty much as their ancestors had. (Today, even they have adopted the automobile for traveling long distances in search of work.)

I left the reservation in 1951 when my family moved to Iowa. I went back only once for an extended stay, in the summer of 1955, while on a furlough, and after that I visited only occasionally during summer vacations. In the meantime, I attended college, served a hitch in the Marines, and went to the seminary. After I graduated from the seminary, I took a job with the United Scholarship Service, a private organization devoted to the college and secondary-school education of American Indian and Mexican students. I had spent my last two years of high school in an Eastern preparatory school and so was probably the only Indian my age who knew what an independent Eastern school was like. As the program developed, we soon had some 30 students placed in Eastern schools.

I insisted that all the students who entered the program be able to qualify for scholarships as students and not simply as Indians. I was pretty sure we could beat the white man at his own educational game, which seemed to me the only way to gain his respect. I was soon to find that this was a dangerous attitude to have. The very people who were supporting the program—non-Indians in the national church establishments—accused me of trying to form a colonialist "élite" by insisting that only kids with strong test scores and academic patterns be sent east to school. They wanted to continue the ancient pattern of soft-hearted paternalism toward Indians. I didn't feel we should cry our way into the schools; that sympathy would destroy the students we were trying to help.

In 1964, while attending the annual convention of the National Congress of American Indians, I was elected its executive director. I learned more about life in the N.C.A.I. in three years than I had in the previous 30. Every conceivable problem that could occur in an Indian society was suddenly thrust at me from 315 different directions. I discovered that I was one of the people who were supposed to solve the problems. The only trouble was that Indian people locally and on the national level were being played off one against the other by clever whites who had either ego or income at stake. While there were many feasible solutions, few could be tried without whites with vested interests working night and day to destroy the unity we were seeking on a national basis.

In the mid-nineteen-sixties, the whole generation that had grown up after World War II and had left the reservations during the fifties to get an education was returning to Indian life as "educated Indians." But we soon knew better. Tribal societies had existed for centuries without going outside themselves for education and information. Yet many of us thought that we would be able to improve the traditional tribal methods. We were wrong.

For three years we ran around the conference circuit attending numerous meetings called to "solve" the Indian problems. We listened to and spoke with anthropologists, historians, sociologists, psychologists, economists, educators and missionaries. We worked with many Government agencies and with every conceivable doctrine, idea and program ever created. At the end of this happy round of consultations the reservation people were still plodding along on their own time schedule, doing the things they considered important. They continued to solve their problems their way in spite of the advice given them by "Indian experts."

By 1967 there was a radical change in thinking on the

part of many of us. Conferences were proving unproductive. Where non-Indians had been pushed out to make room for Indian people, they had wormed their way back into power and again controlled the major programs serving Indians. The poverty programs, reservation and university technical assistance groups were dominated by whites who had pushed Indian administrators aside.

Reservation people, meanwhile, were making steady progress in spite of the numerous setbacks suffered by the national Indian community. So, in large part, younger Indian leaders who had been playing the national conference field began working at the local level to build community movements from the ground up. By consolidating local organizations into power groups they felt that they would be in a better position to influence national thinking.

Robert Hunter, director of the Nevada Intertribal Council, had already begun to build a strong state organization of tribes and communities. In South Dakota, Gerald One Feather, Frank LaPointe and Ray Briggs formed the American Indian Leadership Conference, which quickly welded the educated young Sioux in that state into a strong regional organization active in nearly every phase of Sioux life. Gerald is now running for the prestigious post of chairman of the Oglala Sioux, the largest Sioux tribe, numbering some 15,000 members. Ernie Stevens, an Oneida from Wisconsin, and Lee Cook, a Chippewa from Minnesota, developed a strong program for economic and community development in Arizona. Just recently Ernie has moved into the post of director of the California Intertribal Council, a statewide organization representing some 130,000 California Indians in cities and on the scattered reservations of that state.

By the fall of 1967, it was apparent that the national Indian scene was collapsing in favor of strong regional organizations, although the major national organizations such as the National Congress of American Indians and the National Indian Youth Council continued to grow. There was yet another factor emerging on the Indian scene: the old-timers of the Depression days had educated a group of younger Indians in the old ways and these people were now becoming a major force in Indian life. Led by Thomas Banyaca of the Hopi, Mad Bear Anderson of the Tuscaroras, Clifton Hill of the Creeks, and Rolling Thunder of the Shoshones, the traditional Indians were forcing the whole Indian community to rethink its understanding of Indian life.

The message of the traditionalists is simple. They demand a return to basic Indian philosophy, establishment of ancient methods of government by open council instead of elected officials, a revival of Indian religions and replacement of white laws with Indian customs; in short, a complete return to the ways of the old people. In an age dominated by tribalizing communications media, their message makes a great deal of sense.

But in some areas their thinking is opposed to that of the National Congress of American Indians, which represents officially elected tribal governments organized under the Indian Reorganization Act as Federal corporations. The contemporary problem is therefore one of defining the meaning of "tribe." Is it a traditionally organized band of Indians following customs with medicine men and chiefs dominating the policies of the tribe, or is it a modern corporate structure attempting to compromise at least in part with modern white culture?

The problem has been complicated by private foundations' and Government agencies' funding of Indian programs. In general this process, although it has brought a great amount of money into Indian country, has been one of cooptation. Government agencies must justify their appropriation requests every year and can only take chances on spectacular programs that will serve as showcases of progress. They are not willing to invest the capital funds necessary to build viable self-supporting communities on the reservations because these programs do not have an immediate publicity potential. Thus, the Government agencies are forever committed to conducting conferences to discover that one "key" to Indian life that will give them the edge over their rival agencies in the annual appropriations derby.

Churches and foundations have merely purchased an Indian leader or program that conforms with their ideas of what Indian people should be doing. The large foundations have bought up the well-dressed, handsome "new image" Indian who is comfortable in the big cities but virtually helpless at an Indian meeting. Churches have given money to Indians who have been willing to copy black militant activist tactics, and the more violent and insulting the Indian can be, the more the churches seem to love it. They are wallowing in self-guilt and piety over the lot of the poor, yet funding demagogues of their own choosing to speak for the poor.

I did not run for re-election as executive director of the N.C.A.L. in the fall of 1967, but entered law school at the University of Colorado instead. It was apparent to me that the Indian revolution was well under way and that someone had better get a legal education so that we could have our own legal program for defense of Indian treaty rights. Thanks to a Ford Foundation program, nearly 50 Indians are now in law school, assuring the Indian community of legal talent in the years ahead. Within four years I foresee another radical shift in Indian leadership patterns as the growing local movements are affected by the new Indian lawyers.

There is an increasing scent of victory in the air in Indian country these days. The mood is comparable to the old days of the Depression when the men began to dance once again. As the Indian movement gathers momentum and individual Indians cast their lot with the tribe, it will become apparent that not only will Indians survive the electronic world of Marshall McLuhan, they will thrive in it. At the present time everyone is watching how mainstream America will handle the issues of pollution, poverty, crime and racism when it does not fundamentally understand the issues. Knowing the importance of tribal survival, Indian people are speaking more and more of sovereignty, of the great political technique of the open council, and of the need for gaining the community's consensus on all programs before putting them into effect.

One can watch this same issue emerge in white society as the "Woodstock Nation," the "Blackstone Nation" and the block organizations are developed. This is a full tribalizing process involving a nontribal people, and it is apparent that some people are frightened by it. But it is the kind of social phenomenon upon which Indians feast.

In 1965 I had a long conversation with an old Papago. I was trying to get the tribe to pay its dues to the National Congress of American Indians and I had asked him to speak to the tribal council for me. He said that he would but that the Papagos didn't really need the N.C.A.I. They were like, he told me, the old mountain in the distance. The Spanish had come and dominated them for 300 years and then left. The Mexicans had come and ruled them for a century, but they also left. "The Americans," he said, "have been here only about 80 years. They, too, will vanish, but the Papagos and the mountain will always be here."

This attitude and understanding of life is what American society is searching for.

I wish the Government would give Alcatraz to the Indians now occupying it. They want to create five centers on the island. One center would be for a North American studies program; another would be a spiritual and medical center where Indian religions and medicines would be used and studied. A third center would concentrate on ecological studies based on an Indian view of nature—that man should live *with* the land and not simply *on* it. A job-training center and a museum would also be founded on the island. Certain of these programs would obviously require Federal assistance.

Some people may object to this approach, yet Health, Education and Welfare gave out $10-million last year to non-Indians to study Indians. Not one single dollar went to an Indian scholar or researcher to present the point of view of Indian people. And the studies done by non-Indians added nothing to what was already known about Indians.

Indian people have managed to maintain a viable and cohesive social order in spite of everything the non-Indian society has thrown at them in an effort to break the tribal structure. At the same time, non-Indian society has created a monstrosity of a culture where people starve while the granaries are filled and the sun can never break through the smog.

By making Alcatraz an experimental Indian center operated and planned by Indian people, we would be given a chance to see what we could do toward developing answers to modern social problems. Ancient tribalism can be incorporated with modern technology in an urban setting. Perhaps we would not succeed in the effort, but the Government is spending billions every year and still the situation is rapidly growing worse. It just seems to a lot of Indians that this continent was a lot better off when we were running it.

THE TENTH PRESIDENTIAL
PAPER—MINORITIES

Norman Mailer

The modern American politician—read: the Democratic or Republican liberal—often begins his career with a modest passion to defend the rights of minorities. By the time he is successful, his passion has been converted to platitude.

Minority groups are the artistic nerves of a republic, and like any phenomenon which has to do with art, they are profoundly divided. They are both themselves and the mirror of their culture as it reacts upon them. They are themselves and the negative truth of themselves. No white man, for example, can hate the Negro race with the same passionate hatred and detailed detestation that each Negro feels for himself and for his people; no anti-Semite can begin to comprehend the malicious analysis of his soul which every Jew indulges every day.

For decades the Jews have been militant for their rights, since the Second War the Negroes have emerged as an embattled and disciplined minority. It is thus characteristic of both races that they have a more intense awareness of their own value and their own lack of value than the awareness of the white Anglo-Saxon Protestant for himself. Unlike the Protestant of the center, minorities have a nature which is polarized. So it is natural that their buried themes, precisely those preoccupations which are never mentioned by minority action groups like the Anti-Defamation League or the NAACP, are charged with paradox, with a search for psychic extremes. To a Protestant, secure in the middle of American life, God and the Devil, magic, death and eternity, are matters outside himself. He may contemplate them but he does not habitually absorb them into the living tissue of his brain. Whereas the exceptional member of any minority group feels as if he possesses God and the Devil within himself, that the taste of his own death is already in his cells, that his purchase on eternity rises and falls with the calm or cowardice of his actions. It is a life exposed to the raw living nerve of anxiety, and rare is the average Jew or Negro who can bear it for long— so the larger tendency among minorities is to manufacture a mediocre personality which is a dull replica of the manners of the white man in power. Nothing can be more conformist, more Square, more profoundly depressing than the Jew-in-the-suburb, or the Negro as member of the Black Bourgeoisie. It is the price they pay for the fact that not all self-hatred is invalid—the critical faculty turned upon oneself can serve to create a personality which is exceptional, which mirrors the particular arts and graces of the white gentry, but this is possible only if one can live with one's existential nerve exposed. Man's personality rises to a level of higher and more delicate habits only if he is willing to engage a sequence of painful victories and cruel defeats in his expedition through the locks and ambushes of social life. One does not copy the manner of someone superior; rather one works an art upon it which makes it suitable for oneself. Direct imitation of a superior manner merely produces a synthetic manner. The collective expression of this in a minority group is nothing other than assimilation.

To the degree each American Jew and American Negro is assimilated he is colorless, a part of a collective nausea which is encysted into the future.

PROMISES

Oscar Handlin

When a boy had come, the friends had said, "Now you have a son and a successor."

But the son was no successor.

It might have been once on a cool evening that mercifully broke the summer's torpid grip, when they both leaned back suddenly refreshed in the chairs still sticky with the day's heat, it might have been then that the father thought, "Well, if only it were not so; if only he could walk a part of my way, enough to be sensitive to what emotions stir me, then I could tell him what this journey was, and in the communication that would make it ever of his heritage, I too could find the meaning of these turnings in my life."

The old man never tried. In the young American face was no hint of recognition. Fear of the bland, uncomprehending answer stilled the laboriously marshaled phrases that might have told the story. Silence filled the room as the moment passed. Only later, in some other connection, the inarticulate parent would complain, "We talk never seriously together." And he would thereafter pause often to rehearse the questions in the vain hope that the opportunity might return. Time and again, while the shovel grew loose in his hands, while the treadle rocked away beneath his heedless foot, while the load rested unfelt upon his shoulders, in his mind there was ever that asking.

What Was the Question, Never Asked?

"For I was once a man, established; and had a place; and knew my worth, and was known for it. What of the hardships, if my situation then had a meaning in the wholeness of the community to which I belonged. But I was thrust away and carried cruelly to a distant land, and set to labor, unrewarding labor, for even the glittering prizes the few attained had little value in my eyes and came at a great price. Yes, I was plunged into an altogether foreign scene that yielded never to my understanding. Indeed, I made the effort, wished to be myself; but could not. Into all that was familiar, the New World introduced mutations; I built a church, then saw others fill it with strangeness; I drew close to my friend, then found our association develop toward an unexpected end. Power was cast into my hands which only slowly I learned to use, and never certainly.

"Indeed, in all that happened I was alone, although I did not wish to be. If I turned to those of my family I found them each confined to his own lonely round of concerns. I was separate while other men belonged. When there are none like me left, I shall be forgotten; there will be no successor to go on as I have gone. Such is the extent of my isolation. Were not then all my flutterings random, tricks of a meaningless circumstance?"

What Does the Question Mean?

"I was pushed violently out from the nest of my birth. In the shattering fall and ever thereafter I longed to be back; my heart yearned for the security, for the familiar order of the warm feathery place. As I struggled in the effort to spread my wings and labored in the learning to bear my weight, as I ventured to the far places and saw what never was seen before, I did not cease to dream of home. I did not cease to regret the lost safety that had been before—before the harsh winds of distance had bruised my body, before the impenetrable newness had shut light away from my eyes, before the vast aloneness had closed down around my spirit.

"Though a rest may come, end all these struggles, what shall I have gained thereby?"

The question never set to words never gains an answer. Locked in his own preoccupations, the unlistening son will not reply.

He might have. There was an answer, had he but known

how to speak it. In the meaning of his father's life was a meaning of America.

The Answer.

"No, you may long for it, but you will not take the steps to lead you back; the nest abandoned will never see its brood again.

"And what is this security of which you dream? Its warmth is that of many bodies crowded into a small place; its order is that of the rigid constriction that leaves no room for action; its safety is that of the binding fetter. The security of the nest is a huddled restraint.

"No, the blow that tossed you out, that forever snapped the ancient ties, that blow was an act of liberation. You had not much latitude in your choice of a destination; you knew only you would come to America. But America was not the British colonies or Brazil or Argentina where the governments lavishly held forth inducements to attract you. America was this country which was most hostile to your old way of life. Was it not that separation was also a release? Were you not tempted by a break as complete as possible?

"You long of course for the safety, you cherish still the ideals of the nest. But danger and insecurity are other words for freedom and opportunity. You are alone in a society without order; you miss the support of a community, the assurance of a defined rank. But you are also quit of traditional obligations, of the confinement of a given station. This is no less a liberation because you arrived at it not through joyful striving but through a cataclysmic plunge into the unknown, because it was not welcomed but thrust upon you.

"No longer part within some whole, you mourn the loss beyond all power of repair and, blinded, fail to see the greater gain. You may no longer now recede into the warm obscurity where like and like and like conceal the one's identity. And yet, exposed, alone, the man in you has come to life. With every hostile shock you bore, with every frantic move you made, with every lonely sacrifice, you wakened to the sense of what, long hidden in that ancient whole, you never knew you lacked. Indeed the bitter train of your misfortunes has, in unexpected measure, brought awareness of the oneness that is you; and though the separation pains now will not let you know it, the coming forth endowed you with the human birthright of your individuality."

The Meaning of the Answer.

The life of the immigrant was that of a man diverted by unexpected pressures away from the established channels of his existence. Separated, he was never capable of acting with the assurance of habit; always in motion, he could never rely upon roots to hold him up. Instead he had ever to toil painfully from crisis to crisis, as an individual alone, make his way past the discontinuous obstacles of a strange world.

But America was the land of separated men. Its development in the eighteenth century and the Revolution had set it apart from Europe; expansion kept it in a state of unsettlement. A society already fluid, the immigrants made more fluid still; an economy already growing, they stimulated to yet more rapid growth; into a culture never uniform they introduced a multitude of diversities. The newcomers were on the way toward being Americans almost before they stepped off the boat, because their own experience of displacement had already introduced them to what was essential in the situation of Americans.

A Larger Meaning, and Some Promises.

This answer never was delivered. Perhaps it could not have been while the son was too engrossed in his own distinctiveness to recognize the paternity of his father.

Retrospectively now, with the movement ended, the son may begin to make out its meaning. A time came for many men when the slow glacial shift of economic and social forces suddenly broke loose in some major upheaval that cast loose the human beings from their age-old setting. In an extreme form this was the experience of the immigrants. It was also in some degree the experience of all modern men.

They did not welcome the liberation, almost any of them. Its immediate form was always separation. Its common incidents were the painful transitions from the tried old to the untried new. To earn their bread in novel fashion, to adjust their views of the universe to a new world's sights, to learn to live with each other in unaccustomed surroundings, to discover the uses of power, and to uncover beneath the inherited family patterns intimate personal relationships, these were the adventures all people in motion shared with the immigrants.

To the son now looking back it seems the movement comes untimely to a close. The ideals of the nest, remembered even at the height of flight, have triumphed. Men weary of a century and more of struggle, impatient of the constant newness, more eagerly than ever hunger for the security of belonging. Restriction becomes a part of their lives—and perhaps it must be so.

Yet looking at the old man's bent head in the chair, who came so far at such cost, the son knows at once he must not lose sight of the meaning of that immigrant journey. We are come to rest and push our roots more deeply by the year. But we cannot push away the heritage of having been once all strangers in the land; we cannot forget the experience of having been all rootless, adrift. Building our own nests now in our tiredness of the transient, we will not deny our past as a people in motion and will find still a place in our lives for the values of flight.

That also must be so. In our flight, unattached, we discovered what it was to be an individual, a man apart from place and station. In our flight, through the newness, we discovered the unexpected, invigorating effects of recurrent demands upon the imagination, upon all our human capacities. We will not have our nest become again a moldy prison holding us in with its tangled web of comfortable habits. It may be for us rather a platform from which to launch new ascensions that will extend the discoveries of the immigrants whose painful break with their past is our past. We will justify their pitiable struggle for dignity and meaning by extending it in our lives toward an end they had not the opportunity to envision.

BIOGRAPHICAL NOTES

LOUIS ADAMIC

was born in Blato, Yugoslavia, in 1899. He emigrated to the United States in 1913 and worked as a foreign-language newspaper man before he settled down as a writer of stories and a translator of Slovenian, Croatian, and Serbian stories. His works include *Laughing in the Jungle* (1932), *The Native's Return* (1934), *My America* (1938), and *From Many Lands* (1940).

MARY ANTIN

was born in Poland in 1882 and grew up under the shadow of the Czar Alexander III. Toward the end of the nineteenth century she migrated to America with her father and settled in Chelsea, Massachusetts. Her story, as told in *The Promised Land,* (1912), is a minor classic of Jewish immigration and reveals the many difficulties she and her family confronted as they sought to Americanize themselves.

JAMES BALDWIN

was born in New York City in 1924. He became a minister in the church at the age of fourteen, but he was already intent on a career as a writer. He won a Eugene F. Saxton Memorial Trust Award for an early draft of *Go Tell It On The Mountain,* and in 1953 he published the novel. From 1948–1958 he lived in Paris and wrote some of his most important essays: *Notes of a Native Son* (1956) and *Nobody Knows My Name* (1961) are products of those years. In 1956 he published his second novel, *Giovanni's Room;* in 1962, *Another Country;* in 1963, the long essay *The Fire Next Time;* in 1964, the sociological drama, *Blues for Mr. Charlie;* and in 1968, *Tell Me How Long The Train's Been Gone.*

CHIEF STANDING BEAR

was a Lakota Indian whose autobiography, *The Land of the Spotted Eagle*, was published in 1933.

KAY BENNETT

was a Navajo Indian whose *Kaibah: Recollection of a Navajo Girlhood* (1964) is an accurate reflection of life on a reservation from 1928–1935.

GERTRUDE BONNIN

whose Indian name was Zitkala-Sa, was a Dakota Sioux. Her two most important books are *Old Indian Legends* (1901), a children's book, and *American Indian Stories* (1921), a collection of writings on Indian life at the turn of the twentieth century.

VANCE BOURJAILY

was born in Cleveland in 1922. He graduated from Bowdoin College and went on to become a newspaperman, T.V. dramatist, playwright and professor. Some of his books are *The End of My Life* (1947), *The Violated* (1958), and *Confessions of a Misspent Youth* (1960).

GWENDOLYN BROOKS

was born in Topeka, Kansas, in 1917, and was raised in Chicago where she still lives. After publishing in the literary quarterlies, she achieved fame with *A Street in Bronzeville* (1945). This volume was followed by *Annie Allen* (1949), which won the Pulitzer Prize in 1950, *The Bean Eaters* (1960), and *Selected Poems* (1963). She has also written a poetic novel, *Maud Martha* (1953), and a children's book, *Bronzeville Boys and Girls* (1956).

CLAUDE BROWN

was born in New York in 1937. He wrote plays that were performed by the American Afro-Negro Theater Guild in 1960–61 and then attended Howard University from 1961–65. He received national attention with the publication of his autobiography, *Manchild in the Promised Land* (1965).

CARLOS BULOSAN

was born in Mangusmana in the Philippines in 1914 and came to California in 1931. After working as a fruitpicker, he began to write actively. His poetry may be found in *Letter from America* (1942) and *The Voice of Bataan* (1943); his stories appear in *The Laughter of My Father* (1944). The excerpt included in this volume is from Bulosan's autobiography, *America is in the Heart* (1946). *Sound of Falling Light: Letters in Exile* (1960) was published after Bulosan's death in 1946.

JOHN CIARDI

was born in 1916. He studied at Bates College, Tufts College, and The University of Michigan. Some of his best-known books of poetry are *Homeward to America* (1940); *As If, Poems New and Selected* (1955); *In the Stoneworks* (1961); *In Fact* (1962); and *Person to Person* (1964). He has also served as poetry editor for *Saturday Review*.

ELDRIDGE CLEAVER

was born in Little Rock, Arkansas, in 1935. He grew up in the black ghetto of Los Angeles and spent time at San Quentin, Folsom, and Soledad prisons for reasons ranging from rape to theft. He has been the Minister of Information for the Black Panther Party and its nominee for President of the United States in 1968. His books include *Soul on Ice* (1968) and *Post-prison Writing and Speeches* (1969), edited by Robert Scheer.

ARTHUR A. COHEN

was born in New York in 1928. He received his B. A. and M. A. from the University of Chicago in 1946 and 1949. Cohen began his career in publishing and later wrote many books, among them *Martin Buber* (1958) and *Religion and the Free Society* (1958).

GREGORY CORSO

was born in New York in 1930. He has taught at Buffalo University. His books of poems include *The Vestal Lady in Brattle* (1955); *Gasoline* (1958); *Bomb* (1958); *Marriage* (1959), which won the Longview Foundation Award; *The Happy Birthday of Death* (1960), *Long Live Man* (1962), and *Selected Poems* (1962).

VICTOR HERNANDEZ CRUZ

is a young Spanish-American whose poetry, included in *Snaps* (1969), reflects his life in the barrio of New York City.

COUNTEE CULLEN

was born in New York in 1903. He attended Dewitt Clinton High School, New York University, and Harvard University, where he received his M. A. degree. From 1929 until his death in 1946, Cullen taught in the New York City Public Schools. His first collection of poetry, *Color* (1925), was published the same year that he graduated from New York University. His other books include *Copper Sun* (1927); *The Ballad of the Brown Girl* (1927); *The Medea and Other Poems* (1935); *The Lost Zoo* (1940), a children's book; *My Nine Lives and How I Lost Them* (1942); *One Way to Heaven* (1932), a novel; *St. Louis Woman*, a musical play. His most impressive verse is included in *On These I Stand* (1947).

VINE DELORIA, JR.

an American Indian, wrote *Custer Died for Your Sins: An Indian Manifesto* (1969).

PIETRO DI DONATO

was born in West Hoboken, New Jersey, in 1911. His father was killed in the collapse of a building when di Donato was twelve, and his mother died a few years later. He supported his family of eight by taking up his father's work of bricklaying. At the same time he attended night classes. In 1937 he published "Christ in Concrete" in *Esquire* and two years later a novel of the same name. His other books include *The Woman* (1958) and *Three Circles of Light* (1960).

CHARLES EASTMAN

whose Indian name was Ohiyesa, was a Sioux who fled to Canada because of Sitting Bull's victory at the Little Big Horn. He converted to Christianity and received his B. A. from Dartmouth and his M. D. from Boston University. His works include *Indian Boyhood* (1902), *The Soul of the Indian* (1911), and *From the Deep Woods to Civilization* (1916).

RALPH ELLISON

was born in Oklahoma City, Oklahoma in 1914. From 1933 to 1936 he attended Tuskegee Institute and soon became interested in music and sculpture. In New York, where he went to study, he met Richard Wright and began publishing essays and stories in various journals. In 1952 he published *Invisible Man*, which won the National Book Award for Fiction and was considered, by a *Book Week* poll of critics in 1965, "the most distinguished single work" published in America since 1945.

MARI EVANS

was born in Toledo, Ohio and attended the University of Toledo. In addition to her poetry, which has appeared in numerous journals, Miss Evans has been a producer and director of "The Black Experience," a weekly broadcast on WTTV-Channel 4 in Indianapolis.

JOHN FANTE

was born in Denver, Colorado in 1909. He studied at the University of Colorado and Regis College in Denver. Some of his works are *Wait Until Spring Bondini* (1938), *Ask the Dust* (1939), *Full of Life* (1952), and a collection of stories, *Dago Red* (1940). He has also written numerous screen plays.

JAMES T. FARRELL

was born in Chicago in 1904 and educated at the University of Chicago. His most famous works are *Young Lonigan—A Boy in Chicago Streets* (1932), *The Young Manhood of Studs Lonigan* (1934), and *Collected Short Stories of James T. Farrell* (1937). He has written numerous stories for magazines.

LESLIE FIEDLER

was born in Newark, New Jersey, in 1917. He received his B. A. from N. Y. U. in 1938, his M. A. and Ph. D. from the University of Wisconsin in 1939 and 1941. He has taught at the University of Montana (1941–1964) and the State University of New York at Buffalo (1965–   ). His major publications include *An End to Innocence* (1955), *Love and Death in the American Novel* (1960), and *No! In Thunder* (1960), works of literary criticism; *The Second Stone* (1963), a novel; and *Pull Down Vanity* (1962), a collection of stories.

E. FRANKLIN FRAZIER

was a well-known sociologist who spent most of his career as a professor at Howard University. His many volumes include *The Negro Family in the United States* (1939). *Black Bourgeoisie* (1957), *The Negro in the United States*, and *The Negro Church in America* (1964).

ALLEN GINSBERG

was born in Newark, New Jersey, in 1926. He received his B. A. from Columbia University in 1948. His volumes of poetry include *Howl and Other Poems* (1955), *Empty Mirror* (1960), *Kaddish and Other Poems* (1960), and *Reality Sandwiches* (1963).

NATHAN GLAZER

was born in New York in 1923. He received his B. S. S. at the City College of New York in 1944, his M. A. from the University of Pennsylvania in 1944, and his Ph. D. from Columbia University in 1962. He has written extensively on racial and ethnic subjects. His most important books include *The Lonely Crowd* (1950), which he wrote with David Reisman; *Faces in the Crowd* (1952), again with David Reisman; *American Judaism* (1957); *The Social Basis of American Communism* (1961); *Beyond the Melting Pot* (1963), with Daniel P. Moynihan, a book which won the Anisfield-Wolf Award from the *Saturday Review*.

ARTURO GIOVANNITTI

was born in Ripabottoni, Southern Italy, in 1884. He came to the United States in 1900 and worked in the Pennsylvania coal mines.

He joined the Socialist party and for a time edited an Italian radical paper, *Il Proletario*. His one book of poems is *Arrows in the Gale* (1914).

JOSUE A. GONZALEZ

is a young Mexican-American writer whose poetry has appeared in *El Grito* magazine.

JOHN HAGOPIAN

is a Professor of English, Harpur College, State University of New York. He has published numerous essays in scholarly journals.

OSCAR HANDLIN

was born in Brooklyn, New York, in 1915. He received his B. A. from Brooklyn College in 1934, his M. A. and Ph. D. from Harvard University in 1935 and 1940. He taught for most of his career at Harvard University and has written voluminously on ethnic culture in America. His most famous works are *Boston's Immigrants* (1941), *This Was America* (1949), *The Uprooted* (1951), *Adventure in Freedom* (1954), *Race and Nationality in American Life* (1956), and *Immigration as a Factor in American History* (1959).

LANGSTON HUGHES

was born in Joplin, Missouri, in 1902. After graduating from Cleveland's Central High School in 1920, he studied for a short time at Columbia College and began publishing in a variety of journals. During the next forty-seven years he wrote in every genre. His poetry includes *The Weary Blues* (1926), *Fine Clothes to the Jew* (1927), *Shakespeare in Harlem* (1942), and *Selected Poems of Langston Hughes* (1959); interesting novels are *Not Without Laughter* (1930) and *Tambourines to Glory* (1957); his autobiographies are *The Big Sea* (1940) and *I Wonder as I Wander;* his plays can be found in *Five Plays by Langston Hughes* (1963); some of his short stories have been included in *The Ways of White Folk* (1934) and *Something in Common and Other Stories* (1963); and an example of his satire is *The Best of Simple* (1961). A good sampling of Langston Hughes' diverse work may be found in *The Langston Hughes Reader* (1958).

DAVID HENDERSON

is a young black poet whose work reflects the actualities of New York City street life. A book of his poetry, *Felix of the Silent Forest*, was published in 1967. A new volume will appear shortly.

LEROI JONES

was born in Newark, New Jersey, in 1934 and educated at Rutgers and Howard Universities. After serving in the Strategic Air Command, he taught and wrote poetry at The New School for Social Research. His first professionally produced play, *The Dutchman* (1964), won the Off-Broadway Obie Award; it was followed by *The Slave* and *The Toilet*. His social essays appear in *Home* (1966); his commentaries on jazz music are reflected in *Blues People: Negro Music in White America* (1963) and in *Black Music* (1967). He has also published a semiautobiographical novel, *The System of Dante's Hell* (1965) and a collection of sixteen stories, *Tales* (1967). His poetry is included in *Preface to a Twenty Volume Suicide Note* (1961), *The Dead Lecturer* (1964), and *Black Art* (1966).

ALFRED KAZIN

was born in Brooklyn in 1915. He studied at The City College of New York and Columbia University, where he received his M. A. in 1938. He was literary editor of *The New Republic* (1942–43) and then contributing editor. He has lectured at many colleges and is presently Distinguished Professor of English, State University of New York at Stony Brook. His books include two critical works— *On Native Grounds* (1942) and *Contemporaries* (1962)—and two memoirs, *A Walker in the City* (1951) and *Starting Out in the Thirties* (1965).

WILLIAM MELVIN KELLEY

was born in New York in 1937. A recipient of a Rosenthal Foundation Award in 1963, Kelley has published three novels—*A Different Drummer* (1962), *A Drop of Patience* (1965), *dem* (1967)—and a collection of stories, *Dancers on the Shore* (1964).

JOHN F. KENNEDY

was born in Boston in 1917, the child of a family that had originally migrated to America in the 1840's. After attending Choate, he studied at Princeton and Harvard Universities. His honors thesis at Harvard, *Why England Slept*, was published as a book in 1940. He served in the Navy during the war and upon his return to the United States, he entered politics. In 1946 he became a Boston Congressman; in 1952, a Massachusetts Senator; in 1960, President of the United States. He was assassinated on November 21, 1963. His most important book is *Profiles in Courage* (1954).

EMMA LAZARUS

was born in New York in 1849, the daughter of a wealthy sugar merchant. In her early years she fell under the influence of Emerson, who thought highly of her *Poems and Translations;* she dedicated her second book of poetry, *Admetus and Other Poems* (1871) to Emerson. She became deeply conscious of her Jewish heritage in the 1880's when she was angered by the sight of poverty-stricken

Jews who had come to Wards Island because of Russian persecution: "The New Colossus" is one of many poems that Emma Lazarus wrote in response to the East-European immigration of Jews in the late nineteenth century. It is particularly a part of the American imagination because of its inscription on the pedestal of the Statue of Liberty. Emma Lazarus' finest verse is collected in *The Songs of a Semite*. She died on November 19, 1887, at the age of thirty-eight.

CHIN LEE

was born in Hunan, China, in 1917. He received his B. A. and his M. F. A. from Yale University. An editor of *Young China* from 1954–1955, Lee went on to write *Flower Drum Song* (1957), which was made into a Broadway musical in 1958 by Richard Rodgers and Oscar Hammerstein. He has also written *The Sawba and His Secretary* (1959), *Madam Goldenflower* (1960), *Cripple Mah and the New Society* (1961), and *Virgin Market* (1964).

DON L. LEE

was born in 1942. He has taught at Roosevelt University. His three books of poetry, published by The Broadside Press, are *Black Pride* (1968), *Think Black* (1968), and *Don't Cry! Scream!* (1969).

MAX LERNER

was born in Minsk, Russia, in 1902, and was brought to the United States in 1907. He received his B. A. at Yale in 1923, his M. A. at Washington University in 1925, and his Ph. D. at the Robert Brookings Graduate School of Economics and Government in 1927. He has taught at Brandeis and other universities and has written newspaper columns for the *PM* and *The New York Post*. His many books include *Ideas are Weapons* (1939), and *America as a Civilization* (1957).

OSCAR LEWIS

was born in New York in 1914. He studied at the City College of New York and Columbia University, where he received his Ph. D. in 1940. His many works of anthropology include *Five Families: Mexican Case Studies in the Culture of Poverty; Children of Sanchez,* and *La Vida; A Puerto Rican Family in the Culture of Poverty: San Juan and New York. La Vida* won the National Book Award for nonfiction and the Anisfield-Wolf Award in 1966.

JOHN LOGAN

is an Irish-American poet whose collection of poems, *Ghosts of the Heart,* appeared in 1960.

NORMAN MAILER

was born in Long Branch, New Jersey in 1923. He grew up in Brooklyn and attended Harvard University, graduating in 1944. He served as a rifleman in Leyte, Luzon, and Japan during World War II and used his experiences as the basis for his best-selling novel, *The Naked and the Dead* (1948). Since then he has published widely. His novels include *Barbary Shore* (1951), *The Deer Park* (1955), *An American Dream* (1965), and *Why Are We In Vietnam* (1967). He has written drama—*The Deer Park* (1967)—and poetry, *Death to the Ladies* (1962); but his most important work of the past decade has been in the form of creative journalism: *Advertisements for Myself* (1959), *The Presidential Papers* (1963), *Cannibals and Christians* (1966), *The Armies of the Night* (1968), and *Miami and the Siege of Chicago* (1968).

BERNARD MALAMUD

was born in Brooklyn in 1914. He received his B. A. from The City College of New York in 1936 and his M. A. from Columbia in 1942. He has taught at Oregon State University and Bennington College. He has published four novels: *The Natural* (1952), *The Assistant* (1957), *A New Life* (1961), and *The Fixer* (1967), for which he won the National Book Award and the Pulitzer Prize. His collections of short stories are *The Magic Barrel* (1958), which won the National Book Award, and *Idiots First* (1963).

JULIAN MAYFIELD

was born in Greer, South Carolina, in 1928. He has had a varied career as a radio announcer, teacher, newspaperman, house painter, and shipping clerk as well as a governmental worker in Ghana. He has written novels (*The Hit*, 1957; *The Long Night*, 1958; and *The Grand Parade*, 1961), plays, and movie scripts. His editorials and political essays have appeared in *Puerto Rico World Journal, African Review, Commentary, The New Republic,* and *The Nation.*

N. SCOTT MOMADAY

received his Ph. D. at Stanford University and teaches at the University of California at Santa Barbara. He has published scholarly articles and stories in various journals and has edited *The Complete Poems of Frederick Goddard Tuckerman.* His books include *The Owl in the Cedar Tree* (1965) and *House Made Dawn* (1968).

TOSHIO MORI

was born in California, the child of Japanese immigrants. *Yokohama, California* (1949), his collection of stories, deals with the problems of the Nisei in California.

DANIEL P. MOYNIHAN

was born in Tulsa in 1927. He graduated from Tufts University in 1948 and received his M. A. and Ph. D. degrees from Fletcher School of Law and Diplomacy in 1949 and 1961. He has served as the director of the Joint Center of Urban Studies at M. I. T. and Harvard as well as Professor of Education and Urban Politics at the Kennedy School of Government at Harvard. He is the co-author of *Beyond the Melting Pot* (1960).

HOWARD NEMEROV

was born in New York in 1920. He graduated from Harvard in 1941 and went on to teach at Bennington and Brandeis universities. He has written novels, *The Melodramatists* (1949) and *The Homecoming Game* (1959); plays; and short stories, *A Commodity of Dreams* (1959). His best-known work has been in the genre of poetry —*Image and the Law* (1947), *Guide to the Ruins* (1950), and *Mirrors and Windows* (1958). His finest poetry appears in *New and Selected Poems* (1960).

FRANK O'HARA

was born in Baltimore in 1926 and educated at Harvard University (B.A., 1950) and the University of Michigan (M.A., 1951). His books of poems include *A City and Other Poems* (1952), *Second Avenue* (1960), *Odes* (1960), and *Lunch Poems* (1964). He has also written a number of one-act plays and a monograph on the artist, Jackson Pollock.

ORLANDO ORTIZ

was born in New York in 1946. After growing up in Spanish Harlem, Ortiz held various jobs, among them News Editor and Coordinator for the Student Communications Network. His poetry has appeared in *El Grito: A Journal of Contemporary Mexican-American Thought*.

ELENA PADILLA

is an anthropologist whose book, *Up From Puerto Rico*, "provides a detailed description of the ways of life and changing culture of Puerto Ricans in a New York slum."

JO PAGANO

lives in California. His most important book, *The Paesanos*, is a collection of stories about Italian-American life.

GEORGE PANETTA

was born in New York City in 1911. He worked for WPA and in advertising. His collection of short stories is *Ride a White Donkey* (1944).

HARRY MARK PETRAKIS

was born in St. Louis in 1923. He studied at the University of Illinois from 1940–1941 and has taught creative writing. His books include *Lion at my Heart* (1959) and *The Odyssey of Kostis Volakis* (1963); *Pericles on 31st Street* (1965), which was nominated for the National Book Award; *The Founder's Touch* (1965), and *A Dream of Kings* (1966).

NORMAN PODHORETZ

was born in Brooklyn in 1930 and was educated at Columbia University and Cambridge University in England. The editor of *Commentary* Magazine since 1960, Podhoretz has published many essays, collected in *Doings and Undoings: The Fifties and after in American Writing*. His autobiography, *Making It*, was published in 1967.

MARIO PUZO

studied in the writing workshop of The New School for Social Research after World War II. His first two novels were *The Dark Arena* (1955) and *The Fortunate Pilgrim* (1964); his study of the Mafia, *The Godfather* (1969), was a bestseller.

OLE EDVART ROLVAAG

was born on the island of Dönne, Norway, in 1876 and died in 1931. He came to Elk Point, South Dakota in 1896 and, after a brief attempt at farming, went to Augustan College, Canton, South Dakota. Rolvaag's most famous novel is *Giants in the Earth,* written in Norwegian and translated into English by Lincoln Colcord. It was followed by *Peder Victorius* (1929), *Pure Gold* (1930), and *The Boat of Longing* (1933).

LEO ROSTEN

whose pseudonym is Leonard Q. Ross, was born in Lodz, Poland, in 1908 and was brought to the United States at the age of two. He received his Ph. D. from the University of Chicago in 1937 and after a short teaching career, he worked as a screen writer and a consultant on a variety of Presidential committees. He has written books on Hollywood—*The Movie Colony* and *The Movie Makers*—but his most famous works deal with Hyman Kaplan, the jovial Jewish immigrant who seeks education in evening school. The Kaplan books are *The Education of Hyman Kaplan* (1937), and *The Return of Hyman Kaplan* (1959).

PHILIP ROTH

was born in Newark in 1933. He graduated from Bucknell University in 1954 and received his M. A. from the University of

Chicago in 1955. He has taught at the Iowa Writers Workshop (1960–62) and has been a writer-resident at Princeton University (1962–63). His books include *Goodbye, Columbus* (1959), which won the National Book Award in 1962; *Letting Go* (1962), *When She Was Good* (1967), and *Portnoy's Complaint* (1969).

MURIEL RUKEYSER

was born in New York in 1913. She studied at Vassar and Columbia and has been a poet, biographer, movie script and television writer, and finally a teacher. Her books of poetry include *A Turning Wind* (1939), *Beast in View* (1944), and *Selected Poems* (1951).

CARL SANDBURG

was born in Galesburg, Illinois in 1878. His early career was spent as a journalist for *The Chicago Daily News*, but he soon established himself as a poet. His most famous volumes include *Chicago* (1915), *Corn Huskers* (1918), and *Smoke and Steel* (1920); most of his poems may be found in *Complete Poems* (1950), for which he received the Pulitzer Prize. He is also the author of an impressionistic biography of Abraham Lincoln.

WILLIAM SAROYAN

was born in Fresno, California in 1908. His many works include *The Daring Young Man on the Flying Trapeze* (1934) and *My Name is Aram* (1940), collections of stories; *My Heart's in the Highlands* (1939) and *The Time of Your Life* (1940), plays; and *The Human Comedy* (1942), a novel.

KARL SHAPIRO

was born in Balitmore in 1913. He has taught at John Hopkins University and The University of Nebraska. His books of poems include *Poems* (1935), *Person Place and Thing* (1942), *V-Letter and Other Poems* (1944), and *Poems of a Jew* (1958).

BUFFY SAINTE-MARIE

is a popular folk singer whose American Indian heritage is powerfully expressed in "Now That The Buffalo's Gone," a song included in her record, *It's My Way*.

WILLIAM SHANNON

was born in Worcester, Massachusetts in 1927. He received his B. A. from Clark University in 1947 and his M. A. from Harvard in 1948. His career has been primarily devoted to newspaper work. *The American Irish* was published in 1964.

MAY SWENSON

was born in Logan, Utah, in 1919. After studying at Utah State University, May Swenson came to New York and worked as an editor at New Directions. Her books of poetry include *A Cage of Spires* (1958); *To Mix with Time* (1963); *New and Selected Poems* (1963); *Poems to Solve* (1966); and *Half Sun, Half Sleep* (1967).

PIRI THOMAS

was born in New York City in 1928 and grew up in Spanish Harlem. After a four-year prison term, he turned to literature and wrote the narration for *Petey and Johnny*, a documentary dealing with Spanish Harlem. *Down These Mean Streets*, his autobiography, was published in 1967.

EMILIO DÍAZ VALCÁRCEL

was born in Trujillo Alto, Puerto Rico, in 1929. Much of his work, like "Damián Sánchez, G. I.," has appeared in *San Juan Review*, a journal in English concerned with Puerto Rican culture.

BARTOLOMEO VANZETTI

was born in Villeefalletto, in the region of Piedmont, Italy, in 1888. He came to the United States in 1908 and worked in New York City restaurants; he went to New England and was employed in quarries, brickyards, on street construction and railroads. He settled in Plymouth, Massachusetts, and sold fish from a cart. On June 11, 1920, he was indicted for an attempted payroll robbery in Bridgewater, Massachusetts; on September 11, he and Nicola Sacco were indicted for murder in Braintree, Massachusetts. After one of the most controversial criminal cases in American history, Sacco and Vanzetti were executed on August 23, 1927.

JOSE GARCIA VILLA

was born in Manila, Philippines, and came to the United States in 1930. He studied at the University of Mexico and Columbia University and then began writing stories, which were collected in *Footnote to Youth* (1933). Since these early years, Villa has written mostly poetry. Two of his volumes, *Selected Poems* (1946) and *Selected Poems and New* (1958), contain his most important verse.

SELECTED
BIBLIOGRAPHY

Adamic, Louis. *A Nation of Nations*. New York: Harper & Bros., 1945.
———. *From Many Lands*. New York: Harper & Bros., 1940.
Gitler, Joseph B., Ed. *Minority Groups*. New York: John Wiley & Sons, 1956.
Handlin, Oscar. *Race and Nationality in American Life*. Boston: Little, Brown, 1957.
———. *The Uprooted*. Boston: Little, Brown, 1951.
Hansen, Marcus Lee. *The Immigrant in American History*. New York: Harper & Row, 1940.
Kraus, Michael. *Immigration: The American Mosaic*. Princeton: D. Van Nostrand, 1966.
McWilliams, Carey. *Brothers Under the Skin*. Boston: Little, Brown, 1943, 1944.
Rose, Peter T. *They and We: Racial and Ethnic Relations in the United States*. New York: Random House, 1964.
Simpson, G. E., and J. M. Yinzer. *Racial and Cultural Minorities*. New York: Harper & Bros., 1953.
Williams, Robin M., Jr. *Strangers Next Door: Ethnic Relations in American Communities*. Englewood Cliffs, N.J.: Prentice-Hall, 1964.
Wittke, Carl. *We Who Built America*. New York: Prentice-Hall, 1940.